FASTER CONSTRUCTION PROJECTS WITH CPM SCHEDULING

Murray B. Woolf, PMP

New York   Chicago   San Francisco   Lisbon   London   Madrid   Mexico City
Milan   New Delhi   San Juan   Seoul   Singapore   Sydney   Toronto

The McGraw-Hill Companies

Library of Congress Cataloging-in-Publication Data

Woolf, Murray B.
  Faster construction projects with CPM scheduling / Murray B. Woolf.
     p. cm.
  Includes index.
  ISBN 0-07-148660-7 (alk. paper)
  1. Building—Superintendence 2. Production scheduling. 3. Critical
path analysis. I. Title.
  TH438.4.W65 2007
  690.068'4—dc22

                             2007007213

McGraw-Hill books are available at special quantity discounts to use as premiums and sales
promotions, or for use in corporate training programs. For more information, please write
to the Director of Special Sales, Professional Publishing, McGraw-Hill, Two Penn Plaza,
New York, NY 10121-2298. Or contact your local bookstore.

Faster Construction Projects with CPM Scheduling

1 2 3 4 5 6 7 8 9 0   DOC/DOC   0 1 9 8 7

ISBN-13: 978-0-07-148660-6
ISBN-10:   0-07-148660-7

Sponsoring Editor Cary Sullivan	**Indexer** Valerie Perry
Editorial Supervisor Jody McKenzie	**Production Supervisor** George Anderson
Project Manager Vasundhara Sawhney	**Composition** International Typesetting and Composition
Acquisitions Coordinator Laura Hahn	**Illustration** International Typesetting and Composition
Copy Editor Sally Engelfried	**Art Director, Cover** Anthony Landi
Proofreader Surendra Nath Shivam	**Cover Designer** Pehrsson Design

ABOUT THE AUTHOR

Murray B. Woolf, PMP, is president of the International Center for Scheduling, Inc. He founded ICS as his response to the number of challenges facing the Scheduling Practice in the United States and globally. ICS, although in its infancy, promises to change the face of the Scheduling Practice by providing coordinated support programs, products, and services to Scheduling Practitioners and their customers. Specifically, the ICS model includes education and training, job placement support, research, publications, credentialing, scheduling specifications software, objective quality scoring of schedules and scheduling programs, direct scheduling support, and consulting.

Mr. Woolf has more than 30 years of project management, project controls, training, consulting, and expert witness experience. He spent the early part of his career providing project management and project controls services on more than 125 projects worldwide, with combined value estimated at around $28 billion.

Mr. Woolf is a frequent lecturer and writer on Scheduling Practice topics, and is the inventor of numerous Scheduling Practice innovations, including Momentum Management, and Dilemma Forecasting. He is a member and a vice president of the PMI College of Scheduling and the first Managing Director of the Scheduling Excellence Initiative (a College of Scheduling endeavor to write best practice and guidelines for the Scheduling Practice).

In Memoriam

to

Jo and Cy Woolf

My parents were an inspiration

throughout my entire life.

They taught, by example and word,

that anything in life is possible

if one has the will.

But they also warned that

what one does is less important

than how it is done.

They are my moral compass and will remain

an inspiration and guiding light for all of my days.

Contents

Part 2 Creating a Penchant for Change. 83

5 The New Scheduling Practice Paradigm: Specializations, Positions, Deliverables, and Roles . . 85

6 Introduction to Dilemma Control 121

Part 3 Preserving Project Schedule Integrity. . . 173

10 Anatomy of a Schedule 175

11 Working at Cross-Purposes 193

16 Performance Control 325

Part 5 Epilogue 353

17 Creating Schedules They'll Actually Want to Use! 357

Foreword

A little while back, I received a disturbing e-mail from Murray. To most anyone else, I suppose, the e-mail would have seemed innocent enough. He was asking me to write a Foreword for his new book, a book on project scheduling aimed at the intermediate scheduler. So why was this e-mail so disturbing to me? Because, in it, Murray was asking me a specific question[1] and promising that my answer would be shared with all of the generations of project schedulers that have succeeded me. And while the assignment might have seemed a bit daunting to some, for me it was not the question so much that upset me; it was my discomfort with confronting the truth and implications of the answer. For, within myself, that answer would also disturb the peace I had managed to find in my senior years.

I began in the "scheduling business" even before it was a business, at a time when the very word *scheduling* meant different things to different people—when planning and scheduling were two distinctly different processes. Back in the early 1960s, the scheduling business was in its infancy. For practitioners of the time, the business was being created on the fly; we were winging it. We were developing impromptu processes in response to sudden needs as they arose. There were no manuals, textbooks, college courses, or software help screens to show us the way. In many respects, we were the early explorers of Frontier Scheduling.

Armed only with our wit, and a sharp number 2 pencil, we used our creativity and intuition to find a way to get from here to there. Speaking metaphorically, we would only build a bridge upon encountering an unexpected river, one blocking our path. Some ideas worked; some didn't.

Mostly, we worked in isolation from one another. Schedulers rarely worked in large groups. No scheduling undertaking anywhere on the globe employed more than 1 percent of the world's supply of schedulers. In other words, the scheduling business was being developed in parallel, independent pockets of concentrated effort. There was no unifying center for the scheduling business. Not surprisingly, solutions were popping up all over the place. As a result, it was not uncommon to find the same "discovery" appearing in completely unrelated thought centers around the globe, just as it was equally likely to find incompatible solutions in a competitor's office across town.

But what all schedulers had in common—what all project managers had in common—was a desire for results, for benefit, for value. And it was this singular desire that became the great equalizer—and the great eliminator. Before long, certain processes emerged as "better," while others shriveled up and died. Of course, the names we gave to processes, steps, components, and people remained inconsistent, but the general benefit of the underlying strategies in time began to crystallize. Before long, good or bad scheduling became like pornography. In 1964, Justice Potter Stewart tried to explain "hard-core" pornography, or what is obscene, by saying, "I shall not today attempt further

---

[1] I'll discuss the question and answer later.

to define the kinds of material I understand to be embraced . . . but I know it when I see it." That's how it was with good (or bad) scheduling. You just knew which was which.

But that was a different time, back when scheduling was young and feisty and impatient, and there were no rules, per se. All of the labels were fresh, even the names we gave ourselves. Planners and Schedulers were two such labels. One label that never stuck (thank God) was given to me by one of my first project managers: *The Time Man.* I would pull up to the job-site and he would step out onto the rickety plywood porch of his trailer and shout across the dusty parking lot, "Hey, it's the Time Man."

TIME

I think that of all the things I have learned after 44 years in the business what I have learned about *time* is the most chilling. To be sure, every scheduler is in the Time Business. Today, we delude ourselves into thinking that our goal is to become would-be masters over time. We even dabble with renaming our craft Time Management. But we manage time as much as we manage the wind. We speak of time control. With our methodology, we slice and dice time and call the resultant fragments "durations." We kid ourselves into thinking we have some control over time when we equate time and money. Cost engineers control the money; scheduling engineers control the time—or so the confusion goes.

But time is nothing like money. Money is a human invention and its flow can be started, stopped, limited, inundated, revalued, and devalued. Money flows through a spigot with a shutoff valve. We have the ability to stop funding inviable ventures.

Time, however, has no shutoff valve. Time flows—steadily, unendingly, unavoidably, indiscriminately, and mercilessly—whether we want it to or not. As the soap opera warns us, "Like sand in the hourglass, so are the days of our lives." Indeed, the hourglass is an ample metaphor but better if we cover the upper half with black paint so we cannot see how much time remains.

So the first bubble for me to burst is this one: there is no such thing as Time Management. We do not manage time; we manage our *use* of time. Benjamin Franklin is credited with saying something like, "When someone tells you that they don't have time to do this or that for you, what they are really saying is that you are not important enough to them. We all have the same amount of time. It is what we *choose* to do with it that is our right and responsibility."

Another, more complimentary label I acquired early in my career was *The Idea Man*. I liked that one a lot more. I had always seen the Planner (more so, even, than the Scheduler) as a stenographer, as a note-taker, as a scribe. In other words, we would ask probing questions with the clear intent of picking the brains of those who would be most responsible for the ultimate prosecution of the work, and we would capture their intentions on paper. We would reflect back to them a more crisp and clear view of the inner machinations of their minds than they could ever have acquired, left to their own devices. With the potent clarity of a well-drawn logic diagram, I could show them what their thoughts looked like in a bold, tangible, reviewable form. As one project manager, upon seeing a logic sketch of his strategy, joked with unbridled pride: "Hmm. So there *is* a method to my madness." He then added, "You have a clear grasp of the obvious."

If I *was* the Idea Man, it was mainly that I brought their ideas into clear focus, not that I was this bottomless well of original thought. Although this is not to say that, across the years, I haven't contributed my share of innovative ideas. Walk enough jobsites and you'll invariably get mud in the crevices of your boots. That's how it goes with Logic Sessions. Conduct enough of them and before long, you will be the conduit for knowledge exchange between projects and project teams that had no other connection than your involvement and interaction with each.

IDEAS

Ideas come in two forms: those that call for action, and those that don't. We know the latter as concepts, beliefs, values, philosophies, convictions, and the like. Such ideas, which do not result in or call for actions, are of minor interest to the Planner or Scheduler. Instead, in our business, we traffic in action-oriented ideas. Such ideas have two elements or components: the action itself, and the perceived benefit. It is important to understand how these two components play off of one another. Why? Because ideas of this type—the ones containing proposed actions and perceived benefits—are what we call *plans*. And the process of planning, when you cut through the facade, is essentially a structured and organized attempt to identify possible courses of action and to speculate on possible, likely benefits to be derived from each avenue of endeavor.

That last sentence invites us to recognize four possible combinations of actions and benefits:

- Unattractive actions yielding unattractive benefits
- Attractive actions yielding unattractive benefits
- Unattractive actions yielding attractive benefits
- Attractive actions yielding attractive benefits

The planning process is all about finding as many instances of the fourth condition as we can. Unattractive actions are those that come with significant risk, cost, or effort. Unattractive benefits are those that are immeasurable, unwanted, or of limited value.

In those early days, the number of possible "benefits" was far fewer than they are today. Originally, CPM (as opposed to PERT, for instance) was designed to provide a mechanism for discovering the most cost-effective project implementation option. In other words, resources were assumed to be unlimited, and durations were assumed to be achievable (finite). By adjusting logic and durations, the project length could be regulated. We understood, early on, the tradeoff between direct and indirect costs. A shorter project would reduce indirect costs but increase direct costs—and vice versa.

The point is that most individuals involved in project scheduling limited the benefits of scheduling to project length reduction, cost reduction, and disruption reduction. But that was decades ago. Since then, the schedule has found many other uses and, as a result, many more and different stakeholders than were present in the early days, and each stakeholder has a unique perspective yielding a different set of "benefits." To make matters worse, what one stakeholder might consider a benefit, another might consider a risk or cost or unwanted effort.

Not surprisingly, because of these competing and conflicting perceived benefits, it is far more difficult in today's climate for all parties to a project to agree on the acceptability of a particular plan. This may go a long way to explain why, perhaps subconsciously, we have collectively evolved the profession to where planning is no longer the essential first step in the scheduling process. And that takes me to my answer to Murray's question, which was, "Where do you see the future of scheduling headed?"

Before I answer, though, I'd like to say a few words about change.

CHANGE

Why change? Because change always evolves from the passage of time. Time and change are the two sides of the coin called *life*. Change, like time, is constant, inevitable, and relentless; like time, change happens to us. But *unlike* time, we also can precipitate change. In other words, we can cause change, just as we are affected by change.

A few years ago, I was quoted in an *Engineering News-Record* article. Those quotes led many readers to conclude that I rallied against change and lamented the loss of the "good old days," as it were. I want to set the record straight, here and now. Change can be both bad and good. It's never as black-and-white as the past was good, the present is bad, and the future is doomed. Rather, there were some things about the way we did things back then that I am happy to see gone forever, just as there were some things done back then that I wish I could see resurrected in my lifetime. Likewise, there are many of today's practices that I applaud, while there are some practices I would like to see eliminated.

Each of these items, whether done then or now, must be evaluated and discussed on its own merits and not grouped into a time warp and either accepted or rejected simply based on when it occurred/occurs. It is not as simple as that. This Foreword is hardly the place to address each of those issues. But a few particular points bear clarification, for they are the best way I know of how to answer Murray's question.

ADM vs. PDM

I do not deny that I grew up on ADM, not PDM. But that is not to say that I feel that ADM is perfect and PDM is evil. To be sure, there are a few distinctions between the two methods and only some of them seem problematic to me:

- **Diagramming Notations** Activities are depicted as boxes and relationships as arrows in PDM, whereas in ADM the arrows depict the activities and circles (nodes) depict the relationships. I have no great heartburn over the PDM diagramming notations, as they tend to be easily read and interpreted.
- **Activity Numbering** In ADM, an activity-identifier was a hyphenated number comprised of the two numbers at the tail and head of the activity, respectively. In PDM, the activity-identifier is a single number. I have no problem with the PDM numbering; it is cleaner, simpler.
- **Dummies** ADM required the creation of activities, called "dummies," to get around the situation where multiple parallel activities had the same tail node and head node. PDM's diagramming method eliminates the need for dummies, and I think this is a great improvement.

- **New Relationship Types** In ADM, there was only the finish-to-start relationship. PDM gives us the ability to diagrammatically depict partially or completely simultaneous yet interdependent activities. In my opinion, these additional relationship types (start-to-start, finish-to-finish, and start-to-finish) present both opportunities and challenges for responsible scheduling. I do not condemn PDM as being unacceptable simply because of the allowance of these relationships, but I am concerned about the effects of their irresponsible use.

Other Innovations

Over the years, scheduling software has introduced automated capabilities we did not have in the early days. Since the timeframe of their evolution coincides with the ascent of Primavera to its world-class status as the leading scheduling software, many of these innovations have been wrongly associated with Primavera, per se, when in fact several competing software programs contain the same features. A similar argument can be made for the unfair linking of these features with PDM, even though the innovations could be accomplished with ADM just as readily, if ADM were still in vogue and practice.

- **Multiple Calendars** Today's scheduling software programs allow for the assignment of different automated calendars to different activities and even different resources. This is neither a Primavera-specific feature nor one that could not be applied to an ADM schedule. I am concerned about the unbridled use of multiple calendars.
- **Excessive Date-Constraints** Similarly, virtually all scheduling programs (and not just Primavera) offer a wide variety of date-constraint options. Again, these constraints could just as easily be injected into an ADM schedule as they are in PDM schedules. I am concerned about the unfettered use of constraints in today's schedules, which can skew the results to incorrect answers.
- **Calculation Settings** While there are many software settings that dramatically affect the results of date calculations, some of the most potent are progress override, contiguous durations, and zero-total-float/zero-free-float. I am quite concerned about the irresponsible use of these settings.
- **Output Formats** I am concerned about the present output options available to the scheduler and project team. Bar graphs, while helpful in depicting the general timing of project activity at a summary level or the intricate juxtaposition of activity on a detailed level, can fail to convey the interrelatedness of project activity, as can be shown only through a logic diagram, complete with relationship ties.

This issue is one of practice, not software technology. The software does not insist that we either exploit or ignore bar graphs. Those are human decisions, and the current trend seems to be toward more high-end graphics and fewer tabular listings containing predecessor/successor details.

The most obvious manifestation of this trend is where logical, developmental progression of

Logic Diagram->Data Entry->Tabular Listing->Summary Bar Graph

has been replaced with the Reverse Engineering approach of

Bar Graph->Data Entry->Tabular Listing

I am especially concerned about this trend.

I will stop my list at this point, for the purpose in itemizing any of the preceding is only to clarify that I am not an opponent of change versus the way it was done "back then." I do think we need to step back from our workstations and take a long, sobering, and honest look at where we are headed. And that brings me back to Murray's question.

THE PURPOSE OF SCHEDULING

Originally, it was called the Main Chain, not the Critical Path. Jim Kelley, who, along with his partner from Dupont, Morgan Walker, invented CPM, considered the path of activities with the least float to be the "Main Chain." When the Navy suggested the expression "Critical Path," it had immediate appeal, because those words hinted at the objective of all scheduling: to keep our focus on the end game. Critical *to what,* the term subtly asked.

The *end game* is another way of saying *benefit,* which we have already begun to discuss. What is the purpose of scheduling? If we all had the same single purpose in mind, surely finding agreement on approach would be that much easier. But schedule uses have increased over the years, and that expansion has created much of the discord I see in today's practices.

Some use the schedule to plan. Some use it to control. Some use it to bargain and negotiate. Some use it to ridicule, while others use it to defend. Some use it to manage. Some use it to monitor. One schedule cannot achieve all of these various ends with equal effectiveness. In fact, the route to some ends is mutually exclusive. As you head in one direction, you distance yourself from another destination.

A few of the more recent (last couple decades) uses of schedules have driven the level-of-detail of the schedule to an almost ridiculous level. Let me give you a simple example. Late Saturday night, my wife and I decided, just before retiring, to go to church in the morning. Since there is one shower in the master bath, we had the following discussion:

Jim: Since you need to do your hair after you shower, why don't you shower first?

Rita: Good idea. But don't you like to shave before you shower? You can shave while I'm showering.

Jim: Fine. We need to leave around 9 A.M. to be there on time. When do you want to get up?

Rita: 7:30 ought to be enough time, don't you think?

That's it. We developed a plan. We agreed on a project start time (7:30 A.M.) and project completion time (9:00 A.M.) and a coordinated sequence of activities. Notice that we did not create a whole list of minute steps to be performed or get into assignment of specific start and stop times for each of those steps. We kept it simple! Scheduling is the assignment of start and finish times to activities, whereas planning is the development of an orderly sequence, even if specific activity times are not assigned.

Notice also that we did not require a Work Breakdown Structure. In fact, I would argue that the WBS approach to planning might well be a possible deterrent to effective planning at times. I say that because the WBS approach presupposes that every activity necessarily leads to a deliverable. But have you ever done a jigsaw puzzle? You pick up a piece in your hand, fumble with it in your fingers, turn it every which way, observe its special features, and then intermittently look at the incomplete puzzle on the table and back at the piece in your hand.

That's just about how planning occurs. Planning is this magical combination of experience, understanding, vision, and collaboration. All four ingredients are required. The participants of the planning session bring to the table their respective years of *experience* in the type of work involved in the project. They take the time to *understand* what the project is all about, and then they apply their creative juices to *envision* alternative approaches to the work. As they *collaborate*, they share and respect each other's perceived benefits to be derived from each different approach. In the win-win sprit, the group settles on a plan that yields the greatest benefit to all—individually as well as collectively. Now, tell me what this process has to do with deliverables, per se?

I have seen a lot of schedules developed by others over the years, especially through my company's[2] claims consulting services. If I had to point to the one common thread linking the vast majority of failed projects and slipped schedules, it would have to be inadequate collaborative planning. Today's schedulers have been taught a mechanical approach to scheduling that, to a very great extent, downplays or even ignores the planning process. Schedules are often developed in a vacuum detached from the project team, and even when the team *is* involved, the WBS process works "backward" from the deliverable to the required inputs. But with this approach, the optimum strategy plan for the work is often missed, or only accidentally stumbled upon when it is uncovered.

Finally, we have taken the schedule too far. A trend that I consider extremely troubling is the increasing reliance of the computer to "identify the best way to go." We have somehow accredited the computer with the wisdom of Solomon. We have become convinced that greater precision means increased likelihood of project success. If only we can decompose the activities into greater and greater granularity and if only we can identify, with great specificity, the responsible party for each activity, then surely the schedule, if merely followed, will necessarily lead to a successful project. So the thinking goes.

And so we see a mad rush to greater and greater dependence on the computer. The essential rationale behind the recent Enterprise Project Management current is that we need to "get everything into the computer," into one single database. If only we have *every* project in one database, and if only we subdivide each project into the most minute elemental pieces, then surely we will have complete control over the entire enterprise.

Project management is really people management. And while we cannot control people, we certainly have a far better chance of managing people than we have of managing time. If you are reading my words, then it is because a book about project scheduling is of interest to you, and that means that, in one form or another, *you* are a Time Person. You are someone who has an interest in a project achieving its time objectives.

---

[2]O'Brien-Kreitzberg.

Well, you have found the right book. Murray, too, believes that there is such a thing as too much detail. He also believes that we have lost sight of the primary objective of all scheduling, which is to coordinate, not control. With a friendly, conversational style, he holds our hand and returns us to the basics of *scheduling*—starting with the disappearing art of *planning*.

He also speaks out—no, he preaches—about the sanctity of the activity-duration, that it must remain pure. He insists that behind each duration, whether belonging to an activity or to a relationship, there are underlying assumptions that we must understand and acknowledge. He gives us guidance about the responsible use of calendars and constraints and software settings and PDM relationship types.

But above all, Murray encourages us (maybe even warns us) to step back from the precipice, where we now find our discipline, before it is too late. He calls upon us to rethink many current trends by taking what is good from newer technologies and combining them with what was best from the "old ways" that still have merit and relevance in today's marketplace of ideas and challenges.

For some years now, I have been feeling that the direction in which our discipline appears headed seems sadly removed from what has worked so well in the past, just as it is moving in a direction inconsistent with and different from where Project Management itself is headed. I have wondered how, given the diverging routes that planners, schedulers, project managers, owners, and educators are taking, we will ever again bring to projects the kind of synergistic creativity known in the early days. It is not as if our current breed of schedulers or project managers is all that satisfied with the benefits of our craft, or that any of them would be unwilling to entertain a different approach.

WHY YOU SHOULD READ THIS BOOK!

And that brings us full circle, doesn't it? What we are doing today doesn't seem to be working. What we did in the past embodied a combination of attractive and unattractive approaches. Needed now, more than ever, is a revisiting of the entire matter, of determining the best of all generations, an amalgamation of thought and creativity leading to our best hope for scheduling excellence.

Murray's book is, in my opinion, "the real thing." He has a profound understanding of what we are all about, what we are trying to accomplish, what we are doing right, what we are doing wrong, where we seem to be headed, what course adjustments we need to make, and what re-engineering we need to impose upon ourselves as a discipline to get from the discouraging state we are in to the dynamic state to which all professional schedulers aspire.

The question: *Where do you see the scheduling profession headed?*

My answer: If we continue down the paths indicated by recent trends—in pursuit of absolute control through greater minutia and greater expansion—scheduling, as we knew it and even as we know it, will cease to be. But if we take a restocking of our position and our tack, there is yet time to turn the field around. Murray's book, at the very least, provides a launching ground for informed, educated, and passionate discussion of the issues. At its most hopeful, it may well contain the roadmap to our discipline's complete makeover.

This is a book for Intermediate Schedulers, written by a Master Scheduler. Murray describes his audience this way: "This book . . . is not being written for the 20-year scheduling veteran. Rather, it is aimed at those tasked with creating a Project Schedule who have not had years of experience or training."

I think Murray's self-perception is too limited. For instance, I find that this book is full of ideas and concepts that are interesting and refreshing to me, a 44-year scheduling veteran, and I would suggest that is an equally good set of guidelines for the "rookies." It is also a *must read* for project owners, project directors, and project managers.

Murray contends that today's scheduling terminology is woefully inadequate, so in this book he offers an entirely new set of key definitions. As but one example, he distinguishes between *planning* and *scheduling* in a way that appeals to my common sense. Key to my understanding his unique distinction of the two terms was when he associated planning with *commitment* and scheduling with *execution*.

Murray expresses some serious thoughts about scheduling and schedulers as a "profession," per se. We (schedulers) would like our field to be a profession, but at present it isn't one—at least not yet.

I would like to set a context for Murray's comments. When he became a scheduler in 1977, CPM was in its twentieth year. For the first ten of those years, which I remember well, CPM (as a promising methodology) was an uphill "sell." By 1977, about the time when Murray was drawing his first logic diagram, CPM was already an accepted norm in the construction industry. In 1978, a Project Management Institute (PMI) survey listed 40 CPM computer software programs, including MSCS and Project 2. Primavera did not exist.

Both computer hardware (mainframe) and software (expensive and centralized in computer centers) had evolved considerably by 1977, but still shaped the role of the scheduler who had well-defined duties associated with the preparation and maintenance of the schedule. Murray notes that the arrival of the desktop computer had an immediate impact on scheduling, for now almost anyone could create a schedule (though not necessarily a good one). In his words, the role of the scheduler "began to implode," and indeed it sure seemed that way.

After his early years of CPM scheduling, Murray says that he was "disillusioned." CPM schedules did not seem to be as helpful to project management as he and many other schedulers of his day believed they should or could be. He notes that the monthly "snapshot" of project status was more of a function of recording past events than of projecting future events.

Murray wanted the CPM Schedule to be a more dynamic tool, like a film instead of a snapshot, like a map to show the way to proceed, and he thought the CPM schedule should facilitate work-arounds whenever the unexpected was encountered. He shaped several theories to accomplish this. He initially tested these theories on 14 projects in the Northeast for which he was the Project Controls Manager.

Out of his early efforts, in the first half of the 1980s, came two significant developments, which I earnestly believe hold great promise for the future of both project scheduling and project management. For the latter, he developed a new Scheduling Practice Paradigm. Under this heading, Murray gives us a consolidated set of terminology that describes specialties, subspecialties, procedures, deliverables, and roles. Finally, someone has definitively clarified the meaning of Commitment Planner, Execution Scheduler, and Performance Controller.

But by far, the greater of the two contributions to our discipline is his identification of a "miles-per-hour" value for projects of all types. Called *Performance Intensity*, Murray succeeded in quantifying the invisible—by developing a way to measure, depict, and influence the rate at which work is performed. This invention alone I consider to be one of the greatest breakthroughs in network scheduling since the invention of CPM itself.

Enveloping the Performance Intensity formula, Murray has crafted a complete science called Momentology, or (as I prefer) Momentum Management. Momentology is the applied science of Performance Intensity, along with a cluster of associated calculations, formulas, and variables that collectively combine to provide schedulers with a completely new and refreshing way to plan, schedule, and understand the dynamics of projects of any type.

As a subset of Momentology, Murray introduces a new project management subsystem, which better prepares project managers to handle the unexpected, called *Dilemma Control*. He explains that whereas traditional Risk Management attempts, *before* the project, to develop plans for handling downstream major risks, Dilemma Forecasting provides real-time warnings, *during* the course of the project, about approaching small-scale dilemmas. With sufficient forewarning to allow project management the opportunity to develop appropriate reversing or mitigating responses, Dilemma Control appears more proactive and timely.

As almost an aside, Murray questions our allegiance to Earned Value Measurement (EVM) and Work Breakdown Structure, as well as our easy acceptance of emerging methodologies, such as Critical Chain Project Management (CCPM), which he says poses a grave threat to the integrity of the schedule and contributes to the erosion of our craft.

From what I have described thus far, it might seem to you that Murray has used the guise of a book on scheduling as a soapbox for philosophical and theoretical musings. And while he does beseech us to think outside the box, during the latter two-thirds of the book Murray nonetheless delivers on his promise to provide expert guidance on how to create schedules that will lead to projects executed more efficiently, and thus to projects predisposed to completing sooner, as the book's title promises. In five meaty chapters, Murray gets into the details of schedule design, development, construction, maintenance, analysis, and reporting.

Amidst the detailed discussions, he describes several additional rules, theories, and axioms that he developed to accomplish the basic building blocks of all schedules. He devotes an entire chapter to project planning, a treatment I have felt for quite some time has been missing from the literary landscape.

But Murray also ventures into uncharted territory as he introduces us to:

- A variety of different ways to determine schedule Criticality (beyond total-float)
- His patented way to distribute total-float across all schedule activities (he calls the resultant value Discrete Activity Float (DAF))
- A collection of new methods for performance trending (beyond Earned Value)
- A subset of processes (complete with accompanying terminology and formulas) that allow us to systematically monitor the credibility of the schedule itself, as it continually changes in content, substance, and integrity during the course of the project

MOMENTOLOGY MAY BE THE NEW FACE OF SCHEDULING

What I find the most intriguing of anything I read in this book is how Momentum Management fosters the smooth functionality of the project team working together in a collaborative and constructive way, as opposed to traditional CPM reporting, which is focused on a retrospective analysis of past performance and baseline compliance. In stark contrast, Momentology concentrates on what remains to be done and how to get from the present state to the project's ultimate time objectives as painlessly and as cooperatively as possible.

Momentology promotes teamwork and team-based problem solving, which is far more compatible with the current trend in Project Management than the old Command-and-Control attitudes of 50 years ago, when CPM was first invented. It is time for a rethinking of Scheduling's contribution to Project Management, and this book is my first encounter of a seasoned scheduler trying to help bridge the growing chasm between Project Management and ineffective scheduling practices. Murray suggests, and I wholeheartedly agree, that that ineffectiveness can be attributed to modern innovations and trends that have taken us farther and farther away from the end benefits to which we all initially aspired, as well as to the abandonment of many basic principles inherent in the earliest schedules of the opening years of our profession that have since been lost in our mad obsession with more details and greater reliance on the Almighty Computer.

This text is an excellent stand-alone book, with a promise of good things to follow. It offers so much that it is worth reading once lightly, and then again with a notepad in hand.

Enjoy the journey.

Sincerely,

Jim O'Brien

Preface

THIS BOOK IS JUST THE BEGINNING

This text is the first in a set of books intended to ultimately present a brand-new project management concept called *Momentum Management (Momentology)*. This first book is all about how to create Project Schedules that have credibility, because *Applied Momentum* is only as good as the Project Schedules upon which it is dependent.

Before I proceed any further, there is one more nuance I care to highlight right at the outset, even before I give a brief summary of what *Momentology* is all about. Writing about how to create better Project Schedules naturally requires making frequent references to how Scheduling Practices are currently performed. It also requires reference to commonly accepted terminology. The problem is that I take issue with both of these "standards"—the practices and the terminology. I happen to think that today's scheduling terminology is in dire need of a complete overhaul, just as I think that the Scheduling Practice has lost sight of our prime customer, the project manager, and what he needs.

In reaction to these feelings, over the last few decades I have been working toward developing responses to these deficiencies. As a result, this book contains several new concepts that I wish to introduce to you. Namely:

- A new Scheduling Practice Paradigm, complete with three specialties, seven subspecialties, and an assortment of procedures, position titles, deliverables, and roles.
- A new set of definitions that, at last, distinguish a planner from a scheduler, a plan from a schedule, and planning from scheduling.
- A new project management system, called *Dilemma Control*, that better prepares project managers for the daily uncertainties that all projects experience.
- A new project management methodology, called *Momentology*, that allows project managers to be far more proactive and to foster true collaboration among project participants.

Because this book is simultaneously introducing new concepts and terminology while it attempts to suggest improvements to traditional Scheduling Practice, your job as reader will be made that much harder. You will have to remain open minded as I introduce new concepts. Once you understand them, I will incorporate these new ideas into the context of mainstream functions that all Practitioners perform. What I can promise you is that, by the end of the book, you will surely know what you *can* do to improve the way you design, develop, maintain, and use your Project Schedules. I can promise you that your Execution Schedules *will* be desired and that your project managers *will* praise your efforts as the best Scheduling

Practices they have ever experienced. Just keep an open mind! Now, back to where I was when I rudely interrupted myself . . .

In terms of book organization, I grappled with the question of *when* to introduce these innovative concepts. Should I introduce my foreign ideas first and possibly frustrate you by delaying the practical advice on mainstream Scheduling Practices you are expecting to find? Or should I introduce my ideas at the end of the book, perhaps as appendices, and possibly confuse the reader by referencing currently accepted terminology, concepts, and processes throughout the volume, even though, in the closing chapters, I end up repudiating them? Ultimately, I decided to introduce the new terminology and concepts *before* using them throughout the balance of the text. And so, Part 2, which introduces these new ideas, precedes the nuts and bolts subjects contained in subsequent chapters of Part 3 and beyond. I hope you approve.

As for *Momentum Management*, it refers to a set of principles, theories, concepts, processes, procedures, technologies, and management practices that can be applied to time-sensitive projects. Momentum Management (also called Momentology) operates under the premise that a project's time-performance objectives can be best ensured by constantly monitoring and influencing the project's inherent *Momentum*. Momentum Management is based on rigid scientific principles and is manifested in practical yet immediately intuitive and useful project management products and services. It introduces an entirely fresh set of terms and concepts that are built upon traditional Critical Path Method (CPM) methodology.

This is an important point: *Momentum Theory* is not a replacement for conventional CPM— it is merely an enhancement of it. Momentum Theory does not challenge CPM basics. To the contrary, and quite unlike several recently surfaced methodologies purporting to be based upon the CPM model, Momentum Theory insists that Scheduling Practitioners return to the basics. That is precisely why this first book in the Momentum series is dedicated to ensuring that the Project Schedules underlying Momentum applications are sound.

Momentology is quite innovative in how it extracts vital information from the Execution Schedule, insights that have always been there but that we have been ignoring all along. Momentology merely squeezes the Critical Path Method a bit tighter in order to get more juice from the fruit.

ABOUT BUILDING BETTER PROJECT SCHEDULES

Other books in the Momentum set will follow, providing a complete treatment of Momentum Theory, Momentum Science, and Applied Momentum. Momentology is both a theoretic management science and an applicable set of management tools for the Scheduling Practitioner. Because any project management methodology that depends on a Project Schedule can be no better than the Execution Schedule upon which it is predicated, I have dedicated this first book to building better Project Schedules.

The next book to be published will be an academic text, far more formidable and weighty. It will provide a complete treatment of all aspects of Momentology. So, as you read this text and encounter Momentum terminology or theory, please understand that this book is not meant to provide a full treatment of Momentology. Rather, it mentions Momentum concepts only when such mention is appropriate to the subject matter being discussed.

Following the Momentology book will be the third volume in the set, which will concentrate on an area of Execution Scheduling that has been grossly under-treated in both literary works and formal academic coursework: *Performance Control*. Sadly, the vast majority of schedule update cycles generate little more than hastily statused schedules and a routine set of superficially reviewed reports. The truth is that inherent in each Project Schedule is a treasure trove of insightful information as to how well the project is doing, how well the Project Schedule is performing in its intended roles, and more. To wet your whistle, this first book will also touch on some of these ideas.

Finally, I wish to note that during the course of the publication process, the title of this book changed. In many ways, the working title better describes the spirit and intent of the original manuscript: "How to Create Projects Schedules That They'll Actually Want to Use!"

Indeed, the main goal of this book is to help you develop better schedules, with "better" being confirmed when your project manager anxiously and willingly welcomes your scheduling efforts. Throughout this book you will see reference to schedules "they'll actually want to use," and that is because when I wrote the book, I had the earlier title (and intent) in mind.

A COUPLE CAVEATS

Throughout this book I make frequent reference to projects within the construction industry. This is where I have acquired the majority of my project scheduling experience. The fact is that Schedule Management is now popularly applied in more than 20 major industries; construction is the oldest application environment but is no longer the largest. So, while this book is written specifically for the construction industry as its title indicates, I encourage readers from outside the construction industry to remember that basic Project Scheduling principles vary quite little from one industry to the next. You should be able to make the necessary conversions of thought in order to apply what is discussed herein to your particular industry.

As for gender designations, I made another executive decision: to say "he" rather than "he/she." Please know that this decision does not reflect any belief that one sex is better than another, more prevalent than the other, and so on.

Now, let's get started.
Murray B. Woolf

Acknowledgements

Over the years I've heard the expression, "the book wrote itself." Well, this book didn't quite write itself. It required a fair amount of effort to take the broad, diverse, and complex topic of the Scheduling Practice and somehow reduce it to small enough chunks of thought that we might make sense of it all.

No book ever writes itself, but that is not to say that, from time to time, the words didn't course through the mind faster than the fingers could type. And every once in a while—yes—an idea magically appeared on the screen, as if coming to me from some far away place. I experienced several such moments, and when they struck, I momentarily bathed in the warmth of fond reminiscence. There, against the black backdrop of my mind, I watched the flickering dance of a distance recollection spin and swirl into delightful clarity, and the printed words on the screen were spoken by unheard voices from the past.

I truly believe what some scientists have speculated: that *every single second* of our lives is recorded in our brains and is available for recollection, if only we could learn the technique. I don't claim to know that trick, but I can say with absolute certainly that many past events—some I thought were surely lost to the decades—did come back to life to help me better understand the origins and context of my own beliefs.

And so that is why I simply *must* begin the long list of acknowledgements with written tribute to the many bosses, colleagues, clients, mentors, and even competitors who each, in his or her own way, have helped to hone my craft and humanize my perspective. I am indebted to each one of them for the mark they have left on the fabric of my life. "Thank you" seems inadequate repayment to the folks listed in Table A-1 at the end of this section.

Without hesitation, the very first thank you must go to my dear friend Jim O'Brien, whom I and so many thousands of schedulers worldwide consider the Father of Modern Scheduling. I asked Jim to read my manuscript and he not only graciously agreed to do so, but then went far beyond my wildest expectations. He personally recommended to McGraw-Hill that they publish this text. If not for Jim's support and belief in me, this book wouldn't be in your hands. I will be indebted to Jim for the balance of my life. I wish Jim and his dear wife Rita many years of good health and happiness. I encourage anyone who calls himself or herself a planner or scheduler to learn more about Jim, and the absolutely phenomenal role that he (and dear Rita) have played in bringing our Practice to where it is today.

Next, I would like to thank a group of special friends and colleagues who gave so generously of their time, energy, and insights to help review the many drafts of this book. Their thoughtful comments and profound advice have delivered this book from the cluttered musings of a frustrated Scheduling Practitioner to the final product you now hold in your hands.

Without any exaggeration, while I may have written this book, whatever quality it contains is due, in large part, to the contributions made by Hal Balsinger (EDS), Chris Carson (Alpha Corporation), Ted Douglas (ACTPMA), Dr. Patricia Galloway (Neilson-Wurster Group), Mike Hopkins (Fluor), Keith Howard (Motorola), Jeff Huneycutt (U.S. Army Corp of Engineers), Veena Kumar (Bovis Lend Lease), Richard Long (Long International), Dr. Gunnar Lucko (Catholic University), Craig Miller (Vanir Construction), Anamaria Popescu (CPM Consulting), and Janice Staley (Envision).

Then there are those who comprise what I would call the *Inner Circle*, as it were. These are the special people in my life who have taken turns standing beside me and giving me the inspiration and encouragement I have needed to accomplish what I have over the years. I will always be grateful to Anita and Ken Woolf who, recognizing my potential, advised me to walk away from my *career* as a gas station attendant and instead enter a Construction Management program at the University of Southern Mississippi. I thank Sue Babbitt who, for nearly nine years, kept the home fires burning and often "went it alone" while I plugged on through the night in crazy pursuit of a better Scheduling Practice. And of course, I thank Lynn Clark for her unwavering support and faith in me. She consistently got me through those moments when I thought that the subject matter was simply too overwhelming, by encouraging me to "just take one thing and run with it—and the others things will fall into place." Her wisdom proved true, time and again.

It is my life view that the extent to which one's true potential is manifested is most dramatically governed by the quality of souls with whom we spin through our life dance. On my dance floor, I was richly blessed to waltz with Bob Woolf and Patti Woolf, my dearest confidantes for the longest time. They never stopped believing in me, always said "yes" any time I asked for their guidance or help, and never hesitated to inform the emperor that he was naked. In an equal light of reverence I hold my daughters, Susan and Laura, who sacrificed their very youth for the sake of their father's dreams, only one of which was to write a definitive text on construction planning and scheduling. I thank them for such a precious gift of love.

Project Scheduling is a fascinating art, science, practice, discipline and—maybe one day—profession. But, like the instrumentalist who can never aspire to his personal greatest potential without the partnership of the orchestra, I am forever beholden to *all* of my scheduling colleagues who, as I write this, continue to work diligently each day to improve the collective value of our craft, one Project Schedule at a time.

Here's to all of you—my friends in spirit!

Table A-1

Influential Individuals

Individuals Influential in Shaping My Views on Scheduling and Project Management			
Phil Apprill	Rey Diaz	Richard Lamb	Lee Schumacher
Russ Archibald	Kent Dickinson	Larry Landry	Thomas Shaw
Brad Arnhart	Michael D'Onofrio	Jack Lemley	Rollie Smith
Andrew Avalon	Mark Dochtermann	Bret Leppo	Tony Smith
Tarek Bahgat	Dennis Dorward	Paul Levin	Al Stepaniak
Evans Barba	Tom Dirscoll	Jeff Lindsey	Bruce Stephan
Gwen Barger	Chet Dunlevy	Kirby Loid	Kevin Stubblebine
Susan Barton	Sam Duvall	Rob Low	Lars Tanner
Mike Bertino	Gary Ehrlich	Eric Lowther	Denise Taylor
Mike Bitner	Dick Faris	Dick Macklehatten	Sam Tipton
Mark Boe	Jeff Galyon	David Marchman	Tim Todorow
Mark Bojeun	Jim Garrett	Derek Mason	Bob Tumbarello
Chuck Bolyard	Jeff Gilmore	Tom McCarthy	Eric Uyttewaal
Matt Boot	Earl Glenwright	Paddy McCarthy	Gary Veidt
Barry Bramble	Chuck Guedelhoefer	Pradip Mehta	Craig Veteto
Barry Brower	Bud Guest	George Mills	George Vogler
Alex Brown	John Heeley	Rick Moffat	Alex Waddell
Roger Burnett	Scott Herold	Mike Mosley	Patricia Walsh
John Buziak	Jim Highfill	Saleh Mubarak	Tony Warner
Timothy Calvey	Terry Hill	Stu Ockman	Ronny Warren
Doug Clark	Chris Hite	Glen Palmer	Jeff Werner
Richard Clough	Barbara Hodges	Dave Pattillo	Susan Weston
Mark Cohen	David Hulett	Dan Petry	Jon Wickwire
Ken Cone	Steve Hurlbut	Charlie Phillips	Tammo Wilkens
Gustavo Couto	Chip Hutchison	Keith Pickavance	Laura Williams
John Cronin	Steve Huyghe	Steve Pinnell	Ron Winter
Colin Cropley	Bob Jacobs	Fred Plotnick	Kevin Wise
Sudhir Damle	John Jerz	Ed Putkonin	Ed Wilson
Gordon Davis	David Kaiser	Brian Relle	Hugh Woodward
Dennis Dayton	Barry Kane	Rich Richmond	Richard Wurster
Jesus de la Garza	Dave Kendrick	Ron Rider	Jim Young
Gui Pone de Leon	Truman King	Mike Rutherford	Jim Zack
Leo Della	Nick Koreisha	Al Schaer	Jim Zipperly

Introduction

For a number of years during the late 1970s and early 1980s, I taught a course called *Scheduling* for the Associated General Contractor's Supervisory Training Program (STP)®. To break the ice on the first night, I would approach the lectern, wait for complete silence, and then, in a fake Latino accent[3], utter, "Scheduling . . . has been berra, berra good . . . to *me*."

The truth is that the fascinating art and science of Commitment Planning and Execution Scheduling has been my lifeblood for over a quarter century. I have had hands-on involvement in the planning and/or scheduling of more than 125 projects worldwide, projects ranging in dollar value from small ($250,000) to large ($250,000,000) to megalarge ($14 billion).

In terms of the types of projects I have worked on, they run the gamut: airports; clean rooms; telecommunications; education; skyscrapers; manufacturing; retail; aerospace; defense; subways and light rail; research and office campuses; correctional facilities; chemical, process, and power plants; theme parks; roads and bridges; bus terminals; sports arenas; healthcare facilities; waste water treatment facilities and other civil and heavy construction; pharmaceuticals; hospitality (restaurants and hotels); performance halls; residential; and municipal and government buildings.

PLANNING AND SCHEDULING—WHAT'S NOT TO LOVE?

I love Planning and Scheduling. What's not to love? Commitment Planning and Execution Scheduling are at the very heart of all project management. Without exaggeration, virtually every aspect of project management evolves around the *Execution Schedule.* A popular analogy compares the project manager to the commercial airliner pilot and the Project Scheduler to the pilot's navigational officer. If that is so, then the Execution Schedule itself must be the flight plan. It doesn't get more significant than that!

From a planning perspective, Feasibility Planning is the starting point that leads to ultimate Performance Control. Owners and contractors alike look to Feasibility Planning for answers to questions that will determine whether a project is viable and prudent from a business perspective.

Moving chronologically toward Performance Control, Master Planning generates answers to almost all questions asked during the project conception period. Owners want to know if the project can be finished quickly enough to meet market demands (time), what the estimated price tag will be (cost), and the extent of functionality the finished product will contain (quality).

---

[3]The quote "Baseball . . . been berra berra good . . . to me" comes from Saturday Night Live comedian Garrett Morris, who invented a baseball player named Chico Escuela (he served as the sportscaster on Saturday Night Live's Weekend Update). It is generally thought that the character was loosely based on real-life baseball player Roberto Clemente.

During Strategic Planning, contractors desire to know whether the project is one for which they should compete and how difficult it will be to build. Will the project be potentially profitable and sufficiently prudent from a business perspective to pursue? From the standpoint of optimization, a forerunner to the Execution Schedule is the Strategic Plan, a graphical depiction of the optimum course of action, that is, the infamous contractor "means and methods," followed by the Consensus Plan, which carries the endorsement of the entire project team.

But then comes the Execution Schedule itself. Through rigid design, development, and maintenance processes, the project team devises an execution concept that anticipates potential risk events, maximizes return on monetary investment, incorporates quality and safety measures, coordinates the activities of hundreds or thousands of workers, suggests ideal site utilization strategies, forecasts human and other resource needs, documents budgeted and actual capital expenditures, and addresses numerous other factors. Of course, this anticipation assumes that the schedule is thorough and well thought out. Sadly, not all Execution Schedules have these attributes.

Being an Execution Scheduler is exhilarating. Hardly a day goes by on any well-managed project that the Execution Schedule is not discussed or referenced. Next to the project manager, the Project Scheduler is the individual most exposed to virtually every aspect of project management, from the earliest planning discussions, to direct field execution to contract and change order deliberations and then to closeout and claims negotiations.

Plus, in combinations, Commitment Plans and Execution Schedules are used longer than any other project documentation, spanning the entire length of the project lifecycle. Thoughts about project implementation begin during Feasibility Planning, a point in the project lifecycle quite often predating the arrival of the project manager, the project budget, quality control plans, human resource planning, or even most contracts.

During Strategic Planning, when estimators and procurement personnel are at the height of their involvement, the Execution Planner is a team member with seniority. Then, during the project implementation phase, change management activities may call the estimators back to the jobsite—where the Execution Scheduler has been all along. Field engineers, tasked with managing project documentation, submittals, record keeping, subcontractor and vendor invoicing, and the contractor's own pay requests, use the Project Schedule on a daily basis to perform their duties.

After the project has ended, long after almost all players have moved on to their next project, the project manager and Scheduling Practitioner remain behind, knee deep in post-project benchmarking, analysis, and unfortunately, dispute resolution activities.

I'm a Scheduling Practitioner at heart—and I *love* it. What's not to love?

MUCH HAS CHANGED OVER THE YEARS

For nearly three decades I have observed lots of changes in the field of what was once called Planning and Scheduling. To be sure, much has changed and yet much remains the same. As for the technocrat himself, we used to be called *schedulers*. Then, it became chic to be called *planners/schedulers*. After that, it all got mixed up. With no national standard, some companies called us planners (even if we were doing just scheduling) and some called us schedulers (even if we were doing just planning).

Conditions were hardly better with the Practice itself. In the mid-1980s the term *Project Controls* was introduced. Again, with no universal definition, the term meant different things to different users. Sometimes it meant just schedule controls, most often it meant cost and schedule controls, and on some rare occasions it was much broader in meaning, encompassing cost, schedule, quality, safety, and even estimating, contracts, and claims!

At the technical level, the story is the same: little has changed despite major developments in technology. In terms of Critical Path Method (CPM), the principles are all the same. We still have activities, durations, and relationships. Yes, we went from the dominance of the Arrow Diagramming Method (ADM) to the current Precedence Diagramming Method (PDM). Both methods, with only subtle differences in symbolism and mechanics, yield the same basic Project Schedule values that were available almost 50 years ago: earliest-dates, latest-dates, total-float, free-float, and critical-path.

It is the software that has changed the most over the years. In the early days, Project Scheduling was performed on a mainframe computer located sometimes hundreds of miles away. Long car trips with boxes of IBM punch cards bouncing in the back seat were required to "test" the logic of a new Execution Schedule. In the early days, MSCS (McDonnell-Douglas Schedule and Cost System) was the king of all scheduling software. Graphics were accomplished via MAPS and T-MAPS (McDonnell-Douglas Automated Plotting System, and a subsequent version created by a joint venture of Turner Construction and McDonnell-Douglas).

The first major shakeup in automated scheduling was the invention of the minicomputer, along with concurrent development of corresponding software, such as Artemis. Eventually, the minicomputer gave way to the microcomputer (IBM marketed its personal computer model as the IBM PC) and, along with it, came an onslaught of rushed-to-market scheduling software programs, the early frontrunner being *Primavera*.[4]

One day, we woke up and found scheduling software *on our desk!* For my younger colleagues, those of you who have grown up with one or more computers in your home since you were a baby, it may be difficult to appreciate just how thrilling it was to be able to produce a Project Schedule right from your desk without having to travel anywhere.

Our elation would surely have been dampened had we realized the Trojan Horse that the desktop scheduling software really was. I say that because, thanks to the advent of the desktop scheduling application, even extreme novices could now create what they purported to be Execution Schedules. In all truth, those "schedules" were little more than spreadsheet-type task lists in dire need of CPM Scheduling fundamentals. But in a sudden and frightening wave of false confidence, these self-proclaimed "schedulers," (mostly project managers) could produce their own schedules, without the help of costly Scheduling Practitioners. Within a few years, the population of dedicated Project Schedulers dropped off by more than 75 percent.[5]

---

[4]Primavera Systems, Inc., manufacturer of Primavera Project Planner ("P3")
[5]This is a conservative estimate on my part.

A dozen years later, Microsoft pushed its way into the Project Scheduling market with a very anemic CPM program called MS Project. The earliest versions neither calculated total-float nor contained any provision for a data-date.

DESPITE CPM, PROJECTS ARE SLIPPING AS MUCH AS EVER

The heading of this section brings me to why I wrote this book. "The proof of the pudding is in the eating," they say. Well, the "eating," as it were, is to be found in the following four observations, which came out of Momentum Studies[6] conducted in the 1980s. Taken together, these observations form what I call a Schedule Effectiveness Paradox:

- **Observation #1** The vast majority of multifamily residential projects finish within 2 percent of their planned project length.

- **Observation #2** The vast majority of multifamily residential projects are managed without the use of network schedules.

- **Observation #3** The vast majority of large commercial and industrial projects finish late: between 5–10 percent longer than their planned project length.

- **Observation #4** The vast majority of large commercial and industrial projects are managed with automated CPM Schedules. Note: The results were essentially the same, regardless of CPM diagramming method, ADM or PDM.

Be careful as you struggle to interpret these seemingly disappointing statistics. Study of the raw data underlying these statistics revealed some rather surprising explanations of what I called the Schedule Effectiveness Paradox. Specifically, I found that the key contributor to the difference in residential and commercial performance was *not* the Project Schedule itself, but rather the nature of the project type. In multifamily or production residential construction, the "product" is very much a cookie. That is, most residential developers have less than a dozen different floor plans that they build at different locations across the country.

The only real "surprises" residential builders may encounter come from below-grade activities as a result of geographical differences. Once the slabs are in place, however, the balance of the construction activities are produced in cookie-cutter fashion. There are few, if any, surprises. Material and equipment requirements are well understood from the get-go, as are labor and capital needs. Key management personnel travel from project to project, and few projects are built concurrently.

By stark contrast, every commercial project is a one-of-a-kind undertaking. Each commercial or industrial project has a unique design. There is no prior learning curve from which to gain an advantage. In contrast, residential construction already has an established learning curve from the similar designs of previous projects. A major cause of productivity loss on commercial projects is standby time; the result of unclear or conflicting design or instructional details; missing materials, supplies, or equipment; and so on.

---

[6]See *Momentum Studies* in the Glossary.

In a nutshell, there are more unknowns in commercial construction than in residential construction. While this may not be the fault of the Project Schedule, the preceding observations suggest that it is an obstacle that the CPM methodology does not seem able to overcome. My conclusion is that CPM-type Project Schedules, as designed and used, fail to anticipate most surprises,[7] either in the long term (during Authorization Planning or Strategic Planning) or in the near term (during Execution Scheduling and Performance Control).

Of course, this conclusion didn't require these statistics. Sadly, there is widespread skepticism, even cynicism, across the construction industry about the true value of network-based scheduling. Recent movements in professional circles, including ongoing efforts by the Project Management Institute to establish national scheduling standards and best practices, suggest that the science and art of Commitment Planning and Execution Scheduling have fallen short of user expectations.

WHY OUR PROJECT SCHEDULES CONTINUE TO FAIL US

So what went wrong? That's the million-dollar question, of course, and everybody and his brother has an opinion. I do, too. And that's why I have written this book. I have several thoughts on the matter. I can summarize them here, so as to remove the mystery, but it will take the balance of this book to adequately explain them. But, please don't jump to early conclusions of your own based strictly on these bullets:

- The Project Schedule has been commandeered by nonscheduling disciplines.
- Questionable Schedule Development practices have rendered core Execution Schedule elements (scope, duration, relationship) flawed and unreliable.
- Traditional Project Management fails to address the notification, planning, or response to daily surprises (which I call *dilemmas*).
- The traditional application of CPM is inherently retrospective.[8]
- As currently taught and practiced, our Project Schedules are too detailed, and we have become too obsessed with pointless precision.
- While we fixate on activities, the vast preponderance of schedule delays occur "in between" these Project Schedule elements.

The Project's Only Time Tool Has Been Commandeered

It is not surprising, given the Project Schedule's eminence and potency that so many other project management disciplines choose to use the Execution Schedule to advance *their* causes. Today's Project Schedules are often cost-loaded and manpower-loaded, burdened by sometimes imposing Work Breakdown Structure (WBS) requirements, resource-leveled, and more. Activities are injected into the Project Schedule to accommodate General Condition costs, to incorporate TQM (Total Quality Management) programs, to support Monte Carlo

---

[7]It was this discovery, that CPM schedules don't help the project manager anticipate or react to daily "surprises," that inspired the creation of Dilemma Control (see Chapter 6).

[8]This is one reason, perhaps the primary one, why the traditional CPM schedule becomes little more than a historical report rather than a serious project management tool.

Simulations in connection with risk analysis, to provide sufficient granularity for Earned Value Management System (EVMS) calculations, and so on.

You can't blame any of these other disciplines for wanting to use the Project Schedule as a means to their own ends. The problem is that, when you look at the various Knowledge Areas[9] side by side, the extent of usage seems a bit greedy. Why do I say that? Because each of these other disciplines has its own, exclusive set of specialized work products and tools. By comparison, the Scheduling Practice has only the Project Schedule!

Consider the discipline of cost management, for example. In order to perform its basic functions it uses budgets, work authorization forms, tracking logs, delivery tickets and receipts, cost codes and schedules of values, EVMS, cash flow projections, accounting records, cost control procedures, engineering estimates, and more. Likewise, procurement management has contracts, bid documents, material-receiving reports, change orders, and so on.

Yet, what does the Scheduling Practice have at its disposal to assist the project manager in achieving Performance Control? Only the Project Schedule! The Project Schedule is the *only* tool within the project manager's arsenal that is able to help him effectively orchestrate the actions of hundreds or even thousands of project participants.

When you think about it, orchestrating the performance of project team members constitutes the bulk of the project manager's responsibilities. Without a reliable Project Schedule, he cannot know answers to many questions that begin with the word "when." When should Contractor *X* be expected on site? When will Equipment *Y* need to be delivered? When should vacations be scheduled, or prohibited? When will the money be needed?

Unconventional Schedule Development Practices

Without nationally recognized best practices for Schedule Development standards, core elements across Project Schedule can vary widely. Worse, even within a single Project Schedule, inconsistent treatment of variables can result in an unreliable end product. Specifically, I'm referring to the activity-duration and the activity-relationship (which will be discussed at length throughout this book, and especially in Chapter 10, "Anatomy of a Schedule"). Beyond this, I am referring to a Project Schedule's level-of-detail, Performance Recording practices, Schedule Revision parameters, use of various scheduling software features that can and so often do obliterate the reliability of the Project Schedule, and so forth.

Start with the activity-duration itself. Any Scheduling purist will agree with me that *the duration is sacrosanct*. The supreme importance of the activity-duration should be obvious. Activity-durations generate earliest-dates and latest-dates that, in turn, lead to total-float, which eventually yield the critical-path. If a Project Schedule's activity-durations are bogus, then so are the Execution Schedule's calculated earliest and latest dates, free-float and total-float, critical and near-critical-path determinations, and so on.

Momentum Studies have shown that a paltry 25 percent of those polled who have had Schedule Development responsibilities could accurately define or explain the following terms: *elapsed-duration, contiguous-duration, interruptible-duration*, or *continuous-workdays*.

---

[9]From the Project Management Institute's *Project Management Body of Knowledge* (*PMBOK*).

Let's look at the relationship component of a Project Schedule. Much has been said about PDM's vulnerability to fraud or unintentional error in the area of activity overlapping. Many experts agree that if *relationship-durations* are inaccurately or unreasonably allocated, the Project Schedule's overall reliability is diminished proportionately.

Now, consider this fifth observation from the Momentum Studies:

- **Observation #5** Upward of 90 percent of all *actual* durations are within +/– 5 percent of the original-durations.

Understand what this statistic is saying! The vast majority of activities are completed in a length of time not much different from what was originally estimated. This statistic stands in stark contrast to the preceding Observation #3, which says that the vast majority of projects overran their Project Schedules. Yet Observation #5 says that the vast majority of original-durations are achieved. How is this possible?

The answer lies in the relationship-duration. To understand this, one needs to return to the scene of the crime: back at the jobsite trailer, at the time of Logic Development Sessions, with the subcontractors encircling the table. When Contractor X is asked how long he will need to perform Activity Z, he responds with "give me seven days."

Here's what's happening in his head. He knows he wants to give himself some wiggle room, and since he knows he can get the work done in five days, those two extra days are enough cushion to satisfy him. He'd like to secure a larger buffer, like ten days, but if he tries for it he knows that his tactic will be exposed and reversed. So, he proposes an activity-duration that is somewhat more than what is needed but not so excessive that it draws attention.

Enter Parkinson's Law, which states that, "work expands so as to fill the time available for its completion." For instance, if a report is due one week from now, work on that report will begin just shy of the deadline in order to submit it one week from now. However, if the report is required in two weeks, then it will be submitted at the end of two weeks. Why? Because workers take as much time as they are allowed, according to Parkinson's Law.

We now have two reasons why the vast majority of activities take about as long as their original-durations:

- Activity-durations are fairly reasonable when first created (contractors pad only slightly).
- Contractors typically finish within the time allowed.

By process of elimination, then—that is, if the activity-durations are not the culprit—it must be during the time span of the relationship-duration that project delays are being experienced. Further research into the way relationship-durations are created in the first place confirms this conclusion. Relationship-durations are not established the same way that activity-durations are. There is a general belief that a given relationship-duration represents some portion of the predecessor activity's duration. Often, this initial thinking is expressed in terms of a percentage. For example, say that the prior activity-duration is 20 days, and the subcontractor wants this prior activity to be at least 25 percent complete before he starts his follow-on activity; he will request a relationship-duration of SS5, meaning a start-to-start duration of 5 days.

The inherent fallacy in this approach, even though it is the predominant method for determining relationship-durations, is that there is no clear scope associated with the relationship-duration. Unlike an activity-duration, which generally describes the associated work scope, there is no similar "reasonableness check" for the relationship-duration. Further, Parkinson's Law does not apply, since the scope of work that must be performed before the successor activity can start is not known or understood by the activity performer. Nor is the relationship-duration typically visible in most schedule reports.

There is a third problem with relationship-durations: the Administrative Time Gap. The ATG, which is discussed in detail in Chapter 10, represents a broad and usually unwritten list of "things" that have to be performed prior to an activity's start, up and above the predecessor activity's having "gotten underway." According to the Momentum Studies, it is this unwritten set of tasks, understood to be represented by the relationship-duration, that when not performed in a timely manner creates the bulk of schedule slippage.

Inherently Retrospective CPM Usage Methodology

Go back to the Schedule Effectiveness Paradox: commercial construction projects are fraught with surprises, and the current scheduling technology fails to anticipate those surprises. The truth is that, as currently practiced, CPM-based time management is entirely *after the fact*. Most often, updates are performed monthly. At the end of the reporting cycle, the project manager is informed that his project has lost six days of total-float. Even though computer power and software capability exist with which to monitor and report performance on a weekly or even daily basis, the overwhelming majority of Scheduling reports are issued at the monthly interval.

Even the monthly routine is essentially *reactive* in nature. Two report formats dominate the types requested by most project managers, so much so that they are considered "standard" by Primavera and by most seasoned Scheduling Practitioners: the Total-Float Report and the Earliest-Start Report.

Both reports are used in a nonproactive manner. The Earliest-Start Report lists activities in the order of their implementation sequence, based on underlying logic. The perspective of the report's reader is one of taking each activity "as it comes." In fact, working out-of-sequence is typically viewed as somehow wrong or indicative of poor project execution strategy or ability.

It is the Total-Float Report and how it is used, however, that causes the greatest damage to Performance Control efforts, in my opinion. In this report, activities are sorted by total-float with activities bearing the least (including negative) total-float appearing at the top of the list. Suppose a project is running three weeks behind schedule and that there are 47 activities on this *longest* path. Running down the first page of the report are all activities with total-float of –15 days. The next longest path is –13 days, and there are 29 activities along this path, and so on.

Now, picture the project manager thumbing through this report. He sees 47 activities with total-float of –15 days completely filling all of page 1 and rolling onto page 2. Next he sees another 29 activities with total-float of –13 days. He flips to the bottom of page 3 and notices that activities are still bearing negative total-float values, just as they are on pages 4 and 5. By page 6, total-float is at last appearing positive, if only by a few days.

So, if you were the project manager, where would *you* place your attention—on the activities with some amount of total-float on page 6 and beyond, or on those activities that are behind schedule on pages 1 through 5? Practically all project managers interviewed in the Momentum Studies acknowledged that, given this example, they would concentrate on the negative total-float activities *only*! And what about paying attention to the activities that were still positive but perhaps poised to turn negative if not attended to? The answer was universal: "Wish I could. Too busy putting out fires!"

Even the much-touted Earned Value Management System is entirely retrospective. By formula, it requires a comparison of planned to actual resource consumption upon which it speculates on what it calls "performance measurement." This is clearly an after-the-fact methodology.

But at least EVMS attempts to look at trending, something CPM fails to do at all! Consider the common interpretation of a project reporting total-float of –15 days. Imagine a project in its third month of an 18-month lifecycle. The conventional interpretation would be that the project will complete 3 weeks late—15 months from now! The fact that in the first month the project total-float was –5 days, in the second month it was –10 days, and in this third month it is –15 days is not considered. Yet if you look at the trend, losing 5 days each month, *at this rate* the project will finish 18 weeks behind schedule, not just 3 weeks behind schedule!

Too Much Detail

Somehow, along the way, we have forgotten that so much of what we do is steeped in estimates and guesswork. Seen from this point of view, it really does seem funny—almost ludicrous—that we Scheduling Practitioners spend time debating whether lags should be negative or positive or arguing so passionately that *this* path is critical and *that* path is not, even though only a few days of total-float separate them.

Our Project Schedules are too detailed, in my opinion. When a Project Schedule tries to predict that a particular activity will start on a Wednesday 28 months from now, then that Project Schedule is simply too detailed! Cost engineering demands for fiscal accountability to the single-activity level can be blamed for some amount of today's Project Schedule detail overkill, but other special interests have had their finger in the pie, too. Much more on this point later.

Staking Out the Wrong Door

You've seen it in a hundred movies. The cops are staked out in a car, watching the front door, while the bad guys slide out the back door. That's how I see today's Scheduling Practice. We are obsessed with activities and relationships, even though research has shown that the vast majority of schedule delays do not occur during the activity-tenure or as a result of failed interdependencies. The major causes of schedule delay have to do with circumstances and conditions that are not even depicted in the Project Schedule. Yet there we are, month after month, calculating duration variances and lag variances, noting out-of-sequence work performance, statusing progress with scientific precision, and on. Much more on this point later, as well.

WHY I WROTE THIS BOOK, AND HOW IT'S ORGANIZED

Over the course of my career as a Scheduling Practitioner, I have accumulated hundreds of observations about what works best, better, or not at all when it comes to producing Project Schedules that project managers will actually want to use. From time to time, Junior

Schedulers have asked me for practical advice. At some point, it occurred to me that something in writing was needed that "whispered in the less-experienced Practitioner's ears." The image in my head as I wrote this book was one of a seasoned Scheduler (with 50 or more projects to his credit) sharing "tricks of the trade" with a Junior Scheduler (with between four to six schedules under his belt).

I wrote this book because I wanted to repay a Practice that has been my lifeblood throughout my career, one that has been "berra, berra good to me." I felt that the best way I could give something back was to share battle-born lessons with those who are struggling to improve the quality of our craft through skillful application of its art and its science. There is widespread consensus in recent professional writings that what the Scheduling Practice needs more than anything else, right now, is better *training* materials that will instill proper and consistent processes within the Practice and across multiple, diverse industries.

That is what this book is all about. It is meant to provide a common-sense, real-world treatment of construction Commitment Planning and Execution Scheduling considerations. It is not intended to be a how-to book containing a sequential set of instructions on schedule design, development, maintenance, and usage. To be sure, if this book is viewed along the planning/scheduling continuum, you will find it to have blatant gaps in coverage. There are plenty of how-to books on the bookstore shelves, and besides, this book assumes that the reader has already created a half-dozen or so schedules and is therefore beyond the basics.

Instead, this volume speaks specifically and limitedly to issues that I have found to be significant contributors to why Project Schedules fail to meet their intended objectives and why projects fail to achieve their proposed Project Schedule milestones and promised deliverables.

This book is divided into five parts. Part 1, "Keeping Your Eye on the Donut" (Chapters 1 through 4) looks soberly at the environment in which projects are built and Project Schedules must function. Only by understanding the challenges facing the project manager as he embarks on maneuvering a project through tumultuous political, social, economic, technical, and functional waters can the Project Schedule that is created to serve the project manager be of any real value. Chapters 1–3 explore the many diverse and often-conflicting elements that either influence, or are influenced by, the Project Schedule's design, development, maintenance, use, and quality. Chapter 4 offers a thought-provoking analysis of the current, undeniable conversion from the centuries-old, authority-based Command-and-Control style of project management to the more team-centered Collaborative Management.

Part 2 of this book, "Creating a Penchant for Change," contains five chapters that, collectively, explore innovative new ways to make our customers much happier with what we provide to them:

- Chapter 5 offers what I believe to be the first-ever consolidated set of definitions for the Scheduling Practice, including specialties, positions, procedures, deliverables and roles.
- Chapter 6 introduces Dilemma Control, a new project management capability made possible by Momentology.
- Chapter 7 introduces Momentology, a new project management methodology and technology, including a new set of products and services to be offered by the Scheduling Practitioner.

- Chapter 8 provides a summary of all of the new terminology I am proposing. The preceding three chapters introduce quite a few new concepts and lots of new terms. This short chapter is so helpful that I have repeated it at the end of the book, right ahead of the Glossary.
- Chapter 9 segues the conceptual backdrop of Part 2 into the practical advice found on how to create better Project Schedules, discussed in subsequent chapters.

Part 3, "Preserving Schedule Integrity" (Chapters 10 and 11), addresses several methodological subjects that need to be ironed out before we submerge ourselves in the mechanical aspects of Parts 4 and 5. In this part, we dissect the Project Schedule so that you may see its many components, perhaps in a context never before considered. You will learn about *Administrative* and *Productive Time Gaps*, explore structured ways to determine relationship-durations, and discover the anatomies of relationships and activities. You will be cautioned about forces that can and often do attack and erode your Project Schedules and what you can do to ensure their ongoing integrity.

Chapters 12 through 16, which comprise Part 4, "Execution Scheduling and Performance Control," address dozens of assorted issues that characterize and encompass the design, development, maintenance, and usage of the Execution Schedule. Here, you will find practical hints and worthwhile warnings on a broad range of subjects with equally varied depths of treatment.

Chapters 15 and 16 provide admittedly light treatment of Performance Recording and Performance Control, however, because an upcoming book will be completely dedicated to Performance Control. After all, if we have learned anything over the last 50 years, it is that those superficial CPM printouts that we hand out like confetti each month just don't tell the astute project manager much of anything he didn't already know. Only through advanced Performance Analysis will you be able to give your project manager insights into future events and the ability to truly accomplish Dilemma Control.

Finally, Part 5, "Epilogue," is a one-chapter close to this attempt on my part to help you produce Project Schedules that your customers will actually *want* to use. It contains the "Top Ten Techniques for Sabotaging Your Scheduling Efforts," an antithetical summary of the entire book. Chapter 17 also contains a helpful synopsis of each chapter's key points. Finally, you will find a handy Glossary of unique terms. I have omitted from this Glossary any terms which you should already know the meaning of and that I have not changed.

Speaking as a quarter-century Scheduling veteran who truly believes in the art and science of the Scheduling Practice, I am genuinely frustrated that a project management tool having so much potential can so often be so terribly ineffective. We can do better—all of us—and we must, if we hope to remain valuable to the project management process! I hope this book adds meaning to the wealth of information available to those who want to create Project Schedules that "they will actually want to use." It *is* possible! Good luck.

Part 1 Keeping Your Eye on the Donut

Part 1, *Keeping Your Eye on the Donut* (Chapters 1, 2, 3, and 4) looks soberly at the environment in which projects are built and Project Schedules must function. Only by understanding the challenges facing the project manager, as he struggles to maneuver his project through tumultuous political, social, economic, technical, and functional waters, can the Project Schedule, created to serve him, be of any real value. Chapters 1, 2, and 3 explore the many diverse and often-conflicting elements that either influence, or are influenced by, the Execution Schedule's design, development, maintenance, use, or quality. Chapter 4 offers a thought-provoking analysis of the current, undeniable conversion from the centuries-old, authority-based Command-and-Control style of project management, to the more team-centered Collaborative Management.

1 The Allure of the Project Schedule

Answer this: What project management process or element has been the root of more jokes than the Project Schedule? Invoices? Change orders? The specs? The contract? The computer? The budget? No, it's the Project Schedule, the network-based Critical Path Network schedule to be more precise, that receives a constant undermining dose of ridicule, mockery, and verbal abuse from practically every member of the project team. No wonder Project Schedulers are CPMs (Crazy People Mostly).

All kidding aside, the Project Schedule's poor image is quite ironic, given its tremendous potential to make an overwhelming difference in how your project ends up. The Project Schedule is, without exception, the most powerful weapon in the project manager's arsenal. It has the ability to plan, coordinate, schedule, direct, monitor, inform, analyze, report, and evaluate all project activities.

The Project Schedule has the last laugh, however, for today virtually every major construction project in the United States has a Project Schedule associated with it—before, during, or after the project's life cycle. Of course, the best time to prepare a Project Schedule is *before* the project starts. But, rest assured, if one is not prepared *before,* or even *during* the life of the job, some high-priced claims consultant will be preparing one *afterward*.

THE SUCCESS OF A PROJECT SCHEDULE DEPENDS ON MANY FACTORS

To be sure, the success of a Project Schedule depends on many considerations, as shown in Table 1-1.

Schedule Timing

The earlier in the project life cycle that a Project Schedule is developed, the more significant its contribution will be. This is pretty much common sense. The time to consult

Table 1-1

Project Schedule
Success Factors

Schedule Timing
Schedule Content
Schedule Format
User Resistance
Upper Management Commitment
Schedule Developer Expertise
Schedule User Training
Tie-in to Other Project Controls

a map is *before* the journey begins. The longer one waits, the greater the possibility of having traveled many miles in the wrong direction. Timing, then, is a primary key to successful project schedules.

Schedule Content

Another key variable affecting Project Schedule value and acceptance is content. Does the Project Schedule tell you something you didn't already know? Is the information within it presented at a meaningful and useful level of detail? Is the Project Schedule factually sound and is its inherent logic equally unassailable?

Schedule Format

Format, too, makes a big difference. How a Project Schedule looks can have a tremendous impact on how much or how well it is used. Project Schedules should be easy to follow. Graphical representations should be laid out with an artist's eye, including a fair amount of white space. Subnetworks (also called subnets or fragnets) should be used liberally to assist the brain in visually segmenting the Project Schedule (and, hence, the project) into its logical components.

User Resistance

No amount of creative schedule design can overcome entrenched user resistance. There must be general receptivity to the role and importance of the Project Schedule and to the idiosyncrasies of a network-based schedule, in particular. If members of the project team are opponents of project scheduling, you may as well not waste time or money developing a CPM network at all; it will only end up in the trash anyway. The Project Schedule must provide them an obvious benefit if you wish for them to support its development and usage.

Upper Management Support

Similar to user receptivity, but not the same, is upper management commitment to the project's Scheduling effort. I can't begin to tell you how important it is that the project director and Vice President of Operations back at the home office make both visible and explicit their support of Execution Planning and Scheduling processes and tools. They can do this by attending one or more of the schedule development sessions, by participating in Feasibility Planning, and Strategic Planning, and by using the Project Schedule themselves as a basis for setting priorities and making smart decisions.

Most important of all, they should insist on the inclusion of a Scheduling Practitioner in *all* major project meetings where discussions pertain (in whatever degree) to the Project Schedule or the planning activities. Consider, for example, Strategic Planning sessions, where a contractor decides whether a proposed project is appropriate to pursue. Far too often, management invites everybody and his brother to these meetings. Everybody, that is, except the Project Scheduler: the project manager, estimator, business development manager, buyer, and comptroller are all on the distribution list. But not the Scheduler; go figure! Yet it happens everyday in design and construction war rooms around the country.

Schedule Developer Expertise

As I stated in the Preface, this book was written in response to a call for scheduling experts to share their understanding of what makes for a good Project Schedule and what does not. With a proliferation of scheduling software and an abundance of books on Critical Path Method (CPM) mechanics, why should there be any question as to what goes into a good Project Schedule?

The answer lies in the reality that the majority of things that cause bad Project Schedules don't fall within the mechanics of the Critical Path Method, or software settings. Take, for example, the tremendous importance of Schedule Design. Most texts on CPM scheduling either ignore this process completely or they give it little more than a few paragraphs of coverage. Every seasoned Scheduler already grasps its importance and makes sure that the conclusions reached during Schedule Design are incorporated into the Execution Schedule. Yet someone who is new to the Scheduling Practice might miss the subtle but highly relevant importance of appropriate schedule architecture.

Likewise, look at how these same texts treat the development of relationship-durations. Do they talk about the concepts of concurrent administrative actions that also restrain an activity from starting, beyond the completion of a certain amount of predecessor activity scope? Few texts do.

I guess there is little need for me to say much more about the value of scheduling expertise. If you didn't already appreciate that someone who has done scheduling for 30-plus years might have insights not apparent to someone who is doing their first, second, or third schedule, you wouldn't be reading this book.

Schedule User Training

Not everyone who eventually uses the Project Schedule participates in its creation. In fact, the earlier participants are typically few in number or percentage, compared with all who will eventually look to the Project Schedule for answers. It serves the project well to take the time to educate all of these folks on how to read a logic diagram, how the basic calculations (earliest and latest dates, float, and critical path) are derived, and how to interpret the contents of printouts.

In particular, the latter refers to frequent misinterpretations of total-float. I can't count all the times I've seen executives get all bent out of shape over minor changes in total-float values. If only they realized how erratic that measure truly is, they would focus on other, more meaningful indicators of project performance. Correspondingly, down-stream participants, such as vendors and subcontractors, often use "available" total-float as justification for dragging out their own work and missing earliest-finish dates.

Tie-In to Other Project Controls

This point is covered at some length in Part 3, "Preserving Schedule Integrity," but let me repeat one of its key points here. The Project Schedule is extremely versatile, but it performs many functions that other project management support system components can also do, independent of the schedule. These other components align with the PMBOK® Guide's knowledge areas: scope management, cost management, risk management, human resource management, and procurement management, just to name a few.

These project management subsystems include processes, outputs, techniques, and objectives that can be achieved either:

- Independent of the Project Schedule.
- In conjunction with the Project Schedule.

or

- Solely by the Project Schedule.

Once the decision has been made about where these subsystems will base their operations, coordination is required with the Scheduling side of the house. Obviously, if the third option is chosen, many decisions need to be made as to how input data will be communicated *to* the Project Schedule and how output data will be sent back to the informational partner. The same holds true for components pursued as a joint venture. Information must flow in both directions. As I said earlier, these additional users of the Project Schedule can be accommodated, but they must be prevented from weakening project management's ability to effectively manage Project Momentum.

Finally, protocols should be set in place to establish which project management component will have first-point accountability for which critical project data element. Who will speak for project status, for instance? If an Earned Value Management System (EVMS) is being operated on the project, then the cost management team will have its sense of whether the project is behind or ahead of schedule based on its Schedule Performance Index. Yet the Scheduling Practitioners will have their *own* opinion, based on the latest Schedule Edition and the project's most recent total-float value. Who should speak about project status, the cost folks, or the schedule folks? Likewise, should budget status be derived from the cost-loaded schedule or from any number of other cost management tools?

THE AUTOMATED PROJECT SCHEDULE OFFERS THESE STRENGTHS

One of the reasons that Project Schedules are not as successful as they could be is because their purposes and abilities are understated, if not also misunderstood. The Project Schedule is multidimensional, not only in design, but also in usage. Consider the ways of describing the Project Schedule, as listed in Table 1-2.

It Is a Picture

First and foremost, a Project Schedule is a picture, and we all know a picture's worth. Even a sloppily drawn network of activities can visually convey otherwise complex human thinking in an instinctive and easy-to-understand format. Neat little boxes, nestled among arrows pointing the way from a project's beginning to its hopefully successful end, create a flowchart requiring minimal training in how to interpret.

It Facilitates Group Consensus

Put a dozen constructors in one room and ask about the best way to build this or that, and you'll get more than a dozen responses, each comment punctuated by loud voices, flailing arms, stern faces, and intermittent pauses (sometimes to expel tobacco juice). A frustrated team leader wanting to capture the essence, and hopefully the wisdom, of the combined expertise in the room requires a mechanism for depicting those thoughts in a manner that all can study and refine. A network-based schedule, quite often hastily scratched on a war room wipe-off board, provides just such a vehicle.

Remember this: the heart of all group synergy is effective communication. Recall the biblical tale of the Tower of Babel. A bunch of industrious developers and builders embarked upon perhaps the world's first theme park of global dimension. They envisioned building a tower so high that one could reach and confront God Himself.

Great plan, except that God didn't fancy the notion of uninvited guests. He resolved to thwart the ambitious band of entrepreneurs by causing each of them suddenly to speak in a different language. The results were immediate. Any word spoken by one individual seemed to be so much "babble" to all others. The Critical Path Method maximizes group communication by providing a concise, easily and commonly understood method

It Is a Picture
It Facilitates Group Consensus
It Creates Powerful Perceptions
It Transitions from Plan to Schedule
It Gives Direction
It Supports Resource Optimization
It Provides Irrefutable Evidence
It Is a Dynamic Model of Reality

Table 1-2
The Project Schedule's Versatility

of notation, where sequencing, dependency, and duration of activities are clearly represented—without the babble. An assembled puzzle is far more useful than its scattered pieces.

It Creates Powerful Perceptions

A common chasm between management theory and real-world practice is in how the project manager prioritizes decisions and actions. Modern management theory seems to adopt the notion that the astute project manager should, or at least will, manage by exception. That is, he will concentrate his efforts on those issues that, by an earlier process of elimination, have been determined to be the most needing of his attention.

But that is not how it is done in reality. What managers consistently concentrate on are those issues that they perceive to be important. Perception may be very different from the truth but, if believed strongly enough, it becomes the reality. Perception is everything in management. The key to effective project management is in gaining and maintaining clear and realistic perceptions. The Project Schedule helps here, as well. Most claims consultants can cite countless examples of projects that went awry because the Project Schedule was defective, and yet project management acted on what they *thought* was critical, as opposed to what was actually critical.

An accurate Project Schedule can be used to spot a project's areas of potential disaster *while the project is still a model in the computer*. When such potentials are acknowledged, the collective wisdom of the assembled masses is free to coalesce into optimal solutions. The results are quite often a complete avoidance of the problematic condition altogether. Even when a trouble spot cannot be circumvented entirely, its impact can almost always be mitigated to some significant degree.

It Seamlessly Transitions from Plan to Schedule

Emerging from Strategic Planning sessions, the CPM diagram, in the form of a schematic, appears as a single, massive network of activities. In such a hulking form, it is impressive to few—except perhaps to the Commitment Planner, who sits at a cluttered desk gloating over the sheer immensity of it, this product of his convoluted mind. Fortunately, the CPM network "cleans up nice."

One option is that it can easily be converted from a network-formatted Consensus Plan into a bar chart that is easy to understand. Another, even better, option is that the Consensus Plan can be expounded upon, resulting in a detail-level Execution Schedule. Through a comprehensive effort, the pre-project's general itinerary becomes the project's detailed road map.

A word about information overload: Today's construction projects are more complicated and challenging than ever before. Designs are more incomplete, materials more varied, contractors more independent, workers more hesitant, resources scarcer, budgets tighter, owners more demanding, governments more finicky, building codes more controlling, and so on.

Our challenge is to craft a Consensus Plan (and subsequent Execution Schedule) that is practical, achievable, profitable, and also addresses all of the above considerations. By way of an elaborate classification and coding system, the computerized network is designed to minimize information overload for any single project participant.

A cardinal rule of Scheduling that I have taught students for over three decades is this: *give the people all the information they need to do their job—no more, no less, and always in a form they can readily understand and use.* Fortunately, most Project Schedules are automated, and information contained within them can easily be sorted, selected, and printed in practically any combination or order imaginable—and all at the speed of light.

It Gives Direction

"Just tell me what you want, and I'll get it done," complains the project superintendent. Execution Schedule Extractions, made possible by smart coding, mean that each person gets the information he needs to do his job. At the daily level, each crew foreman has a list of tasks his team is expected to complete by the end of the day, or week. And stapled to the drywall, adjacent to the man hoist at each level of the building is a printout of what needs to happen on *that* floor *that* day or *that* week.

Each subcontractor gets two lists; one itemizing field activities required by week's end and the other for the home office, listing submittals and deliveries expected during that same time frame. The first list is handed to the subcontractor's superintendent; the latter is sent to his home office.

Each of the general contractor's superintendents has a list of what the subcontractors in his charge are expected to do. The chief superintendent, in turn, enjoys a more summary list of what each of his superintendents are responsible for achieving. Finally, the project manager's list is a digest of his chief superintendent's list, at an even more general level.

Back at their respective home offices, the project engineer has a list of shop drawings to be chased, the architect has a list of submittals in his shop for review, and the owner has a list of action items to complete in order not to hold up the job. You get the idea.

It Supports Resource Optimization

Every project requires money, time, materials, labor, and equipment. A well-defined Project Schedule can easily and effectively incorporate a project's resource requirements into the master strategy. Based on the demands made by a combination of all of the network's activities, an Execution Schedule can generate a very specific (and extremely useful) projection of resource demand levels at any point along the project life cycle.

It Provides Irrefutable Evidence

In today's far too litigious climate, it is vital that a project's day-to-day progress be carefully recorded. Here, too, the Project Schedule comes into play. Through Performance Recording, an exercise already necessary for appropriate use of the Execution Schedule as a project management tool, every significant aspect of the project's life is documented. Not just in terms of what took place and when it took place, but also (and more importantly) how it affected other aspects of the project.

It Is a Dynamic Model of Reality

The Project Schedule's record of project events is hardly static like some still picture of a jobsite. Rather, the Project Schedule is a living, breathing entity that is continually updated to reflect the current status and conditions of the project. The great value of this process is that with the occurrence of changes—in design, owner priorities, contract scope, contractor approach, project conditions, or resource availability—the Project Schedule can accurately and meaningfully reflect such changes and thereby provide a current roadmap to be followed.

I'm not merely talking about claims justification or avoidance, nor even about time impact analysis in conjunction with a change order proposal or evaluation. Beyond these aspects, I'm referring to the project manager having the ability to quickly and positively respond to that sudden, unexpected, potentially disruptive "dilemma" that so distinguishes the construction project from all other types of manufacturing.

2 Understanding the Scheduling Theater

I remember as a kid hearing about World War II. In class we read about the great achievement of the Allies in the "Pacific Theater." I thought then (and I still think) that this was a strange word to use. After all, isn't a theater where one goes to be entertained?

But a theater is a place where people converge, where human drama plays out. Where some come to speak, and others come to listen. Some come to be entertained. Others come to escape. The theater is where the playwright's deep, dark secrets are aired in the most public forum. It is where the director is his most assertive, as he attempts to manipulate the tongues, hearts, and passions of those who defy taming.

Years later, sitting in a Construction Management class in college, I again thought about the word *theater*—this time, in the context of the construction project. What I noted was that the construction site is very much like a stage. It is a place where some people perform, while others watch and wait with anticipation. There is a script, a director, actors, and an audience. There are expectations. And there are an infinite number of subplots, both fictitious and real.

Come with me as I transform this metaphor into an entirely different view of the world in which you and I endeavor to make a difference. It should be obvious why such an excursion is necessary. If you do not have a clear understanding of the environment in which you struggle to bring order, then how successful can you possibly hope to be? Notwithstanding the innocence of this analogy, this chapter is intended to help you better understand just what you're up against, as you attempt to create a schedule they'll actually want to use.

THE STAGE: THE ENVIRONMENT IN WHICH CONSTRUCTION TAKES PLACE

First, there is the stage itself. This is where the action takes place. In construction this is most assuredly the jobsite. For all practical purposes, though, it is also the community in which the jobsite is located. Let's consider the project as a stand-alone entity.

11

Each Project Is Unique

No two projects are the same. Unlike manufacturing, in which the plant is equipped with machinery specifically designed to create the company's most popular widgets, the construction "plant" is different each and every time. And the community in which the project is being built is unique as well.

Unique in Design

The product is different each and every time. Each construction project differs in one or more of these elements: design, size, purpose, and location. The Project Schedule must consider the unique design of the project, including such things as constructability, availability of resources, long-lead item implications, installation of new or untested materials, worker and material movement logistics, concurrent uninterrupted owner/tenant use of facilities, and so on.

Unique in Size

As for size, high-rise buildings impose an entirely different set of considerations than, say, a sprawling research campus might. Even width has its considerations: an interesting example of this is the Saturn Automobile plant in Spring Hill, Tennessee. The four main structures, each over 1,000,000 square feet, sit on a 1.5-mile building pad. The walls at the extreme opposite ends of the project are out of plumb from one another, due to the curvature of the earth!

Unique in Purpose

Purpose determines much about the manner in which a project is constructed. Pharmaceutical labs, computer chip manufacturing plants, and other "clean room" operations require an extra degree of quality control. In these, as in most health care projects, dust containment is vital during construction. Additionally, in most occupied spaces, but especially in health care facilities, sound abatement is critical. The Project Schedule must allow for steps taken to incorporate these considerations.

Unique in Location

Location plays a critical role in how a project is accomplished. Weather, terrain, access to site, proximity of resources, and community restrictions are just some of the variables to be considered by the Project Schedule.

Unique in Financing

Each project is financed differently and comes under a different set of public or private overseers. Accountability for the construction effort also places demands on the Project Schedule. It is the Schedule that answers many important questions with respect to the timing of major milestones. In most public projects where funding is by way of government bonds, money is released in major chunks across a long span of time when certain of these milestones are met. The Project Schedule must accommodate the owner's (in this case, the government's) ability to pay for construction efforts. Therefore, cash flow management is extremely important in this case.

Unique in Management Control Requirements

Closely akin to accountability are costing and other components of record keeping, the specific requirements of which differ from project to project. A construction project is the organized assembly of hundreds or thousands of individual parts. Someone wants to know—and a good Schedule should be able to tell—about each and every part's whereabouts: has it been designed (shop drawings), has that design been approved, has the part been ordered, has it been fabricated, has it been delivered, has it been installed (and if not, where is it being stored?), has it been inspected, has its installation been approved, and so on?

Each project requires a unique set of critical resources: workers, equipment, and materials. The Project Schedule must reflect these requirements and provide for their orderly assimilation. Clearly, shortages of critical resources can have a tremendous effect on the outcome of any project, and the Schedule that fails to address resource management is destined to become a useless document. And don't forget the most important of all resources: information.

Each Community Is Unique

Within the geographic area surrounding the jobsite are homes and businesses that may impose requirements and limits on how the work can be prosecuted. On a hospital project in Melbourne, Florida, resident complaints about dynamite blasting of coquina rock forced the contractor to resort to use of a headache ball and jackhammers, which caused a two-month time extension to the Project Schedule.

Different locations have different government overseers, complete with different building codes, different inspection frequency requirements, and so on. Two projects, in all other ways identical, can easily take different lengths of time, depending on coding and inspection differences from one locale to the other.

A Project Is a Dynamic Organism

All projects are more than just people, equipment, and materials sharing the same long-term objectives. They are an elaborate set of processes, representing overlapping and interdependent activity strings that culminate, hopefully, in the physical manifestation of a conceptual design.

A project's rate of progress is hardly guaranteed. It is often interrupted and diverted, with characteristic ebbing and surging. The project manager's role, as facilitator, is to safeguard that project's pace and direction, which I call *momentum*. Project Momentum can be affected by major as well as minor factors. Major factors include project mobilization/demobilization, strikes, labor shortages, acts of God (also called force majeure) such as severe weather or the weakening of a project's financial underpinning. One might easily and incorrectly assume that focus on major factors will best protect the project.

However, historical evidence suggests that a project's overall momentum is more likely to be influenced by the combined impact of a thousand individual catalysts, each somehow limited in scope, location, timing, or magnitude, than by a handful of major factors. Fortunately, even though these minor factors are anything but obvious, in the vast majority of cases, their effect on momentum can be mitigated or eliminated altogether.

While the project manager's challenge is to regulate momentum, it is important to remember that momentum is an effect, not a cause. Influencing momentum, then, involves influencing the one single factor that overwhelmingly influences all project momentum: the human factor.

A Collision of Competing Interests

The project manager's primary goal is to consistently and positively inspire the conduct of dozens, hundreds, or even thousands of individually-minded project participants. This must be accomplished against the unrelenting dynamics of infinite individual, group, and organization impulses, almost all of which can run counter to those of the owner. Consider three centers of competing motivational focus:

- **The Individual** Humans are highly individualistic. No two people have an identically matched set of values, beliefs, priorities, and interests.
- **The Organization** Individuals naturally adopt a certain loyalty to the group in which they work. Its goals, characteristics, and cultures strongly influence the individual's attitude. Behavioral psychologists call this tendency "group think."
- **The Project** Adjust your perspective one last time, and recognize the various groups more as individuals, with the project itself being the embracing group. Each organization has its own unique culture, focus, orientation, personality, and goals.

The concept of competing interests may well explain why complex projects rarely achieve all of their stated objectives. Quite often, initial owner objectives are dwarfed by the quantity, strength, and diversity of dynamic forces acting on any multi-participant project. The sad reality is this: if a multidiscipline project is a tug-of-war between powerful, competing interests, the owner's wishes are quite often the rope!

This is where the comparison of the project manager to the orchestral conductor falls short. In an orchestra, the musicians *want* to play together; harmony *is* the objective. But on the typical construction project, as seen through the eyes of the typical construction project manager, harmony is a means to an end, and the "musicians" would rather be somewhere else.

Project Momentum

Every project has momentum. We observe momentum throughout the project life cycle. Examples include:

- **Mobilization and demobilization actions** These reflect changing patterns of work intensity.
- **Work slowdowns** These often occur before approaching holidays, hunting season, or anticipated work stoppages.
- **Disruptive crew movements** This includes moving from one physical area of a project to another, which affects the momentum of the impacted work.
- **Work interruptions** These are often due to missing or unclear information, which breaks the momentum of design work on concept projects.

All projects experience momentum, and by definition, momentum requires action. My non-technical definition of momentum is *pace and direction*. Action in turn requires energy, which can be categorized by the types of energy sources causing the ebbs and flows of work crews in, through, and around each project. I call these energy sources *project dynamics*.

In order for the project manager to influence the outcome of the project, he must influence these project dynamics. Such dynamics include the competing interests of individuals and organizations discussed earlier, external factors that affect the project, decisions of any participants whose choices might make differences in how the project is executed and, finally, any unexpected development (dilemma) that can affect the success of the project if not anticipated and adequately managed.

Project Management as an Environmental Variable

At first blush, it may seem odd for me to include the overall discipline of project management as an environmental consideration for the Project Schedule. But if you stop to think about it, the Scheduling Practice is a project management methodology and tool. As is strongly emphasized throughout this book, good Project Schedules are ones that support the project management effort, so it is important to have a clear understanding of what the project manager faces in the course of doing his job.

The project manager is an individual with ultimate accountability for the successful achievement of a company's contractual responsibilities on the project. Project management is that set of people, processes, techniques, tools, and priorities that lead to the achievement of the project's objectives.

There are many ways to describe project management, but I have chosen its functional objectives because with projects, as in most things in life, it is not so much what one does, as it is why he does it. Project management is an ongoing series of responses to surprises, and it is vital that the project manager never lose sight of his primary functional objectives, which are to make decisions and solve problems in order to:

- Orchestrate the timely execution of the work in a proactive manner
- Prevent or mitigate legal, financial, or contractual risk or damage
- Capture knowledge and experience from project execution that will be of value to the acquisition and successful performance of future work

It used to be that the project manager's job was to essentially drive the herd to market, to merely serve as conductor of an orchestra of talented workers. But nowadays it is the rare project that does not experience scope growth, or which does not end in some dispute over time and/or money. As a result, today's project managers must do more than simply coordinate the work; they must also administer the project with an ever-trained eye on the contractual and legal implications of their actions and the actions of others. Thus, the dual focus of the project manager becomes evident:

- **As work coordinator** The first-rate project manager strives to remain proactive as he coordinates project activities. His goal is to bring about orderly, harmonious, and mutually beneficial performance by all parties to the project.

- **As contract administrator** The top-drawer project manager is focused on being preventive, as he works to ensure that all project entities perform their contractual duties in a quality, timely, safe, and minimally disruptive manner.

These two roles will be discussed in more depth later in this chapter.

Dynamic Project Management

Discussed throughout this text, every project is a living, breathing organism, often seeming to have a mind of its own. Execution Schedules, no matter how thoroughly developed or universally endorsed, become obsolete almost before Day One. Experienced project managers understand that successful project management can be reduced to effective response to dilemmas.

The other side of the same coin is how the project manager's primary functions can be distinguished in the context of an ever-changing environment, that is, in the context of a dynamic project. This characterization I call Dynamic Project Management, and central to its success is a dynamic Project Schedule.

Four Elements of Dynamic Project Management

How to achieve highly effective project management, time after time, is not a mystery. It merely requires managing the influence of the following four essential ingredients, which together spell P-R-O-J-E-C-T. This anagram helps us understand the bottom-line assignment of the project manager:

- **Planned Resources** First and foremost, there must be a plan; a method to the madness. "Plan your work, and work your plan." A well-conceived Project Schedule will consider, allocate, and choreograph the deployment and utilization of all resources: time, labor, materials, equipment, and money.
- **Objective Judgments** Second, there must be strong leadership. Successful project management is distinguished by decision-making grounded in objective, proactive, prudent, and timely thinking. Vital to this are the project manager's individual attributes: education, experience, organizational autonomy, and skills in finance, scheduling, contracts, problem solving, decision-making, accountability, disputes, leadership, and communications.
- **Effective Communications** Third, information must flow. What good are Project Schedules, early warnings, inquiries, or instructions, if they aren't communicated to the relevant parties? To be effective, however, the information being communicated, like the communiqué itself, must be timely, coherent, accurate, meaningful, germane, and understandable. A managed mechanism is needed for receiving, validating, consolidating, storing, summarizing, analyzing, and disseminating information. A comprehensive Project Schedule is an excellent choice. Finally, the various communication formats and venues must be integrated so as to reduce misunderstandings, ensure follow-through, and provide adequate inspiration for compliance.
- **Troubleshooting** Fourth, plans go awry. The adept project manager is constantly watching to identify troubles in their infancy, with the hopes of preventing them altogether. While a project that follows its plans is impressive (and rare), a project

that responds and adapts to sudden and unexpected dilemmas is the full measure of Dynamic Project Management. The trick is to know when to respond, and when to stay the course. Sound Performance Analysis, a key part of Performance Control, can really help here. (More on this in Chapter 5.)

Scheduling Software

This text would be remiss if it did not include scheduling software as one of the environments in which the Scheduling Practice functions. In keeping with the theme of this book, which is to highlight ways to produce better Project Schedules, I will limit my comments to those aspects of scheduling software that can affect the quality of Scheduling products. In no particular order, I offer these thoughts:

- **How understandable is it?** Does the scheduling software explain itself adequately? Sadly, some software programs, although loaded with very powerful and useful features, do a poor job of explaining how their various features work, and the user is forced to operate on a basis of blind faith—or ignorance. This is unacceptable if the result is that you generate reports you cannot adequately modify or explain, or you produce statistics you cannot vouch for, simply because you do not know how the values were derived.

- **Do you understand its technical underpinnings?** Assuming the software has passed the first test—that it can be understood—do *you* understand it? Can you answer the questions in this list?

- **How does the program calculate total-float?** Does it give you the option of choosing start-float, finish-float, or most-critical-float? If not, to which one does it default?

- **How does the program handle multiple calendars?** How does it compute dates when the activity utilizes multiple resources and each is on a different calendar?

- **How does the program handle out-of-sequence work?** Does it give you the option of either progress-override or retained-logic? If not, which one does it use?

- **How does the program calculate the critical-path?** Is it the longest path on the network or the one with the least total-float?

- **How does the program handle date-constraints?** What kind of date-constraints does it let you use? How is total-float calculated when applying these date-constraints?

- **How does it interpret a start-to-start relationship?** Can Activity B start five days after Activity A starts, even if Activity A stops working on Day Two?

- **Is information portable?** Can you easily exchange data with spreadsheet and database programs (for example, Excel and Access) in support of analysis and reporting functions?

- **Does the program support global changes?** Can global changes be accomplished with the program, or through export to supporting software?

- **How robust are its activity coding options?** Does the software allow for many or few coding options, and are they well integrated into the software's other functional features?

When Is Enough, Enough?

As a Practitioner "old-timer," my view of technology has changed along the way. In the beginning, I admit, I was mesmerized by every new innovation and technological breakthrough. Perhaps no one moment stands out in my mind more than a Tuesday morning in July 1983 when, for the first time, I started up a PC-based scheduling software program. No longer did I have to make the 225-mile round trip between Harrisburg, Pennsylvania to Philadelphia, the back seat loaded with IBM punch cards, just to run a schedule update at some central computer center. No more card readers, keypunch machines, high-speed printers, or reams of printouts.

Over the years, PC-based software evolved, paralleling advances in hardware technology. When I went to college, our computer lab had no monitors, so all inputs were on punch cards and all outputs were on green bar paper with holes on the side. When the first PC-based scheduling software arrived, they hadn't yet invented the hard drive, and RAM was 64K. Imagine scheduling a project with only 64K to work with!

ADM (Arrow Diagramming Method) was king, and PDM (Precedence Diagramming Method) was this wild concept that, like my buddies, I thought would never work. Not long after, the mouse came into existence and many of us diehards who knew how to work with a "C prompt" rejected the mouse as a *toy* for amateurs.

But fast-forward to the early 1990s, and there you find that the majority of Scheduling veterans somehow survived the revolution, now content with both the mouse and PDM. Then came a second wave of revolutionary concepts, and once again the pioneers from the early days balked. I was one of them. While the complaints were too many to mention here, the thread that wove the complaints together is a much shorter list, as I discuss in the following sections.

Bells and Whistles

You've heard the expression "too much of a good thing." How can there ever be *too much* of something that is good? Pampered children of wealthy, indulgent parents are one answer to that question. Today's computer hardware and software may be another. Christmas was just last week and for the previous two months, kids all across our great country were begging their parents to buy them the latest models of PlayStation and X Box. But when I looked at the output quality of these "new and improved" machines, they were hardly different from their predecessors. The same can be said for DVD quality versus CD quality music, when either is compared to vinyl albums (remember LPs?). I won't disagree that CD quality is far better than grooved records, but is DVD-quality music *that* much better than CD quality? Can you really tell the difference?

As Tom Cruise said in the movie, Jerry McGuire, "Follow the money!" The only one to benefit from swapping out ten million copies of PlayStation II with PlayStation III is the manufacturer of PlayStation. Now, look at the constant stream of upgrades in scheduling software (or software of any kind, for that matter) and ask yourself if you really need all of those bells and whistles.

The question is more than rhetorical, though. The proliferation of marginally useful technology is not just a case of excess; it's also a case of erosion. Not long ago, after giving a speech, I was approached by a young scheduler who asked me if I thought the advent of PDM was the Scheduling Practice's Achilles Heel. "No," I responded without hesitation, "it was the introduction of the date-constraint." He asked me to explain.

The sheer magic and power of CPM is in its ability to simulate reality, *future* reality.[1] At the center of that magic is the logic tie, the link between two activities that states, arithmetically, that Activity B is somehow dependent upon Activity A. CPM is simple and yet brilliant. With only activities and their durations, plus logic ties and their durations (PDM only), virtually any dependent relationship can be depicted.

At first glance, date constraints seem to be an improvement; a bolster to achievement of the same desired ends. After all, isn't it useful to be able to impose a start or finish date in defiance of the forward or backward pass calculations? My answer is "yes," if the interjection is responsible; but "no" if it is harmful. The problem is that damage can come to a Project Schedule, intentionally or unintentionally, from excessive or inappropriate date-constraint use. When Schedule Developers do not understand the full implication of date-constraints yet still pepper their Project Schedules with an excess of imposed dates, they often destroy its very credibility. I talk more about this elsewhere in this book, so for now I will leave it at that.

The use of date-constraints is just one schedule element that has the potential to improve or destroy a Project Schedule. Multiple calendars are another. Still more damaging, without question, are the variety of schedule calculation settings, such as retained-logic, progress-override, continuous-durations, zero-free-float, and zero-total-float, just to name a few. Unless the Schedule's developers and users are keenly sensitive to the effects that these settings can have on the software's ability to predict the future, the situation is not much different from a child playing with the wires in the back of the TV set!

Sizzle, Not Steak I blame upper management for much of the erosion of the Scheduling Practice as a useful science. I can draw examples from as early as the late 1970s of owners being more impressed with glossy bar charts than content-pertinent logic diagrams. Management has always wanted things distilled for them. Disinterested in understanding the details underlying time-related conclusions, for whatever reasons, they have left themselves wide open to acts of deception and misrepresentation by those having something to gain by keeping the boss convinced that "all is going well." The bells and whistles have made it entirely too easy to create false images of reality, with bogus predictions of future success.

Once upon a time, a savvy executive might have been able to ask for the backup and actually have been able to trace the foundation of the predictions back to their mathematical origins. Sadly, those days have long since disappeared. Now, it is darned near impossible for even a seasoned Scheduler to find the true impact of a myriad of specific settings and dubious date-constraints that convolute a Project Schedule from whatever it was that its creators intended for it to say.

---

[1]Documenting the past is no great achievement, as man has been doing so for thousands of years. Predicting the future, now that's a breakthrough!

Here Are the Keys to the Safe   For the unscrupulous contractor, the keys to the bank have been left on top of the Welcome mat, not even hidden underneath it anymore. Experienced contractors know how to stack the deck—how to build a Schedule that insulates them from the negative effects of their own future slippages—while at the same time virtually ensuring a time extension for even the slightest owner-caused delay.

I've seen Execution Schedules with average durations of less than two days and average total-float across 3,000 activities of less than four days! Imagine every activity in the Schedule having total-float of eight days or less! Look, if you have ten tasks to perform today, and *all* are Priority One, then you have no priorities! And in a Project Schedule with average total-float under four days, you have no criticality. In the end, not only is the contractor manipulating the Project Schedule for his own greedy ends, no one is effectively managing the project because there is no reliable Execution Schedule by which to manage.

Under the Totem Pole   Scheduling Practitioners have always held the bottom spot on the project team totem pole. But when PC-based scheduling software came out and project managers assured their bosses that they could produce the Schedule themselves, Schedulers were buried *under* the totem pole. I estimate that by the late 1980s perhaps as many as 90 percent of all Scheduling Practioners had changed jobs, becoming project managers, cost engineers, procurement agents, field engineers—becoming anything, just not a scheduler!

The tragic error of management was in not recognizing that seasoned Schedulers brought more to the project than just the ability to draw boxes and type on a keyboard. They understood the cause-and-effect dynamics of the project in a way that few others, including the project manager, ever could. Those of us who were stubborn (or stupid) enough to stick with it licked each other's wounds for more than a decade. We mumbled to each other about how projects would not be better off without our input.

Today, we are the gray-haired relics of another era. But we have also enjoyed partial vindication, as the statistics show that, despite continued "advances" in scheduling software and a proliferation of scheduling training, projects continue to finish "late." Project deadlines continue to be missed, resources continue to work overtime to compensate for poor planning, and budgets continue to overrun because of poor project management practices.

My final advice, under this heading of "when is enough, enough?" is simply this: "keep your eye on the donut, and not on the hole." By that I mean don't venture far from basic logic and durations. All the rest is trappings, and you should be asking yourself at all times: who set the trap?

These are just a few questions and comments about scheduling software, but from them you can get my drift. If you don't understand what the software is doing, how confidently can you use the computed data it generates? Are you willing to go to the mat over information you can't explain, or replicate manually?

THE ACTORS AND AUDIENCE: UNDERSTANDING THEIR ROLES AND CHARACTERS

I happen to believe that Project Schedules quite often fail because they ignore or downplay the human element. As a project management consultant, I am often retained by construction companies having difficulty getting their projects to complete "on time and within budget" despite elaborate Execution Schedules. Time and time again I find the same exact scenario: the Project Schedule was not tailored to its end users (in other words, Schedule Design was skipped).

Here's the key point: lots of different people, with vastly differing levels of education and responsibility, have individual needs yet must use the same Project Schedule. Therefore, the Project Schedule must be designed and developed in such a way that each player gets out of it what he needs. And just who are these players?

Those Who Do the Physical Work

The physical workers include the laborer, the apprentice, the journeyman, and the foreman. Yes, these individuals should come in contact with outputs from the Project Schedule. If you think that they are too far down on the food chain to be receiving a printout of some fashion, then we've probably uncovered one reason why your Project Schedules aren't working hard enough for you.

The worker's attitude is really quite simple: "I'm here to earn a buck. Just tell me what you want done, how you want it done, when you want it done, where you want it done, and then . . . step back and leave me alone. It'll get done." Nothing frustrates (or irritates) a dedicated worker more than ambiguity or vacillation by supervision on any of these fundamental directions.

It should be clear that, for the worker, a simple list of *things to do* is precisely what the worker wants—and what you should deliver from your Project Schedule. To be most effective, the list should never exceed a single sheet of paper and should never span more than one week. A format I find very effective shows five-days' work on one sheet, each day's work under the name of the day. The list should be limited to tasks in which the worker has involvement.

Those Who Supervise the Physical Work

The people who supervise the physical work are the superintendents of both the subcontractor and the general contractor. The internal motivation of the superintendent is similar to that of the worker, with one major distinction. The superintendent wants some authority. He prides himself on his ability to take charge, to make things happen, and to *deliver the desired product*. He requires, therefore, a clear understanding of what is expected of his crews.

He'll have questions about materials, manpower, and other intervening events, such as prior and concurrent activities, as well as follow-up activities. The Project Schedule should adequately answer these questions before they are asked. The superintendent's need to know is only slightly broader than those he supervises. I would include in his Execution Schedule Extraction, items such as the expected delivery of critical equipment and materials, the timing of nearby work not under his control yet that might affect his work, and so on.

The Project Manager

In a category all his own, the project manager's[2] need to know exceeds all others, and no single Schedule Extraction report is adequate for him.

Two Different Roles

To be sure, the project manager's assignment is nearly impossible: to develop and maintain harmonious momentum on a project populated by opposing forces and competing interests. As we stated earlier, the project manager's prospects for success are further challenged by the fact that the project manager actually wears two different, and sometimes conflicting, hats.

First, one must realize that the contractor's scope is always something less than the full scope of the project. When the contract type is construction only, this is more than obvious. To be sure, the project begins with design, and the contractor's involvement begins after design has completed. Second, even during construction, there are others who perform work on the project, such as other prime contractors, owner-supplied materials, equipment, and services vendors, design professionals, and the owner as well. But even when the contract type is a form of turnkey or Engineering-Procurement-Construction (EPC), there are almost always elements of the project (often owner activities) that are beyond the scope of the EPC contractor.

Additionally, there often can be other competing projects happening before, during, or after the contractor's project that must be monitored and coordinated within the project manager's job. These may include projects within the owner's portfolio or other projects in the area that are unrelated to the owner, with which the project manager will be competing for limited resources: labor, materials, equipment, construction financing, and so on.

As Contract Administrator

As relates to overseeing the performance of the project, the project manager's role is that of contract administrator, in which he ensures that all parties to the project perform their respective contractual duties with quality, timeliness, efficiency, safety, and minimum disruption to others. His primary concern is protection of his company's commercial interests. In order to do this, the project manager must, at a minimum, accomplish the objectives shown in Table 2-1, each of which is tied to the creation and use of the Project Schedule.

As Work Coordinator

As just noted, a contractor's contractual scope is rarely equivalent to the overall magnitude of the project. The project manager, now having single-point responsibility for

---

[2]Throughout this text, reference to a "project manager" refers to the individual heading the project management team for either a contractor or construction manager.

PM Objective	Schedule's Help
Understand the Contract	Schedule Considers Contract Requirements
Understand the Design	Schedule Anticipates Design Implications
Understand the Schedule	Schedule Reflects Management Understanding
Remove Progress Obstacles	Schedule Development Identifies Obstacles
Discern Progress Being Made	Schedule Maintenance Monitors Progress
Recognize Scope Changes	Schedule Maintenance Reflects Scope Changes
Detect Seeds of Conflict	Schedule Usage Detects and Mitigates Conflict
Sustain Project Momentum	Schedule Maintenance Exposes Momentum
Communicate Feverishly	Schedule is Comprehensive Information Conduit

Table 2-1

Management Responsibilities and How Schedule Can Help

all aspects of daily operations of the entire project, must do more than merely oversee the performance of the general contractor. More correctly, the project manager must take a far more proactive role by coordinating the activities of *all* other contributors to the construction project up and above what the general contractor is doing.

The name of the game is *coordination*. The goal of the project manager is to ensure the smooth, coordinated performance of all participating parties. Expressed in the jargon of our opening discussion, the project manager's job is to manage the project's *momentum*, and his motivation is to succeed, to defy the odds. A seasoned project manager is assertive but not aggressive, organized yet flexible, and very charismatic and people-oriented.

This last point is quite often ignored. The results are almost always the same: show me a tension-ridden jobsite and I'll show you a dictator of a project manager at the helm. It's true what they say about catching more flies with honey than vinegar. Still, far too many project managers use brute force to drive their agendas. Despite all the noise and bulging blood vessels, the work gets done no faster, no better, and no more cost effectively than had the project manager never bellowed in the first place.

So let us talk about the professional project manager. He believes in *communicating* with people, not shouting at them. He believes in *reasoning* with them, not threatening them. In order to communicate reasonably, he needs to see and convey the big picture, so that all parties understand how their particular activities fit within the whole of the project. And he must do this succinctly.

For the project manager, the Project Schedule must present itself in many different formats, as a series of tailored reports (called Execution Schedule Extractions). These different reports will tell the project manager what the designers ought to be working on, advise the owner as to what he needs to be thinking about, informs what each of his superintendents is pursuing, details the status of key deliverables, establishes what upper management knows (or thinks) to be the situation at the jobsite, and so on.

Those Who Support the Project Manager

The group that supports the project manager includes the estimator, scheduler, cost engineer, field engineer, buyer, comptroller, and the like. They are all support personnel who provide needed services to the project manager. Their motivation is more often than not a personal pride in their technical acumen. They are good at what they do, and they experience job dissatisfaction when their input is not sought or the products of their hands and minds are not utilized. In a word, they want to make a difference. They want to feel that the project is somehow better off, thanks to their efforts, than it would have been otherwise.

For them, the Project Schedule is a needed tool of their trade. They reference it for information vital to the performance of their work. In it, these individuals find volumes of data about how the job should be going, how it *is* going, how it could be going, and how it will most likely end up. A good Project Schedule will present this information to each of these parties at a level of detail and at a frequency supportive of their respective needs.

Those Who Oversee the Project Manager

Here, we are talking about management, people with position titles like project director, project executive, Vice President of Construction, Vice President of Operations, or Chief Operations Officer. As much as (and perhaps more than) any other, the purpose for developing a comprehensive Project Schedule cuts across all techniques, in terms of choice, degree, and emphasis. What goes into a Project Schedule is directly related to what is expected from it. Sadly, the expectations for a Project Schedule are typically at the whim of management, notwithstanding well-articulated recommendations by Scheduling aficionados. To a great extent the Project Schedule's role becomes an extension (and expression) of management style.

Some construction executives like a statistical backdrop to their decision-making, and some even relish the notion of a project-independent, home office–based scheduling department to provide a check-and-balance against the project manager. Others see the Project Schedule as being the project manager's responsibility, with Scheduling personnel merely providing clerical/technical assistance. Still others dislike the dry, narrow, and often cold appearance of Scheduling products and services and thus use them, ever so sparingly, only to support management reports.

All Other Project Stakeholders

This overview would be incomplete if I did not also acknowledge all others who share a stake in the project with the prime contractor. There are those who conceived the project in the first place, such as the owner, operators, tenants, architects, engineers, and consultants. Their informational needs peak twice during the project's life: first during conception when critical advanced planning is necessary, and again during project execution phases as plans for acceptance of the finished project begin to materialize.

Those Who Supply the Project

The subcontractors, the manufacturers, the suppliers, and the vendors are those who supply the project. These groups have a need to know how the project is progressing so they can more effectively plan their activities to coincide with and support overall project momentum. They have a genuine need to see the *big picture*, the Execution Schedule, but they also have supreme interest in an Execution Schedule Extraction, one that they can use to plan and track the delivery of labor and materials to the site. Between the Execution Schedule and Schedule Extractions, they will be able to plan resource utilization more effectively.

Those Who Monitor the Project

Included in the final group are the building inspectors, fire marshals, OSHA agents, union representatives, and even financiers. Each has a fiduciary interest in how the project is faring. Each has occasional need for information that is found only in the Project Schedule. And, perhaps more importantly, each has the potential to dramatically impact (positively or negatively) the time and budget achievements of the project.

THE SCRIPT: THE PROJECT SCHEDULE'S MANY USES

So far, I have noted that Execution Schedules, like the construction projects with which they are associated, exist in an environment harboring many obstacles, opportunities, demands, and challenges. I've also noted that Project Schedules have many intended users, each with specific and diverse informational needs. Now I must acknowledge the many different ways a Project Schedule can be used.

As a Planning Tool

The first use, and some say the best use, of a Project Schedule is to plan a logical course of future action. Thanks to CPM's ability to intertwine activities based on their logistic, geographic, tactical, or resource relationships, an early plan for project execution offers an exceptional opportunity for identifying problematic aspects of the game plan long *before* they manifest themselves in real life.

As a Coordination Tool

The Project Schedule can be used to orchestrate the separate yet interrelated efforts of a multitude of people in order to affect a successful project. The Project Schedule functions much like a choreographer who designs and regulates the pace and direction of the dancers on stage. Not only do they not run into one another, they are often at precisely the right location to be of mutual support to one another.

The notion of *pace* and *direction* deserves a few extra words. I liken the role of the Project Schedule on a construction project to that of the map used by a long distance truck driver. The map allows the driver to lay a course, monitor his direction, establish a performance schedule, check his pace, and make corrective maneuvers, as needed, in order to accommodate unexpected changes in conditions along the way.

But what good is a map if the driver has no steering wheel? The steering wheel is the device the driver uses to control *direction*. Knowing that he must turn north is one thing; being able to do so is quite another. Now, suppose he has a steering wheel but no accelerator pedal. If he falls behind, how can he increase his speed in order to catch up? In the inverse, without a brake pedal, how can he slow down if his pace is too aggressive?

Brake and accelerator pedals for *pace* and steering wheel for *direction:* all are needed in order to control a vehicle. But something else is needed also! Can you guess what?

Information: all sorts of information. Start with the windshield. Try covering the windshield with black paper so that the driver cannot see where he is going. Now is he still in control, even with brakes, an accelerator, and steering wheel? What about the rear view mirrors? What about the instrument panel that reports rate of speed, remaining fuel, engine performance, and time? Aren't these insights into critical information necessary for meaningful control of the vehicle? What about the side windows, through which are seen road signs, surrounding weather, other vehicles, and road conditions?

What we conclude from this example is that true project *control* involves two key factors, both important to the effective project manager. First, he must have the *ability* to influence the pace and direction (momentum) of those who perform on his project (I'll get to this next). Second, he must have adequate and meaningful information concerning *how* to influence them. On a construction project, that information resides in the Project Schedule.

As a Communication Tool

Just how important is this information? Without exception, everything the project manager does, or is obligated to do, involves information, either in its raw form (data) or as conveyed (communication). Said differently, everything the project manager does consists of receiving, processing, and communicating information.

Information Alone Is of Little Value

Information is rarely useful in its raw form. Instead, it must be validated, simplified, synthesized, and, above all else, communicated. Such communication takes many written and verbal forms. And information can be communicated for many different reasons. For instance, written communications may be intended to compel (contracts), clarify (plans and specifications), query (RFIs), persuade (some correspondence), notify (transmittal forms), and inform (reports, minutes). Of course, quite often, effective communication attempts to satisfy multiple objectives.

Likewise, communication can have varying degrees of premeditation, from the spontaneous (phone calls) to the planned (meetings) to the rehearsed (speeches). Communications can be official or off-the-record, although nothing is really off the record, except perhaps what is legally privileged.

The Project Manager Is the Great Communicator

The essential value of communicated information to the project manager is more than conceptual. Table 2-2, which references the project manager's list of primary responsibilities

PM Responsibility	Communication Need
The Contract	The contract is a form of written communications.
The Design	The design is a set of written communications, called plans and specifications.
The Schedule	The schedule is a form of written communication.
Remove Obstacles to Progress	This entails verbal and written communications between the involved parties. Further, the early warnings that alert of impending problems (dilemmas) are presented as vital information.
Monitor and Analyze Progress	This involves empirical information, combined with raw data and written and verbal communications.
Scope Changes	This involves a comparison of sets of information; contract versus written modifications to design or approach, suggested to be additional.
Detect Seeds of Conflict	Such seeds are buried in written and verbal communications, usually found "between the lines."
Reward and Penalize Performance	Always done in written form; often verbally as well.
Inform the Parties	This is communications at its most apparent.
Manage Procurement and Delivery	This relies on critical information and involves communications to carry out the management tasks.
Coordinate the Work	Central to this effort is the schedule, a key communication tool in written form.

Table 2-2

Schedule's Role in Project Management Communication

listed in Table 2-1, confirms that one is hard pressed to find a single responsibility that does not require the exchange of information, or that does not directly or indirectly call on the Project Schedule for help.

Suffice it to say that the project manager simply cannot carry out his duties without reliance on available information and without utilizing various communication formats. It should logically follow that the project manager's success depends fully on the quality and effectiveness of that information. When you stop to think about it, the Project Schedule, as an information clearinghouse, is critical to each of these 11 key project management functions.

As a Work Organization Tool

Sound Schedule Development protocol routinely includes organizing the project's scope of work into a Work Breakdown Structure (WBS). This becomes an excellent catalyst for and assistant to the budgeting process. In conjunction with the financial group's cost coding requirements, and within the context of some broadly recognized categorization of work (quite often the CSI[3] code), the Project Schedule offers an ideal way of dividing the project into small enough chunks to be easily monitored, managed, and controlled.

As a Resource Management Tool

The automated Project Schedule allows the prudent project manager to plan the best use of critical project resources *before* they are set into motion. By utilizing information existing only in the Project Schedule, the project manager is able to maximize worker productivity and efficiency, minimize idle or "standby" time, and increase the cost-effective use of capital resources.

As a Performance Measurement Tool

The Project Schedule is the best place—and some may argue the *only* place—to track actual performance against planned progress. Each discrete activity in the Project Schedule represents an equally distinct scope of work against which actual-start-dates and actual-finish-dates can be recorded. Further, the actual sequencing of activities, as in compliance with or disregard for planned logic, can also be notated for future reference.

As a Forecasting Tool

Using the Execution Schedule as a forecasting tool to routinely predict project outcomes is very popular. Information derived from Execution Schedule Editions can be used to identify status and trends and then speculate on likely project completion or future work performance.

As a Reporting Tool

Clearly, the Project Schedule and its computer host provide a most efficient tool for reporting schedule-resident information. Standard scheduling reports litter all project offices where automated Scheduling is applied.

As a Contract Administration Tool

The Project Schedule is almost always a legal document, made so when it is incorporated into the contract by reference. This special standing introduces possible *conflicts of interest* on the part of project participants, as they design, develop, use, and reference the Project Schedule. An obvious comparison to this condition is the management

---

[3]The Construction Specifications Institute's breakdown of construction components into 16 logical categories, and numerous subcategories beneath that.

report produced by a project manager for the readership of his superiors. These superiors look to the report for an accurate characterization of the project, but they also use the status of the project as the basis for the project manager's financial compensation. What prudent project manager will willingly report bad news about the project that he thinks he can otherwise cover up or eventually correct?

The essential core of the Project Schedule is the activity duration, a subjective value provided by the one who has responsibility for performance of that scope of work. Because of the contract's legal role, the temptation for a project participant is to skew information (such as the duration) entered into the Project Schedule so that resultant reports are as favorable to him as possible. This tendency to distort occurs both during Schedule Development as well as during Performance Recording.

I would like to note that, while it is a legal tool, the Execution Schedule is seldom held to the same standards as the rest of the contract and very seldom does anyone hold up a payment to the contractor because the Execution Schedule was not submitted on time, or did not comply with the specifications. This said, the Execution Schedule should be treated with the same respect as other elements of the contract. But most important— and this is something you need to remember—is that, to be construed by the courts as a viable contemporaneous tool, the Execution Schedule must be an effective tool for coordinating, influencing, measuring, and reporting project activity.

As a Cost Control Tool

Certain basic functions of cost control require information found only in the Project Schedule. It doesn't matter whether cost control functions are ultimately performed entirely within the Schedule, in joint venture between the Project Schedule and other cost control tools, or entirely in other cost control tools—the Schedule is vital to certain cost control processes.

I have long argued that there is no such thing as cost *control*, simply because so few costs are actually controllable. Prices for materials and equipment are set by the marketplace, as is the prevailing wage. With project designs being created in computers that generate precise material quantity estimates, one has to wonder why any two bidders' estimates are different at all.

The key variable, which I'm sure you realize, is the human element. The price of a brick or a crane or a laborer is essentially identical from one bidder to the next. What differs is how humans employ those bricks and cranes. Broadly, I'm talking about the bidder's *project execution strategy*; one may be more innovative (and efficient) than another. More specifically, I'm referring to the skill and experience level of the worker and his supervisor. With greater experience and skill come fewer mistakes and greater commitment to quality, efficiency, and accountability.

Human dynamics such as motivation, drive, strong work ethic, attention to detail, and tenacity not only affect labor hours expended and labor dollars spent, but they also affect material and equipment *costs*. Prices and rates may be set in the marketplace, but field-level efficiency creates the ultimate costs at the jobsite. Efficiency is a human function. So, who controls the actions of a worker?

Answer: the worker. Not the crew foreman, not the superintendent, not the project manager, and certainly not the cost engineer. Only the worker himself can and will motivate his own arms and legs. If his heart is in his work, quality will be there, and so will be efficiency. With the project's success in his hands, quite literally, those who oversee his performance should have an intense desire to *influence* his behavior. But *influence* is a far cry from *control*.

The Execution Schedule is the project manager's primary device for maintaining the momentum of the project, and that momentum is the result of motivated action. Momentum results from motivation.[4] The pace set by the Project Schedule directly influences costs that arise from efforts involved in placement of the work (breakage, rework, direct labor, and so on) and indirectly affects costs compounded by the passage of time (rentals, amortizations, cost of capital, overhead costs, indirect costs, and so on).

Budgets created without reference to a time-based schedule are likely to reflect a theoretical set of assumptions much different from what is presumed by the Project Schedule. One way to ensure alignment between cost and schedule assumptions is to cost-load the Execution Schedule. But as I said at the outset, whether the Project Schedule participates directly or indirectly, its importance to cost management cannot be overstated.

As a Marketing Tool

As already noted, products of the Scheduling Practice are excellent at communicating: by detailing execution strategies, demonstrative graphics in support of traffic and site utilization scenarios, concurrent major scope components, the sequence of key deadlines, and more. Often, especially during the project's earliest commitment stage, there is need to depict the project in a summary form.

Another way the Scheduling Practice contributes to the securing of new work is as a component of a contractor's bid or response to a Request for Proposals (RFPs). The Consensus Plan is typically more finite than the summary bar charts of the Master Plan, but the purpose is the same: to depict a proposed strategy.

Important to our discussion of how the different uses of the Scheduling Practice in turn impose constraints on its associated design and implementation is recognition of the dual role of the Authorization Plan. On the one hand, it presents a theoretical scenario at a level of detail inadequate for project direction and coordination. Further, it is developed at a time when, with much critical information not known, many important assumptions have to be made. On the other hand, more and more owners expect the final Execution Schedule to comply with the overall parameters of the Authorization Plan. In this sense, the Authorization Plan, at a parametric level, becomes a self-fulfilling prophecy.

---

[4]Both words, *motivation* and *motion*, are from the same Latin root, *motivus*, meaning to move.

As a Financial Planning Tool

Financial folks use various Scheduling deliverables to plan, monitor, and evaluate (the effectiveness of) capital expenditures. Feasibility Plans are often cost-loaded and used to plan funding commitments. Once the funding allocations have been "locked down" in the Master Plan, the project is released. Not surprising, many projects are subsequently accelerated or slowed down in accordance with preplanned release of funds. Here again, the early planning becomes a self-fulfilling prophecy. Later Execution Schedules are robbed of flexibility because these *critical thresholds* are tied to calendar dates, and the Execution Schedule must work within the bounds of those dates.

As a Record-Keeping Tool

Using the Project Schedule as a record-keeping tool emanates from sheer convenience. In some respects, the original suggestion to use the Project Schedule as record-keeping database was just too easy. Think about it: the Project Schedule contains a detailed listing that itemizes every single task to be performed, who is expected to do it[5], and when it has to be done. Further, through Performance Recording, the Project Schedule maintains a record on what was done, when, and how far each individual task has progressed. What better repository could there be for project-level information than the Project Schedule?

If you want to understand how Project Schedules began to lose their time-management potency, start here. Once the Project Schedule was given this additional role, its integrity began to deteriorate as one discipline after another imposed requirements on the Project Schedule, treating it as its own records database. Separate, redundant, conflicting, and often excessive coding requirements, in particular, quickly bogged down the Project Schedule as a lean, time-calculating machine. A level of detail that was too meticulous for one interest group was too sketchy for another.

Even the schedule's *logic* was affected by demands that the Project Schedule be used to generate a daily "to do" list. Some entities wanted certain tasks included in the Project Schedule, even if the tasks had no necessary order of performance, no particular sequence. What relationship tie would you use to connect these activities to one another? One option is to include the various tasks as "things to do" in an innocuous activity code field. Another choice is to depict them all as concurrent, all restrained by the same start, and completing in advance of the same successor.

Further compounding the rush for schedule database real estate was contemporaneous interest in WBS, OBS, and EVMS. Now, all activities that were simply floating at the microscopic level had to be resource-allocated and categorically aligned with the Work Breakdown Structure. The trick is to define a WBS that is (a) scope-based, (b) defined at a reasonable level and, (c) optionally aligned with a Cost-Breakdown Structure, when the latter is appropriately necessary. A WBS provides a useful service in organizing project activities, but it needs to be correlated with project scope deliverables, not cost containers.

---

[5]Assuming the Project Schedule identifies the responsible party through coding.

As a Dispute Resolution Tool

The final nail in the Project Schedule's coffin was when it became a key weapon in the lawyer's arsenal. First came the eventually universal acceptance of the contractor's initially approved ("as-planned") Baseline Schedule as a conceptually, if not literally, contractual commitment. This alone greatly impacted the Execution Scheduler's ability to obtain durations that weren't strategically padded or logic that wasn't intended to manipulate the Project Schedule's calculations, including which activities and paths were, or might become, critical.

Next came the use of other project data resident in the Project Schedule (see the previous section), to bolster the positions of claimants in a dispute. Suddenly, anything entered into the Project Schedule, even seemingly innocent activity codes, could be used against a contractor or owner in a court of law.

Of course the most important information in the Project Schedule, from a claims perspective, are Performance Recording entries (actual-start-dates, actual-finish-dates; and percent-complete/remaining-duration estimates) and the Schedule Revisions (in the form of additions, deletions, or modifications of activity data, including activities and relationships themselves). What the lawyers and others often forget is that the original Schedule was an *estimate* of the time and sequence of work required to perform each task and that Project Schedules are living documents that will require revisions as the project goes forward.

3 Why Our Schedules Disappoint Our Customers

This chapter suggests several reasons why our Project Schedules so often disappoint our customers. The ugly truth is that, over the decades, we have allowed our Practice to fall into disrepair. Today, it needs attention—even an extensive overhaul—and urgently so. This chapter will discuss three things we can and *must* immediately do in order to restore credibility to ourselves and our various products and services:

- We must replace confusing terminology with words that really describe who we are, what we do, and what we produce.
- We must refocus on our primary customer, the project manager. We have blurred his identity just as we have lost sight of his informational needs and wants.
- We must redesign our work products. We must tailor our work products and services to meet our customer's needs. And we must re-engineer our overall processes to more effectively produce those work products.

CUSTOMER DISSATISFACTION REASON #1: THE TERMINOLOGY QUAGMIRE

Let me start with a question: *Can one Project Schedule do it all?* Referring back to the previous chapter and all that we've discussed so far, the question I am asking here is whether a *single* scheduling product can adequately satisfy all of its many stakeholders with their many diverse and specific informational needs and still effectively perform all of its intended roles. Frankly, I don't think that one can, and I submit that one of the reasons that our Project Schedules fail to satisfy our broad stakeholder base is because *we expect too much out of a single work product*, instead of creating a set of related work products.

Distinguishing Between Internal and External Work Products

Let us distinguish internal from external work products and then confess that we have lazily chosen to call them all by one name, the "schedule." That's where the confusion begins. Can we agree that there is an *internal* schedule, a computerized database in which each record represents a discrete scope of work? For the sake of the limited discussion under this heading, let us call this database the *internal schedule*. Now, let us acknowledge that when our customers see tailored manifestations of this internal schedule, whether on paper or a computer screen, they refer to each of these as a "schedule." Let us call each outer depiction an *external schedule*.

Immediately we have the start of a conflict of meaning. Suppose the internal schedule contains 120 records (activities). Now suppose we present the *entire* schedule in two different formats: a 120-activity bar chart and a 120-activity tabular listing. Do the bar chart and tabular listing represent two different schedules? As trained schedulers, you and I would probably agree that there is only one underlying schedule and that it is merely being presented in two different formats.

Distinguishing Between Different External Work Products

Next, let's discuss those creative extracts from that single database. Exploiting the computer's exclusive ability to isolate and present thousands of lines of selected information in an artfully arranged presentation, one can create any number of specialized reports. Since many of our customers do not possess our understanding that a schedule is merely a database of information presented in a structured format, to them any one of these printouts can be perceived as being a schedule in its own right.

You and I, of course, know that our customer's perception is technically incorrect. After all, an excerpt from Schedule A does not really create Schedule B. Agreed? My point, however, should not be lost entirely. To our customers, it's all about whether the output seems unique. Perhaps the uniqueness is in *how* it appears—a bar chart versus a tabular listing of the same activities. Or perhaps it is in *what* it contains—two tabular listings, one of expected deliveries and the other of owner activities. They would likely call these a procurement schedule and an owner's schedule, respectively.

Can you really blame our customers for construing these as two different schedules, even though they are derived from a single database? Hey, if I tear a paper napkin in two, giving half to my daughter and keeping half for myself, don't we now each have a napkin? Of course we do! Each of us has something to wipe our mouth with; each half serves the purpose of a napkin. Likewise, if a schedule is a body of time-related information intended to serve one or more of the purposes identified in the last chapter, then any portion of a schedule meeting this definition qualifies as a schedule in its own right. Right?

This Is My Brother Darryl, and This Is My Other Brother Darryl

Some of you may remember, back in the 1980s, that comedian Bob Newhart had a popular TV show on which there were three country bumpkin brothers, only one of whom spoke. He would introduce his siblings as "my brother Darryl, and this is my other brother Darryl." I always thought the real laugh was on the parents—who obviously had so little creativity that they couldn't come up with more than one name for two sons!

In Chapter 5, "Introduction to the Scheduling Practice," I list more than a dozen discrete deliverables produced by Scheduling Practitioners, eight of which are referred to as

Table 3-1
The Practice's Key Deliverables

Numerous different work products are each called "the project plan," and/or "the project schedule" in the current vernacular

Feasibility Plans
Master Plans
Strategic Plans
Consensus Plans
Execution Schedules
Schedule Editions
Schedule Extractions
Schedule Revisions

either plans or schedules, in today's jargon (see Table 3-1). While these work products are developed at different points in the project life cycle, involving different development partners, and intended for different purposes and different end users, in the current vernacular, they are each called either a "plan" or a "schedule." When you consider that presently there is no universally accepted distinction between a plan and a schedule, it appears that we have essentially one perceived label for multiple documents.

And therein lies one of the first reasons why our "schedules" are so often a disappointment to our stakeholders. Why shouldn't they be? Each individual recipient is expecting a specific-looking or specific-functioning document—one that will serve *his* needs—and instead he gets something else!

> Conclusion #1: By calling all of our work products by the same name, we create unreasonable expectations and invite disappointment. That is why I created *different* names for each of the primary work products that our Practice produces (see Chapter 5).

A few paragraphs back I wrote that, "we expect too much out of a single work product, instead of creating a *set* of related work products." Then I went on to say that, in fact, we *have* created a set of related work products. Am I contradicting myself? No, not really. For while the Scheduling Practice does produce a number of different products, we still mistakenly call them all by the same name.

We Are Also Confusing Ourselves

Let me go one step further and also suggest that a great number of my respected colleagues don't agree with me that there are more than a dozen distinctly different work products, as enumerated in Chapter 5. And this is what I believe to be another part of the same confusion that we foist upon our customers. Among ourselves, too many of us tend to see both planning and scheduling, or plans and schedules, as being the same animal, just at different stages of growth. Those holding this view see a schedule as the outgrowth of a plan; in other words, the same document at different stages of development.

Finally, just to make sure everyone is completely confused, they mindlessly interchange the words *plan* and *schedule*. They speak intermittently of a feasibility *schedule*, a feasibility *plan*, a master *plan*, a detailed work *plan*, "working your plan," and so on.

> Conclusion #2: We need to reach consensus among ourselves that these work products do not necessarily beget one another. As will be amply discussed in Chapter 5, the many work products that we produce need not evolve from one another, although there is obvious commonality among them in terms of subject matter, mechanics of development and depiction (logic diagrams), and appearance of outputs, just to name a few.

Consistently Inconsistent Definitions

But the confusion involving terminology extends well beyond primary words such as *plan, schedule, planner,* and *scheduler.* I recently reviewed several dozen CPM scheduling textbooks and reference manuals and found that the definitions of key terms are, as the saying goes, "all over the map." The only consistency I found across the broad range of terms was just how inconsistently they were being defined. We're not talking about differing eyewitness accounts of a car accident. We're talking about technical terms, such as *critical-path* and *total-float,* having different meanings!

Table 3-2 lists the terms for which I found inconsistent definitions among some of the leading textbooks, software help screens/manuals, and professional reference materials. The problem is more than one of mere inconsistency; it's also one of inaccuracy! When someone says that a right angle is 75 degrees, while another "authority" says it is 85 degrees, it isn't just a case of inconsistency, is it?

Since I consider it grossly unfair to lodge a sweeping complaint without giving any tangible examples, consider Figure 3-1 with examples of definitions for rather common scheduling terms that, taken collectively, are overwhelmingly conflicting and confusing. The point of this display is simply to show the disparity that exists in current literature, and not to pick a fight with anyone, and so I will not list the sources. (But I found them by Googling these terms, and you can do the same, if you so desire.)

The Scheduling Method/Model Notion

Over the last few years, steam has been building around a new set of terms to describe the practices, components, tools, and deliverables of the Scheduling Practice. It is my opinion that this proposed set of terms soon will be joining all of its predecessors in the heap of terms that (a) did not clarify the topic, but instead (b) added even more confusion.

Yet Another Set of Confusing Terms

Before offering my commentary on this set of terms, let me first present the definitions being advanced as fairly and accurately as I can. I have added numbers to the statements and definitions, to aid with correlating my subsequent commentaries to them.

> Statement 1: "The schedule development process includes selecting a *scheduling method, scheduling model,* followed by incorporating project specific data within that *scheduling model,* and generating *project schedule(s).* This process results in a model for project execution which reacts predictably to progress and changes. Once developed, the project schedule model is regularly updated to reflect progress and changes, such as scope or logic."

		Table 3-2 Confusing Terminology
Plan v. Schedule	Acceleration	
Planner v. Scheduler	Recovery	
Planning v. Scheduling	Milestone	
Float v. Slack	Relationship	
Modification v. Revision	Restraint	
Constraint	Event	
Critical-Path	Activity	
Soft Logic	Task	
Hard Logic	PERT Diagram	
Data Date	Logic Diagram	
Time-Now-Date	Network Diagram	
As-Of-Date	Hammock	
Progress-Date	Dependency v. Interdependency	
Statusing	Logic Tie	
Updating	Total-Float	
Leads v. Lags		

Statement 2: "Scheduling methods provide the framework within which schedule models are developed. One of the most common is the critical path method; another example is Critical Chain."

Statement 3: "The Critical Path Method (CPM) is a schedule network analysis technique used to determine the minimum total project duration and the earliest possible finish date of the project as well as the amount of scheduling flexibility (the amount of float) in the project schedule network."

Statement 4: "The Scheduling Model contains schedule components and the rules for relating and using the components to represent the process for completing a project. This is easily visualized by running a scheduling program and, before the addition of any activities or other project specific data, observing the various components in that tool which are available to build the Project Schedule Model. The Scheduling Model is the basic tool used to assemble the Project Schedule Model and provide the means of adjusting various parameters and components that is typical in a modeling process."

Statement 5: "The introduction of project-specific data, such as the activities, durations and resources, into the Scheduling Model creates a Project Schedule Model that is specific to a particular project. This Project Schedule Model, in turn, is used to generate various sets of dates, depending on the intent of a specific modeling iteration. Thus the Project Schedule Model produces a Project Schedule, which contains the planned dates for completing project activities."

Statement 6: "The Project Schedule Model can be used to produce critical paths and instances of schedules, as well as resource profiles, task assignments, records of accomplishments, etc. and provide time based forecasts, reacting to inputs and adjustments made throughout the project's life cycle."

Statement 7: "A Project Schedule, in its simplest form, is a table of activities with their scheduled dates when activities and milestones are to take place. In current project

Figure 3-1

Examples of Conflicting or Confusing Definitions

Critical-Path

1. The series of tasks that must finish on time for the entire project to finish on time.
2. In a network diagram, the longest path from start to finish or the path without any slack, and thus the path corresponding to the shortest time in which the project can be completed.
3. In a network diagram, the path with the longest duration.
4. The line of project activities having the least float, especially when float is close to, or below, zero.
5. The route through the network that has only critical activities.
6. The series of interdependent activities of a project connected end-to-end, which determines the shortest total length of the project.
7. The path (sequence) of activities which represent the longest total time required to complete the project.
8. The longest connected route through the CPM network.
9. The sequence of activities through a project network from start to finish, the sum of whose durations determines the overall project duration. There may be more than one critical path depending on workflow logic. A delay to progress of any activity on the critical path will, without acceleration or resequencing, cause the overall project duration to be extended, and is therefore referred to as a "critical delay."
10. The series of interrelated tasks that comprises the longest duration to complete a project, where a delay in any task will extend the overall schedule.
11. An analysis technique used to predict project duration. Analysis of activities, sequencing, and paths and determining which path has the least amount of schedule flexibility (float).
12. In project management, a critical path is the sequence of project network activities with the longest overall duration, determining the shortest time possible to complete the project. Any delay of an activity on the critical path directly impacts the planned project completion date (i.e., there is no float on the critical path). A project can have several, parallel critical paths. An additional parallel path through the network with the total durations shorter than the critical path is called a sub-critical or non-critical path.

Figure 3-1

Examples of Conflicting or Confusing Definitions (*continued*)

Lead

1. In a network diagram, the minimum necessary lapse of time between the start of one activity and the start of an overlapping activity.
2. A modification of a logical relationship which allows an acceleration of the successor task. For example, in a finish-to-start dependency with a ten-day lead, the successor activity can start 10 days before the predecessor has finished.
3. An acceleration of the successor activity allowing it to start before completion of its predecessor activity.
4. The opposite of lag, but in practice having the same meaning. A preceding activity may have a lag to a successor activity – from the perspective of the successor activity that is a lead.

Lag

1. The amount of time after one task has started or finished before the next task can be started or finished.
2. A modification of a logical relationship which directs a delay in the successor task. For example, in a finish-to-start dependency with a ten-day lag, the successor activity cannot start until 10 days after the predecessor has finished.
3. The logical relationship between the start and/or finish of one activity and the start and/or finish of another activity.
4. The time delay between the start or finish of an activity and the start or finish of its successor(s). See finish-to-finish lag, finish-to-start lag, and start-to-start lag.
5. Duration between activities traditionally imposed on following or successor activities.
6. Lag in a network diagram is the minimum necessary lapse of time between the finish of one activity and the finish of another overlapping activity. It may also be described as the amount of time required between the start or finish of a predecessor task and the start or finish of a successor task. (See logic link)

Negative Lag

1. The arrangement or sequence in which the successor activity is allowed to start chronologically before the predecessor activity has been completed.

Figure 3-1

Examples of Conflicting or Confusing Definitions (*continued*)

Network Diagram

1.   Any schematic display of the logical relationships of project activities. Always drawn from left to right to reflect project chronology. Often incorrectly referred to as a "PERT Chart."
2.   Drawn from left to right to show project chronology, a Project Network Diagram displays the logical relationships between project activities.

Network

1.   Connected sequence of arrows representing the project. This is the basis of CPM and PERT. The network must have one start point and one terminal point.

Dependency Diagram

1.   Another name for a network or precedence diagram that shows the dependencies (precedence) between tasks.

PERT Chart

1.   A flowchart that shows all tasks and task dependencies. Tasks are represented by boxes and task dependencies are represented by lines connecting the boxes.

Relationship

1.   A logical connection between two activities.
2.   A logical or natural association between two or more things; relevance of one to another; connection.

Dependency

1.   A relation between activities, such that one requires input from the other.
2.   A relationship between two modeling elements, in which a change to one modeling element (the independent element) will affect the other modeling element (the dependent element).
4.   See "Logical Relationship," — which is a dependency between two project schedule activities, or between a project schedule activity and a schedule milestone.
5.   In a project network, a dependency is a link amongst a project's terminal elements.

Logical Relationship

1.   Dependency between two schedule activities; four possible types are finish-to-start, finish-to-finish, start-to-start, and start-to-finish.

Figure 3-1

Examples of Conflicting or Confusing Definitions (*continued*)

Statusing

1. Indicating most current project status.

Status

1. The comparison of actual progress against the plan to determine variance and corrective action.
2. The condition of the project at a specified point in time.

Update

1. Revision of the schedule to reflect the most current information on the project.

Updating

1. Revising; amending.
2. Revision of a schedule or network to reflect progress to date. Fully completed items are eliminated and the date of the update becomes the new reference date for the project.
3. Regular, periodic review, analysis, evaluation, and recomputation of a CPM schedule.

Data-Date

1. The calendar date that separates actual (historical) data from scheduled data.
2. The date up to or through which the project's reporting system has provided actual status and accompllishments. In some reporting systems, the status information for the data date is included in the past and in some systems the status information is in the future. Also called as-of date and time-now date.
3. Starting calendar date for a network calculation.

Time-Now-Date

1. The current calendar date from which a network analysis, report, or update is being made.
2. The time at which all remaining work starts.
3. Specified date from which the forward analysis is deemed to commence.

Progress-Date

1. The date used in order to calculate the progress of the project.

Figure 3-1

Examples of Conflicting or Confusing Definitions (*continued*)

Revision

1.   A change to a document or design.
2.   In the context of scheduling, a change in the network logic or in resources which requires redrawing part or all of the network.

Modification

1.   Changes to an existing product, item, document or design.

Slack

1.   Term used in PERT for float.
2.   Originally the flexibility in the dates of an event in an activity-on-arrow network (i.e., late event time/early event time). Recently used synonymously with float, mainly in software originating in America.
3.   In PERT, the scheduling flexibility available for an event, equivalent to total-float in CPM.

Float

1.   The difference between the time available for performing a task and the time required to complete it.
2.   Available time for activity execution less the time taken by the activity.
3.   The amount of time that an activity can slip past its duration without delaying the rest of the project.
4.   The additional time available to complete non-critical activities or work items without affecting the critical path.
5.   The amount of time that an activity may be delayed from its early start without delaying the project finish date.
6.   A measure of the time flexibility available in the performance of an activity.
7.   The flexibility that an activity has versus the critical path. See total-float and slack.
8.   The time available for an activity in addition to its planned duration. See free-float and total-float.
9.   Float in project management is the amount of time that a terminal element in a project network can be delayed by, without causing a delay to subsequent terminal elements (free float) or project completion date (total-float).

Figure 3-1

Examples of Conflicting or Confusing Definitions (*continued*)

Total-Float

1. The maximum number of work periods by which an activity can be delayed without delaying project completion or violating a target finish date.
2. The amount that an activity can be lengthened without delaying the project completion, assuming that all other activities are done in their normal time.
3. The amount of time (in work units) that an activity may be delayed from its early start without delaying the project finish date.
4. The excess time available for an activity to be expanded or delayed without affecting the rest of the project, assuming it begins at its earliest time.
5. Measure of scheduling flexibility available on a network path.
6. The amount of time that an activity may be delayed beyond its early start/early finish dates without delaying the contract completion date.

Negative-Total-Float

1. Expression sometimes used to describe the time by which the duration of an activity or path has to be reduced in order to permit a limiting imposed date to be achieved. Negative-total-float only occurs when an activity on the critical path is behind programme. It is a programming concept, the manifestation of which is, of course, delay.

Free-Float

1. The amount of time an activity can be delayed beyond its early start/finish dates without delaying the early start or early finish of any activity.

Activity-Float

1. The duration contingency directly related to a single activity built into the planned duration of that activity. Activity float is established simply by dictating an activity duration that is greater than the actual time needed to complete that activity.

Plan

1. The sequence in which a project is to be done. It is independent of the schedule.

Planning

1. The process of identifying the means, resources, and actions necessary to accomplish an objective.
2. Proposing the timing, staffing (and possibly budget) breakdown of work to be done.
3. A systematic arrangement of tasks to accomplish an objective.

Figure 3-1

Examples of Conflicting or Confusing Definitions (*continued*)

Schedule

1. A time sequence of activities and events that represents an operating timetable.
2. A display or project time allocation.
3. The timing and sequence of tasks within a project, as well as the project duration.
4. The timetable for a project. It shows how project tasks and milestones are planned out over a period of time.
5. A series of things to be done in sequence of events within a given period.
6. The planned dates for performing schedule activities and the planned dates for meeting schedule milestones.
7. Planned dates for performing scheduled activities and meeting schedule milestones usually derived from a planned logical network.

Scheduling

1. The process of converting a general or outline plan for a project into a time-based schedule, based on available resources and time constraints.
2. The process of determining when project activities will take place depending on defined durations and precedent activities.
3. The recognition of realistic time and resource restraints which will, in some way, influence the execution of the plan.
4. The determination of when a series of activities should start, and when they should finish, typically in relation to many other activities and depending on the availability of resources.
5. Determination of the best means for achieving a project's general and specific schedule objectives.
6. Scheduling is the discipline of organizing and time-phasing the activities required to complete the objectives of an effort.

Imposed Date

1. A predetermined calendar date set (usually extremely) without regard to logical considerations of the network.
2. A fixed date imposed on a schedule activity or schedule milestone, usually in the form of a "start no earlier than" and "finish no later than" date.
3. A fixed date, usually in the form of a "start no earlier than" (SNET) date, or "finish no later than" (FNLT) date.

Figure 3-1

Examples of Conflicting or Confusing Definitions (*continued*)

Constraints

1. A restriction that must be balanced with all other constraints to achieve project success. The four primary and universal project constraints are scope, quality grade, time and resources.
2. A restriction or limitation you set on the start or finish date of a task.
3. Applicable restriction which will affect the scope. Any factor which affects when an activity can be scheduled. See restraint.
4. A factor that will limit the project management team's options. For example, a predefined budget is a constraint that may limit the team's scope, staffing, and schedule options.
5. Restrictions or boundaries impacting overall capability, priority, and resources.
6. A generic term for factors affecting the possible start and finish dates of an activity, including logic and imposed dates.
7. The state, quality, or sense of being restricted to a given course of action or inaction. An applicable restriction or limitation, either internal or external to the project, that will affect the performance of the project or a process. For example, a schedule constraint is any limitation or restraint placed on the project schedule that affects when a schedule activity can be scheduled and is usually in the form of fixed imposed dates. A cost constraint is any limitation or restraint placed on the project budget such as funds available for overtime. A project resource constraint is any limitation or restraint placed on resource usage, such as what resource skills or disciplines are available and the amount of a given resource available during a specified time frame.
8. An artificial limitation based upon information not recorded in the logic network that affects when an activity can be scheduled.

Acceleration

1. The use of methods for completing the work in a shorter time than previously planned or required by the contract.
2. The execution of the planned scope of work in a shorted time than anticipated or the execution of an increased scope within the originally planned duration.

Figure 3-1

Examples of Conflicting or Confusing Definitions (*continued*)

Crashing

1. Action to decrease the duration of an activity or project by increasing the expenditure of resources.
2. In project planning, an activity can be conducted at a normal pace, or at an accelerated pace, known as "crashing" the activity of the project. Crashing is completed at a greater cost than a normal-paced project.
3. Taking action to decrease the total project duration by analyzing a number of alternatives to determine how to get the maximum duration compression for the least cost.
4. A specific type of project schedule compression technique performed by taking action to decrease the total project schedule duration after analyzing a number of alternatives to determine how to get the maximum schedule duration compression for the least additional cost. Typical approaches for crashing a schedule include reducing schedule activity durations and increasing the assignment of resources on schedule activities.
5. A technique of reducing overall schedule time frame by either re-sequencing activities and/or reducing activity times by expenditures such as overtime.

Terminal Element

1. In project management, a terminal element is the lowest element (activity or deliverable) in a work breakdown structure (WBS); it is not further subdivided.

Activity

1. A task or set of tasks that are carried out in order to create a deliverable.
2. A single task within a project.
3. A specific project task that requires resources and time to complete.
4. An element of work performed during the course of a project. An activity normally has an expected duration, an expected cost, and expected resource requirements.
5. Subtask within a project.
6. An individual task needed for the completion of a project.
7. A component of work performed during the course of a project.
8. The work item that is the basic component of the project schedule.
9. An operation or process consuming time and possibly other resources. An individual or work team can manage an activity. It is a measurable element of the total project programme.

Figure 3-1

Examples of Conflicting or Confusing Definitions (*continued*)

Task

1. A cohesive, individual unit of work that is part of the total work needed to accomplish a project.
2. A small part of a project.
3. A subdivision of an activity.
4. Also called an activity.
5. The term usually used to refer to a piece of work contained within a work package.
6. A term for work whose meaning and placement within a structured plan for project work varies by area, industry, and brand of project management software.
7. A component scope of work that is part of an activity.

Event

1. A point in time when certain conditions have been fulfilled, such as the start or completion of one or more activities.
2. A happening or occurrence; outcome of an activity or decision point between activities.
3. In CPM or PERT networks, the end state for one or more activities that occurs at a specific point in time.
4. Something that happens at a point or moment in time. A significant event is often called a "milestone."
5. Something that happens; an occurrence, an outcome.
6. A point in time representing the intersection of two or more arrows. The event has no time duration. It can be a milestone. Junction between two or more activities in a logical network.

Milestone

1. A point in time representing a key or important intermediate event in the life of a project.
2. A key or important intermediate goal in the network.
3. A major event in a project, typically one requiring the customer or upper management to approve further work.
4. An activity with zero duration (usually marking the end of a period).
5. A significant point or event in the project.
6. Significant event in the project.
7. A key event selected for its importance in the project. Commonly used in relation to progress, a milestone is often used to signify a key date.

management practice, the term schedule is often used interchangeably to mean both the tool (typically a computerized CPM scheduling tool) and the activities and associated dates. [We define] the project specific data within the tool as a Project Schedule Model and the resulting list of activities with dates as a Project Schedule. Project Schedules include simple lists, bar charts with dates, and network logic diagrams with dates, to name just a few."

Statement 8: "Project Schedules can take the form of an early start schedule, late start schedule, baseline schedule, resource-limited schedule, or target schedule. Other types of schedules are actually derivatives of these five basic schedules. Such derivatives include master schedules, milestone schedules and various summary schedules."

Statement 9: "On regular intervals, as the project progresses, the Project Schedule Model must be updated. The project team needs to develop and maintain a process for Project Schedule Model changes. These changes can be the result of logic or scope revisions, but regardless of the source, the project team must plan for their occurrence."

Confused? I know I am! I consider myself a fairly intelligent fellow, who has been around the Scheduling block more than a few times, yet I have to confess that I am simply unable to get my mental arms around scheduling method, scheduling model, project schedule model, and project schedule. So I turned to the Glossary at the end of the cited document, with hopes of getting clarification. Well—let's see if you can do any better than I was able to:

Definition 1: "*Plan*—Not defined."

Definition 2: "*Project Schedule*—The planned dates for performing schedule activities and the planned dates for meeting schedule milestones. Also used with a modifier, such as early, late, current, baseline, resource limited, milestone, or target to identify various instances of the project schedule. See also, project schedule model."

Definition 3: "*Project Schedule Model*—A dynamic representation of the project's plan for executing the project's activities developed by the project team's applying the scheduling method to a scheduling model using project specific data such as activity lists and activity attributes. The project schedule model can produce critical paths and instances of project schedules, as well as resource profiles, activity assignments, records of accomplishments, etc. and can provide time-based forecasts, by reacting to inputs and adjustments made throughout the project's life cycle. (Scheduling Method plus Schedule Model plus Project Specific Data equal Project Schedule Model)"

Definition 4: "*Project Schedule Network Diagram*—Any schematic display of the logical relationships among the project schedule activities. Always drawn from left to right to reflect project work chronology."

Definition 5: "*Schedule*—See project schedule and see also project schedule model."

Definition 6: "*Scheduling Method*—A system of practices, techniques, procedures and rules used by project scheduling practitioners. This methodology can be performed either manually or with project management software specifically used for scheduling."

Definition 7: "*Scheduling Model*—A tool which provides schedule component names, definitions, structural relationships, and formats that support the application of a scheduling method. A model used in conjunction with manual methods or project management software to perform schedule network analysis to generate the project schedule for use in managing the execution of a project. See also project schedule."

Definition 8: "*Schedule Network Analysis*—The technique of identifying early and late start dates, as well as early and late finish dates, for the uncompleted portions of project schedule activities. See Also Critical Chain Method, Critical Path Method, Resource Leveling."

Definition 9: "*Network*—See Project Schedule Network Diagram."

Definition 10: "*Network Analysis*—See Schedule Network Analysis."

My Commentary on the New Set of Terms

In no particular order, I offer the following comments concerning the new set of terms that have their proponents hoping that they will bring *clarity* to our Practice.

1. The terms sound too similar to one another, and thereby immediately invoke confusion. The expressions—scheduling method, scheduling model, project schedule model, project schedule, and schedule—seem to all wash together. Because of how similar they sound, one is required to apply undivided mental concentration to their use.

2. The terms are not intuitive. These are not terms that have evolved over time. Rather, they are essentially foreign to the construction industry. The subtle distinction between words like method or model will be lost on the average contractor.
   - Will the typical schedule stakeholder appreciate that Scheduling Model and Project Schedule Model refer to two entirely different things?
   - Will these same stakeholders understand that a Project Schedule Model is different that a Project Schedule?

3. Some of the terms seem to be used in ways that contradict the meanings given for them in the Dictionary. For instance, scheduling software is called a Scheduling Model and defined in the Glossary as a tool. Yet here is what the Dictionary says about models and tools:

   Model: a standard or example for imitation or comparison; a simplified representation of a system or phenomenon.

   Tool: anything used as a means of accomplishing a task or purpose.

   To be sure, folks in construction as well as in the Scheduling Practice have long understood that the Critical Path Method provides a means of developing a simulation model designed for processing through computer algorithms for the purpose of analyzing project strategies, conditions, and opportunities. But in this context, it is the schedule itself that is the model of the project—as in "a simplified representation." This understanding would never include the scheduling software—independent of project-specific data, no less—as being the model (as Statement 4 requires).

4. For decades, Scheduling Practitioners have argued about whether a schedule is a database of information or if it is one or more of the various printouts of data extracted from that database. Well, this set of terms informs us that the database is called the Project Schedule Model, which in turn manifests itself as either a Project Schedule (when tabular; see Statement 7) or Project Network Diagram (when graphic; see Definition 4).

No distinct label is given for the monthly updates, or the various specialized reports that derive from that same database; these are also called Project Schedules (see Statements 8 and 9, and Definition 2.)

5. The Glossary merely compounds the confusion by cross-referencing most of the already similar-sounding terms to one another.
   • Project Schedule—See project schedule model. (Definition 2)
   • Schedule—See project schedule and project schedule model (Definition 5)
   • Scheduling Model—See project schedule (Definition 7)
   • Schedule Network Analysis—See critical chain method, critical path method, resource leveling. (Definition 8)
   • Network—See project schedule network diagram (Definition 9)
   • Network Analysis—See schedule network analysis (Definition 10)

So here we are at the start of 2007 and the latest attempt by Scheduling Practitioners to bring clarity to our Practice seems like just one more layer of confusion and contradictions that are burying us alive. Some of you may be wondering how I can have the audacity to think that my proposals in Chapter 5 are somehow superior to the materials we just examined, or any of the other noble attempts to bring clarity to the Practice.

My short answer is that I really don't know how my ideas will fair under critical scrutiny. My longer answer (some might call it a *defense*) is that Chapter 5, and this book as a whole, is written for the construction industry, whereas most (if not all) of the latest attempts at standards and best practices are aimed at the IT world. The exposure draft just examined is replete with examples of influence by the software world, where terms like "instances" and "models" and "methods" have a more familiar ring.

In Chapter 5, I keep the terms *plan* and *schedule, planner* and *scheduler, planning,* and *scheduling*—and offer clear distinctions between them. I refer to the monthly versions of the schedule as Schedule Editions, and the various tailored reports derived from the schedule database as Schedule Extractions. According to the Dictionary, an edition is:

"One of a series of printings of the same book, newspaper, etc., each issued at a different time and differing from another by alterations, additions, etc."

That about sums it up, don't you think? Each update is issued at a different time, and each differs as the result of alterations, additions, etc. And why the word "extraction"? It derives from the word *extract*, which means:

"To get, pull, or draw out, usually with special effort, skill, or force; to deduce (a doctrine, principle, interpretation, etc); to derive or obtain from a particular source; to take or copy out material, as from a book; to make excerpts from a book."

By using words that have common meaning, enjoy broad acceptance, and are instantly intuitive—such as extraction and edition—we help to clarify, not stupefy.

CUSTOMER DISSATISFACTION REASON #2:
NOT SERVING OUR CUSTOMER

When you step back and view the Scheduling Practice through critical eyes, you see that we have allowed it to become convoluted and weakened by side assignments and challenges. In the end, we have unintentionally abandoned our prime customer, the project manager. In the beginning, the Project Schedule was produced as an aid for the project manager, but it didn't take long for the project manager to be pushed to the back of the bread line.

- Almost from the start, the scheduling software itself became our new master and we found ourselves having to tell the project manager, "I can't do what you are asking for, because the software wouldn't let me."

- Next in line to assault the Project Schedule were a host of other "interested parties" wanting something from the Project Schedule, most notably the project owner. Suddenly we started coding our Project Schedules so as to generate the reports these others wanted. Their informational needs and wants forced us to adjust the level of detail we might otherwise prefer for an Execution Schedule.

- New uses for the Project Schedule created additional pressures. By cost-loading the Project Schedule, we could support EVMS; by resource-loading it we could perform Monte Carlo simulations; and, by further coding, we could even validate progress payments. As these other management functions became dependent upon Project Schedule outputs, they also became the primary customers to whom we now had to cater.

- Organizationally, the individual Scheduler was assigned to a Scheduling department, which established rules and standards that all schedules had to satisfy. Once again, we found ourselves having to tell the project manager, "I can't."

- Continuous and ever more radical changes in software architecture, design, and functionality further hindered our ability to give the project manager what he was asking for. Today, we wrestle with lumbering Enterprise Project Management software just to generate a 100-activity schedule for a tiny project. What used to take two hours to produce now takes much, much longer!

- The chasm between what our prime customer wants and what we are able—or willing—to deliver widens.

Conclusion #3: We need to remember that our primary customer is the project manager and his requirements come first and foremost. Only after we have satisfied his informational needs and wants are we free to assist others.

Conclusion #4: We must never forget that Practitioners don't control, direct, coordinate, or manage project activities. Those functions fall within the purview of the project manager. We help the manager control, direct, coordinate, or manage by providing products, services, and information that facilitate those actions. We may comment, suggest, and even advise. But we are *not* managers! We provide commentary on the shots; we do not *call the shots*.

CUSTOMER DISSATISFACTION REASON #3: OUTDATED PRODUCTS AND SERVICES

Finally, it is time for us to take a good long look at what we produce—products and services—and see if they meet our primary customer's needs. Is it possible to develop *one* Project Schedule that is versatile enough to serve the many different functions we identified and satisfy the many different end users we have named, while at the same timing still packing a noticeable punch? You bet it is!

To meet all of the demands placed on our work products, once we have made sure to identify, to ourselves and our stakeholders, each unique work product by a unique name, all we then need to do is make certain that the following happens:

- That the Project Schedule is intelligently designed.
- That the Project Schedule is thoughtfully developed.
- That the Project Schedule is attentively maintained.
- That the Project Schedule is skillfully used.

That's it, the long and the short of it! These four simple guidelines will lead to successful Project Schedules every time.

Is the Project Schedule Intelligently Designed?

First, do some advance work: find out who will be using your Project Schedule, and *how*. Understand the users' informational needs and the urgency and frequency of those needs. Determine the level of detail your Project Schedule must maintain in order to supply the right level of information to each customer. Based on this research, design the Schedule's architecture, complete with information sourcing, coding conventions, and report formats, in such a way that it will achieve all stated objectives. (For more on Schedule Design, see Chapter 12)

Is the Project Schedule Thoughtfully Developed?

Proper Schedule Development should also ensure that the Schedule's design is not compromised. At all costs, protect the integrity of the Project Schedule! Do not let practical, political, financial, or organizational influences erode the legitimacy or viability of the Project Schedule. One of the biggest killers of Project Schedules is front-end pressure (usually from management types) to dispense with some aspect of schedule design or content in order to meet other business objectives. We'll talk more about this later, when we look at Schedule Development issues such as float, relationships, and durations, in Chapter 13.

The other essential ingredient of good Project Schedules is up-front buy-in by all stakeholders. This means that, before it is finalized, the Project Schedule is reviewed and approved by all who will be obligated to its mandates. This buy-in extends beyond the obvious stakeholders, the general contractor and his subcontractors. It also includes the owner, designers, and any others who have an active part in the project. And this buy-in begins with Consensus Planning.

Is the Project Schedule Skillfully Used?

Once the Project Schedule has been incorporated into the project management process, it will be *accessed* by way of a variety of output products: logic diagrams, bar charts, tabular printouts, resource curves (histograms), Schedule Performance Analyses, and the like. The single-most important guiding principle I can impart to you concerning how to create Project Schedules that people will actually want to use is this: *the Project Schedule should provide each project member with all the information he needs to do his job- no more, no less. And the information should always be in a form that is relevant, meaningful, timely, and accurate.*

To some, this may sound harder than it really is. Smart coding systems on the front end will yield well-tailored Execution Schedule Extractions on the back end. To others, this rule may seem much easier than it really is, for what is continually needed is a certain amount of *human* involvement (namely, a Scheduling Practitioner). All too often, we over-rely on the computer's ability to mechanically sort and filter data for extraction, based on preset selection criteria. Don't forget that the computer has *no* scheduling experience!

Construction projects are living creatures, with new surprises every Monday morning and new obstacles every Thursday afternoon. Construction projects may be many things, but one thing they are not is predictable. The Project Schedule that seeks to simulate events and predict outcomes can never be dead-on every time—even with the most cleverly crafted, forward-thinking set of database manipulation codes and parameters.

Is the Project Schedule Attentively Maintained?

What I have uncovered, virtually every time I have been asked to analyze a contractor's failing scheduling program, is that there had been "no one minding the store." By this I mean that, at the outset, the Project Schedule may be smartly designed and developed, but then, once the project begins, some data entry clerk with no scheduling training is given the task of producing printouts on a monthly basis. As the course of the project changes (while schedule content does not), reports begin to have less and less resemblance to the realities of the project, and hence less value to those receiving the reports. Narratives are rarely written, limited Schedule Maintenance is inadequate, and no diagnostic analyses are performed.

It should go without saying that a Project Schedule is like a map: no matter how well designed, developed, or conveyed, it is essentially useless if it remains hidden in the glove compartment—or if its information is obsolete. A Project Schedule is a living and breathing member of the construction management team. It should be consulted frequently and *routinely*. Listen: everything about the construction project is dynamic; nothing is static. The work doesn't stand still, time doesn't stand still, the elements don't stand still, the owner doesn't stand still, the status of the project doesn't stand still—and neither should the Project Schedule.

Too many Project Schedule stakeholders, even including many well-trained and highly seasoned Practitioners, view each Execution Schedule Edition as a stand-alone view of the world. Through their eyes, the latest Project Schedule update is a snapshot of how things are on the job. By contrast, I consider this snapshot mentality as nothing short of tunnel vision. It's like looking at one frame from a long roll of movie film. A snapshot does not convey movement—momentum—and if a project is any one thing, it is planned and executed momentum.

That is why it is essential that the project management team interprets each Project Schedule Extraction in the context of a continuum, as one of an ongoing series of snapshots—together creating a *motion* picture—one that conveys the pace and direction of project momentum.

4

The Changing Style of Project Management

Over the last few years, project management, across an array of industries, has been experiencing a seismic shift in style and approach that reflects a corresponding change in management philosophy. Being gradually abandoned is the Command-and-Control management style/philosophy that has dominated general business management, and, more specifically, project management, for centuries, up through and including all of the twentieth century. It is of historical significance that the Critical Path Method was born during the heyday of the Command-and-Control era, and its Newtonian origins reflect management's insatiable desire to know all and dictate all. In the last ten years or so, a new management philosophy has been gaining a significant foothold and, according to many experts, its swift climb in popularity suggests that both general management and project management approaches will dramatically and permanently transition from the failed methods of Command-and-Control to the promising style of what I refer to, herein, as Collaborative Management.

The Scheduling Practice always has been, and always will be, a set of products and services intended to support project management. Logically, then, as project management philosophies, methods, and styles change, so too must our products and services, if we are to remain relevant and of benefit to our primary customer, the project manager. In this sense, there may be no more obvious or important sentence in this entire book than the following: *If our customers' needs and wants are dramatically changing and yet we, nonetheless, continue to do things in the same manner that we have always done them, then we are certain to become obsolete, irrelevant, and unwanted.* Maybe that inevitability is already occurring.

In the following pages, I make many sweeping assertions; some complimentary of the way things are done, some critical. I wish to clarify that I do not see things as being as black-and-white as these pages may imply. For instance, when I assert that a particular practice does, will, or can result in such-and-such, in the back of my mind I am keenly aware that there are exceptions to everything. To be sure, for any bold statement there can be found exceptions. I acknowledge that, despite my insistence that, "our schedules are not working," or "too much detail will kill a schedule," or "workers are not unethical, lazy, or incompetent," exceptions can be cited.

PROJECT MANAGEMENT PARADIGM SHIFT

What you need to know is that a major paradigm shift is occurring in the project management field. In a nutshell, the iron grip of the Newtonian Model is giving way to the influence of the New Sciences on how projects are being managed. So let's take a brief look at what the Newtonian Model is all about, and contrast that understanding with New Sciences' drastically different view of projects, as complex adaptive systems.

The Newtonian Model

In the seventeenth century, Sir Isaac Newton gave the world a systematic way to understand complex systems or entities by breaking them down into smaller and smaller subelements. This approach, which we can describe as *understanding the whole by understanding its parts*, made a lot of intuitive sense and quickly caught on, so much so that the Newtonian thinking paved the way for the Industrial Revolution. Manufacturing adopted an assembly line process in which individual parts were built and then assembled into the whole.

In management, a parallel approach took root. Managing an organization amounted to managing the individual parts of the organization. The familiar *organizational chart* became the logo for the Newtonian Model, and its practical implementation became the structure for virtually all modern business enterprises. A corporation is comprised of companies (or subsidiaries), and companies are made up of divisions. Departments comprise divisions, and sections make up departments. Teams make up sections, and so it goes. According to the Newtonian theory, if each team is fully controlled, then collectively the entire enterprise is fully controlled.

The influence of the Newtonian whole-parts model is evident even in the language of modern management. The very word de*partment* hints at the component aspect of organizations, and individuals who are highly compatible with a given role are said to make a good "fit." Casually, problematic employees are called "cogs in the wheel," and descriptors of organizational performance have strong mechanical references, such as process "gates," performance thresholds, and the like.

As long as the deliverables of business were chiefly physical, the Newtonian model seemed to be a well-suited management framework. But the Industrial Revolution eventually gave way to the Information Age, and nowadays the emphasis has shifted from production of things to the exchange of knowledge. And therein lies the rub, as Shakespeare would alert us. Knowledge and communication are interactive at their essence, whereas products are tangible, linear, and unique. A widget cannot be in two places at one time, but information can. Knowledge is more like the flame of a candle. It can be used to create another flame, without diminishing itself. Knowledge can expand in its reach without ever diluting itself. Try that with a widget!

And knowledge grows! Knowledge is an *active a*gent, to use a popular term from our times. That is, knowledge can evolve into an infinite number of conclusions, depending on the minds in which it lights. Since every person is unique, in terms of reasoning, experience, values, and skills, the same bit of information can (and will) have a different impact and cause an entirely different ripple of downstream effects on each unique person who comes upon that information.

The Newtonian model called for silos, each subelement being design and developed in an essential vacuum, to be united with other subelements at the time of assembly. But despite what I just said about the differences between widgets and information, until recently, even information-based businesses followed the Newtonian model. Consider a large insurance company. It has a sales department, an underwriting department, a claims department, a marketing department, a legal department, and so forth. Each department functions rather independently. That model persists in other industries as well, including banking, auto sales, manufacturing, the military, and so many others. The Newtonian model is alive and well in the twenty-first century!

In construction, the Newtonian Model was instantly embraced, and evidence of its influence is to be found everywhere. The conventional *contract model*, the infamous triangle, depicts owner-architect-contractor. Each of the players has a distinct role and the boundaries between them are carefully guarded. Responsibility for the general contractor's scope is further divided into subcontracts, to be performed by subcontractors. Vendors and suppliers are identified as yet other subcomponents of the whole (the project).

In our world of Scheduling, the Critical Path Method (CPM) came along to provide a practical manifestation of the Newtonian model. The project was depicted as a collection of activities, first grouped into subnetworks and further into strings of sequential steps (activities). Today's work breakdown structure is the epitome of the Newtonian Model, and modern-day cost control principles (even—and perhaps especially—including the Earned Value Management System) are based on the reasoning that to control the pieces is to control the whole.

Interestingly, it was the advent of the *project* concept that represented one of the first formal rejections of the Newtonian Model. Introduced as an alternative to the silo-styled business structure, representatives from the previously isolated and independent functional departments were invited to join forces on what was called "the project." Working synergistically, the project team would endeavor to blend and amalgamate the interests, concerns, and talents of each distinct functional discipline toward the common goals of the whole.

The Project Schedule became the unfortunate rope in the business model tug-of-war. Why do I say this? Because the demand of the project was to first understand and then depict the collaborative vision of the project team, but the underlying methodology of CPM called for fragmentation of project scope. And over the last two decades, the rope has only been strained more and more, as demands for greater granularity in schedules has coincided with one management theory after another calling for team empowerment, management by objectives, total quality management, and more. How might the Project Schedule foster teamwork, even as it continues to subdivide the work down to a single-performer (read: single point of accountability) level?

The New Sciences and What They Teach Management

They are called the *New Sciences* because they have come around in the last 25 years, roughly since 1980. Actually the sciences themselves have been around for centuries, but the recent rash of outlandish discoveries have given the old sciences a new face; hence, the New Sciences. Major discoveries have emerged virtually simultaneously in five separate traditional sciences: physics, chemistry, biology, psychology, and mathematics.

The Dynamic Nature of Projects

Before we attempt to highlight what the New Sciences are able to teach us, we need to establish a few key definitions. Let us start by recognizing that a project meets the New Sciences definition of a *complex adaptive system*. According to most definitions, a complex adaptive system has these attributes:

- It is an open system, meaning that it interacts with the environment in which it exists and operates. Few would disagree that projects are constantly subject to change resulting from corresponding changes in the environment in which the project exists. Owners change project scope, communities or government entities cause changes in project scope or progress, the economic climate can affect the scope or achievement of a project, and so on.
- It is comprised of a large number of interdependent parts. More than other characteristics, this one captures the major essence of all projects.
- It is characteristically dynamic—constantly changing—and such changes are rarely linear. The nonlinear aspect of projects is well known. Often called the *ripple effect*, a change in one variable commonly sets off a host of other changes, and the changes fan out in numerous directions at once, unlike the linear cause-and-effect represented by an engine pushing or pulling a string of railroad cars.

The common thread among the lessons to be learned from the New Sciences about complex adaptive systems is that these dynamic systems cannot be understood by simply understanding the individual parts. And this is where the New Sciences part company with Sir Isaac. To give a modern, tangible example, one can analyze a windshield wiper motor forever and never understand the workings of an automobile. In fact, even if one deduces from the motor the functionality of the windshield wiper, and from that the windshield, and from that a moving vehicle, one still has no way of distinguishing an automobile from a truck, or a motor boat, or an airplane, or a locomotive, all of which have windshields.

As you will soon see, each of the New Sciences gives us greater understanding of *how*, in all complex adaptive systems, the parts of the whole interact in ways that constantly change the whole. Even the *timing* of the interactions creates changes in the whole. An example I like to use to describe the profound significance of the dynamic aspects of parts integration is a food recipe. Most recipes have two sections: the list of ingredients, and the manner in which they are to be combined. It is the latter that turns the same ingredients into different foods. That is how dynamic systems work. To a great extent, they are comprised of the same parts, and it is only in the manner in which the parts are combined that unique end products emerge.

No Objective Reality

From the field of physics comes Quantum Theory, first contemplated by Albert Einstein (among others) almost a hundred years ago. Recent discoveries, thanks in large part to computers and other microchip technologies, are showing us that, as one scientist put it, "what we have always believed to be reality is not; and what we thought was unreal, is."

Consider, for instance, what is called *Observation Theory*. Observation theory says that the very act of observing something causes that *something* to alter its behavior. Using an electron microscope, scientists have discovered that protons can manifest in two different forms: as particles or as waves of energy. Now here is the spooky part: the protons appear to be able to change their form depending on whether or not they are being observed! Further research is underway to understand how this occurs, but the pattern of reaction to observation is incontrovertible.

Dr. Masaru Emoto, who has made great strides in understanding the behavior of water molecules when being observed, has advanced a possible (but unlikely to be the only) explanation. He discovered that water molecules react to the vibrations emanating from humans, the wave patterns of which change with different emotions within the human. When a person is angry, they emit a certain wave pattern that is different from the wave patterns when they are happy or scared or curious or bored. Since the human body, not to mention the entire Earth, is mostly comprised of water, the implications of his findings are profoundly significant. (For more on Dr. Emoto's ground breaking discoveries, go to www.masaru-emoto.net.)

Additional support for the observation theory comes from psychology, with some studies dating back nearly a hundred years. Consistently, they have shown that humans behave in anticipation of what is expected of them. For instance, in the late 1960s, Robert Rosenthal, a researcher from Harvard University published a controversial study, called *Pygmalion in the Classroom*. In it he argued that, "when teachers expect students to do well and show intellectual growth, they do; when teachers do not have such expectations, performance and growth are not so encouraged and may in fact be discouraged in a variety of ways."

As a third persuasive argument in favor of observation theory, consider what is called the Time Irreversibility Rule. This postulates, in unequivocal terms, that the same identical context never occurs twice. Each gathering of cars at a red light is unique, even if they are the same cars (which, in itself, is unlikely), because each car is in a uniquely different state at every minute, each hour, every day. A common analogy states, "you never step into the same river twice." This is true not only because the river composition is constantly changing, but because you are too.

These three different perspectives teach the project manager and project scheduler a most valuable lesson: *there is no objective reality*. The obvious implication is that the "project" we envision during initial planning is *not* the project that the team will encounter as the project unfolds. No matter what we may anticipate or speculate about how the project will unfold day to day, the reality of the moment will be different than anything we can anticipate. Of course, we've known this truth all along and have been in denial of it for as long as we have steadfastly defended the practice of "planning the work and working the plan." But now, with the New Sciences, we have an additional argument we may not have realized previously: simply by observing (let alone directly interacting with) the project, we effectively alter the reality of the project based on who we are, how we feel, how we act, what we do, what we think, how we interact with others, and on and on and on.

Bounded Disorder

From Chaos Theory we learn about the natural behavior of open systems. For one thing, systems are *bound* at one level to rules of conduct, and yet at a more detailed level, they act rather randomly. The name for this type of bounded disorder is *chaordic*, meaning that there is chaos within order. In this usage, "chaos" does not mean ruckus and dysfunction, but instead unpredictability.

The example I prefer to use to clarify the contrast of chaos and order is lightning. At a general level, modern meteorologists understand enough about the conditions that spawn lightning storms to be able to predict their occurrence. On the nightly local news, we are told when the storm is expected to roll into town and whether it will be accompanied by lightning. The accuracy of these predictions is impressive, to say the least. But notwithstanding what must be a fairly good understanding of the conditions that produce lightning, weather scientists would never attempt to predict precisely when or where the lightning strikes will hit: down to the square mile, square yard, square foot, or square inch, or down to the minute or second. Why don't they know those details as well?

The answer lies in the chaordic behavior of natural systems. They all operate according to certain general rules, but within those general rules (boundaries) they act randomly (chaos). We recognize projects as natural open systems because they are animated by human beings, natural creatures, and exist in natural environments. The important lesson to learn about the management of projects—which is, above all else, the management of people—is that too much control backfires. Man's repeated tampering with, and disruption of, the world's ecosystems amply confirm this truism.

Self-Reference and Self-Renewal

Understanding why our attempts to re-engineer the environment continually fail leads us to another discovery from the New Sciences. Natural systems routinely conduct *self-reference* and *self-renewal*. Put simply, systems know when they are out of sync and correct themselves. As a simple example, consider how a river behaves. A river follows some basic rules (boundaries), such as water seeking its own level, water seeking the path of least resistance, and water adhering to the power of gravity. With those three basic rules, rivers find their own routes from high ground to low ground, twisting and turning as they go, and occasionally overflowing their banks. In areas where overflow is a common occurrence, the ground is marshier, and the life forms that live there are accustomed to and dependent on the ground moisture.

Consider what happens when Man decides to reroute a river segment and construct a canal in its place. The canal, being made of concrete, cannot reform its curves or redirect itself. Overflow becomes the only option available to the water, and the areas it floods are *not* ones accustomed to the overflow (such as adjacent populated areas).

To counter this possibility, Man next constructs dams and sluice gates and water level sensors, and so on. Of course, the more we try to control the conditions, the more we realize that we cannot anticipate every eventuality, and sooner or later our "failsafe" systems fail us.

Now consider what we do in project management that is similar. Projects are made up of humans who, more than anything else, make projects *natural* open systems. Projects are also prone to constant change (see the section "No Objective Reality"), and so there is a constant need for humans to respond to ever-changing conditions. If only allowed to do so, most workers will solve the problems they encounter. But instead, management puts in place rigid plans and schedules and demands that those preconceived plans be adhered to, no matter what the current reality otherwise suggests to the worker. We ridicule and condemn "out-of-sequence" work as bad, even though it is most often merely residual evidence of a natural system practicing self-reference and self-renewal.

Fractals: There's No Such Thing As Ever Fully Knowing

The idea underlying fractals is that they contain a large degree of self-similarity, as if they are comprised of little copies of themselves. In an extreme case, humans contain the seeds of their replication. But more traditional examples are canyons or rivers or trees. The closer you look at these features, the more the smaller aspects of them look similar to their host. There is the textbook example of the implications of fractals, which cites the coastline of England. If you measure the coastline, using a zoomed-out map, you will derive a much smaller number than if you use an extremely precise map, one showing every bay, inlet, harbor, and such.

What do fractals have to do with project management and the Scheduling Practice? Simply put, they teach us not to get too caught up in our quest for greater precision, because there really is no precise answer. We can start with a general activity—say, Interior Rough-Ins, Third Floor—and assign a duration of three months, and this value would be an approximation of how long such rough-ins should take. We could, of course, divide that single activity into several dozen *smaller* activities, one of which might be Rough-In Interior Walls, Third Floor, and assign a duration of six workdays. But is this a precisely accurate duration?

We might further divide this activity into a few more subactivities, one of which might be Erect Metal Studs, Third Floor. Or maybe we get more specific geographically, as well, and define an activity—Erect Metal Studs, West Wing, Third Floor—and assign a duration of two workdays. But is *this* duration the most accurate estimate of the time needed to perform the work? What if we decomposed the scope to something as specific as Erect Metal Studs, Column X to Column Y, and the length of that wall segment is 20 feet, and the estimated duration is four hours? Is *this* estimate any more accurate relative to its scope than the three-month duration was relative to its scope? Surely you can see that we can continue to drill down into more and more specificity and still never improve the reliability of our schedules.

Change and Complexity Reduction

Another discovery of the New Sciences has to do with the phenomenon of change. In fact, a whole new discipline has emerged, called *Change Science*. One of its observations is that the *rate* of change is increasing over time. About 150 years ago, it is estimated, the average person experienced less than a dozen significant changes in a lifetime. By significant, it is meant events such as deaths, births, marriages, major technological changes, and so on. Today, it is estimated we experience more than a dozen major changes each week. Yes, the births and deaths might only be ones we hear about, but in those olden days, the news from even the next town over came slowly. Today, if a factory burns down in Taiwan, we know about it before the smoke has cleared the air.

The effect of change on the human psyche is a major focus of change science. One discovery of the New Sciences is a human response phenomenon called *complexity reduction*. The theory behind this concept is that humans have a maximum capacity for change. At first, a change constitutes a substitution of an older way for a newer way. But each such adaptation requires internal conditioning. You might think of this as "getting used to" something new. Adaptation takes time, and if the changes do not occur too frequently, humans can absorb the changes.

But when changes occur suddenly and often, we humans reach a maximum capacity beyond which we simply shut down. The manner in which we turn a deaf ear to the changes, as if we are pulling the covers over our heads, differs from person to person, to be sure, but in terms of business practices, two common techniques involve selective consideration and summarization. The important point about complexity reduction is that it is a coping mechanism; it is *not* a skilled response to change. In fact, complexity reduction essential denies the change altogether.

Using *selective consideration* (my term), we pick and choose which changes to acknowledge and which ones we will pretend don't exist. To understand this technique, let's be clear about how change may appear to us. You've heard of an airplane pilot "flying on instruments." This is an alternative to "flying on sight." What's the difference, in terms of reality? Well, you might say that the latter involves dealing directly with reality (what the pilot sees), whereas flying on instruments involves dealing with an artificial representation of reality (instruments and gauges). A physicist might argue, somewhat esoterically, that what our eyes "see" is also an indirect representation of what actually exists.

Let's take this concept of selective consideration and relate it to project management. Let us address the question, "What is the project's current status?" First, set aside the matter that this question can have numerous different meanings and let us agree, for the sake of this discussion, that we simply want to know whether the project is on schedule or not. How can we determine the truth of this reality? If Sir Isaac were answering this question, he would insist that we determine the status of each activity in the schedule. And because our current scheduling methods are entirely Newtonian, that is precisely how we approach the question today.

But we also apply several layers of complexity reduction. First, even though there are countless ways to evaluate the status of a project, we quickly and arbitrarily decide that our answer will be given in the context of time. That takes us to the schedule for our answer. Next we decide that, in terms of how such performance affects timely completion, we will use a strictly numeric approach, one relying on the total-float value. Third, because our minds cannot simultaneously juggle more than a few dozen variables at once, we decide that we must further reduce the list of "critical" activities to those with a total-float value below a particular threshold. Finally, because this list is still more than we can deal with, we further limit the list to those activities occurring in the near term. Through complexity reduction, we have effectively dismissed 95 percent of the activities, turning our complete attention to an unbelievably small subset of activities ready for selective consideration.

The other way we deal with what my children call TMI (too much information) or my generation calls "information overload" is by various summarizing techniques. Perhaps the most popular application of this technique is averaging. The latest buzzword in project management reporting is the *project dashboard*. The idea is to reduce an entire project to a small set of indicators, each one of which is a summary of averaged data sets. Again, we distance ourselves from the details and make decisions based on generalizations. Complexity reduction is a major factor in why the *reality* we think we see is anything but the reality that is really out there on our projects.

Fields Theory

This last category of the New Sciences is one that may seem way out there for many of you; it was for me, at first. This theory states that all around us are invisible fields that cause living organisms to behave in ways that have nothing to do with mental thought or physical connectedness. The most often given example of this is a flock of geese in flight or a school of fish swimming as a group. The group seems to be following the lead goose or lead fish. As if acting out of a thousands years of rehearsal, the entire group suddenly darts left or right. Until recently it was believed that the group was simply following the leader at the front of the formation, but the New Sciences have discovered that they all, including the leader, are reacting to invisible fields.

These fields are waves of invisible energy that have a collective effect on all members of the group. At first, like I said, I didn't buy the concept. But then someone explained that magnetism and gravity are two such fields. Suddenly I began to understand that, indeed, there is much that is going on all around us that can and does effect how we act, dynamics that we choose to forget are out there. Some people have arthritis, and damp weather makes the joints hurt. During the course of the day, an afflicted person might be tenser, less friendly, more impatient and never know why. Dew point is a measure of moisture in the air, and moisture is a field.

Maybe emotions are a field. We are all aware that our moods rub off on one another. And sometimes we feel down for no good reason and cannot explain why. But when we bring our melancholy to work, it is contagious.

The importance of fields theory to project management is that, perhaps more than any other theory, it explains why the project we experience today is not the same as the project we left at quitting time yesterday, or the one we will encounter tomorrow. Tomorrow is a new day, right? Fields theory, even as ambiguous and esoteric as it is, still rings true because we all know that there is this intangible, unexplainable phenomenon in all of our lives, something going on that we cannot explain. "I've got a feeling," we say, "but I can't put my finger on it." Or maybe we have an epiphany, or the light bulb goes off, or we experience déjà vu, or we think about something completely random and it happens right in front of our eyes.

The point is that there is an unspoken, unseen, and grossly not understood dynamic that energizes all projects. The creative mind, the spark of genius, the great solution, these happen all the time on all projects. If our attempts at project control serve to stifle the natural eruption of inspired or inventive thought, we do the project a grave disservice.

The Devil's in the Relationship

The collective lesson to be learned from all of these New Sciences discoveries—the dynamic nature of projects, no objective reality, bounded disorder, self-renewal, fractals, complexity reduction, and fields theory—is that the real driver of all projects is the interaction of the parties. It is not some set of activities in a Project Schedule, identified through algorithms as "drivers." The reality of the project is the one that unfolds day by day, hour by hour, and challenge by challenge. The real energy of the project cannot be predicted or planned. And it sure as heck cannot be controlled. We shouldn't *want* to control it. Imagine someone standing outside Thomas Edison's laboratory and insisting that his latest discovery was "late," or more ridiculously, "out of sequence."

Humans learn from one another, draw off of one another's ideas and moods, and affect one another. Humans interact. Systems interact with their environments, just as environments are affected by the systems alive within them. This free flow of energy is there for us to tap, as sails do with wind. The new project management paradigm is moving away from the Command-and-Control mentality of the centuries, to a new model where the system corrects itself. This translates into team empowerment on the project, less management autocracy, and less fixation with baselines and deviations from the plan.

The Momentum Studies of the mid-1980s, admittedly coming from an entirely different angle, reached the same conclusions that the New Sciences have reached with respect to how projects ought to be run. It was discovered that the vast majority of project delays were caused by catalysts occurring *in between* activities, not during the activities. In CPM jargon, between activities are relationships. It is interesting that the New Sciences alert us to the invisible power of relationships. In fact, as one of the best descriptions of the contrast between the Newtonian Model and the New Sciences Model, may I suggest that:

"According to Newton, the whole is understood by understanding the parts. According to the New Sciences thinking, the whole is understood by understanding the relationships between and among the parts . . . to each other and to the whole."

CHARACTERISTICS OF PROJECT MANAGEMENT PARADIGM SHIFT

In the previous section, I discussed a major shift in project management philosophy changing the way projects are being managed all around the world. Since the project manager is the primary customer of the Scheduling Practice, it behooves us to understand what that change is all about and how we can and must adapt our methods to accommodate the new philosophy.

To this end, in this section we are concerned with better understanding how the new project management paradigm will look and behave. For starters, it would well serve this discussion to give meaningful names to the two opposing management styles. I will call the outgoing method *Command-and-Control Model, or Management* and the new method *Collaborative Model, or Management.*

Under the Command-and-Control Model, the strategy has been to dictate and control the behavior of each and every activity on the project and, in doing so, collectively control the project itself. Contrast that with the Collaborative Model, where the strategy is to allow for the contemporaneous resolution of problems and response to change by those who create the active reality and who affect it by their mere interaction.

The New Sciences provide convincing explanations for the ineffectiveness of the Command-and-Control approach that we have observed for some time. They also justify the need for a paradigm shift to a Collaborative Management strategy, one that fosters team ownership of the project. When we take in everything we have just learned, the essential instructions to the open-minded project manager begin to crystallize.

- **Set the Context, and Then Step Back** Trust the teams to solve their own problems. That is not to say that we shouldn't set boundaries for that trust. Create a chaordic jobsite: you set short-term goals (order) and give the project team the freedom to determine their own route to goal achievement (chaos).

- **As Management, Set Goals and Parameters** Goals refer to *what* is to be accomplished, while parameters mandate *how* the work is to be accomplished in terms of general sequencing and timing. The new role of the Scheduling Practitioner is to facilitate the implementation of the new project management paradigm.

- **Trust the Team** Appreciate the collective knowledge and wisdom of the team, and remember that they just created the very reality that you are now so concerned with managing. Understand that the team will be best qualified to *sense* the solution. Have faith in the ethics and commitment of the team.[1] Stop obsessing over absolute compliance. Out of sequence isn't always bad.

---

[1]It is interesting to note that the recently introduced Critical Chain Project Management method is predicated on the notion that the team cannot be trusted. Central to its reasoning are contentions such as: durations are padded; workers will drag out their work if allowed to; and float cannot be entrusted to those performing the work, but must be managed at the project level (as buffers).

- **Orchestrate, Don't Dictate** Learn to facilitate the smooth unfolding of the project. Know that history has shown that efforts to micromanage systematically fail. Eliminate compartmentalization and silos. They stifle teamwork and creativity. Pave the way for self-organization, self-reference, and self-renewal.

- **Acquire Improvisational Skills** The word *improvise* comes from Latin and means "not foreseen." The Momentum Studies confirm that the majority of schedule delays result from unforeseen "small stuff"—what I call *dilemmas*. The best counter to dilemmas is the acquisition of skills and practiced responses to the unforeseen. I call this Improvisational Management. Develop a heightened sense of awareness of open systems and appreciate the ability of systems to correct themselves. Control has always been a fantasy. Utilize the project's natural momentum to the project's advantage.

- **Affect the Paradigm Shift** The tectonic shift in project management style will occur one project at a time (see Table 4-1).
  - **Purpose** Simply dismiss the futile notion that the worker can be controlled. Dismiss the notion that the project itself is controllable simply by controlling all of its various parts. Instead, see the project manager's function as one of *facilitation*, much like the conductor of an orchestra, who lifts his baton to signal an instrument's moment to begin playing and the tempo at which playing should continue. It is left to the musician to know when to wet his lips, lift his instrument to mouth, and take his deep breath.
  - **Emphasis** Focus less on the activities themselves and more on what happens between activities. In our schedules, these are depicted as relationships, but so much more than relationships alone transpire—or *should* transpire—between activities. Management must focus on the invisible barriers that obstruct, thwart, and impede the start of all activities.
  - **Authority** Recognize that decision making should be paired with responsibility and that those who do the work are—or should be held—most accountable for the actual performance of work on the project. Quality control, momentum, cost control, safety, productivity, accuracy, punctuality, timeliness, thoroughness, attention to detail, cooperation, creative solutions, impact avoidance and mitigation, dispute resolution, risk identification, and so much more depend on the mental, emotional, and psychological commitment of the individual. We do the project a great disservice when we view the worker as a "human *resource*" because we see them only as a *physical* factor and completely ignore their many other, more significant, attributes.

Table 4-1

Project Management Paradigm Shift

In Terms of . . .	Move Away From . . .	. . . And Move Toward
Purpose	Control	Facilitation
Emphasis	Activities	Relationships
Authority	Top-centered	Bottom-shared
Perspective	Deterministic and Linear	Chaordic and Complex
The Future	Prediction	Early Warnings
Reaction	Planned Responses	Spontaneous Responses
Focus	Compliance	Creativity

We must trust those on the front line and vest authority in them. Those in the ivory towers may have power of the purse, but that doesn't give them superior knowledge, and the knowledge they acquire indirectly (through reports or even site visits) is unquestionably summarized, distilled, and even skewed.

- **Perspective** Once and for all, see the project as chaordic and complex. Sir Isaac also got it partially wrong with his Third Law: "For every action, there is an equal and opposite reaction." Now, I admit that I am playing with semantics, here, but I take issue with the word *an*. On projects, for every action there are *multiple* reactions. And these reactions are interwoven in such a way that each initial reaction becomes a precipitating action in its own right, which causes additional reactions. We must stop seeing the project as deterministic, as if we can draw a neat flow chart and capture every significant relationship. Projects are natural open systems and as such are not linear. This fact alone may well explain why our current scheduling methods, despite the computer giving them specious credibility, nevertheless fail to prevent project slippage.

- **The Future** For the very same reasons we have just discussed, we must quit trying to predict project completion dates. First, our bases of predictions are all wet. Second, who cares? A professional bowler does not aim for the pins; he aims for the arrow-shaped markers on his end of the 60-foot bowling lane. He knows the key to successful bowling: "hit your mark, and the pins will fall." Our fixation on the infamous "end date" has distracted our attention from the factors that cause us to achieve or miss those end dates. Instead, we should be watching for telltale signs of impending dilemmas, plan for their arrival, and make quick work of them when they arrive.

- **Reaction** Because our ability to predict the small stuff is so poor, we should instead develop a repertoire of *planned responses*, so that, no matter what eventuality comes our way, we know how we will respond. Instead, we ignore the preponderance of dilemmas and focus on the uncertain arrival of a handful of major risks (risk management). More people get wet from the collective moisture of a billion raindrops than they do from the inundation of a sweeping flash flood. That's why we carry umbrellas but we don't drive in unsinkable cars.

- **Focus** We must tap the bottomless well of human imagination. All problems can be solved, and those involved at the most grassroots level of the project are the spawning ground for all great ideas. When we shut them out of the problem solving process—which is what happens when we communicate with them only to assess and critique their compliance with predetermined planned actions—we deny the project its greatest source of knowledge, security, and energy. How smart is that?

- **Lose Faith in Details** To inspire and drive these changes in attitude, project managers will want to change how they do business, as discussed in this and the next section. To begin, let's quit bowing down to details. The word "detail" comes from Old French, and means, "a piece cut off." When we extract a detail, we are creating a sample of the whole, but something is lost—something is always lost. Then, when we extrapolate a more minute detail from the sampling, something further is lost. We can improve our craft by:
  - Understanding and accepting that the deeper you dig, the more inaccurate you become.

- Halting and reversing recent trends toward greater minutia beyond our ability to comprehend, what I call our *awareness zone*.
- Rejecting any management methodology that wrestles control away from those on the front lines (for example, the critical chain).
- Restricting the unbridled influence of WBS (Work Breakdown Structure): it is as Newtonian as it gets!
- Rethinking EVMS (earned value) and (total-float), which are both retrospective methods. Neither they nor Critical Chain adequately prepare management for the project's inevitable daily dilemmas. They merely react to them *after the fact.*

- **Support Team Ownership of the Project** Over the last decade we have seen a meteoric rise in appreciation for the value of synergy, teamwork. We would be wise to move in that direction as well. Establish a reasonable context for performance. Establish boundary goals and parameters:
  - Project Schedules should be no more detailed than Level 2. This will set goals without micromanaging goal achievement.
  - At the time of project execution, abandon dogmatic loyalty to prior intent (Commitment Plans). Recognize the serendipitous nature of all projects. Neither dilemmas nor witty solutions can ever be adequately planned. (I plan to be sick next week. I plan to recover by taking aspirins for two days.)

- **Respect the NERD (nutshell, extreme, remote data) Threshold**:
  - **Avoid nutshell data** Stop summarizing as a form of complexity reduction. Abandon management by exception and other process-of-elimination methods (for example, total-float reports).
  - **Avoid extreme data** There is such a thing as too much detail. Remember that humans have a limited capacity for details, beyond which information is simply ignored or dismissed.
  - **Avoid remote data** Close the gap between where decisions are made (in the ivory towers) and where reality is being observed, created, and responded to (in the trenches).

IMPLICATIONS FOR MODIFIED SCHEDULING METHODS

As noted at the outset of this chapter, if our customers are making dramatic changes in the way projects are being managed, then it behooves us to make corresponding changes in the way we design, develop, maintain, and use Project Schedules in support of our customers. For if we continue on with business as usual, we run the very real risk of becoming obsolete. Judging by recent surveys, it would seem that we are well on our way to extinction.

Okay—so we must change our ways. But what should those changes be? To answer this question, let's review the different ways Project Schedules are commonly used and see if we can allocate those uses to the two different project management philosophies: Command-and-Control, and Collaborative.

Let us begin by seeing if we can summarize what I have just said about the Command-and-Control and Collaborative Management philosophies. I will do so in three separate steps. First, I will summarize the *Beliefs* that underlie each school of thought. Second, under *Behaviors*, I will explain how these beliefs translate into management behaviors having distinct characteristics. Third, and finally, under *Merits*, I will list the reasons the Command-and-Control philosophy is quickly falling out of favor, while the Collaborative philosophy is taking its place as the dominant project management strategy for the foreseeable future.

Management Philosophy Beliefs

The Command-and-Control Management style did not survive hundreds of years without some very powerful and worthwhile beliefs about the way humans behave. We must remember that project management, and even general management, ultimately boils down to people management. But this same criterion for validation—human behavior—forms the foundation of the more recent Collaborative Management style. An examination of these underlying beliefs will help us better understand why the paradigm shift in management approach is happening in our lifetime.

Command-and-Control Beliefs

Those who subscribe to the Command-and-Control Management philosophy share some or all of the following general beliefs and attitudes.

Newtonian Model   Command-and-Control managers subscribe to the Newtonian Model, whether they know it under that label or not. That is why the Critical Path Method is so compatible with this management style, and why the WBS approach to Scheduling provides such a sense of comprehensiveness. WBS ensures that *everything* has been considered, and the network's most significant feature, the logic tie, ensures that the relationships between *everything* have been taken into account as well.

Plan Your Work; Work Your Plan   The Newtonian Model could have no better marketing slogan, in terms of application to projects, than this most famous of all project management teachings: *plan your work, and then work your plan.* That's the whole game, in a nutshell. You simply get everyone to agree to a plan that contains every component of project scope and every significant relationship between those components, and then you force compliance with the plan. If everyone does their fair share, in the order they promised, and at the times they promised, with the quality they promised, using the resources they promised, then the project will complete as shown in the plan: on time, within budget, and with required quality. (Yeah, right!)

Importance of Order   Of course, vital to the Command-and-Control Management philosophy is a zealous loyalty to structure and order. The plan reigns supreme. With apologies to Benjamin Franklin for slightly modifying his famous quote, it would seem that the Command-and-Control philosophy believes in, "A place for every project performer, and every project performer in his place"—with "place" referring to the timing and sequence of activities as mandated in the Project Schedule.

Lack of Respect   Whether lack of respect for those who perform the work existed coincidentally or as a natural extension of the Command-and-Control mentality, it nevertheless dominates the attitude of Command-and-Control managers and proponents. Two general beliefs are that workers lack drive, and workers lack understanding.

Concerning the former, among believers it is argued that the worker will always find the easiest way out of any task, is always looking for shortcuts, and will work as slowly and incompletely as he can get away with. I find it interesting that the recently introduced Critical Chain Project Management (CCPM) method trumpets these allegations. For instance, a review of over a dozen different papers on this method cite Parkinson's Law, which is most commonly given as, "Work expands to fill the time allowed." [Do your own research: Google 'critical chain parkinson']

Coined by Northcote Parkinson in 1958, the principle evolved from a study that observed that the number of British Civil Service employees had no correlation to the expanse of the British Empire. In fact, as the latter declined, the former grew. Today, the principle is often cited as a truism about the willingness of people to take as long as they can get away with, to perform any required task. Anyway you cut it, the implication is that the worker cannot be trusted to work diligently, efficiently, and as productively as possible. Instead, they can be counted on to be lax, even lethargic, and that management oversight is the only remedy. CCPM adopts this attitude when it argues that the activity-duration must be taken away from the performer and placed in a *buffer* for responsible oversight and distribution by management.

The other belief that leads to a lack of respect for the worker is that the more power one has, the more knowledgeable he must also have. And thus, following the second belief, project managers *must* know more than project superintendents who, in turn, must know more than foremen, who must know more than the common worker. Is that why those above the subordinates are called "superiors?"

This same attitude about the tiers of wisdom and awareness reinforces the hierarchical elements of the organizational structure, only further reinforced by contractual relationships. The general contractor perceives the lowly subcontractor as only seeing a piece of the puzzle. Yet the owner feels the same way about the general contractor or the architect, for the owner understands the value and need for the project in ways that the others simply cannot.

Hopefully, you can see how, for those who lack respect for the workers' commitment or understanding, it is essential that tight controls be implemented and administered at all times during the life of the project.

Lack of Trust   The final nail in the coffin is yet another lack of faith in the worker, and this one has to do with ethics. A general fear of dishonest behavior permeates construction (as well as other types of) projects. Contracts long ago displaced handshakes because of this belief. The semi-colon in "plan your work; work your plan" symbolizes the linkage between commitments and the need to enforce them (because they will not voluntarily occur unless enforced). Contracts, work authorizations, change orders, and meeting minutes all exist to compensate for a lack of trust in both directions up and down the command chain.

Collaborative Beliefs

Those who subscribe to the Collaborative Management philosophy share some or all of the following general beliefs and attitudes.

Authority/Accountability Balance   Collaborative Management proponents subscribe to a principle of human psychology taught by behavioral psychologists that there must be a balance between authority and accountability. Ample studies have shown that when either side of this seesaw is emphasized over the other, troubles are not far behind. Those who wield unchecked authority are viewed as tyrants and despots. It is generally agreed that there must be check-and-balance at all levels of an organization, and that no one should be allowed to act with impunity. In the other direction, it seems intuitively unfair for someone to be held accountable for events or conditions outside his control (beyond his authority).

Collaborative managers recognize the essential need and the profound value in soliciting the input of all parties to the project. Those who will be evaluated on the merits of their performance must be allowed a voice in what those expectations will be. You might be thinking that that is precisely what Consensus Planning and Execution Scheduling are all about: getting the input from those who will perform the work. And you would be right—but you'd also be missing the key point I am trying to make.

The overall effectiveness of Pre-Execution Scheduling is extremely low, simply because the future is unforeseen to us. The Latin word for *unforeseen* gives us the English word *improvise*. And for every development on a project that suddenly "happens" because it was unforeseen, we must quickly conceive a response (improvise). It is in *this* planning, at the moment and in response to the immediate, that the worker is summarily ignored, and his input is dismissed or overlooked. At this critical juncture, as a response plan is being developed, under the Command-and-Control Model, management sees itself as holding the superior knowledge. By contrast, the Collaborative Model eagerly invites the contributions of the project team. Underlying this invitation is not only an ethical propriety, but also an acknowledgement that accountability and authority must go hand in hand.

Faith in People   Obviously, the Collaborative Management style embraces the very positive beliefs that workers are inherently courageous, energetic, intelligent, motivated, prideful, and reasonable. Given the chance, workers will outperform all expectations, time and time again. Andrew Carnegie gave legendary examples of the true character of the worker in his seminal work, *How to Win Friends and Influence People*, written in 1936. For the cynics among you who think that "times have changed," look at his list of recommendations, and ask yourself how many would work on you!

In terms of managing people:

- Don't criticize, condemn, or complain.
- Give honest and sincere appreciation.
- Arouse in the other person an eager want.

In terms of converting others to your point of view:

- Show respect for the other person's point of view, and avoid saying, "You're wrong."
- When you are wrong, swiftly say so, and be bold in your acknowledgement.
- Always begin in a friendly manner.
- Get the other person into early agreement, saying "yes" to various obvious statements.
- Allow the other person to do much of the talking.
- Maneuver the discussion so that the other person thinks the idea was his.
- Endeavor to understand the other person's point of view.
- Be sympathetic to the other person's needs, wants, desires, and concepts.
- Appeal to the highest standards of ethics and value in all arguments.
- Dramatize your ideas; give them life.
- Always put forth a challenge. Inject something tangible, an action to be taken.

In terms of being an effective leader:

- Begin with praise and honest appreciation.
- Call attention to others' mistakes in an indirect way. Meanwhile, talk about your own mistakes openly and first.
- Ask questions rather than giving orders.
- Provide a way for the other person to save face.
- Praise constantly: look for and highlight the smallest improvement, and make sure to acknowledge every improvement.
- Constantly encourage others. Make any problem easy to overcome and any fault of character easy to correct.
- Find ways to make the other person happy to do the things you suggest or request.

I have interviewed many, many successful project managers and they have consistently confirmed that positive reinforcement works. This means that workers are fundamentally the same today as they must have been back in 1936. People *want* to do a good job. They *want* to be given a chance and a challenge. But they also want to be recognized for their contribution. They want to be respected.

Preparedness versus Prediction A core tenet of the Collaborative Management philosophy is that the future cannot be predicted and, therefore, blind reliance on Authorization Planning or Execution Planning will not help us survive the storm. Instead, we must conduct a program of preparedness for the inevitable unknowns that will strike our project. In Momentum Management, I incorporate what I call *Dilemma Forecasting*, which is a somewhat formulaic attempt to provide *early warning* of dilemmas that are approaching. Notice that Dilemma Forecasting is somewhere in between the silly effort to predict future events that underlies pre-project planning and the other end of the spectrum, where we simply wait for the fire to break out, all the while ignoring the telltale trails of smoke squirming into the air.

Dilemma Forecasting is an ongoing program that spots the conditions that most often spawn dilemmas and reports these to project management in sufficient time for the project team to take appropriate actions; such actions centering on avoidance, mitigation, and recovery. For such response plans to work, prior rehearsals are necessary. Think of the fire drill back in school, or similar drills experts recommend all families practice. Emergency preparedness is an entirely different concept than attempting to draw a flowchart that, through clairvoyance, somehow anticipates every eventuality.

Power of Synergy   Another tenet of Collaborative Management is that the best ideas seem to emerge from a *meeting of the minds*. The old adage, "two heads are better than one," is founded on the idea that each person has a unique perspective. Remember the nineteenth century poem by American poet John Godfrey Saxe called *The Blind Men and the Elephant*. It is fun to recall it here:

It was six men of Indostan to learning much inclined,
Who went to see the Elephant (Though all of them were blind),
That each by observation might satisfy his mind.

The First approached the Elephant, and happening to fall
Against his broad and sturdy side, at once began to bawl:
"God bless me! but the Elephant is very like a wall!"

The Second, feeling of the tusk, cried, "Ho! what have we here
So very round and smooth and sharp? To me 'tis mighty clear
This wonder of an Elephant is very like a spear!"

The Third approached the animal, and happening to take
The squirming trunk within his hands, thus boldly up and spake:
"I see," quoth he, "the Elephant is very like a snake!"

The Fourth reached out an eager hand, and felt about the knee.
"What most this wondrous beast is like is mighty plain," quoth he;
" 'Tis clear enough the Elephant is very like a tree!"

The Fifth, who chanced to touch the ear, said: "E'en the blindest man
Can tell what this resembles most; deny the fact who can.
This marvel of an Elephant is very like a fan!"

The Sixth no sooner had begun about the beast to grope,
Than, seizing on the swinging tail that fell within his scope,
"I see," quoth he, "the Elephant is very like a rope!"

And so these men of Indostan disputed loud and long,
Each in his own opinion exceeding stiff and strong,
Though each was partly in the right, and all were in the wrong!

Moral:

So oft in theologic wars, the disputants, I ween,
Rail on in utter ignorance of what each other mean,
And prate about an Elephant not one of them has seen!

When we factor in the revelations of the New Sciences—that those who participate on a project serve to create, or at least modify, the reality of the project—it becomes abundantly clear why the collective knowledge of the entire project team affords the project manager the very best chance of understanding the true state of the project and the best ways to overcome its obstacles and exploit its opportunities.

No Bottom Line   Collaborative Management subscribes to the belief that chasing the "absolute answer" is futile, for there is no such thing as the "bottom line." Fractals teach us that there is never an absolute answer and at whatever level we stop our chase, we will in any event be working with an approximation of a representation of reality. Statistics are seen for what they are: human attempts at complexity reduction. And complexity reduction techniques—all of them—have the equal effect of leaving more truth behind than they bring to the forefront. The "reality" depicted by statistics is just a picture of an elephant—not even the real thing!

Experience the Unfolding   Finally, there is a humbling realization by believers in Collaborative Management that there are forces on every project that, quite simply, are unseen or beyond the control of Man. In a very real way, we are *all* passengers in the vehicle of life. None of us controls the steering wheel. Managers who understand this are prepared to approach each new day with childlike awe of, combined with seasoned preparedness for, whatever is in store.

Management Philosophy Behaviors

We have just explored how Command-and-Control and Collaborative managers harbor fundamentally different—even fairly opposite—beliefs concerning the best way to manage projects. Now we will examine how those various beliefs translate into predictable, identifiable behaviors. As you read this section, you will surely recognize projects you have been on, or wish you could be on!

Command-and-Control Behaviors

When the Command-and-Control Management style is applied on a project, one or more of the following behaviors and characteristics will be apparent.

Detailed or No Planning   Now here is a dichotomy if I ever saw one. Either a project receives *no* planning (even if it subsequently pursues meticulous Scheduling), or the pendulum swings 180 degrees in the other direction and the project receives extremely detailed planning. How can we reconcile these two apparently contradictory behaviors? Actually they stem from some of the beliefs I identified above, especially the lack of trust. The parties to the contract, the members of the project team, don't trust one another. They expect to be exploited by the other project team members.

One way not to be exploited is not to commit to anything. Don't promise anything and you can't be taken to the woodshed for not delivering on the promise. But if you are forced to commit, then cross every "T" and dot every "I." In other words, if you *must* engage in planning, then make darned sure that every possible eventuality is contemplated and make sure you have built into that plan sufficient wiggle room to get yourself out from under the pile.

Meticulous Scheduling   For this same reason, scheduling is typically very detailed. Contractors are suspicious of the owner, and vice versa, so everyone tends to schedule defensively. Those charged with overseeing the project have an additional need to build extreme detail into the Project Schedule, and that harkens back to the Newtonian Model. If every single step in the overall project is spelled out in excruciating detail, down to the day (sometimes hour), down to a single point of accountability (one responsible performer), and down to a clearly defined scope (for that activity)—and if each activity's performance is monitored for compliance with the Project Schedule, then how can the project result in anything other than complete success?

Now take an honest look at the overall trend in the Scheduling Practice, and you will see that the project management field is only moving farther down this path to greater control. WBS was one of the first innovations meant to drive detail into the scheduling process. Next came EVMS, which espoused various principles that require activities to be driven to a level where only *one* project participant performs *one* single task. Enterprise Project Management is another innovation, the ultimate objective of which is to inflexibly tie the performance of the smallest portion of project scope to the highest levels of managerial oversight at the program level.

Rigid Project Controls   But Command-and-Control proponents have complete faith in details, for that is the Holy Grail of Newtonian thinking. The whole is equal to its parts and to control the whole (project) is to control the parts. It didn't take long for an entirely new discipline to evolve to help project managers command and control: it is called projects controls.

The components of project controls are, minimally, cost control and schedule control, but in many organizations, other "controls" are included as well, such as quality control, safety control, human resource management, fiscal controls, owner/stakeholder satisfaction, governmental controls, and so on. Under the general label *control*, the perception is that anything can be controlled if enough detail is brought to bear.

Frequent Order-Giving   The other half of the Command-and-Control Management style is *command*. Fueled by the belief that workers cannot be trusted or respected, they must clearly be "managed." And *managed* means that they must be directed, from one day to the next, as to what needs to be done. Meetings are a common technique for sustaining a commander/commanded relationship up and down the organizational structure. Those who command are presumed to know more because they have the bigger picture view. They see themselves as wiser and therefore their solutions to problems must, necessarily, be superior to anything that might emerge from subordinates.

This condition occurs, in great part, because Command-and-Control managers share information on a need-to-know basis, and quite often they feel that subordinates do not need to know. This harkens back to two fundamental Command-and-Control beliefs: *knowledge is power* and *what they don't know, won't hurt them*—but the latter belief is to be interpreted this way: what they (the subordinates) don't know, won't hurt them (the superiors).

There is a fascinating story from the Civil War that exemplifies the shortsightedness of this management practice. At the Battle of Petersburg, which proved to be the longest siege in American history, the Union and Confederate armies found themselves in a ten-month standoff, neither side able to dislodge the other. The situation was this: the Confederate encampment was a fort atop a hill, with troops flanking out in each direction, forming a wide, impenetrable line. From the top of the hill, the Confederates could spot and repel any assault launched by the Union forces, whose camps were nestled in the woods several hundred yards away.

For ten months the stalemate continued, with no apparent solution in sight. Leadership (read: "management") never thought to discuss the problem with the lowly soldiers. But, as fate would have it, a "lowly" private overheard the officers talking and ventured a solution: "We could blow that damn fort out of existence if we could run a mine shaft under it!" And that is precisely what they did. 511 feet and 37 days later, the fuse was lit beneath the Confederate fort, and today there is a crater 170 feet long, 80 feet wide, and 30 feet deep. The point of the story is that, had the officers included the subordinates in their "problem-solving brainstorming session" (to use today's jargon), the same string of events might have played out ten months sooner!

Back to today and project management, our scheduling printouts are tailored to support project management's secretive need/desire to issue directives, set deadlines, demand compliance, and monitor for deviations from the plan. Statistical dashboards, routine metrics, and weekly or monthly progress reviews are all part of the Command-and-Control approach to project management.

Monitoring to Confirm Compliance   Let us not forget the contractual undertone of most construction projects. I suspect that the prevalence of contracts came about because of the Command-and-Control dominance in construction: either as a means of achieving control, or as a defense against the abuses of such a management style. Either way, the net effect is that the contractual and litigious environment cultivated by contracts only reinforces the need for Command-and-Control.

Enforcement of contracts boils down to monitoring performance for the limited purpose of recognizing and exposing failures to comply. Compliance is the primary purpose of monitoring, and the Scheduling Practice's recent attempts to write practice standards seem merely to reinforce the various ways that compliance can be tracked. Rigorous procedures and controls govern how Project Schedules are to be updated and maintained, in order to know, at any point in time, whether the baseline schedule (and all of its inherent promises) is being honored. The close ties between good scheduling practice and contract enforcement, in my humble opinion, have made for a dubious marriage, one that has effectively destroyed the Project Schedule's utility as a *project management* tool. Instead, the Project Schedule has become the whip in the taskmaster's fist.

Heavy Reliance on Statistics   The logical, ultimate extension of all of the preceding is a push for more and more detail. At all points along the Scheduling continuum, details rule! During the developmental stage, Project Schedules are being pushed into more and more granularity. During the Performance Recording stage, precision is preached for all progress measurement methods. During the Performance Control stage, metrics, and statistics carry the ultimate weight, and continued attachment of heads to shoulders hangs on the most subtle change in slope of a progress curve.

Collaborative Behaviors

When the Collaborative Management style is applied on a project, one or more of the following behaviors and characteristics will be apparent.

Strategic Planning   The understood objective of pre-execution planning is to forge consensus on an overall implementation strategy. It begins with Strategic Planning, where the level of detail will not be as decomposed as it is under the Command-and-Control Model, because, under the latter management style, if planning *is* done, the intent it to posture for downstream delays and claims.

Consensus Planning   Following the same intent as Strategic Planning, the purpose of pre-execution Consensus Planning is to establish goals and parameters, as discussed earlier in this chapter, which all parties can live with. The level of detail will dig only as deep as is necessary to establish "push pin" short-range goals for a group of activities all *directly* affecting the achievement of that goal. Consensus Planning emphasizes collaboration and commitment between project participants. As a result, intra-participant activity decomposition, such as the previous example of Erect Metal Studs and Hang Drywall activities, are avoided.

Monitor to Know Current Reality   The purpose of Performance Analysis is *not* to uncover inconsistencies between planned and actual performance, as if they are such egregious crimes. In fact, the Collaborative Model *anticipates* such deviations and frankly would find it problematic (and indicative of information distortion) if actual progress exactly or even closely mirrored Commitment Plans devised years or months earlier! Instead, Performance Analyses are performed to determine and report on the *rate* of progress, and then interpolate from actual performance statistics the reasonable implications of such performance on the volume of remaining work.

Performance Analysis also includes various feedback mechanisms that allow for identification and incorporation of *changes* in reality, even from the previous reporting period, let alone from the beginning of the project. Most importantly, it leads to Change Optimization scenarios, including Dilemma Forecasting which converts telltale signs into early warnings of dilemmas on the near-term horizon. Such advisories provide project management with the opportunity to prepare for the storm *before* it hits.

Heavy Reliance on Synergy   Finally, Collaborative Management embraces the idea that the team will have the best answers to problems and challenges that arise on the project. To maximize the exploitation of group wisdom, management methods systematically incorporate team planning for near-term project execution. Combined with the types of reality monitoring described in the previous subsection, the team can conceive a short-range response plan and monitor for team performance without ever having to be told by a Command-and-Control manager what needs to be done next. Instead, the project manager facilitates the Collaborative Management strategy by administering a variety of Collaborative Management techniques.

Management Philosophy Merits

Obviously, each type of manager believes in the style he or she has adopted—but not always. Quite often a particular management style is engrained in the culture of the company, and a manager with a different management style is prohibited from behaving in accordance with his personal beliefs. In this last section we will candidly discuss the drawbacks of Command-and-Control Management as well as the attractive aspects of Collaborative Management. Taken together with the two previous subsections, you will fully understand why each management style exists, how each translates into behaviors we find on projects, and why there is now a movement from one paradigm to the other.

Command-and-Control Flaws

Here are the most commonly cited reasons why the Command-and-Control Management approach is losing its grip on project management thought. As you'll see, several of the premises of Command-and-Control are simply unfounded.

Workers Are Not Inherently Lazy, Ignorant, or Unethical   Now here is a flawed premise that only foments tension and distrust across the project. When managers dictate the obvious to the contractor, the blatant implication is that respect is missing. So commonplace is this management practice, that we (Practitioners and project managers) have become desensitized to its offense and no longer recognize examples right before our eyes.

Here is a quick illustration. Do we really need to tell a drywall contractor that, before he hangs his drywall, he needs to erect the wall framing on which it is to hang? If not, then why do we have these two steps as separate activities? Who benefits by the schedule containing an Erect Metal Studs activity with a finish-to-start tie into Hang Drywall? Who benefits?

When management takes away a significant portion of an activity's duration and sequesters it in a buffer controlled by management (as is mandated by CCPM process), the message is obvious: *You (the contractor) lied when you created your duration.* When management hides calendar dates from schedule reports (another CCPM process), the message is clear: *You (the contractor) will take as long as you can, so I won't let you know how long you have.*

The Whole Is Greater Than the Sum of Its Parts   The New Sciences teach us many things, but perhaps the most important is that there are intangible aspects to all projects and, compared to the tangible elements, they are the more potent. Our Project Schedules only address the tangible elements of the project. Yet, it is the relationships *between* players, the interaction *between* activities, and the unrelenting ebb and flow of change across time, that have the greatest impact on project performance. If there is more to a project than the tangible, and if we are only tracking the tangible, then our attempts at control will always prove inadequate.

The "Plan Your Work; Work Your Plan" Strategy Is Flawed Of all the reasons I cite why the Command-and-Control approach doesn't work, this is the most significant one. You cannot plan for the unknown. Not a human alive has the power to see into the future and know what will transpire. Our plans, as such, are an act of faith. We trust that each day on the upcoming project will cast no stones in our path and that the things we plan to accomplish each day will be restricted only by our own unwillingness or inability to do so.

Yet this faith is unwarranted, as we have a billion lifetimes of examples that mumble, "who knows what tomorrow will bring!" Plus, as the New Sciences confirm, the reality of tomorrow cannot ever be the same as the reality we envision, simply because reality is created as it occurs, and its precise manifestation is modified by the combined influences of the people who create it and the ever-changing environment in which it is being created.

That is why, in the real world of human experience, we end most attempts to micro-manage in advance with a sweeping rejection of further help, by uttering to our well-meaning supporter, "Thanks, but I think I'll cross that bridge when I come to it."

People Don't Like To Be Commanded or Controlled The days of fist-pounding managers are gone. Today, people want to be respected for their knowledge and appreciated for their willing contributions. Domineering, autocratic, and arrogant managers are simply ignored by the worker, and their bellows are met with secret sabotage. As I explained in Chapter 2, there is no such thing as project control, cost control, quality control, or schedule control. Control, per se, of these variables lies with the worker alone, if he so desires. We can seek to influence his attitude toward these concerns, but influence alone and no more is within the purview of the manager. It is said that you get more with honey than vinegar, and fist-pounding, no matter how frightful, will never get the results the pounding manager seeks. Threats of lawsuits are just a white-collar form of fist-pounding.

Projects Continue to Finish Late Whether I have exposed the most compelling reasons why the prevalent Command-and-Control approach doesn't work is somewhat moot. The fact remains that projects continue to finish late, so it appears that the current approach doesn't work. It is time for a different approach.

Project Players Are More Contentious and Distrusting Than Ever The natural evolution of Command-and-Control is a complete dissolution of trust and teamwork. On today's projects, the attitudes of disrespect, distrust, and defensiveness have been formalized. Whereas long ago, the reactions to the Command-and-Control Management style were just that, reactionary, today it is preemptive and anticipatory. Before the first spade of dirt is turned, the contracts have already been negotiated and positions taken. Heels have been dug in, and the name of the game from Day One forward is, "Watch your back." The Project Schedule has become the inevitable battleground, planning has become posturing exercises, and updates have become equilibrium sessions.

In The Management/Claims Tug-of-War, the Scheduling "Rope" is about to Snap
In the end, the Project Schedule has become a useless tool for either purpose. Surely,

with all of the posturing incorporated into the Schedule during both design and updating, it has become an essentially worthless tool for reasonably identifying progress obstacles and opportunities. And, in the inverse, as a claims tool it has been neutralized because the net effect of the posturing is to create a schedule that has little semblance to the intended approach to the work.

In claims, there is a principle that delay and other time-related allegations are proved or disproved by the evidence of the contemporaneous intentions of the parties and conditions of the project. But when the official Project Schedule fails to reflect either or both of the variables, it proves useless in the advance or defense of a claim. More and more, claims consultants are discovering that the project had *two* Project Schedules: the official one and a secret one that the contractor kept to himself. Because the contractor's motive for the latter schedule was to have a tool with which to *manage* the project, he dutifully maintained this schedule. Since scheduling resources are typically in limited supply, quite often the *claims* schedule was not equally maintained. As a result, the official schedule often fails to reflect the conditions and intentions of the moment, and the secret schedule fails to contain anything other than the contractor's work activities. This is because owner activities cannot be obtained from the owner without disclosing the existence of the secret schedule.

It should be obvious to you, but I will state it nonetheless: having an incomplete Project Schedule (as the secret schedule necessarily must be), or a convoluted schedule (as the official schedule often is), is worse than having no Project Schedule at all. You are familiar with the espionage tactic of leaking faulty information to the enemy. This works because the enemy knows we are up to something. As long as we try to keep our plans from them, they will continue to seek them. But if we give them our "plans" (or what we convince them are our plans), then (a) they will stop spying on us, and (b) they will be sufficiently misled. Such is the equivalent effect of bad Project Schedules. The project team is misled into following a flawed strategy, which is worse than following no strategy at all.

Collaborative Merits

Here are the strongest arguments in favor of the Collaborative Management style:

Current Debates over Scheduling Methodology Become Largely Moot   By raising the level of detail in Project Schedules from Levels 3 or 4 to something closer to Level 2, many of the current issues that so often separate even seasoned Scheduling Practitioners will instantly disappear. This is because the *purpose* of Scheduling will have changed in ways that will deflate the critical arguments against certain methodologies. Allow me to expound on this distinction. Have you ever attended a PowerPoint presentation, where the speaker moves from slide to slide while presenting additional content beyond the cryptic bullets on the screen? Accompanied by his verbal narrative, the bullets make perfect sense. Yet later, in response to requests for a copy of the presentation, the speaker proudly distributes the PowerPoint file. Recipients who did not attend the presentation attempt to make sense of the bullets, but cannot. This is a simple example of how the same content and format can be completely effective for one purpose, while completely useless in another.

CPM is a notation method, nothing more. It is a symbolic language that allows its users to capture the essence of thought and convert it to a simulation model to which a computer can apply mathematical functions. In the end, any evaluation of schedule logic must look at once to both why and how the logic is devised.

Under the Command-and-Control Model, the logic is devised so that the resultant schedule can be used to control the project. Such control requires a rather extreme level of detail, but it would do little good to have very precise activity-durations while having contrastingly general relationship-durations. And so the debates rage on as to how best to notate what occurs *between* activities. But if the purpose of the Project Schedule is simply to establish what I call "push pin" dates along the project continuum for the sole purpose of coordinating the work of a multiple of contributors, then it matters little which of several available techniques is used to yield a specific date. I might use constraints in combination with open ends, or I might use hard logic. I might use a negative finish-to-start or I might use a positive start-to-start.

Similarly, there will be no cause to debate the relative merits of ADM or PDM, for either method can be used to generate the push pin dates. The entire argument—about whether PDM's start-to-start and finish-to-finish relationships disconnect work scope from assigned duration—simple evaporates.

Changes in Scheduling Methods Will Put a Quick End to Current, Devastating Trends While there are many—maybe even a majority of—Practitioners and project managers who will disagree with me, I contend that several of the recent trends in project management are leading us to the slaughterhouse. As I have amply and repeatedly argued in this book, I warn against what I see as the inevitable, likely long-term consequences of such methodological applications as WBS, Enterprise Project Management, excessive resource management, and excessive dissection of relationships. I have also warned about the diminished utility of the Project Schedule as a time management tool resulting from the encroachment of competing technologies who have commandeered the Project Schedule, such as Earned Value, Critical Chain, cost engineering, claims, and the like.

If my concerns are at all justified, then we should find comfort in knowing that the refreshingly different scheduling practices that are required to support the Collaborative Management Model will stop these devastating trends dead in their tracks.

To be sure, a central value of Enterprise Project Management is the ability to effectively manage human resources *across* projects. In order to achieve this aim, two requirements are imposed on the scheduling effort. First, each Project Schedule must be resource loaded, and the level of detail of the Project Schedule must be rather precise. Second, all Project Schedules within the enterprise must be combined in a single, central database. Even outside the EPM model, a vast majority of Execution Schedulers contend that unless a Project Schedule is resource-loaded it is invalid, not to be relied upon.

My counter to these currents is that what all proponents of resource-loaded schedules have in common is an underlying desire to control the project—or, in the case of EPM, the entire enterprise (including all projects). Collaborative Management takes an alternative tack. It argues that resource management, as an administrative function, is both local and momentary. Let me give you a simple example. Most of you have traveled on business. Imagine a situation where the itinerary calls for you to arrive early evening and meet the client at his office at 9 A.M. the next morning.

Before retiring for the night, you call down to the front desk to arrange for a wake-up call. First, though, you do a quick calculation of when you need to awake, and you do this by working backward. The client's office is 15 minutes from the hotel. You need an hour to get dressed and 30 minutes to have breakfast downstairs. You set the wake-up call for 7:15 A.M.. What I have just described is a simple planning process for the limited purpose of coordinating your activities with those of others (the front desk). Would this objective in any way be enhanced if you were to subdivide "get dressed" into seven specific activities: wake up, go to bathroom, shave, shower, iron clothes, dress, and straighten up room, each with its own start and finish times?

You could also subdivide having breakfast into numerous activities as well. But should you? Who would benefit? You might argue that it would be good practice (maybe even a best practice) to subdivide your tasks, so that you don't fall behind. I agree. But that brings us to an important distinction: control versus self-control. When people speak disparagingly about a control freak, or someone who is controlling, it is implied that they are controlling others. When someone controls himself, we consider this admirable and call it *responsibility*.

That distinction is important to a discussion we will soon have about level-of-detail. For what purpose would we care to subdivide the activities of *others,* except to control or monitor their performance? I think that is a big problem with Project Schedules today. We use them to control others, and we design them to meet this intended use.

Project Management Will Be Able to "Try Something Different" Einstein is the one who defined insanity as "doing the same thing over and over and expecting a different outcome." Since empirical evidence seems to confirm that our current methods don't appear to be resulting in a majority of projects meeting their time goals, how would it hurt to try something completely different?

Collaborative Management Feels Right Aside from everything else we have discussed, there is something quite natural about adopting a Scheduling approach that encourages positive reinforcement, teamwork, and forward-thinking, as opposed to enforcing a regime that constantly looks backward, seeks to command and control, and is centered around spotting and exposing violations and noncompliance.

Part 2 Creating a Penchant
for Change

B y implementing the many practical suggestions made through this book, I am
confident that you will create Project Schedules that *will* be used by those who
reply upon your work products to do their job. The notion of customer satisfaction is
but a metaphor for all that we do as skilled Practitioners in service to our primary customer, the project manager. The broader goal, then, is to find ways to steadily improve
the quality and appeal of our suite of products and services so that our primary customer
has a true yearning for them.

As I stated in the Preface, this book does more than simply discuss ways of creating better Project Schedules. In no small way, this text proposes sweeping changes in how our
profession is organized, how it is presented and perceived, what we offer as our work
products, and what words we use to describe ourselves, our processes, and our products
and services.

Part 2 of this book, "Creating a Penchant for Change," contains five chapters that, collectively, explore innovative new ways to make our customers much happier with what
we provide to them:

- Chapter 5 offers what I believe to be the first-ever consolidated set of definitions for
  the Scheduling Practice, including specialties, positions, procedures, deliverables
  and roles.
- Chapter 6 introduces Dilemma Control, a new project management capability made
  possible by Momentology.
- Chapter 7 introduces Momentology, a new project management methodology and
  technology, including a new set of products and services to be offered by the
  Scheduling Practitioner.

- Chapter 8 provides a summary of all of the new terminology I am proposing. The preceding three chapters introduce quite a few new concepts and lots of new terms.
- Chapter 9 segues the conceptual backdrop of Part 2 into the practical advice found on how to create better Project Schedules, discussed in subsequent chapters.

As I set out to write this book I grappled with the question of *when* to introduce these innovative concepts. Should I introduce my foreign ideas first and possibly frustrate you by delaying the practical advice on mainstream scheduling practices that you are expecting to find? Or should I introduce my ideas at the end of the book, perhaps as appendices, and possibly confuse the reader by referencing currently accepted terminology, concepts, and processes throughout the volume, even though, in the closing chapters, I repudiate many of them? Ultimately, I decided to introduce the new terminology and concepts first, and then use them throughout the balance of the text. And so, Part 2, which introduces these new ideas, precedes the nuts and bolts subjects contained in subsequent chapters of Part 3, and beyond. I hope you approve.

I wish to thank John Wiley & Sons, Inc, for their permission to quote from the following books:

- Construction Project Administration: Edward R. Fisk, 1978
- Construction Project Management: Richard H. Clough, 1972
- Critical Path Methods in Construction Practice: James M. Antil and Ronald W. Woodhead, 1982

I wish to thank McGraw-Hill Companies, Inc, for their permission to quote from:

- CPM in Construction Management: James J. O'Brien, 1971

I wish to thank the International Center for Scheduling, Inc. for their permission to quote extensively from:

- The ICS Compendium, ICS-Global, 2006

I wish to thank the Project Management Institute, Inc, for their permission to quote from:

- Project Management Institute, A Guide to the Project Management Body of Knowledge (PMBOK® Guide)-2000 Edition

With respect to all of the above publications, I happily acknowledge that copyright and all rights have been reserved by the respective publishers, and that materials from these publications have been reproduced in Chapters 5 and 6 with their written permission.

5 The New Scheduling Practice Paradigm: Specializations, Positions, Deliverables, and Roles

This may be the most important chapter in this book—not only to Scheduling Practitioners, but to the very future of the Scheduling Practice itself. For this chapter grapples with the most daunting, sweeping, and significant question of all: what *is* the Scheduling Practice? Not to be missed is the sad truth that this question actually exists and still needs to be asked—some 50 years after the inception of the Critical Path Method.

This chapter has two sections. The first half explores the differences of opinion across the Practice as to what we mean when we refer to our Practice by any of its popular names: Planning, Scheduling, Planning/Scheduling, Schedule Control, and so on. The first part of this chapter will shine bright lights on the many tears in our collective fabric and serve as a context for the solution proposed in the second half of the chapter.

The chapter's latter portion offers what I believe to be the first all-inclusive treatment of this very important issue. Here, we will reconcile between the various camps of thought that currently spar with one another at every gathering of Scheduling Practitioners. We will set forth a concise, simple, and yet comprehensive definition of the Scheduling Practice, in terms of specializations, positions, deliverables, and roles. So let's begin by understanding the mess in which we find ourselves.

DESCRIBING THE QUAGMIRE

One cannot possibly overstate the impact of this confusion. Imagine the medical community being uncertain as to the differences between doctoring and nursing—or the design community not being able to clearly define the boundaries between architecture and engineering. Yet, consider the current state of understanding within the Scheduling Practice in the opening days of 2007:

- There is open confusion over the meaning of the terms *planning* and *scheduling.*
  - Some see the terms as synonymous.
  - Some see planning and scheduling as distinctly different.

- Some see planning as a prerequisite to scheduling.
- Some see scheduling as a functional subcomponent of planning.
- There is disagreement over the meaning of planning itself.
  - Some see it as pre-project planning.
  - Some see it as execution planning.
- There is disagreement over the meaning of scheduling.
  - Some see it as schedule development only.
  - Others take a less literal view and include in its meaning the maintenance of schedules, and thus consider *analysis* as something beyond scheduling, per se.
  - Some see scheduling as also including delay analysis as part of dispute resolution, while others do not.
- There is no consensus about the terms *planner* and *scheduler*—or *plan* and *schedule*, but this simply follows from the contradictory and inconsistent relationship between the terms *planning* and *scheduling.*

Is it possible to reconcile all of these differing points of view? To this mind, we not only can, we *must*, if ever the Scheduling Practice is going to survive for another day. We must end the confusion, conflict, and chaos that have gripped the Practice for the last decade in particular. Infighting will spell the demise of the Schedule Practice in the very near term. We simply must come to a common understanding if we wish to remain a scheduling community. Let us not forget that the root word in *community* is "common."

But before we leap into the den to wrestle with the lion, perhaps we should take a few minutes to reaffirm for ourselves that this excursion is worth the effort it will take for me to write and you to read.

Let me first address two questions that ask *why*:

- Why do we need an answer to the question, *what is the Scheduling Practice?*
- Why choose this book, which is supposed to be about the production of schedules, to introduce a new Scheduling Practice Paradigm?

Explaining the Urgency of the Matter

Look—you regard yourself as a scheduling professional, right? Well, consider these two points, both of which will be fully developed in this chapter:

- Scheduling is *not* a profession.
- Even if it were, what we do as *schedulers* extends well beyond literal *scheduling.*

Here is my point: Our "profession" is imploding and has been for some time now. All around us is evidence of a discipline on the verge of extinction. Our infrastructure, collapsing under the weight of unmanaged growth and change, works at cross-purposes with our *reason for existence*, itself anything but universally agreed upon. Our terminology is outdated, self-contradictory, and inadequately descriptive of what we actually do for a living. Our public image is tainted by squabbling over philosophy, priorities, methodology, customer relations, and our rightful role in project management.

The tremendous expansion in popularity and application of scheduling tools, methods, and personnel has brought us to the current precipice. At this pivotal point in our collective history, the question before us is *what are we prepared to do to save ourselves?* What can we do to stop the hemorrhaging? What can we do to repair the damage caused by decades of custodial neglect? What can we do to mitigate further damage? What can we do to better position ourselves for a future of continued growth and diversity?

Offering a comprehensive definition of the Scheduling Practice, which I will do shortly, is my proposed response to the above questions. For some it will come as a breath of fresh air. For others, it will be a difficult, if not impossible, pill to swallow. I am not so arrogant as to think that I alone have stumbled upon the only answer; nor do I think that there is necessarily one right, or one best, answer. I am setting forth my thoughts so as to inspire dialogue, deliberation, and action—while there is still time to save our Practice.

Even as I write this, evidence of erosion is all around. The professional void created by years of exploitation and lack of guardian attention has led to a free-for-all, where virtually every aspect of our discipline is experiencing a land-grab fever that looks an awful lot like the 1849 Gold Rush.

- **Authority Up For Grabs** A tug-of-war is currently underway between the Project Management Institute's (PMI) Practice Standards for Scheduling, the PMI's College of Scheduling (PMICoS), the Association for the Advancement of Cost Engineering International (AACEI), and a number of other entities. While, in all cases, the intentions are noble and the efforts gallant on the part of many hundreds of dedicated volunteers from all around the world, the net effect nonetheless is a clamoring of each of these groups to establish themselves as the definitive voice for the international scheduling community. Their weapons of choice are certification programs and issuance of standards, either of which might posture them to *be* the authority for the Scheduling Practice.

- **Methodology Up For Grabs** *What we do* and *how we should do it* are being preached to us by software developers, university professors, and freelance authors (me included), who view themselves as self-appointed authorities on the subject. Yet there is no validation process to filter out renegade thought or even faulty information.

- **Applications Up For Grabs** Scheduling work products, most notably the Project Schedule itself, are being adopted by nonscheduling interests as *their* child. And with their self-appointed foster-parenting, they have assumed the right to change how Project Schedules are designed, developed, maintained, and used. Cost engineers, like risk managers and claims consultants, equally insist that *their* informational needs amply justify dictating how Project Schedules are to be built and used.

Whether the Scheduling Practice definition provided in this chapter is the best, or even a good, answer is something I will leave to you, my respected colleagues, to judge. To you who are reading this book, I encourage you to put *your* thoughts on the table. If this chapter invites open debate and leads to plugging the holes in the dike, then its inclusion in a book on how to create better schedules will have been justified.

This Book Is an Odd Place to Make Such a Proposal

Beyond the philosophical and lofty, however, I can offer tangible reasons why this book is a perfectly legitimate place to be proposing sweeping changes in how the Scheduling Practice sees itself, or explains itself to others—most especially the Project Schedule's many stakeholders. The inclusion is reasonable, however, because this book is all about creating Project Schedules that *they* will want to use.

In Chapter 2 we spent considerable time discussing who "they" are. Let me ask you an equally important question: *who* is creating the schedules that "they" will want to use? That would be "*we*," right? Well, who is "*we*?" How do we recognize one another? If we can't identify one another as professional colleagues, then how can we collaborate? How can we learn from one another? How can we avoid spending precious time and energy recreating wheels that have already been fashioned elsewhere?

This argument may be sufficient to suggest that, at some point in time, a discussion is appropriate—indeed overdue—as to why and how the Scheduling Practice should recast itself into a more cohesive, consistent, and functional entity. But it still doesn't explain why I would attempt to do so in a book aimed at developing better Project Schedules. The answer is that I cannot communicate with *you*, and you cannot understand *me*, if we speak in different tongues.

Here is a seemingly straightforward statement: *A list of critical tasks should be generated and sent to the project manager in a timely manner.* In this sentence, there are several opportunities for misunderstanding. Consider how many different interpretations of this sentence there could be, if the following words had multiple meanings:

- **List** Obviously the listing contains references to the *tasks*, but what information should be contained in the list?
- **Tasks** Some people consider *tasks* and *activities* as synonymous. Others contend that *tasks* are more specific actions that, combined, make up an *activity*.
- **Critical** How do we determine what is critical? Are the only critical activities those that reside on the critical-path? How do we identify a near-critical activity—what is its definition?
- **Should** Does the word *should* imply a standard, a requirement, or just a preference?
- **Project Manager** Is this choice of recipient meant literally or figuratively? A *project manager* in one organization may be a *superintendent* in another, or a *project director* in a third.
- **Timely** How should we determine what is *timely*? Is it related to information freshness, or is it tied to informational need?

You get the point. If a single sentence can be interpreted different ways, depending on the context and understandings of both the one making the statement and the one receiving it, just multiply that sentence times a thousand. Throughout this book, I propose unique and proven ways to perform basic and advanced processes that lead to Project Schedules "they'll actually want to use." Doing so, I employ terminology for which I *assume* you and I have the same meanings.

Yet, as will be explored in the following pages, many terms that should be *common* to every Scheduling Practitioner simply are not. It's as if we speak different languages. Consider the book's title, which speaks of CPM *scheduling*. Does this title mean to ignore *planning* activities, or are the two labels *planning* and *scheduling*— used interchangeably in this book?

Babbling Advisors Are Rarely Effective

There is an even more fundamental reason why this book *should* wrestle with certain aspects of Practice redesign. You, as a Scheduling Practitioner, cannot do your job effectively if you cannot communicate with your customer. Central to all that we do as Practitioners is the ability to communicate with our stakeholders in a clear and consistent manner.

We must remain consistent, not just semantically, but philosophically as well. The expression "don't put the cart before the horse" only makes sense if we agree that the horse is expected to *pull* the cart. How can this book recommend a "best" order in which to perform various scheduling tasks if we do not share a common understanding as to which *causes* result in which *effects* throughout the various Scheduling processes?

For instance, how would you answer this question: *Does an Execution Schedule necessarily and naturally evolve from a Commitment Plan?* In other words, is a Commitment Plan a mandatory precursor to an Execution Schedule, or are they essentially independent documents with only a referential relationship or visual likeness? Suppose you think that they are not necessarily related to one another, but your project manager does—and this disconnect remains undetected by either of you throughout the pre-execution phase Planning processes. How would his expectations for the planning exercises possibly disrupt or confuse your efforts as a Commitment Planner?

An even more potent example of the divide that can occur through inconsistent and nonuniversal terminology might be one related to the quality of advice you offer your project manager in the course of cyclical Performance Control. How effective will you be as an advisor if the two of you have completely different definitions for words like critical, deadline, urgent, timely, recovery, accelerate, change, status, performance, and so on?

The Scheduling Practice Lacks Cohesiveness and the Synergy Such Would Spawn

It should be apparent that, as individuals, we are able to accomplish far more when we draw from the wisdom and experiences of like-minded others. It should be obvious that, both collectively and individually, Practitioners can provide much better products and services to our customers when our activities emanate from a cohesive center.

If we were a true profession, we would have a universally recognized body of knowledge, an authoritative glossary of terms and definitions, consistently applied best practices, and a single, universally recognized certification program. If we were a true profession, our customers would not experience the inconsistent and variable levels of service they receive today. Until we standardize, for our customers it will remain a hit-or-miss proposition when they request the services of a Scheduling Practitioner.

It is for these reasons that I use this book as a platform from which to introduce, for what I believe to be the first time, a comprehensive definition of the Scheduling Practice, as a definable discipline. "Just how comprehensive?" you might ask. While a full discussion of the Scheduling Practice would require a book in its own right, in this text I will minimally propose the following:

- **A new name for our discipline** I suggest that we refer to our area of specialized knowledge, products, and services as the Scheduling Practice.
- **Crisp definitions** I propose new terminology that will put to rest, once and for all, the confusion surrounding the terms: *plan* and *schedule*, *planner* and *scheduler*, and *planning* and *scheduling*. I call these the *P/S Enigmas*.
- **A new paradigm** I categorize and define the specializations, positions, procedures, deliverables, and roles of the Scheduling Practice, thus providing a foundation upon which subsequent academic works can develop structured practices, processes, and protocols.

WE CAN'T FIX WHAT WE DON'T ACKNOWLEDGE

Before we can repair a problem we have to agree that we *have* a problem. So let me provide some specifics to back up my gloom-and-doom rhetoric from the opening paragraphs of this chapter. To summarize, as I see it, our Practice is suffering both functionally and organizationally:

- Functionally, we are in disarray. Our terminology, position titles, work product labels, and primary procedures, are overwhelmingly redundant and nonspecific. We enjoy little agreement on our processes, basic methodologies, or techniques. Our software tools are competitive and inconsistent.
- Organizationally, we are in disarray as well. We are not a profession, even though we would like to be. We have no regulation of entry into the field. We have no higher educational requirements or consistent training, and the only universally recognized training is for software use, for goodness sake! This is like having no medical credentials, but instead certifying surgeons in the use of scalpels and monitors.

We do not self-police. We have no universally recognized, self-administered[1] certification program. We lack cohesion: our focus is scattered and noneffective. Other (nonscheduling) project management entities are chipping away at our base. We have forgotten that the project manager is our primary customer. We are confusing to ourselves, as well as to our stakeholders.

---

[1]Administered by a *scheduling* organization. As of this writing, the only known scheduling certification is offered by AACEI, a *cost* engineering association—and even its credentialing program is hardly universally recognized.

Scheduling is Not a Profession

Throughout this book I refer to the Scheduling Practice. This is because we do not meet the rigid parameters to be called a profession. I have researched the term *profession* at length and determined that there is no absolute definition upon which all agree. However, Table 5-1 is a list of characteristics most commonly associated with a *profession,* which I include because these characteristics will inform us as to where the Scheduling Practice needs to improve if ever we are to become a profession.

	Yes	No	Some
Membership			
Always Held by Individual	X		
Membership Exclusive; Self-Restricting		X	
Entrance through Screening or Accreditation		X	
Professional Society			
Authoritative Body of Skilled Practitioners	X		
Self-Regulating of its Members		X	
Produces Seminal Body of Specialized Knowledge		X	
Administers Certification Program			X
Knowledge			
Education Vigorously Supervised		X	
Recognized Body of Learning; Knowledge Unique and Special		X	
Specialized Education and Training at High Level			X
Ethics			
Set of Services Beneficial to Society	X		
Open Avowal of Some Belief(s) or Principle(s)		X	
High Moral and Ethical Principles and Standards			X
Profession's Interest Override Individual Interests			X
Practice			
Self-Regulated		X	
Operates with Great Deal of Autonomy			X
Enforces Discipline on Itself		X	
Engages in Self-Reflection; Self-Critique		X	
Involves Intellectual Activity; Especially Moral Judgments			X
Scope and Purpose of Profession			
Necessarily Limited		X	
Characterized by Specialties			X
Common Values Across Many Specialties		X	
General Public Clear About What Profession Does		X	

Table 5-1

Criteria for Being Considered a "Profession"

Current Terminology Broken Beyond Repair

Psychologists say that how others perceive us is most directly influenced by how we see ourselves. There could not be a more true statement regarding the Scheduling Practice. If ever we wonder why we are not more appreciated by colleagues on the project team, perhaps it is because we lack a solid self-identity:

- We call ourselves by inconsistent names: planner, scheduler, planner/scheduler, project controls engineer, scheduling engineer, scheduling professional, senior scheduler, junior scheduler, planning engineer, planning/scheduling engineer, scheduling specialist, planning specialist, and so on.

- We call our functional departments by different names as well: Project Planning & Analysis, Project Controls, Scheduling, Cost & Schedule, Technical Support, and others.

- We describe our chief products with interchangeable names: plan or schedule, just to name two. We internally argue over whether the monthly iterations of the project schedule are schedules as well.

- Even though we perform a variety of important functions on the project other than just creating schedules, we label our discipline according to only one: *scheduling* (or is it planning?). The Project Management Institute formed the College of *Scheduling*, yet its membership is heavily engaged, on a daily basis, in performing *planning* (and other) activities as well. And the overwhelmingly dominant scheduling software for the last two decades is Primavera Project *Planner* (P3).

- We use conflicting terminology, too. Is it *slack* or *float*? Is it *lead* or *lag*? Is it *task* or *activity*? *Data-Date* or *Time-Now-Date*?

- We disagree on basic methodology. Which is better: retained-logic or progress-override? Start-float or finish-float or least-float? What is best practice: percent-complete or remaining-duration?

WHAT IS PLANNING?

I could go on, but you see what I mean. There is little that Scheduling Practitioners agree on, even within the same industry and on the same project. Now, factor in that we have differences imposed by different industries, different countries, and different software. This book will not attempt to resolve all, or even very many, of the differences that currently separate us. Instead, here in this chapter, this text will try to put to rest only six terms. But they are what I call the Big Six Terms:

- *Plan* versus *Schedule*
- *Planner* versus *Scheduler*
- *Planning* versus *Scheduling*

Why these six terms? Because, taken together, they make a *statement* about us— and a statement is comprised of a subject, a verb, and an object. These six terms, what I call in this book the P/S Terms, cut to the core of:

- **Who we are** Planner or scheduler (subject)
- **What we do** Planning or scheduling (verb)
- **What we produce** Plan or schedule (object)

That's reason enough to focus a few pages on them, don't you think? An *enigma,* according to the dictionary, "is something that baffles understanding and cannot be explained." It is also something "that is puzzling, ambiguous, or inexplicable."[2] For this reason, I will also make reference to the Plan-Schedule Enigma, the Planning-Scheduling Enigma, and the Planner-Scheduler Enigma. Jointly I may speak about the P/S Enigmas.

Of the three enigmas, the central one is Planning-Scheduling, for once we understand the meaning of *planning* and *scheduling*, we will understand the meaning of *planner* and *scheduler* as well as *plans* and *schedules*. So we begin this discussion by asking: *what is planning?*

Historical Inconsistencies in the Use of the Word Planning

Even viewed from an historical perspective, there has rarely been much consensus as to what *planning* entails. To understand the earliest disparity of definitions, recall the history of the Scheduling Practice, starting with the initial development of CPM in the late 1950s. Its first application was in the construction industry, and for the next 25–35 years the overwhelming majority of CPM applications remained in this one industry. Bear in mind, from our earlier discussion of the environment of Scheduling (see Chapter 2), that each construction project is unique, unlike the cookie-cutter pursuits of manufacturing.

Now, this uniqueness requires a process, a prerequisite to the scheduling of project execution, intended to identify an optimum approach to the project. Such an approach would logically include appreciating the physical, logistic, and pragmatic constraints that must be taken into consideration *before* stringing together the performance activities of the Project Schedule. Thought would be given to how the work would be staged, where materials would be stored until needed, how equipment and labor movements would be choreographed, traffic patterns, how ongoing occupation and use of the facility would be maintained during construction, and so on. It is these considerations that early schedulers referred to as *planning*.

From the previous paragraphs you might think that planning boiled down to a series of essentially esoteric discussions, devoid of rigid CPM mechanics. But, in practice, these early planning efforts paralleled certain developmental steps that, in today's parlance, are considered part of the *scheduling* effort (more on this later). As a result, many of those who date themselves back to the "early days" of the Practice remain insistent that certain steps—such as Work Breakdown Structure (WBS), activity description wording, activity duration estimating, and even relationship definition—are part of project *planning*, not project *scheduling*.

---

[2]Dictionary definitions throughout this book come from dictionary.com, which provides definitions from various dictionaries.

To them, *scheduling* begins after these other factors have been evaluated and logistic assumptions or decisions have been made. They point to the appearance of calculated dates as the line of demarcation between planning and scheduling activities. In order to understand why so many Scheduling Practice veterans considered the first steps in Schedule Development to be *planning*, look at the instructional texts from which they learned their craft. We will look at four very popular books on project scheduling, each published in the 1970s and 1980s:

- ***Construction Project Administration*** Edward R. Fisk (John Wiley & Sons, 1978).
- ***Construction Project Management*** Richard H. Clough (John Wiley & Sons, 1972).
- ***Critical Path Methods in Construction Practice*** James M. Antill and Ronald W. Woodhead (John Wiley & Sons, 1982).
- ***CPM in Construction Management*** James O'Brien (McGraw-Hill Book Company, 1971).

As you read the following short discussion about the various definitions for the P/S Enigmas that these five experts employed, don't lose sight of the fact that all four books are focused on the construction industry.

In *Construction Project Administration*, author Edward Fisk defines planning as "simply an application of the thought process that must be entered into before the actual scheduling begins." He then suggests things to think about, including:

> Long-lead purchases, utility interruptions, temporary utilities, temporary construction utility service, labor availability, work and storage areas, traffic requirements, temporary access, other contractors, interdependency of tasks, environmental controls, special regulations, special construction equipment, and time for construction.

Richard Clough, in *Construction Project Management*, states, "Planning establishes, on the basis of a detailed study of job requirements, what is to be done, how it is to be done, and the order in which it will proceed." Elsewhere, he notes:

> Planning is the devising of a workable scheme of operations which is designed to accomplish an established objective when put into action," and that it is "concerned primarily with establishing the sequential order in which various operations will be carried out on the jobsite.

Conveniently, Clough reduces construction planning to three basic steps:

1. Determination of the job steps or activities that must be performed in order to construct the project.
2. Ascertainment of the sequential relationships among these activities.
3. The presentation of this planning information in the form of a network diagram.

Clough defines the line separating scheduling from planning as when date calculations are performed.

> Project planning is only concerned with dividing the job into its elemental parts or activities and specifying the sequential order in which they are to be done. At this stage (scheduling),

a new element is introduced into the planning process: time. On no occasion during the development of the job plan was time taken into account, not with regard to the overall construction period required, nor the times necessary for completion of the individual activities.

He adds, "A project schedule is simply a projected timetable of construction operations."

There seems to be disagreement between Fisk and Clough on where planning stops and scheduling starts. Fisk says that planning is the thinking process, and scheduling begins with identification of activities. Clough believes that planning includes the identification of activities (what needs to be done) as well as the logic (how it is do be done, and in what sequence), and he considers scheduling as having begun once durations are added.

It appears that Antill and Woodhead agree with Clough. In *Critical Path Methods in Construction Practice* they provide these fundamental definitions:

> Planning is the process of choosing one method and order of work to be adopted for a project from all the various ways and sequences in which it could be done. The sequence of steps required to achieve the optimum result is the proper plan for the works, and this can be schematically shown on the CPM network diagrams.

> Scheduling is the determination of the timing of operations comprising the project and their assembling to give the overall completion time. Scheduling can be done only after a particular project plan has been defined and modeled in such a way that it can be committed to paper in the form of a network diagram.

James J. O'Brien, in an early version of his seminal *CPM in Construction Management*, writes:

> CPM separates planning from scheduling. With the collected project information and time estimates, activity times can be computed. Where does planning cease and scheduling start? The first computation marks the end of the planning phase. Once there is a project duration to compare with the desired schedule, the scheduling effort starts.

O'Brien appears to agree with Clough that it is the introduction of dates that constitutes scheduling. Yet O'Brien seems to blur the dividing line when he adds, "The first CPM computation is a plan, not a schedule."

Nevertheless, he goes on to describe the iterative nature of planning and scheduling, consistent with an understanding of the era, that planning incorporates the creation of activities, logic, durations, constraints, and calendars, and that all of these must be in place before you "compute" the schedule.

Distinguishing between the Venerable and Current Definitions

The previous citations from some of the earliest teachers of CPM scheduling suggest that planning is tantamount to what today would be considered the opening steps of Schedule Development. Under this heading I would like to contrast the way the original Practitioners used the terms *planning* and *scheduling* with how current Practitioners interpret the same terms.

As will be amply discussed in the following paragraphs, the historical reality is that the perspective of earlier Practitioners, while no doubt appropriate and germane for those times, is in important ways incompatible with prevailing thought. Two observations can be made with respect to the viewpoints of our Practice's founders:

- Their interpretations are venerable, having served our Practice well for many decades and having surely earned our respect. (According to the dictionary, the word *venerable* means, "commanding respect by virtue of age, dignity, character, or position.")

- Their interpretations have become fairly outmoded against the context of contemporary project management models including, and perhaps most notably, the PMBOK® Guide.

Accordingly, throughout this book I will refer to the earlier view as the *Venerable Model*. In contrast, the current thinking will be called the *Current Model*. Referring to Figure 5-1, according to the Current Model there are essentially ten major steps in the development of a Project Schedule. All ten steps are considered part of the *scheduling* process, and they result in the creation of a key deliverable, the Project Schedule.

Figure 5-1

Planning and Scheduling Meaning per Venerable and Current Models

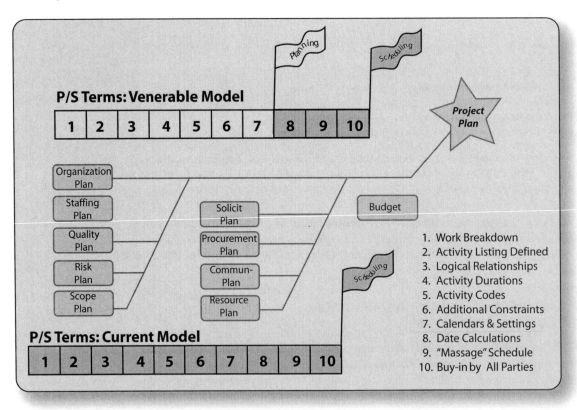

By contrast, the Venerable Model considers the first seven steps to be planning activities, while the latter three steps are considered scheduling activities. According to the Venerable Model, the primary purpose for performing the first seven steps is to lay the foundation for the remaining three steps. The fact that the planning steps generate an interim plan is only incidental, not essential.

You might think, from the earlier four citations, that there was virtually unanimous agreement on the use of the P/S Terms; but you'd be wrong. In those early days of our Practice (and, regrettably, even into the twenty-first century), there has been no unified[3] effort to standardize terminology or methodologies. Each Practitioner has been an evolving expert is his or her own right.

Besides, even if there *had been* 100 percent consensus on terminology for the first 35 years, when the PMBOK® Guide came out in 1996 the entire understanding still would have been turned on its head—as it actually was. Keep in mind that, over the three decades following its invention, the critical center of CPM usage shifted dramatically from the construction industry to several high technology industries. At the start of the 1960s, I estimate that 95–98 percent of all CPM usage was centered in the construction industry. By the early 1990s, a majority of CPM usage was outside of construction.

The PMBOK® Guide, no doubt reflecting the significant nonconstruction population within its ranks, embraced the Project Plan, a concept slow to be adopted within the construction trade. The PMBOK® Guide defined the Project Plan as:

> A formal, approved document used to guide both execution and project control. The primary uses of the project plan are to document planning assumptions and decisions; facilitate communication among stakeholders, and document approved scope, cost, and schedule baselines. A project plan may be summary or detailed.

As a logical extension, the PMBOK® Guide went on to define project planning as "the development and maintenance of the project plan." One can hardly argue with the obvious and easy connection between the process (planning) and the product that the process produces (the plan). But how does the project *schedule* relate to the project *plan*, according to the PMBOK® Guide? As Figure 5-1 illustrates with the Current Model, the answer is that the schedule is one—but hardly the only, or even the primary—element within the Project Plan. The PMBOK® Guide's interpretation of the word *planning* is fairly clear:

> Planning is of major importance to a project because the project involves doing something that has not been done before. As a result, there are relatively more processes in this section.[4] However, the number of processes does not mean that project management is primarily planning—the amount of planning performed should be commensurate with the scope of the project and the usefulness of the information developed. Planning is an ongoing effort throughout the life of the project.

---

[3]Even within the Project Management Institute, one component (Practice Standards for Scheduling) has been tasked with writing standards, while another component (College of Scheduling) has been charged with writing best practices.

[4]That is, more processes associated with Planning than with the other process groupings of Initiation, Execution, Controlling, and Closing.

The PMBOK® Guide proceeds to identify a number of planning processes, only a handful of which relate to Schedule Development, highlighted with asterisks in Tables 5-2.

Interestingly, the stark divide between the Venerable Model and the Current Model can still be found in the current construction industry's interpretation of the terms planning and scheduling.

For instance, the latest edition of *CPM in Construction Management* (copyright 2006) contains a glossary with the following definitions:

Plan The sequence in which a project is to be done. It is independent of the schedule.

Schedule Planned dates for performing scheduled activities and meeting schedule milestones usually derived from a planned logical network.

We recognize in these definitions a lingering perception that a *plan* is a pure logic diagram ("sequence") devoid of dates whereas the *schedule* is distinguished by "planned dates." The second definition further clarifies that the plan is "derived from" the schedule. And so, the P/S Enigma lives on.

Not surprisingly, Practitioners from nonconstruction industries who more recently adopted CPM scheduling have experienced little heartburn over differences between the Current Model and their own understanding of the terms *plan* and *schedule*. The simple explanation is that, overwhelmingly, their adoption of the CPM methodology occurred in the mid- to late 1990s, by which time the Current Model, as would soon be formalized by the PMBOK® Guide, was the prevailing norm.

From the preceding citations, two immediate conclusions can be reached:

- According to the Current Model, planning and scheduling are concentric, not linear, processes. That is, the Project Plan is management's master strategy for successful project achievement. The Project Schedule contains management's tactical details for efficient project execution. The Project Schedule is part of the Project Plan, not subsequent to it.
- What the five authors collectively refer to as the combined processes of "planning and scheduling," the PMBOK® Guide in the majority[5] calls Time Management. The PMBOK® Guide explains Time Management as including "the processes required to ensure timely completion of the project" and specifically lists within those processes "activity definition, activity sequencing, activity duration estimating, schedule development, and schedule control."

Can the Venerable and Current Models Be Reconciled?

The question posed by the heading for this section hints at a deep chasm, one that separates the Venerable and Current Models even today. It asks whether we might ever be

---

[5]Mostly, but not entirely! Some aspects of traditional schedule development, such as Work Breakdown Structure, and updating/reporting, are to be found in other knowledge areas.

Planning Process	Brief Explanation of Process
Scope Planning	Developing a written scope statement as the basis for future project decisions.
Scope Definition	Subdividing the major project deliverables into smaller, more manageable components.
Activity Definition	Identifying the specific activities that must be performed to produce the various project deliverables.
Activity Sequencing	Identifying and documenting interactivity dependencies.
Activity Duration Estimating	Estimating the number of work periods that will be needed to complete individual activities.
Schedule Development	Analyzing activity sequences, activity durations, and resource requirements to create the project schedule.
Risk Management Planning	Deciding how to approach and plan for risk management.
Resource Planning	Determining what resources (people, equipment, materials, etc.) and what quantities of each should be used to perform project activities.
Cost Estimating	Developing an approximation (estimate) of the costs of the resources required to complete project activities.
Cost Budgeting	Allocating the overall cost estimates to individual work packages.
Project Plan Development	Taking the results of other planning processes and putting them into a consistent, coherent document.
Quality Planning	Identifying which quality standards are relevant to the project and determining how to satisfy them.
Organizational Planning	Identifying, documenting, and assigning project roles, responsibilities, and reporting relationships.
Staff Acquisition	Getting human resources needed assigned to and working on the project.
Communications Planning	Determining the informational and communications needs of the stakeholders: who needs what information, when will they need it, and how will it be given to them.
Risk Identification	Determining risks likely to affect the project and documenting the characteristics of each.
Qualitative Risk Analysis	Performing a qualitative analysis of risks and conditions to prioritize their effects on project objectives.
Quantitative Risk Analysis	Measuring the probability and impact of risks and estimating their implications for project objectives.
Risk Response Planning	Developing procedures and techniques to enhance opportunities and to reduce threats to the project's objectives from risks.
Procurement Planning	Determining what to procure, how much to procure, and when.
Solicitation Planning	Documenting product requirements and identifying potential sources.

Table 5-2

PMBOK Planning Processes Involving The Schedule

Planning processes that involve Schedule Development are shown in bold.

able to construct definitions for the word planning around which the majority of Scheduling Practitioners might rally. To be sure, there is a wide range of views with respect to the meaning of the word *planning*, as the previous discussion has elucidated. We can summarize the viewpoints of what appear to be four distinct schools of thought concerning the meaning of the term *planning*, at least in the context of its counterpart, *scheduling*:

- **They are different** The majority of Scheduling Practitioners who I interviewed believe that the two terms mean different things, although there is little consensus on what those differences are.
- **They are the same** There is a small minority who insist that the two processes are so intertwined that it is impossible to draw lines of clear demarcation between them.
- **Planning is part of scheduling** This is the understanding of the Venerable Model, whose adherents remain influential in both numbers and passion.
- **Scheduling is part of planning** This is the understanding of the Current Model, formalized in the PMBOK® Guide.

WHAT IS SCHEDULING?

The confusion surrounding the term *planning* accounts for only half of the quagmire. There is equal uncertainty concerning the label *scheduling,* in terms of both scope and manner.

The Scope of Scheduling

Concerning *scope*, to some, the word should be taken literally and therefore *scheduling* refers only to those processes that develop the Project Schedule but nothing else or beyond. They argue that *scheduling*, like *planning,* refers to processes that necessarily precede the execution of the work they are either planning or scheduling. One would not say, "I am scheduling my vacation," while one is *on* one's vacation.

Others, however, adopt a more figurative interpretation of the word *scheduling*. They believe that all of the processes involved in the design, development, maintenance, and usage of Project Schedules are to be included in a more encompassing use of the word *scheduling*.

The Manner of Scheduling

As for the *manner* of scheduling, there is divergence of opinion about the proper role of the Scheduler. A rather substantial portion of the Scheduling community feels that the Scheduler's role should be that of a scribe and little more. Consider these excerpts from e-mails that crossed my desk in the last six months. Edward, John, and David (whose names have been changed for purposes of anonymity) are well-known leaders in the Scheduling Practice and enjoy a global reputation. Edward writes:

> Because I am an engineer, and most construction site persons doing scheduling work used to be, I used to call myself a Scheduling Engineer. Recently though, Scheduling Practitioner has become a more appropriate term or title. We are NOT "the planner" even if you prefix it

with the word schedule, but we might be a "schedule manager" in that we do manage the schedule work (albeit "manager" must be with a lowercase "m"). As I see it, we are "facilitators and scribes" for the project team for the schedule aspects. We do not make the schedule!

John writes, in response to an article by "Bill":

> [Bill's] entire article was based on the schedules he "prepared," which were totally unrelated to the way the project proceeded. Of course they were! The scheduler prepared the schedule—this is a mortal sin!! The scheduler is a recorder of and not the creator of schedules. The scheduler is part of the project management team and as such, he/she should work closely with the team that's going to build the job to help them through the pre-planning process. Schedulers are not (and never should be) in charge of planning how a job is to be put together—that's what project managers do. Schedulers are tasked with the responsibility of taking the project manager's and their team's plan and putting it into a mathematical model (a network) to see if it's workable, achievable, possible, etc. Once the original schedule is created and approved by the project team, the scheduler monitors and tracks progress against this schedule. Schedulers need to understand their role in the project team and adhere strictly to that role.[6]

As I read these two e-mails, the confusion, contradiction, and misunderstandings that dominate our Practice came into clearer light:

- According to Edward, we are not the planner; we might be a schedule manager; we are facilitators and scribes, but we do not make the schedule—only the project team can do that.

- According to John, it is a mortal sin for a scheduler to *prepare* a schedule; the scheduler is a recorder not a creator of a schedule; schedulers are not (and never should be) in charge of planning; and schedulers merely convert the project team's vision into a mathematical model.

The two e-mails gave me reason to pause and consider the various roles that a Scheduling Practitioner assumes in the course of performing his duties. Admittedly semantic, the question I posed to myself was whether the Practitioner is merely a recorder (note-taker), or something more. John and Edward seem to agree that the Practitioner is just a note-taker: John says *recorder* and Edward says *scribe*.

I set the e-mails aside for a few days and then, as if fate wanted to sweeten the pot, a third e-mail flashed across my screen. David was responding to a comment I had made in an academic exchange we were having on whether the nuances of different project types are sufficient to render a Practitioner, competent in one area, potentially incompetent in another. David wrote:

> I'm surprised we differ on the degree of difference in scheduling approaches for different types of projects. I have found that just two types of job require different schedule structures: alignment projects (railbeds, freeways, pipelines, etc), and dispersed logistical projects such as telecommunication network build-outs. I regard pre- and post-award planning and scheduling, and the accursed claims business, as different branches of the same tree.

---

[6]Notice that the P/S Enigmas is alive and well in this e-mail. The writer speaks of planning and scheduling in the same context, and even in the same sentences.

For my part, I was not as surprised as David that he and I had different views. David, just like Edward and John, is a Venerable, who tends to view the Practitioner as little more than a scribe. I deduced this from David's simplistic view of only two different notation methods: one for linear (alignment) projects and another for nonlinear (dispersed) projects.

Let me give you a few examples. When I schedule the construction of a skyscraper, two bits of information I need to know right up front are whether the structure is a steel frame or a concrete frame and whether the mechanical rooms are located in a rooftop penthouse or in a basement or separate mechanical building. From experience, I know that the answer to these two questions can amount to as much as two or three months of additional construction time. If we are building a correctional facility, from experience I know to ask about the availability of masons in the project's labor market; that will most likely drive the critical-path. If we are contemplating a road and bridge project, I ask about the availability of heavy equipment. If the project entails renovation of an operating hospital, I'm concerned about sound and dust abatement. A seasoned Scheduler, with accumulated experience in a specific project type, has learned which variables will most dramatically impact Project performance *from a time perspective*.

If the Scheduler is treated merely as a scribe and not allowed or expected to contribute his insights, then his accumulated Planning and Scheduling experience in the particular project type is lost entirely. You may be thinking that the project manager should be asking these questions. I agree. But what happens if he doesn't? Should the Practitioner remain mute, because, after all, he's just a scribe?

The truth is that most project managers do not appreciate or recognize the implications to project timing, sequencing, and performance that certain project attributes hold, whereas to the seasoned Practitioner, the implications practically leap off the page. Other times, however, even the Practitioner may not immediately detect the full impact of a particular execution strategy. But when he does, should he share what he has discovered with the project team, or merely keep it to himself?

Let me tell you about how, on a hospital project in Illinois, an escalator in the basement held up the completion of wall finishes five floors above. The convoluted sequence linking these two seemingly unrelated work areas begins with the delivery and installation of the escalator chassis, which would connect the basement slab on grade to the first elevated slab, immediately above (first floor). Since the basement level housed the cafeteria, morgue, and mechanical rooms, a significant amount of under-slab utilities needed to be installed before pouring the slab on grade. However, until the heavy escalator was delivered and dragged into place, the underground utilities could not be completed.

Meanwhile, due to the building's orientation in combination with seasonal weather patterns, there was major concern that the soil upon which the basement slab was to be poured would not dry out if the second floor slab were already in place (blocking the sun). And so, until the under-slab plumbing was done, and before the escalator trusses were set, the second floor slab could not be poured.

Structurally, the second floor slab was designed to resist lateral pressures from the backfill against the foundation walls. Until the second floor slab was poured, the excavation (overdig) that surrounded the entire building footprint could not be backfilled, and this held up the erection of scaffolding needed by the brick masons. The exterior skin of the building called for brickwork seated on the spread footings at the basement level and stacking skyward to the parapet walls six floors above. The wall design did not call for intermittent brick ledges, and so the brickwork could not be started anywhere but at the lowest level.

The connection details at the parapet wall/roof and roofing juncture required that the parapet wall be constructed first, with the parapet wall coping and the roof flashing being one homogeneous piece. As a result, the roofing could not be completed without the flashing, and the flashing (which was also the parapet wall coping) could not be installed until the brickwork was finished. Of course, without roofing, the building was not watertight, and finishes on the top floor could not commence. And so, an escalator in the basement was holding up finishes on the sixth floor.

When I discovered this odd set of dependencies, I immediately brought the matter to the project manager's attention. Would I have been able to do so if I also reported to a Scheduling Manager who believed, as Edward and John do, that Schedulers are to be seen but not heard? I doubt seriously that anyone, even those who subscribe to the "schedulers are scribes" philosophy, would want me to not share what I knew with a project manager. But that only proves that the scribe concept comes with some qualifications.

On a midtown skyscraper project, I remember asking the project manager how much time he wanted to allow as a lag between floors. The building had 41 stories, and he blurted out, without much thought (I felt), "I don't know, let's make it a week." From that instruction I would have assigned an SS5 between the Floor Layout activities for each of the 41 floors. But I understood the extreme importance of this single variable, and so I pursued the question by explaining that changing the SS5 by even one day (to an SS4 or an SS6) would reduce or increase the project length by two months, respectively. Had I adopted the *scribe-only* posture, I would've simply written SS5 and moved on.

Another observation can be made from these two examples, beyond the need for Schedulers to be more than just tightlipped scribes. That is, these examples suggest that David's division of scheduling into only two categories (linear and dispersed) might be too simplistic. After all, the two cited examples are both of disbursed projects, and yet specialized experience in one project type does not give one specialized experience in another. Likewise, theme park schedules are dramatically affected by design changes, whereas road and bridge projects are most dramatically affected by equipment availability. Tunneling projects are sensitive to trade stacking.

The point I'm trying to make is that Scheduling Practitioners bring *expertise* to the table. All of the preceding quoted "authorities" seem to miss this point, and some even go as far as to consciously deny Practitioners any right to contribute, insisting that they should not be more. While this may be a shrewd defensive tactic, it does not serve the best interests of the project.

Finally, there is also a semantic rebuttal to John's and Edward's arguments. Consider these definitions from the *American Heritage Dictionary*:

- *Create* 1. To cause to come into being, as something unique that would not naturally evolve or that is not made by ordinary processes. 2. To cause to happen, bring about, arrange, as by intention or design.
- *Manage* 1. To bring about or succeed in accomplishing, sometimes despite difficulty or hardship. 2. To take charge or care of. 3. To dominate or influence by tact, flattery, or artifice. 4. To handle, direct, govern, or control in action or use.
- *Make* 1. To bring into existence by shaping or changing material, combining parts. 2. To produce, cause to exist or happen, bring about. 3. To put in the proper condition or state. 4. To bring into a certain form. 5. To convert from one state, condition, or category to another. 6. To write or compose. 7. To bring together separate parts so as to produce a whole; compose; form.

Edward says that we *may* be schedule managers, yet John says we are never "in charge." The dictionary says that management *means* taking charge. Edward says that we do not make the schedule, yet the dictionary defines "making" as many of the things that Schedulers do.

I well appreciate the spirit behind these two gentlemen's remarks. They would have the Practitioner function much like the accountant or lawyer, professionals who do not make the business decisions but merely convert those decisions into tools and instruments of their trade. The lawyer forms wills, contracts, and other legally binding documents in reflection of decisions made by the client. To this extent he is a scribe, by converting the client's desires into legally acceptable form.

The accountant prepares financial statements and tax returns, likewise in reflection of decisions made by the client. In this sense, he too is a scribe. But both professionals also offer advice, and at such times they are more than just scribes. John, Edward, and even David (I believe) seem to dismiss the advisory role of the Scheduling Practitioner, and I think this is a critical distinction not to be missed.

As for who is *responsible* for development and maintenance of the Project Schedule, in a purely organizational sense the Project Scheduler *is* responsible producing the Schedule, just as the accounts receivable clerk is responsible for preparing and issuing invoices—even though, ultimately, decisions over *whether* to invoice a client for a particular charge or *how much* to charge might be made by higher authorities. Consistent with the company's standard operating procedures, the accounts receivables clerk is entrusted with the authority and responsibility to make certain that invoices are prepared in a timely manner, that all invoices which should be sent are sent, that invoices are prepared in accordance with generally accepting accounting procedures, and so on.

I think it is simply incorrect to relieve the Project Scheduler of his or her responsibility for the proper development and maintenance of the Project Schedule. Certainly good/best practice mandates that the Practitioner elicit contributions from the project team, and the content of the Project Schedule should reflect the insights and intentions of the project team—but Schedule Design and Schedule Development activities *are* the responsibility of the Execution Scheduler.

Edward says, "We do not make the schedule." But please—look at the preceding definitions for the word *make* and tell me who else makes the schedule. If *make* means bringing into existence by shaping and changing materials; or producing; or putting in the proper condition and shape; or bringing into a certain form; or composing; or bringing together separate parts so as to produce a whole, who does that? Are those not the very steps of schedule construction at the most fundamental level?

I have left for last Edward's contention that we are not planners. A planner is one who plans. But what is the meaning of "planning?" Again, according to the dictionary:

> *Planning*—1. To formulate a scheme or program for the accomplishment, enactment, or attainment of. 2. To arrange a method or scheme beforehand for (any work, enterprise, or proceeding). 3. To draw or make a graphic representation of. 4. To draw or make a diagram or layout.

Edward's argument only holds water if we limit our understanding of the word *planning* to just the first definition (and possibly the second). In other words, if *planning* refers only to mentally conceiving creative, original thought, then planning is most certainly accomplished by the project team, for the planning ideas bearing the highest probability of subsequent achievement are ones derived from the collective wisdom of those who will be performing the work. But *planning* is also a set of physical processes (the other two definitions), and Scheduling Practitioners do perform those processes.

There is also that subtle distinction I tried to make earlier about the Practitioner's expertise. In the course of devising the optimum Strategic Plan, much more needs to be considered than merely strict construction logistics. As an illustration, consider the innovation of the *constructability review* process, which came about when the construction industry realized that a design professional's understanding of a project is much different than a builder's. What might look fantastic on a blueprint might be extremely expensive, or even impossible, to build from the perspective of the contractor.

The same can be said about differing viewpoints between the project manager and the Scheduling Practitioner. What might seem like a perfectly wonderful execution strategy to the project manager might seem terribly inefficient, convoluted, and even impractical from the Practitioner's perspective. If the spirit of the "planning" implies *beneficial* planning, then the Practitioner *must* be involved, just as much as (if not even more than) the other project team members. And such involvement entails more than mere note taking.

The Other Two Enigmas

To briefly review what I have stated thus far in this first half of the chapter, the Scheduling Practice is currently plagued by overwhelming confusion, conflict, and chaos concerning some of the most fundamental terms used to describe what we do (verbs), what we produce (objects), and who produces them (subjects). So far, we have discussed the Planning-Scheduling Enigma, which pertains to the *verb* portion of the question at hand.

We need only acknowledge the parallel confusion surrounding the other two Enigmas, and our discussion of the terminology quagmire afflicting our Practice will be complete. Simply stated, if we are confused as to what planning and scheduling mean, we must be equally confused as to the differences between a planner and a scheduler, or between a plan and a schedule.

Refer to my parenthetical comment concerning John's e-mail and how he kept using derivatives of plan and schedule interchangeably. He writes:

> The scheduler is part of the project management team and as such, he/she should work closely with the team that's going to build the job to help them through the pre-planning process.

First of all, if we take him literally, he is describing a point in the project before planning has begun, which would be some time long before the project's Go/No Go Decision. Then he adds:

> Schedulers are not (and never should be) in charge of planning how a job is to be put together—that's what project managers do.

Now he is talking about planning, whereas in the previous sentence he was at the pre-planning stage. And he is arguing that a *scheduler* doesn't do planning. While I agree with John, unfortunately, his point is not that schedulers or planners do planning, but that the project managers do.

Finally, he exhibits complete confusion when he notes:

> Schedulers are tasked with the responsibility of taking the project manager's and their team's plan and putting it into a mathematical model (a network) to see if it's workable, achievable, possible, etc.

He assigns to the Scheduler the task of understanding the project team's plan and then building a mathematical model. Perhaps he was using the word *plan* to mean *thinking*.

DEFINING THE SCHEDULING PRACTICE

There is an old saying that one should not tear down a bridge unless he is prepared to build a new one in its place. Now that I have sufficiently exposed the deplorable state of the Scheduling Practice (at least, in terms of terminology and consensual understanding), in this second half of the chapter I am obligated to propose a solution. This proposal is presented for your respected consideration and reaction.[7] Personally, I think it goes quite far in resolving the P/S Enigmas.

What follows is the culmination of months of research, thinking, deliberation with colleagues, and hard work. I'm proud to offer a refreshingly new and comprehensive set

---

[7]Please write to me at mwoolf@ics-global.com.

of definitions to describe the Scheduling Practice in terms of specializations, positions, deliverables, and roles. But the discussion must begin with the very label *Scheduling Practice*, itself.

Why "Scheduling Practice"?

I have already explained why the word *practice* is better than the word *profession;* our discipline does not meet the requirements of a profession. Further, I could think of no other word that seems better at describing the collection of people, processes, theories, deliverables, and customers involved in the delivery of Scheduling Practice products and services, than the word *practice.*

The choice of the word *scheduling* was not so easily made, however. I admit that, for a long time, I was one of those literalists who argued passionately that scheduling is what you do *prior to* the execution of the work. Hence, I would not consider Scheduling Practice activities performed after schedule creation as being *scheduling* activities, per se. So I spent considerable time trying to find one or more words that might represent what Practitioners do for the majority of the project life cycle.

I began by examining labels that others had given to the primary functions of the Practitioner. Book titles made for a convenient list of possibilities, and most authors felt compelled to describe three aspects to our discipline: planning, scheduling, and control. By all rights, we should call it the *Planning, Scheduling, and Control Practice*. But that is quite a mouthful. How about the *Planning and Scheduling Practice*? Or perhaps the *Schedule and Control Practice*?

Obviously, it would be better if we could have a short title for our discipline, but what word should we put in front of the word *practice*? I settled on the word *scheduling* once I let go of a need for literal interpretation of the word. When I considered other fields, I found that a verb-type word often includes in its meaning ancillary activities that are not literally what the word describes. For instance, nursing involves more than direct patient contact. It includes ancillary activities such as inventorying meds, record keeping, scheduling, paperwork, and so on. The same conclusion can be reached from words like gardening, landscaping, farming, shipping, and so on.

From a philosophical point of view I recognized that Planning only makes sense if Scheduling is subsequently performed. Likewise, the activities commonly associated with control (analysis and reporting) cannot be achieved without the prior creation and ongoing maintenance of the schedule, clearly Scheduling activities. These observations led to my comfort in using the word *Scheduling* as an umbrella term to refer to all aspects of schedule design, development, maintenance, and usage.

The Three Specialities of the Scheduling Practice

I had dinner with a colleague the other night and, at some point, we found ourselves locked in disagreement over whether planning and scheduling require different or common skills sets (He is a Venerable; can you tell?). From that discussion I was reminded that some people simply will reject the new Scheduling Practice Paradigm that this chapter proposes.

However, I'm confident that the majority of Practitioners will understand and appreciate the value in giving unique names to the fundamentally dissimilar products and services that we render in the course of our work.

For the following discussion, please refer to Table 5-3, which suggests that the Scheduling Practice has three distinct specialties:

- Commitment Planning
- Execution Scheduling
- Performance Control

To fully understand each of these three specializations, we need to examine them one at a time. However, before we do, we must define four phases of the project lifecycle, *as seen from the perspective of the Scheduling Practice*. In terms of the involvement of Scheduling Practitioners in the project lifecycle, the project passes through four phases:

- **Authorization Phase** This is the initial stage of the project lifecycle during which the project owner decides whether or not to authorize the project. This stage culminates with the Go/No Go decision.
- **Pre-Execution Phase** With authorization to proceed granted, the project team conducts both Planning and Scheduling activities in advance of work execution.
- **Execution Phase** This is the longest of the four stages in the project lifecycle, during which the work is actually performed.
- **Post-Execution Phase** With project execution completed, the final stage brings closure to the project, including resolution of any outstanding conflicts. (This fourth phase is not shown in Table 5-3)

Commitment Planning

To appreciate the choice of the word *commitment*, we need to first delineate the specialties of this group: Authorization Planning and Execution Planning.

Authorization Planning Authorization Planning occurs during the Authorization Phase; this makes logical sense. The prevailing question is *whether* the project should be authorized or not. Scheduling Practitioners, among others, are enlisted to help the owner's program management team decide whether or not to proceed with the project. Two common procedures performed at this stage by the Scheduling Practitioner are Feasibility Planning and Master Planning:

- **Feasibility Planning** This type of planning is performed in order to determine whether the project is feasible in the first place. As an example, a few years ago the company for which I worked was retained by the John F. Kennedy Center for the Performing Arts to conduct a feasibility study in order to determine whether the Concert Hall could be renovated in ten months or less. That narrow window of time was constricted by the departure of the National Orchestra on world tour and by the Kennedy Center Honors program ten months later. Working in a solitary mode, I determined that ten months offered sufficient time for a competent contractor to perform the work as depicted in the preliminary design documents. (In case you're interested, the actual work was performed in 9.5 months.)

Table 5-3

Scheduling Practice Specialities and Phases

Specialty	Authorization Phase	Pre-Execution Phase	Execution Phase
Commitment Planning			
Authorization Planning	Feasibility Planning Master Planning		
Execution Planning		Strategic Planning Consensus Planning	
Execution Scheduling			
Schedule Production		Schedule Design Schedule Development	
Performance Recording			Statused Schedule
Performance Control			
Performance Analysis			Schedule Performance Analysis Management Performance Analysis Execution Performance Analysis
Change Optimization			Scope Optimization Approach Optimization Conditions Optimization Execution Schedule Revisement
Performance Advisement			Performance Reporting Performance Consulting

- **Master Planning** The purpose of Master Planning is to memorialize the numerous assumptions and decisions made by the owner's planning team during the course of Authorization Planning. The work product is a summarizing document that visually depicts the overall timing, sequencing, and logistics of the project, notwithstanding that the project design is highly conceptual at this early stage. Note: A Master Plan is not developed in isolation, whereas a Feasibility Plan might be (as in the Kennedy Center example).

Execution Planning Execution Planning is performed by the parties charged with performing the work. Contrast this to Commitment Planning, which is performed by the owner organization. The purpose of Execution Planning is to deliberate upon and identify the one project strategy that seems most beneficial to most parties. Underlying Execution Planning is a belief in the value of a win-win scenario. This philosophy states that it is better, for the long-term benefit of the project, that every party obtain most of what they seek than it is for some parties to gain all that they want while others gain little or nothing of what they value. Execution Planning passes through two stages:

- **Strategic Planning** Strategic Planning is performed in order to derive the optimum approach to Project Execution; the one that best benefits the project as a whole, participant benefits notwithstanding.

- **Consensus Planning** Consensus Planning modifies the strategic plan, as little as necessary, in order for a leveling of the playing field. In other words, where the Strategic Plan might have benefited some entities more than others, adjustments are made so that each party benefits as equally as possible (or, as much as the owner is willing to allow). An offsetting consequence is that the project loses some of the potential benefits inherent in the optimum Strategic Plan.

Resolving the Venerable/Current Model Standoff It should be noted that Authorization Planning is performed by the owner organization, while Execution Planning is performed by the entities responsible for project execution. What both Authorization and Execution Planning have in common is that they each culminate in a self-imposed *commitment*, on the part of the owner and work performers, respectively. Hence, it makes sense to call the overall specialization Commitment Planning.

The value of the two subspecializations is that they help us resolve the conflict between the Venerable and Current Models. Supporters of the Venerable Model will recognize Execution Planning as the type of planning they think of as the prelude to Execution Scheduling. Advocates of the Current Model will appreciate the distinction of a separate Authorization Planning category, which some refer to as *pre-project planning*.

To be sure, I am proud of having at last brought peace between the two passionate groups of Scheduling Practitioners. However, I'm even more excited that the classification of Commitment Planning and its subcomponents makes a bold distinction between *planning* and *scheduling*, for those who had been unable to separate the two.

Execution Scheduling

Execution Scheduling involves the Schedule Design and Schedule Development. Obviously, these are what most people would consider the primary functions of the Project Scheduler. I also refer to Schedule Development synonymously as Schedule Production as *my* answer to that entire debate over whether Execution Schedulers make, are in charge of, manage, produce, or create the Project Schedule. My opinion is that the Execution Scheduler is responsible for *producing* the schedule and toward this meaning, I cite the following definitions from the *American Heritage* dictionary:

> *Produce*—1. To bring into existence by intellectual or creative ability. (dictionary.com) 2. To make or manufacture. (dictionary.com) 3. To create by physical or mental effort (produce a tapestry)(american heritage). 4. To create or manufacture a man-made product. (worldnet)

Consider the tapestry example. One need not be the originator or creator of either the threads or the pattern in order to be the producer of the tapestry. Likewise, the ideas and concepts and strategies that make their way into the Project Schedule need not originate from the Scheduler as original thought, but can, often do, and by all means should come from the project team. Nevertheless, the physical development of the Project Schedule remains the primary responsibility of the Project Scheduler.

Performance Control

The third specialty within the Scheduling Practice is Performance Control. These two words were chosen after *extensive* discussion and debate among a dozen or more colleagues over a period of months.

Let's start with the second word; the one intended to describe what we do. If we follow the pattern established by the two other specializations, planning and scheduling, then here we need a verb that captures the essence of what Practitioners do with a Project Schedule once it has been developed. The term *control* has gained a strong foothold in the Scheduling world and was a natural first choice—but only if used with an acceptable modifier. That modifier would have to adequately describe what we are attempting to control. To be sure, the most popular suggestion among my colleagues was *Project* Control, but this term bothered me because this term is generally used to refer to the combined and coordinated efforts of *both* cost and schedule control. To now suggest that project control is a subset of the Scheduling Practice seemed both awkward and confusing to me. Besides, if any one position *does* control the project it's the project manager, not the Scheduler.

The next suggestion was *Schedule* Control, but this was rejected because it would imply that we create and maintain schedules merely to control their use but nothing more (having to do with the project itself). At this point, as I recall, the discussions grew silent. You could see the smoke rising from our ears as my colleagues and I tried to capture just what it is that we seek to control. I'll spare you all of the other words that came next, but in the end we settled on *Performance* Control. Part of the difficulty of this entire exercise was choosing a specialty name that would have an equally workable specialist title. What troubled all of us was the position title Controller. It was felt that the Scheduling Practitioner does not *control* much of anything, per se.

What broke the impasse was a gradual realization that while Scheduling Practitioners do not *control*, nor do we *plan* or *schedule*, in a vacuum; that is, both are ultimately project manager responsibilities. In other words, the project manager must plan his project, and the project manager must schedule it as well. As technical support personnel, Scheduling Practitioners assist with the development of the Execution *Plan*, and the production and maintenance of the Execution *Schedule*. Once viewed in this light, it became clear that, as a Performance Controller, we were merely supporting the project manager in the project manager's performance *control* responsibilities, as well.

Why *performance?* We looked at other combinations such as Achievement Control, Advancement Control, and even Momentum Control. While each offered certain advantages, we settled on *performance* because *that* is what we spend most of our time monitoring, analyzing, and reporting. Performance Control has four subspecialties: Performance Recording, Performance Analysis, Change Optimization, and Performance Advisement.

Performance Recording   Performance Recording refers to the maintenance activities performed by the Performance Recorder during the cyclical Performance Control cycle. I chose the word *recording* because it helps us to focus on the primary objectives and role of the Performance Controller during schedule maintenance. According to the *American Heritage* dictionary:

> *Record.* (*verb*) 1. To set down in writing or the like, as for the purpose of preserving evidence. 2. To set down or register in some permanent form. (*noun*) 1. An account, as of information or facts, set down especially in writing as a means of preserving knowledge. 2. Anything (such as a document or a phonographic record or a photograph) providing permanent evidence or information about past events.

Clearly, what the Scheduling Practitioner does during the routine cyclical maintenance of the Project Schedule conforms to these definitions. Distinguishing between the Execution Scheduler's production responsibilities, and the Performance Recorder's recording responsibilities reminds us that each calls upon different skill sets, mandates a different focus, and aims toward different objectives.

Performance Analysis   The objective of Performance Analysis is to examine the three central categories of project performance:

- **Schedule Performance Analysis** Studies the performance of the Execution Schedule as a management tool and ensures its ongoing functionality, viability, and integrity. Such routine examination exposes any disparities between planned and actual performance, arbitrary adjustments or changes to schedule logic and content, and so forth.

- **Management Performance Analysis** Like Schedule Performance Analysis, this is an area of review quite often overlooked by Scheduling Practitioners. An important discovery made by the Momentum Studies is that schedule delays are more often caused by management factors than by productivity factors. The probability of successful achievement of project goals is dramatically increased when management performance is carefully monitored.

- **Execution Performance Analysis** Refers to the default topics we commonly associate with the single word *analysis*. Here, the Scheduling Practitioner carefully examines the raw data captured during Performance Recording and may further develop additional data in the form of trends and ratios to enhance his or her understanding of execution performance.

Change Optimization   We can agree that analysis for the sake of analyzing accomplishes little. The reason we analyze project information is in order to constantly improve our abilities and maximize our efforts toward successful project achievement. The dictionary offers a delightful word:

> *Optimize*—1. To make as effective, perfect, or useful as possible. 2. To make the best of. 3. (Computers) To write or rewrite (the instructions in a program) so as to maximize efficiency and speed in retrieval, storage, or execution. 4. To make optimal; get the most out of; use best; "optimize your resources." 5. Modify to achieve maximum efficiency in storage capacity or time or cost

So, where Performance Analysis helps us understand the true nature of what is occurring on the project, Change Optimization provides an opportunity to convert that knowledge into meaningful adjustments in future plans so that we can "get the most out of" the remainder of available time and resources.

Change Optimization divides into three procedures that correspond with Change Capture:

- **Scope Optimization** The title for procedures performed to determine the best way to respond to changes in scope, whether they increases or decreases. Contemporaneous Time Impact Analyses (TIAs) are performed during these procedures.

- **Approach Optimization** The name for procedures that evaluate the acceptability of actual performance variances from plan, as well as the merits of future variances from plan.

- **Conditions Optimization** Refers to those adjustments to future plans necessitated by changes in conditions.

- **Execution Schedule Amendment** Refers to the production of major Execution Schedule Revisions, as a natural outgrowth of any or all of the above three Change Optimization procedures. Schedule Revisions typically replace the Baseline Schedule (or most recent Execution Schedule Revision) as the primary basis for comparison during Performance Control. Examples of Execution Schedule Revisions would include recovery, acceleration, or workaround schedule releases.

Performance Advisement This final subspecialty under Performance Control covers consulting and reporting and is the logical extension of all that precedes it. The emphasis is on performance, and we unabashedly identify one of our roles as that of an advisor. Scheduling Practitioners bring an impressive package of education, experience, skills, and energy to the job of Scheduling Practitioner, and they have meaningful advice to give. We are not just scribes!

Definable Positions and Deliverables

With the Scheduling Practice clearly defined by three specialties (and their subspecialties and subordinate procedures), we are now able to identify various specialist positions within the Scheduling Practice.

Specialist Positions of the Scheduling Practice

Referring to Table 5-4, we have three primary specialties:

- **Commitment Planner** The *Planner* (for short) is capable of performing all facets of Commitment Planning. In larger organizations, however, the position may be subdivided into subspecialties, such as Authorization Planner or Execution Planner.

- **Execution Scheduler** The *Scheduler* (for short) performs that set of functions most closely associated with the Scheduling Practice, namely Schedule Design and Schedule Development. In larger organizations two subspecialties might be Schedule Designer and Schedule Developer.

Table 5-4

Scheduling Practice Specialties and Positions

Specialty	Position
Commitment Planning	**Commitment Planner**
Authorization Planning	Authorization Planner
Execution Planning	Execution Planner
Execution Scheduling	**Execution Scheduler**
Schedule Production	Schedule Producer
Performance Recording	Performance Recorder
Performance Control	**Performance Controller**
Performance Analysis	Performance Analyst
Change Optimization	Change Optimizer
Performance Advisement	Performance Advisor

- **Performance Controller** The *Controller* (for short) performs the advanced functions of analysis, optimization, reporting, and consulting. In larger organizations, it may be practical to divide into three subspecialties: Performance Recorder, Performance Analyst, Change Optimizer, and Performance Advisor.

At last, we have done it. We have salvaged the labels *planner* and *scheduler* in such a way that each means something specific and that each corresponds to a distinctly different specialization area. At long last, our Practice can stop arguing about whether Planning and Scheduling are the same, or about whether Planners and Schedulers are the same, and about whether the Scheduler is merely a scribe, or something more— *much* more. In the final section of this chapter we will examine nine different roles that are played by the Scheduling Practitioner. But for the moment, we can rejoice in seeing the title *Analyst* appearing proudly, side-by-side, with *Planner* and *Scheduler*. Quickly, let's also look at the new names for our deliverables.

The Key Deliverables of the Scheduling Practice

The clarification of Scheduling Practice deliverables is now possible, as well. The labels follow logically from the names of the specialties: Feasibility Plan, Master Plan, Strategic Plan, Consensus Plan, Execution Schedule, Performance Analyses, Optimization Scenarios, Execution Schedule Revisions and various Performance Reports (Execution Schedule Editions, Extractions, and Narratives). (Refer to Table 8-1 in Chapter 8 for a detailed breakdown of these items.)

Plans and Schedules Look an Awful Lot Alike   We are still left to ponder whether it is possible to assign physical attributes to plans and schedules, such that we might tell them apart by mere observation. To investigate this possibility, I began by listing the various ways to characterize a Plan or a Schedule and, for each, I examined whether a hard-and-fast rule could be constructed that would mutually exclude one of the two objects each and every time. This exercise, while exhaustive, proved fruitless. Here are the highlights of the conclusions I reached:

- **Appearance** Plans and schedules can both appear as tabular reports, logic diagrams, or Gantt charts. In other words, they can and often do look quite similar. *Appearance* does not suffice as a differentiating attribute.

- **Level- of detail** While there seemed to be a prevailing opinion among Scheduling Practitioners that plans are typically more general (less detailed) than schedules, this distinction was offset by the variable nature of project types and sizes. For example, a larger or more complex project might generate a Master Plan having more detail than an Execution Schedule developed for a smaller, less complex project. Furthermore, this method of object identification would necessarily be a comparative one. *Level of detail* does not suffice as a differentiating attribute.

- **Timing** The timing variable adopts the Venerable Model's assumption that the Execution Plan will evolve before the Execution Schedule. In the Venerable Model's heyday this may have been a reasonable assumption, when design-bid-build was the standard contract delivery method. Today, however, there are a number of other popular delivery methods that allow some portions of the work to commence while other portions are still in design. For instance, a "rolling wave" Schedule Development approach is sometimes employed, where portions of the Schedule are highly detailed while other portions are still quite general. This nuance invalidates both *level of detail* and *timing* as ways to distinguish a Plan from a Schedule. Concerning the latter, it's possible for one portion of a project to be in Planning, even after another portion had completed with Scheduling. And I'm talking *planning,* as the Venerable Model understands the term! *Timing* does not suffice as a differentiating attribute.

- **Source** Aside from the fact that one cannot merely look at a Plan or Schedule and determine who created it, quite often the same source that creates a Plan creates a Schedule. *Source* does not suffice as a differentiating attribute.

   Conclusion: It is not possible to differentiate between the two objects, the *plan* or the *schedule,* strictly on the basis of physical attributes.

Plans and Schedules Have Different Quality Standards   While, as I noted previously, there are exceptions to the statement that plans and schedules have different quality standards, for the most part Commitment Plans tend to be more general than Execution Schedules. This is especially true of Authorization Plans, which are developed at a point in the project lifecycle when project scope, design, and purpose are not well understood. Schedules, on the other hand, are developed immediately prior to project execution and, given that one of the main reasons for an Execution Schedule is to coordinate and direct the work, a Schedule's level of detail tends to be more specific than the Commitment Plans upon which it was based.

An important corollary to the generality of Commitment Plans is that many of the hard-and-fast rules, standards, and best practices most often assigned to Schedules may not apply as readily to Plans. For example, there is general agreement in the Scheduling community that an Execution Schedule should not contain open-ended activities (except for the Project Start and Project Completion activities). However, in Commitment Plans it is not uncommon to use a fairly large number of date constraints in lieu of hard logic, given the early stage of project definition. Another example might be the average activity-duration, being much larger in Commitment Plans than in Execution Schedules. An important note to make, as we close this section, is that the current rash of efforts to write Best Practices still tend to combine planning and scheduling together, and yet the best practices or standards for Scheduling rarely apply to Planning with equal reasonableness.

The Nine Roles of Scheduling Practitioners

To this point, I have described the Scheduling Practice in terms of specialties, subspecialties, procedures, positions, and deliverables. However, the Practice also can be characterized in terms of nine distinct roles that a Scheduling Practitioner is called upon to play in the course of performing his duties. It is helpful to identify these roles for two important reasons. First, by describing and justifying each role, we give legitimacy to their portrayal and thereby put to rest pointless arguments among Practitioners, such as whether schedulers are merely scribes. Second, with clarified roles, we are able to better understand the positions and specializations that comprise the Scheduling Practice.

As we consider the nine roles of the Scheduling Practitioner, you may wish to refer to Table 5-5.

- **Educator** The Scheduling Practitioner is often called upon to explain to his customers various aspects of Scheduling principles, methods, concepts, and the like. Both Planning and Scheduling sessions are more productive and the results more meaningful when contributors to the process understand how all of the pieces come together.

- **Strategist** There is an art to Strategic Planning, whether for the purposes of authorization or commitment, and the Practitioner can contribute his experience and knowledge to the team's efforts to devise the optimum plan.

Table 5-5

Scheduling Practice Specialities and Roles

SPECIALTY	Educator	Strategist	Interpreter	Scribe	Investigator	Analyst	Advisor	Diplomat	Communicator
Commitment Planning	✔	✔	✔	✔			✔	✔	✔
Authorization Planning	✔	✔	✔	✔			✔	✔	✔
Execution Planning	✔	✔	✔	✔			✔	✔	✔
Execution Scheduling	✔		✔	✔	✔				
Schedule Production	✔		✔	✔					
Performance Recording			✔	✔	✔				
Performance Control	✔	✔			✔	✔	✔	✔	✔
Performance Analysis						✔			
Change Optimization		✔			✔	✔	✔	✔	
Performance Advisement	✔						✔	✔	✔

- **Interpreter** During Planning and Scheduling procedures, project team members orally describe the thoughts that are in their heads. The Practitioner's challenge is to translate those thoughts into the symbolic language of the Critical Path Method without changing the meaning during the translation process. This underscores the importance of accurate *interpretation*, in order to capture the essence and spirit of what is being conveyed, such that the ultimate schematic depiction carries the same meaning as what was first articulated.

- **Scribe** The Practitioner is also a dutiful scribe, capturing in the symbolic language of the Critical Path Method what is being conveyed in spoken or written words and numbers. Much of Schedule Development, and most of Performance Recording, involves unadulterated note taking.

- **Investigator** During Performance Recording, the Practitioner should act like a journalist, following leads, learning the truth, and recording the facts—just the facts. One day, the Scheduling Practice may rise to the level of a true profession. When that day comes, codes of ethical conduct surely will be established, and here, pertaining to the Practitioner's role as an investigator, ethical standards will be most prominent and most germane.

- **Analyst** It is difficult to decide which of the Scheduling Practitioner's nine roles is most important, but *Analyst* has to be near the top of the list. To a great extent, Performance Recording alone rarely reveals much that the astute project manager did not already know. I have found that, most of the times when I was able to present to the project manager insights he didn't already have, my commentaries came from conclusions derived through analytic processes.

- **Advisor** Many Scheduling Practitioners are uncomfortable seeing themselves as advisors. They have gradually acquiesced to the faulty premise that the layers of the project's organization chart somehow correlate with degrees of insight, awareness, and wisdom. They assume that anything they know, the project manager must already know. What, then, could they possible advise about? But experienced and observant Practitioners see the same things that project managers do; only they see them from the perspective of temporal cause and effect.

  Project managers typically view the world one snapshot at a time. This explains why they tend to wait for a fire to erupt, and spend their days extinguishing them. Scheduling Practitioners watch for trends, identify causative agents, and suggest mitigation strategies. A professional colleague for whom I have the utmost respect said this to me, about the Practitioner's analytic role:

  > One of the things I tell my new hires that come out of project management backgrounds is that we need to reorient their thinking to that of a *scheduler,* rather than that of a project manager, the difference being that PM's look at a situation and immediately start to solve it, whereas Schedulers look at the full ramifications through analysis of the situation.

- **Diplomat** My father used to say, "It's not *what* you say that is most important, it is *how* you say it." Scheduling Practitioners—the successful ones—have learned how to speak to owners and workers with equal confidence and finesse. Getting inherently distrusting parties to come together is what Scheduling is all about, and a fair amount of diplomacy is essential to many of the jobs Practitioners are called upon to perform.

- **Communicator** All of the deliverables of the Scheduling Practice are used to communicate, and that is why it has been rightly noted that the Scheduling Practice is in the communication business. An essential attribute of the successful Practitioner is the ability to speak and write effectively.

Why a Fresh Definition of the Scheduling Practice Makes Good Sense

At the beginning of this chapter, I listed the main challenges facing the Scheduling Practice. Here I list the many important ways that the Paradigm of this chapter responds to that first list. Specifically, the new Scheduling Practice Paradigm accomplishes the following:

- It clears up many of the most important terminology problems.
- It clarifies what we do (our products and services) and how we do it.
- It provides a framework for future growth and unification.
- Its definitions support the eventual creation of a true profession, one that bridges industries.
- It resolves the three P/S Enigmas.
- It succeeds in distinguishing between a *Planner* and a *Scheduler*: they are no longer synonymous.
- It limits the titles *Planner* and *Scheduler* to specific procedures during which Planning and Scheduling are actually happening. As noted elsewhere in this book, both Planning and Scheduling are, by definition, pre-execution activities. One does not plan or schedule a party one is already attending. It is semantically incorrect to refer to any of the activities in the Performance Control specialty as being planning or scheduling activities—and with the introduction of the Controller position, we no longer have to.

We are at last able to introduce new position titles that are more descriptive of the work being performed by the Scheduling Practitioner—that is, now that we are no longer stuck with using just two terms, *Planner* or *Scheduler*!

To fully appreciate how much confusion the new Scheduling Practice Paradigm clears up, I draw your attention to Table 5-6, which compares the existing, redundant terminology to the new, proposed terminology. Viewed side-by-side, the benefits of the new Paradigm are glowingly apparent. As you study the table, please notice the self-evident nature of the new labels and the redundant, ambiguous, and even confusing nature of the existing labels.

Lastly, as a final sanity check on our efforts, let us confirm that the new Scheduling Practice Paradigm supports and complements the new Project Management Paradigm. Figure 5-2 divides project management responsibilities into two groups: project administration and project execution. The Scheduling Practice provides informational support to both groups. Of the two, however, project execution is where the rubber meets the road, and that is where the Scheduling Practice must be most relevant. Figure 5-3 depicts the alignment of the Scheduling Practice with the project manager's six primary functions under project execution.

Table 5-6
Terminology: Current versus New Scheduling Practice Paradigm

Existing Redundant Terminology		New Scheduling Practice Terminology		
PHASE	*POSITION*			
Planning	**Project Planner**	Authorization Planning	**Authorization Planner**	Feasibility Plans Master Plan
		Execution Planning	**Execution Planner**	Strategic Plan Consensus Plan
Planning and Scheduling	**Planner and/or Scheduler**	Schedule Production	**Schedule Producer**	Schedule Specs Execution Schedule
		Performance Recording	**Performance Recorder**	Statused Schedule
Updating	**Scheduler**	Performance Analysis	**Performance Analyst**	Performance Analyses
		Change Optimization	**Change Optimizer**	Optimized Scenarios Schedule Revisions
		Performance Advisement	**Performance Reporter**	Schedule Editions Schedule Extractions Performance Reports & Presentations
			Performance Consultant	Consultations

Figure 5-2

The Scheduling Practice Supports Project Management

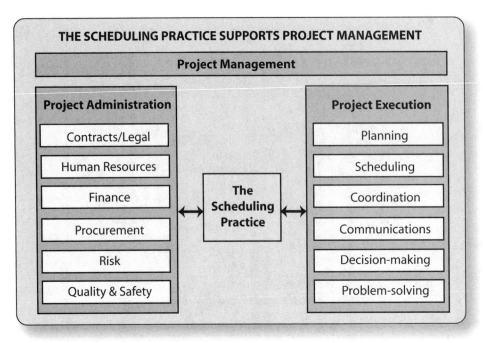

Figure 5-3

The Scheduling Practice Supports Project Execution

THE SCHEDULING PRACTICE SUPPORTS PROJECT EXECUTION	Planning	Scheduling	Coordination	Communications	Decision-making	Problem-solving
Commitment Planning	✔			✔		
Authorization Planning						
Execution Planning	✔			✔		
Execution Scheduling		✔	✔	✔		
Schedule Production		✔	✔	✔		
Status Recording			✔	✔		
Performance Control		✔	✔	✔	✔	✔
Performance Analysis			✔		✔	✔
Change Optimization		✔	✔		✔	✔
Performance Advisement				✔		

6

Introduction to Dilemma Control

While I have made a particular point of denouncing the use of the word "control" in the context of project control, cost control, or even time control, I am comfortable referring to this new area of project management focus as *Dilemma Control*. According to the dictionary, one definition for control is, "to reduce or prevent the spread of; as in *control insects; controlled the fire by dousing it with water*." It is in this context that I use the word "control" to refer to the processes involved in limiting the unwanted effects of dilemma influx.

Dilemma Control is the title for a new project management system that, by no coincidence, is conducted in conjunction with processes administered during Performance Analytics, a Momentology process. Dilemma Control deals with planning for and responding to project dilemmas.

It is not a substitute name for Risk Management, as the two programs, while having some similarities, are essentially different in scope, focus, methodology, and timing. In order to understand what Dilemma Control is, and how it differs from Risk Management, we should spend a few minutes characterizing Risk Management. Afterward, I will explain how Dilemma Control provides benefits that Risk Management does not.

RISK MANAGEMENT AND ITS DISTINGUISHING CHARACTERISTICS

In this section I will briefly explain Risk Management, in terms of traditional processes and distinguishing characteristics.

Risk Management's Traditional Processes

According to the PMBOK® Guide a risk is "an uncertain event or condition that, if it occurs, has a positive or negative effect on a project objective." The PMBOK® Guide goes on to describe Risk Management as "the systematic process of identifying, analyzing, and responding to project risk," and divides Risk Management into six major processes:

- **Risk Management Planning** Deciding how to approach and plan the Risk Management activities of the project.
- **Risk Identification** Determining which risks might affect the project and documenting their characteristics.
- **Qualitative Risk Analysis** Performing a qualitative analysis of risks and conditions to prioritize their effects on project objectives.
- **Quantitative Risk Analysis** Measuring the probability and consequences of risks and estimating their implications for project objectives.
- **Risk Response Planning** Developing procedures and techniques to enhance opportunities and reduce threats to the project's objectives.
- **Risk Monitoring and Control** Monitoring residual risks, identifying new risks, executing risk reduction plans, and evaluating their effectiveness throughout the project life cycle.

Risk Management's Distinguishing Characteristics

This subsection will discuss a number of Risk Management characteristics, the specifics of which subsequently will help us appreciate how Risk Management and Dilemma Control differ in far more ways than they are alike.

Timing

Risk Management is primarily a pre-project planning methodology. By this I mean that of its six key processes, five take place predominantly before work begins. Only Risk Monitoring and Control deals specifically with what to do once the project has begun. However, Risk Management is an iterative process, which involves performing risk identification during the project as well.

According to the PMBOK® Guide, risk identification entails "determining which risks might affect the project and documenting their characteristics." The operative word here is "might." The intent of risk identification is to speculate on which risks might occur in the future. While Risk Management literature also recommends repeating the risk identification process iteratively across the length of the project lifecycle, even then the point is to speculate on possible future risks.

Specifically, we observe that Risk Management involves six basic processes, only one of which takes place after work has commenced:

- **Risk Management Planning** As its name suggests, this includes a number of activities performed in advance of the work itself. The objective is to decide how to approach and plan for Risk Management as a project management methodology.
- **Risk identification** Popular techniques for risk identification include brainstorming, Delphi, and interviewing. As noted previously, the typical timing for risk identification is before the work begins.

- **Qualitative and Quantitative Risk Analysis** Both processes are designed to mathematically scale the degree of significance of risks identified during the risk identification process. The reasons given for performing these analyses is to prioritize risks and estimate their likely effects on project objectives. It would make little sense to conduct such analyses without allowing sufficient time to develop subsequent Risk Response Plans. Thus, these, too, must be performed *before* work begins.

- **Risk Response Planning** Entails the development of specific steps that can be taken in the event an identified risk actually occurs. Again, the nature of this procedure requires that it occur before the emergence of a risk event.

- **Risk Monitoring and Control** The only one of the six Risk Management processes that clearly takes place during the life of the project.

Risk Threshold

Risk Management is primarily focused on *major* risks. This only makes logical sense, since the process of Risk Management is fairly elaborate and the minimal benefits gained by application of Risk Management practices to minor events would likely be dwarfed by the expense in time, energy, and money to perform those steps.

That risks to be addressed by Risk Management are limited to major events is apparent both explicitly and implicitly in the PMBOK® Guide.

Explicit Indications of a Minimum Inclusion Threshold Direct references to a minimum threshold level include the following citations. I've added italics to these citations to make my point.

- "Project risk is an uncertain event or condition that, if it occurs, has a positive or negative effect on a *project* objective." By this definition, therefore, if an event or condition does not benefit or threaten a *project* objective, it falls below an inclusion threshold.

- Concerning the Delphi technique, "A facilitator uses a questionnaire to solicit ideas about the *important* project risks. The responses are submitted and put into risk categories by the facilitator. These risks are then circulated to the experts for further comment. Consensus on the *main* project risks may be reached in a few rounds of this process."

- "Qualitative risk analysis is one way of determining the *importance* of addressing specific risks and guiding risk responses."

- The PMBOK® Guide describes a process of determining the relative significance of impacts using a "Probability/Impact Risk Rating Matrix. A matrix may be constructed that assigns risk ratings (very low, low, moderate, high, and very high) to risks or conditions based on combining probability and impact scales." It then recommends a screening to reduce the ultimate target list of risks to those that are high and possibly moderate. Low risks are not pursued. To further this point, the PMBOK® Guide notes, "risks classified as *high* or *moderate* would be prime candidates for more analysis, including quantitative risk analysis, and for Risk Management action."

- "Sensitivity analysis helps to determine which risks have the *most potential* impact on the project." Also, concerning the prioritized list of quantified risks, "this list of risks includes those that pose the *greatest* threat or present the *greatest* opportunity to the project together with a measure of their impact."

Examples that Implicitly Indicate a Minimum Inclusion Threshold The PMBOK® Guide's Risk Management section groups risks into four categories. As you read this excerpt, notice how none of them are examples of a typical "day-to-day" event, which is my informal definition of a *dilemma*.

"Risks that may affect the project for better or worse can be identified and organized into risk categories. Risk categories should be well defined and should reflect common sources of risk for the industry or application area. Categories include the following:

- "Technical, Quality, or Performance Risks: such as reliance on unproven or complex technology, unrealistic performance goals, changes to the technology used or to industry standards during the project.
- "Project Management Risks: such as poor allocation of time and resources, inadequate quality of the project plan, poor use of project management disciplines.
- "Organizational Risks: such as cost, time, and scope objectives that are internally inconsistent, lack of prioritization of projects, inadequacy or interruption of funds, and resource conflicts with other projects in the organization.
- "External Risks: such as shifting legal or regulatory environment, labor issues, changing priorities, country risk, and weather. Force majeure risks such as earthquakes, floods, and civil unrest generally require disaster recovery actions rather than Risk Management."

Deciding Factor
A principal criterion for risk determination is whether the event threatens, or provides opportunities for achievement of, project objectives.

As has been quoted heavily in the previous paragraphs, the PMBOK® Guide, in its chapter on Risk Management, continuously links the identification, quantification, and qualification of risks with their potential effect on *project objectives*. It should be apparent that risks that do not pose an obvious or immediate threat to project objectives would not qualify for inclusion in the ultimate prioritized list of risks.

Orientation
While not necessarily stated in its literature, Risk Management appears to be oriented on the occurrence of *events*, as opposed to focusing on performance by *people*.

This is another observation that I am making, and one that I invite you to evaluate as well. It appears to me that the thrust of Risk Management is on the identification of risks, as well as on planning for response to such risks, should they occur. Both qualitative and quantitative analyses are statistical processes for which risks, not people, are the subject of analysis. Later, when we discuss Dilemma Control, an important distinction between *event*-oriented and *people*-oriented focus will emerge.

Objectivity
Notwithstanding its scientific flavor, Risk Management is essentially a speculative methodology that, as a result, is highly subjective.

This is an important point to make. When one reads about qualitative and quantitative analysis, Monte Carlo analysis, linear regression, cost-risk simulations, decision tree analysis, probability distributions, and the like, it is easy to assume that the overall process is essentially objective. In fact, the overall process is overwhelmingly *subjective*. I say this because all of the statistical procedures I just discussed are being applied to lists of potential risks and assignments of potential risk severity, yet both risk identification and severity assessments are subjectively derived.

Proof of this comes from the description of the risk identification process itself. First of all, the *inputs* to risk identification are the project charter, the Work Breakdown Structure, the product description, the Project Schedule's logic, costs and duration estimates, the resource plan, the procurement plan, assumptions lists, and constraints lists. Which of these inputs directly supplies identification of risks to project objectives? None, right? Obviously, instead, each serves as a *reference document* to those who will subsequently speculate on possible risks.

There is only one truly objective source for risk identification and that is historical information gleaned from prior projects. However, even this information requires subjective interpolation as to whether the comparison is appropriate, since no two projects are the same.

As for the traditional, recommended approach to risk identification, the PMBOK® Guide reports that, "under the leadership of a facilitator, these people generate ideas about project risk. Sources of risk are identified in broad scope and posted for all to examine during the meeting. Risks are then categorized by type of risk, and their definitions are sharpened." These three sentences are the only ones I could find throughout the PMBOK® Guide to explain *how* risks are actually derived. It is obvious that if a risk is not thought of by any of the individuals participating in the risk identification process, that risk will not appear on the final risk list.

The second introduction of subjectivity is with respect to assessing estimates of impact severity and probability of occurrence. As the PMBOK® Guide rightfully notes, "assessing risk probability may be difficult because expert judgment is used, often without benefit of historical data."

Scope

Two observations can be made with respect to the scope of risks included in the Risk Management methodology. First, the list of risks is finite, based on what is flagged during risk identification. Second, identified risks may or may not have anything to do with project momentum.

As has been repeatedly presented elsewhere in this subsection, the combined set of Risk Management procedures are applied to a finite list of risks as developed during the risk identification process. In other words, if an event is not initially identified as a risk, then that event will not be subjected to the follow-on Risk Management processes of quantitative and qualitative analysis, risk response planning, and risk monitoring and control.

Furthermore, Risk Management considers for inclusion events that may or may not have any bearing on the achievement of time-related performance on the project. Remember that the key factor for deciding what constitutes a risk is whether project objectives are threatened or made more possible. Project objectives can include cost, schedule, quality, or any number of other variables of value to the project's owners and sponsors, beyond timely completion.

Monitoring

In Risk Management, monitoring entails attention to a watch list that is directly tied to previously identified risks. As for identification of new risks, these are flagged only if they satisfy the same criteria as used during initial risk identification.

Risk monitoring and control, which constitutes the culmination of all prior planning, qualifying, and quantifying activities, is applied to whatever risks are on the radar screen. In other words, if a risk has been previously identified (during risk identification) and chosen for subsequent observation (during qualitative and quantitative analysis), then that risk is subjected to monitoring and control. However, if a risk surfaces during the life of the project, unless that risk is detected during iterative risk identification cycles, it will not be monitored or controlled.

Response

A noteworthy feature of Risk Management is that its response program is well planned and orchestrated long before the appearance of the risk.

A significant characteristic of Risk Management is that it attempts to pre-plan that which is essentially unknown. To illustrate this point, consider how football players plan for their next engagement. In a grueling and repetitive set of practices, the team rehearses different defensive and offensive plays. They run different patterns that they coordinate with unique signals.

But what they will not do is attempt to speculate on what the other team will do, play-by-play, and how they will respond in like kind. Just imagine how ridiculous it would be for a team's playbook to include predictions of the other team's likely plays—moment to moment, in sequence, and in detail. Clearly, the most that any team can do to prepare for the next game is develop a set of well-honed maneuvers that can be called into action on a moment's notice, as deemed appropriate by the head coach or the quarterback, in response to the conditions on the playing field at that time!

As you will soon learn, Dilemma Control involves the development of canned responses, which is in stark contrast to Risk Management's strategy. The latter requires predicting which events will occur and planning structured responses to them well in advance of their occurrence.

Risk Management's philosophy on *response* boils down to four options: avoidance, transference, mitigation, and acceptance. Risk avoidance involves "changing the project plan to eliminate the risk or condition or to protect the project objectives from its impact." Risk transfer amounts to "seeking to shift the consequences of a risk to a third party together with ownership of the response." Risk mitigation "seeks to reduce the probability and/or consequences of an adverse risk event to an acceptable threshold." Risk acceptance means that the "project team has decided not to change the project plan to deal with a risk or is unable to identify any other suitable response strategy."

Complexity

As a general observation, Risk Management is fairly complex. It involves six steps, each with numerous substeps, qualitative and quantitative analyses, the convening of subject matter experts, and fairly rigorous operational structure. Not lean, Risk Management is an inconvenient and inappropriate methodology for response to daily issues.

Risk Management involves quite a few technical steps that are required to link the earliest speculation of a potential risk with the final response to that same risk. Specifically, it involves:

- Determining a risk that might affect the project
- Documenting the characteristics of a risk
- Performing a qualitative analysis of the risk
- Prioritizing the effects of a risk on project objectives
- Measuring the probability and consequences of a risk
- Estimating the implications of the risk on project objectives
- Developing procedures and techniques to enhance opportunities and reduce threats to project objectives, as pertaining to the identified risk
- Monitoring residual risks that emanate from the identified risk
- Executing risk reduction plans
- Evaluating the effectiveness of the risk reduction plan

It should be obvious that this series of structured steps is not compatible with a program of flexible and timely response to countless issues that arise on any project on any given day.

DILEMMA CONTROL, A NEW PROJECT MANAGEMENT METHODOLOGY

In this section we will describe Dilemma Control, including an explanation of how it differs from Risk Management, a recognized set of project management processes.

Comparison of Risk Management and Dilemma Control

In a moment I will describe Dilemma Control, so you understand what it is and what it does. Before I do, however, I'd like to contrast Risk Management and Dilemma Control so there is no confusion as to how they differ. From Table 6.1, it should become apparent that they are not the same thing!

Table 6-1

Comparison of
Risk Management
and Dilemma
Control

Variable	Risk Management	Dilemma Control
Threshold	Focused on major issues, called risks	Focused on minor issues, called dilemmas
Timing	Primarily a pre-project planning methodology	Primarily a real time methodology employed *during* the project
Deciding Factor	Project objectives	Project momentum
Orientation	On events	On people
Objectivity	Notwithstanding scientific flavor, based on speculation and subjectivity	Essentially objective, based on empirical data plus formulas
Scope	Finite; may have time component, may not	Infinite; always has a time component; may or may not consider other project objectives
Monitoring	Watch list tied to previously identified risks; awareness of new risks tied to threshold criteria and Deciding Factors	No Watch list; monitoring part of Performance Analytics
Response	Pre-planned; only prepared for what was planned for	Training allows for on-the-spot decision-making and response to whatever comes along
Complexity	Very complex; not lean enough to respond to daily issues	Lean, flexible, simple, responsive

Risk/Dilemma Threshold

Dilemma Control concentrates on the many small things that can go wrong on a project. The Momentum Studies proved that projects are more often, more consistently, and more significantly delayed by the individual or cumulative effect of countless small matters than they are by a handful of major catastrophes. Risk Management is an appropriate and necessary methodology for managing major risks. However, it is not designed or effective as a management tool for what I call *small issues*. Dilemma Control and Risk Management complement one another in that each one covers a category of unknowns that the other does not.

Timing

Dilemma Control is predominantly a real-time methodology that is implemented during the project life cycle and capitalizes on two primary features of Dilemma Control: dilemma response training and *Dilemma Forecasting* (more on these later in this chapter). Where Risk Management is a calculated, planned, and structured program for responding to *major* threats to project *objectives*, Dilemma Control is a program for response to *minor* threats to project *momentum*.

Deciding Factor

As just noted, Dilemma Control focuses on dilemmas that, either individually or collectively, threaten project momentum. By contrast, Risk Management focuses on major risks that threaten project objectives. Dilemma Control is fully compatible with Momentology, which itself is a management methodology that emphasizes cause over effect. An underlying principle of Momentology is that by regulating project momentum desired project time-related objectives are insured.

Orientation

Dilemma Control focuses on the ability of project management participants to respond, in a timely and effective manner, to the sudden appearance of unexpected and typically minor dilemmas. Risk Management, on the other hand, focuses on the identification of potential risks well in advance of their appearance and develops a structured and calculated response intended to avoid, mitigate, or recover from such major risks.

Objectivity

Risk Management, despite a noticeable air of sophistication and scientific basis, is essentially a subjective and speculative methodology. Whatever scientific or mathematical processes exist as part of Risk Management are applied to raw data derived by speculation and subjective judgments. Included in such data would be risk identification, risk probability, risk impact, and risk prioritization. Dilemma Control is a program that responds to dilemmas that have been empirically derived through the course of Performance Diagnostics development. In other words, it is the process of Performance Analytics that generates the list of dilemmas to which Dilemma Control responds. There is no subjectivity involved.

Scope

We can make two important distinctions about the scope of items managed by either system. First, Risk Management is a set of processes that operate on a finite list of risks, as initially identified by subject matter experts. Once this list has been developed, it essentially represents the universe of issues to be handled by Risk Management. In contrast, Dilemma Control does not begin with any list whatsoever. Instead, as dilemmas are identified through Dilemma Forecasting reports, project management reacts to dilemmas using rehearsed response patterns.

Second, Dilemma Control is a methodology devoted to the control of dilemmas that threaten project momentum. Therefore, Dilemma Control is confined to a more limited scope of issues than its counterpart, Risk Management. The latter is concerned with any risks that threaten or enhance project objectives. Since project objectives include more than just completing the project on time, risks may or may not have anything to do with project momentum.

Monitoring

Risk Management includes a process for monitoring the project with an eye toward recognition of the first signs of a risk's emergence. Risk Management can be likened to a tornado watcher, who stares at the clouds in search of signs of an impending tornado and fails to notice the bank robbery happening just below his line of sight. Dilemma Control does not incorporate preconceived notions as to what might be a threat to project momentum. Instead, it relies upon forecasts and insights provided during Performance Analytics and monitors real-time conditions for statistical evidence of a dilemma's first likely arrival.

Response

A key feature of Dilemma Control is the early training of project management personnel in how to handle whatever and as many dilemmas as might come along. Once a dilemma has been forecasted, management can activate preventative and mitigating measures while there is still ample time to make a difference. Once the dilemma occurs, management can implement repair and recovery activities. Contrast this with Risk Management, which develops a response plan at the beginning of the project so that, should the risk occur, a structured response can be employed. An obvious negative to this strategy is that, between when the time that the risk plan is formulated and when the risk actually appears, the pre-planned response may have become outmoded or ineffective.

Complexity

It should be obvious that Risk Management is a fairly sophisticated and complex set of procedures. Because of this, Risk Management is an inappropriate program for responding to the day-to-day, smaller issues that plague every project. Instead, Dilemma Control is a flexible and responsive program of activities designed to handle day-to-day surprises as they come up.

Brief Description of Dilemma Control

So what is Dilemma Control? At the heart of Dilemma Control is an ability to predict dilemmas long before they occur. First, let us define a dilemma. According to the dictionary, a dilemma is, "a situation that requires a choice between options that are or seem equally unfavorable or mutually exclusive." It goes on to say that a dilemma is, "a problem that seems to defy a satisfactory solution."

We need only to clarify what we would consider a "situation" or a "problem," and our definition is complete. Because Dilemma Control is a methodology designed to manage threats to project momentum, a dilemma is any situation, problem, development, or condition that, if ignored, would likely impact project momentum. In terms of structured procedures, Dilemma Control involves six steps:

- Extemporaneous response training
- Dilemma forecasting
- Dilemma response options
- Dilemma elimination or avoidance
- Dilemma mitigation
- Dilemma repair and recovery

Extemporaneous Response Training

A fundamental tenet of Dilemma Control is the necessary training and development of techniques among project management personnel that results in them being skilled at rehearsed, but not planned, responses. The reasoning here is much like that of the baseball player whose daily practice involves learning how to respond to any possible type of pitch. Note that the player does not attempt to speculate on which types of pitch he will experience in a real game, or in what order those pitches will be delivered. Instead, he simply increases his ability to respond to whatever pitch is thrown his way be it curve ball, fast ball, knuckle ball, inside pitch, or up high pitch.

Dilemma Forecasting

Once the project is underway and routine Performance Analytics are performed, thanks to the power of Momentum Science, it is possible for a Performance Analyst to provide project management with reliable forecasts of anticipated or approaching dilemmas. Dilemma Forecasting is the operational trigger for subsequent dilemma response options.

Dilemma Response Options

At this point, project management has the opportunity to respond to the news of an anticipated or approaching dilemma.

Dilemma Elimination or Avoidance

Obviously, this is the preferred response option because it negates any unwanted impact on momentum, by eliminating or bypassing the precipitating event.

Dilemma Mitigation

If the dilemma cannot be completely eliminated or avoided, then the next option would be to take steps to reduce the cumulative effect of the dilemma on project momentum.

Dilemma Repair and Recovery

Unless the dilemma was completely eliminated, dilemma mitigation efforts might not completely neutralize the negative effects of the dilemma on project momentum. Accordingly, some amount of damage to project momentum may occur, and these response options seek to restore project momentum to its predilemma state. For example, suppose that a storm blows a tree branch through your living room window. In this case, "repair" involves replacing the broken pane of glass. However, before you could even temporarily board up the window, your carpets may have sustained significant water damage. As a result, additional "recovery" activities are required to remove and replace the soiled carpet with new flooring.

Benefits of Dilemma Controls

The most significant benefits of Dilemma Control are probably self-apparent. I will list them, nonetheless, if only to give further value to the concept of Momentology.

Fills a Managerial Void

I know of no other project management methodology that deals specifically with the detection, monitoring, and forecasting of, or response to, dilemmas that threaten project momentum. When we recall that projects are more often delayed by the individual or cumulative impact of minor dilemmas than they are by the occasional impact of major risks, Dilemma Control becomes a powerful, new arrow in the project manager's quiver.

Part of Performance Diagnostics

The opportunity to control dilemmas is made possible by the ability of Momentology to accurately and reliably predict dilemmas long before they occur. In Momentology jargon this is called *Dilemma Forecasting*. Remember the discussion in the Preface about how we, as schedulers, rarely tell the project manager anything he does not already know? With Dilemma Forecasting, we can break that mold once and for all.

7

Introduction to Momentology

Anyone who has ever worked on a project intuitively knows that *every project has a certain momentum*. You can just *feel* it! The project's overall momentum is affected by worker attitudes that result in slowdowns before holidays, hunting season, and anticipated strikes. It is equally affected by ramp-ups that reflect learning curves, a return to work from vacation, and so on.

More precisely, it has multiple, overlapping momentums of ever-changing rates. Moreover, not only does the project *itself* have a momentum, so do its component parts. Each subcontractor's work has a momentum, just as each geographic or functional part of the project has its own unique momentum. Momentum is also affected by the quantity and quality of labor, supervision, materials, equipment, and information.

It has often been said that a project manager is similar to a conductor of an orchestra. His job is to keep everybody in tempo, playing the same tune at the same rate (hence, the baton). Indeed, most project management concerns center around the coordinated flow of work. This is what I call Management by Momentum, or Momentum Management.

Momentum Management provides a helpful and innovative way to manage projects. It offers a refreshing yet intuitive context in which project management functions are carried out. Professional bowlers rarely aim for the pins; they aim for lane markings, called arrows. If the ball rolls across a specific arrow, then the pins *will* fall, and this illustrates the main concept behind Momentum Management. It allows management to focus on the short-term causes, rather than the long-term effects, of momentum shift. No longer must the project manager wait for the impacts of such catalysts to manifest in the form of slipping total-float or SPI levels[1] before devising a reactive plan.

---

[1]The Schedule Performance Index is an indicator of project status generated through EVMS.

On time-sensitive projects, Momentum Management allows project managers to achieve promised dates by managing the project's momentum. Its main features include the following:

- A measurable rate of project *Performance Intensity*
- Proportional (free and total) float allocation per activity (Discrete Activity Float)
- The ability to determine the project's Schedule Achievement Potential
- Several innovative and powerful definitions of Criticality
- A structured process for creation of relationship-durations
- A methodology for control of field administrative responsibilities
- An ability to predict schedule slippage before it happens
- The ability to influence outcomes in a way never before possible
- The ability to generate outcome projections, sooner and more accurately

Momentum is a measure of action and is expressed as a rate. When I set out in 1983 to find a way to measure and depict project momentum, the initial challenge was to discover a single unit of measure that would work equally well on all project types, sizes, and locations. It had to take into account different crew configurations, different cost parameters, different contractual constraints, and so on. After two years, I found the unit of measure. From there, it was all downhill. Equipped with a measurable momentum unit, it was possible to establish required rates and compare those to actual rates. As a simple example, assume I need to travel at 50 miles per hour for three hours in order to arrive in Salt Lake City for a meeting. If, after the first hour, I have traveled only 48 miles, then I know that during the second hour I need to travel an additional 52 miles, in order to get back on schedule.

Momentum Management, then, boils down to monitoring performance on a real-time basis. No longer must a project manager wait until the end of the month to learn that his project has lost six days of total-float. With Momentum Management, he can monitor performance rates on a daily basis, per contractor, and take corrective actions before any time is lost. In this critical sense, Momentum Management is a proactive science that gives us catch-up rates, cruise control settings, and Dilemma Forecasting.

BRIEF HISTORY OF MOMENTOLOGY

I created Momentology to fill an obvious void in project management's ability to effectively coordinate and orchestrate the disparate and often conflicting performance efforts of the project's many participants. Momentology is a catchy word that represents the entire combination of Momentum Theory, Momentum Science, and Applied Momentum.

Momentology grew out of early observations, after about five years in the Scheduling Practice, that conventional scheduling efforts really didn't add much value to the execution phase of the project. In fact, I found that schedule significance and project maturity were inversely proportional. That is, the overall utility of the project schedule in its traditional application seemed to diminish at a steady rate, as the project moved along the continuum from start to finish.[2]

---

[2]No doubt, one explanation for this phenomenon is that the further into the project life cycle one goes, the more "stale" the original plan becomes.

Momentology was created to fix what was broken about the way we were (and, sadly, still are) managing our schedules. My early observations concluded that traditional Scheduling Practice methods failed to support project management's need and desire to act proactively. They failed to shed much new light, offer new insights, or suggest new solutions. Mostly, they simply regurgitated what project management somehow already knew.

In the follow subsections I will summarize those early observations and the conclusions I reached about what might be needed if we were/are to improve the Scheduling Practice. I will conclude this overview by presenting a high-level summary of Momentology.

Notes on Scheduling Deficiencies

I began my scheduling career in 1977. My first project was the 72-acre, $72 million, and seven-building world headquarters for McDonnell Douglas Automation at st. Lousi, Missouri. Over the next few years, I was involved in several dozen projects ranging from $2 million to $200 million. Project types included healthcare, defense, transportation, manufacturing, retail, and high-rise construction. These projects were located all across the United States and were run by project managers whose experience levels extended from the novice to the well seasoned. I provide this brief synopsis of the projects and their leadership to lend credence to the following statement: *My schedules didn't seem to be doing my customers much good.* It didn't matter what the project type or the project manager's experience level. Even though I was providing properly developed and executed schedules, they weren't helping. They weren't telling the project manager anything he didn't already know. Beyond that, my schedules didn't seem to provide any special insights that he couldn't get from any number of other sources, including his own gut instincts.

For my part, I found that my daily activities were more focused on keeping the schedule reflective of what was happening on the project than the other way around. This seemed wrong to me, as if the tail were wagging the dog. In college I had been taught that the desired sequence was *"plan the work, and then work the plan."* Yet here, out in the real world, it seemed that the rule was *"perform the work, then reflect it in the plan."* I was disillusioned.

Sometime in 1981 I conducted a study of assorted projects with the intent of identifying where traditional Scheduling efforts fell short of what was expected and finding legitimate ways to improve our craft. What follows are some of the more significant observations I made by interviewing my schedule's stakeholders and by studying the details of the projects (and their schedules), specifically. They are presented here, in no particular order:

- Logic sessions were poorly attended.
- Upper management remained aloof from Scheduling processes and discussions.
- Scheduling data were, all too often, a secondary consideration in project management decision-making.
- Scheduling products were mostly standardized, not customized.

- Only about 50 percent of the time was the Scheduler invited to participate in Strategic Planning sessions.
- The primary demands upon the Project Scheduler, once the project began, were to estimate project completion and identify activity criticality.
- Scheduling reports were rarely studied; most often they were just referenced, and then only randomly, not systematically.
- Scheduling reports were little more than after-the-fact statements of project status.
- There was no formal monitoring and measuring of schedule compliance in terms of pace or direction, what I would later call *Momentum*.
- Performance measurement focused on snapshot status, not ongoing trends.
- Project performers viewed (and therefore consumed) total-float with a use-it-or-lose-it attitude.
- The concept of the critical-path was all-important to the Scheduler, while it was of dubious value or interest to the project manager.

The more I considered these observations, the more certain I was that, as Project Schedulers, we were not meeting the informational needs of our chief customer, the project manager.

Conclusions About How to Improve Schedule Management

To be sure, these reflections made it rather easy to develop a list of things one could do to improve the Practice, if one was so inclined. What I was especially interested in was finding that *one* major, unique innovation that would dramatically and forever improve the Practice's quality and value to project management.

Here are the most significant conclusions I reached from the preceding observations, as I searched for that one major, unique innovation:

- Effective project management requires being proactive and deliberate, not reactionary and impulsive.
- The single, most-important function of project management is to orchestrate the work.
- Worker productivity is most easily measured and most dramatically influenced by changes in project momentum.
- Project management, to be most effective, should concentrate on project momentum.
- The function of the Project Schedule, first and foremost and at all times, is to support the *time*-related aspects of project management.
- To help project management incubate and sustain project momentum, Project Schedules must be able to measure and depict the *rate* at which work is being performed. I later came to call that rate Performance Intensity.
- True performance measurement must reconcile the *rate* of work placement with that rate's relationship to time-based goals. Earned Value did not accomplish this.
- The relationship between work performance intensity and its consequential effects on project momentum must be made apparent to project management and work performers alike, in a timely and accurate manner.

- Work performers must be held accountable for gains or losses in that all-critical public asset, total-float.

- Higher priority should be placed on the achievement of short-term objectives than on long-term goals.

- With consistent accuracy and reliability, Scheduling products should identify future obstacles to, and opportunities for, momentum gain and maintenance. I later called these Soft Ground Advisories.

- The Scheduling Practice should provide project management with reasonably accurate warnings of future threats to project momentum, long before their actual occurrence. This was later called Dilemma Forecasting.

- Project management should be alerted to changes in performance intensity, even subtle ones, just as soon as they occur. No more month-end sports casting, where the gain or loss of precious time is announced uselessly and after-the-fact.

OVERVIEW OF MOMENTUM THEORY

It came rather easily, actually: an understanding of what that *one major, unique innovation* would be. I wanted to create a measure of performance intensity.[3] Such a measure would be equivalent to the more familiar *miles per hour*. That was it: I wanted to invent a miles-per-hour value for the monitoring and measuring of true project advancement.

Momentum Theory is based on the notion that, with the passage of time, unperformed but scheduled work results in an increasing ratio between *required performance* and *time available* to perform the required work. On a cross-country trip, each time you pull off the road to eat or rest, the ratio between the amount of remaining miles and the amount of remaining time (assuming the arrival deadline does not slip) increases. I call this the Theory of Workload Backlog.

Duration-Day: The Numerator

Of course, the immediate challenge was to find a common unit of measure that would be equally meaningful no matter what the activity's scope. This unit of measure would have to correlate gallons of paint, tons of steel, yards of concrete, feet of cable, truckloads of dirt, and so on.[4]

My early work took me to Philadelphia where I consulted with mathematicians at Pennsylvania State University. I remember sitting in a student desk and watching two or three scientists argue with one another, their hands busily scribbling formulas on a chalkboard. It didn't take long for me to realize that the ultimate formula for Performance

---

[3]Performance Intensity is not a productivity measure, the latter being a quantity-based measure of installed work volume.

[4]This is where Performance Intensity differs from traditional labor productivity. Productivity is not comparable across disparate activities; one cannot compare the productivity of dissimilar activities, such as the pulling of cable or the installation of sinks. By contrast, Performance Intensity provides comparability across all activities, regardless of the nature of the scope they represent.

Intensity could not contain square root symbols. No, I wanted something immediately understandable to the average project member, the ones wearing jeans and work boots.

I thanked the wiry-haired geniuses for their time and returned home, where I commenced work on defining Performance Intensity. Before long I had settled on the notion that the activity-duration itself could be used to depict a quantity of work performance. It took a little while for me to overcome the deep-rooted perspective that the activity-duration was a measure of *time*, not *quantity*. But once I accepted the new paradigm, things began to fall into place.

In order to distinguish the two uses of the numerical value associated with an activity, I established a new term: the Duration-Day. The label, used to describe the numeric value representing an estimate of time required to perform the work of an activity, continued to be called a "duration." However, when that same numeric value is construed as a *quantity* of work performance, it was called a "Duration-Day."

Workdays: The Denominator

Having defined the numerator in the Performance Intensity rate formula, I next needed to identify a unit of measure to serve as the denominator. In other words, just as one drives so many miles (quantity) per hour (time), Performance Intensity described the achievement of a certain quantity of performed work over a period of time. With the Duration-Day, I already had the "quantity of work performance." I needed to define a unit of time to act as a denominator.

I found a solution in an already established scheduling term, *workday*. Most scheduling software programs provide a calendar feature that allows for distinguishing between workdays and non-workdays, the latter being days not available for work performance. I had my denominator.

Performance Intensity: The Elusive Miles-Per-Hour

The basic formula for Performance Intensity is simply Work Performance divided by Time Consumption (see Figure 7-1). The process for determining Performance Intensity involved aggregating the Duration-Days for a particular set of activities (work performance) and dividing by the number of workdays required for their performance (time consumption).

The default formula is for future work and yields *planned* Performance Intensity. For example, on a new schedule before work begins, one would aggregate the Original Duration-Days for all activities in the schedule (planned performance) and divide by the number of available workdays provided by contract (allocated time). The result, which is the *average* Performance Intensity for the entire project, is called the Cruise Control Setting. This is a theoretical value since work intensity on most projects follows a bell curve shape, not a straight-line average. Nevertheless, the cruise control setting is a simple and quick way to measure and discuss Performance Intensity requirements and achievement.

Performance Intensity (P.I.)

Basic Formula

Work Performance
Time Consumption

Definitions

Performance = Aggregate
 Duration-Days

Duration-Day = the amount of work
performance required to reduce a
remaining duration by one day; also,
a Crew Day

Time= designated 24-hour periods
during which work is not precluded

Primary PI Uses

Planned P.I.
$$\frac{\text{Planned Performance}}{\text{Allocated TIme}} = \text{PPI}$$

Actual P.I.
$$\frac{\text{ActualPerformance}}{\text{Time Consumed}} = \text{API}$$

Catch-Up P..I.
$$\frac{\text{Planned Performance}}{\text{Time Available}} = \text{CPI}$$

Cruise Control Setting
PPI on Initial Schedule = CCS

Figure 7-1

Performance
Intensity
Definitions

Other uses of the Performance Intensity measure include Actual and Catch-Up Performance Intensity. Actual Performance Intensity is computed by dividing the number of Duration-Days accomplished (actual performance) by the number of workdays required for that performance (time consumed). Catch-up Performance Intensity involves dividing the number of available remaining workdays (time available) into the aggregate Remaining Duration-Days for activities less than 100 percent complete (required performance).

Momentum: Purposeful Performance Intensity

It has been noted elsewhere in this book that momentum is casually defined as *pace and direction*. I arrived at this definition upon acknowledging a deficiency in the Earned Value Management System, namely that its measure of schedule performance fails to take into account *where* the work is being performed.

The Schedule Performance Index (SPI) is a ratio of Earned Value and the planned value of completed works and is derived from the formula SPI = BCWP divided by BCWS. The Budgeted Cost for Work Scheduled (BCWS) is derived from the budgets for all activities whose completion has been planned. BCWP represents the planned cost of the work allocated to the completed activities and is called the *Earned Value*.

To better explain my complaint, consider the analogy of a cross-country truck driver, whose progress we are monitoring using Earned Value formulas. We begin by estimating that the distance to be traveled is 200 miles and we determine that the truck's fuel economy is 10 miles per gallon. We therefore expect the trip to consume 20 gallons of fuel. During the course of the trip, it is reported that the truck has traveled 100 miles and has consumed 10 gallons of fuel. Applying the preceding SPI formula, we would conclude that the "project" is on schedule. However, this formula fails to take into account that the 100 miles driven were *traveled in the wrong direction!*

As I pondered this deficiency in the Earned Value methodology, I resolved to not let momentum make the same mistake. *Direction,* I quickly noted, was as important to the definition of momentum as was *pace* (Performance Intensity). Later, I went on to establish parameters for measuring and monitoring the relative priority (direction) of work performed. For now, it is adequate that you simply understand that momentum considers both the rate (pace) and the priority (direction) of performed work.

OVERVIEW OF MOMENTUM SCIENCE

By 1983 I had successfully incorporated the fundamental momentum concepts and formulas into the mainstream Scheduling Practice. As corporate director of Project Controls for a national construction management company, I was given permission to apply Momentum Theory and Science to all projects in the Northeast region. At once, 14 projects became the guinea pigs to test Momentology on real live jobsites.

During the routine monthly schedule updates for these projects, project momentum statistics were computed and reported. By using the scheduling software's ability to filter and sort activities geographically, by responsibility, and by phase, I was able to provide

Momentum data about each responsible party, each intermediate and contractual milestone, and each physical portion of the overall project. A particular episode stands out in my mind as an excellent example of how Momentum Analysis can improve the project manager's ability to coordinate and direct work execution.

An Interesting Story

It was in the summer of 1984 when I received a call from a very distraught project manager, John Cronin. I had just been to his jobsite a week earlier to conduct the regular monthly schedule update, so I was surprised to hear from him so soon thereafter. He was calling to inform me that he expected an Operators' strike to commence on the following Monday morning and asked what we should do. I told him that I would return to his jobsite on Friday in order to "capture" project status as of the last workday before the strike's commencement.

The strike lasted three weeks and I returned on the day immediately following the end of the strike in order to capture the project's status once again. By comparing the status immediately before and immediately after the strike using momentum formulas, I was able to measure and depict the clearly depressed levels of work performance during the strike. This information was useful in subsequent negotiations between the subcontractors, the general contractor, and the owner, with respect to impact claims now on the table. But the real value of the momentum statistics generated through these updates had nothing at all to do with the strike.

About a week after the strike ended, I returned to the jobsite to perform the next scheduled monthly update. Back at home, on a Sunday afternoon while watching football, I decided to do some crude comparisons among the four updates (two before the strike and two after the strike). To my surprise and excitement, I discovered that there was a distinct and dramatic reduction in Performance Intensity with respect to a particular subcontractor.

By now, I had mastered the technique of Momentum Vectoring, whereby I would triangulate Performance Intensity values according to geography *and* responsibility *and* time frame. Doing so, I determined that there was a noticeable slowdown by the mechanical subcontractor at the west wing of the second floor. On Monday I called John with this discovery. Honoring my request, he visited the second floor, west wing, and reported back to me a few hours later that, "nothing was out of the ordinary." I hung up the phone, disappointed, and tried to forget the matter. But the next day I called John again and asked him to pay another visit to the second floor. He did so and his findings were the same. Disgusted, I boxed up my momentum paperwork and shoved them onto a dusty basement bookshelf.

You can imagine my surprise when, a few days later, I received an anxious call from John Cronin. If there is such a thing as blushing over the phone, John was doing it. He was talking excitedly and saying something about a Coca-Cola can. I asked him to slow down and start from the beginning. He said that he had had a dream the night before and when he awoke he could only remember one tidbit: a Coca-Cola can precariously balanced atop an unfinished plumbing pipe. As he lay in bed he remembered that each time he had visited the second floor, west wing, he had noticed, up in the overhead space, an empty soda can perched high above, on an unfinished plumbing pipe. Now suspicious that work was, in fact, *not* being performed, he decided to conduct a surprise inspection of the west wing by approaching the floor from an undetected route.

"Do you know what a lookout is, Murray?" he asked. I responded that I did and described someone who watches for the boss while other members of the team play cards, sleep, or simply chew the fat. If the lookout spots the approach of supervision, the colleagues are alerted and the workers quickly begin to look busy.

"So what's the real scoop?" I asked. John proceeded to inform me that the mechanical subcontractor's foreman had been gone for a number of days, as his wife had just had a baby. "I am so embarrassed," John continued. "How in the world could you know, from 800 miles away, what was happening on *my* jobsite, when I didn't know what was going on just outside my trailer window?" Obviously I was elated that my momentum calculations were, in fact, reliable after all.

Other Improvements Under the Name of Momentum

Inspired by this and other early successes, I decided to intensify the use of Momentum by expanding its application to all of the projects in the Southeast region of the company. Over the next few years I accumulated additional experience applying Momentum to real projects. I also collected extensive empirical data that would be beneficial in subsequent development of Momentum Science, the name I gave to the technical aspects of Momentology.

Specifically, Momentum Science includes a refinement of all underlying formulas as well as customized software to perform routine momentum calculations quickly and easily. Keep in mind that when I first created Performance Intensity, the personal computer had not yet been invented, and I made all calculations on a hand calculator. But, over the first few years of Momentology, computer technology advanced to where I had a computer humming on the floor, and momentum curves crawling across my desktop monitor like an EKG.

You may be wondering why, if the breakthroughs I just described occurred in the mid-1980s, I am only now unveiling Momentum to the project management community. The answer to that question has to do with innovative urges that were still pulsing through my veins, as I worked on the Momentum algorithms.

Specifically, I began to think of *other* ways to improve the Critical Path Method. Keep in mind that at this point in time, CPM had been around for roughly 25 years and, unfortunately, little had changed in the way we were using it. I reasoned that the rollout of Momentology would provide the perfect excuse to introduce other innovations, ones aimed directly at correcting deficiencies in the contemporaneous Scheduling Practice.

I started by making a list of the more irritating aspects of CPM about which my colleagues and I had spent many a lunch hour complaining. Here is what my list looked like:

- Total-float is a measure of uncommitted time available to a *string* of activities, and yet it is routinely reported (redundantly) against *individual* activities.

- Relationship-durations seem to be defined rather arbitrarily. I could find no clear instructions in *any* of the college textbooks I examined as to how to properly derive relationship-durations.

- The term "critical" was excessively and inconsistently used. Activities were deemed *critical* simply because they resided on a critical-path. However, my common sense said that activities at the far end of the critical-path, perhaps two years away, could hardly be considered "critical." Moreover, keenly aware of the dubious basis for most activity-durations, I was more than tempered in my declarations that one path was "critical" and another path was not.

- Common practice of the day (unfortunately, not much different today) did not include any structured assessment of performer adherence to the Schedule. Sporadic acknowledgement of out-of-sequence work was as close as it came.

- Likewise, there was no process for evaluating the ability of the Schedule to bounce back from a delay or, for that matter, to predict a delay in advance of its occurrence.

- The project manager's daily To Do List was quite often independent of the project schedule. Priorities for the project manager's daily activities in no way correlated with the priorities reflected in the Schedule, as indicated through total-float values.

I could go on, but I believe you get the point. As I struggled to put finishing touches to the momentum algorithms, it occurred to me that the introduction of Momentum Theory might also be the perfect opportunity to introduce improvements to the CPM method. This realization was the genesis for what turned out to be another ten years of developmental work.

Three Major Innovations

By the mid-1990s I had completed development of a half-dozen or more ancillary innovations, all sharing the common goal of providing the project manager with better information than he had ever had with which he could coordinate and orchestrate the work. At last, I was prepared to package the entire set of innovations under the name Momentology. For a short while I grappled with the question of whether to change the umbrella term from Momentology to something else, since many of the intrinsic innovations did not deal *directly* with Momentum formulas. In the end, however, I decided to stay with the Momentology label since all the innovations contributed to more effective Momentum Management.

In this chapter I will only present a glimpse of three such ancillary innovations and leave the remainder for treatment in a subsequent volume of this Momentum series. I hope these synopses inspire within you a renewed appreciation for the types of information we can provide to our primary customer, the project manager—if only we try.

Discrete Activity Float

I had always felt that it was important that each activity have its own Discrete Activity Float value, and so I set out to construct a formula that would proportionately allocate a string's total-float to each resident activity. I had no idea how difficult this assignment would be, and it took me several years to work out the algorithm for Discrete Activity Float. Simplifying the math for purposes of this chapter, in order for each activity on a path to be assigned a proportionate share of the path's total-float value I used the duration as the basis for proportioning. This new value accomplished a few things:

- It brought *fairness* to project performance. No longer would an upstream activity be allowed to consume a path's float, leaving downstream activities to "work without a net."

- It brought *realism* to scheduling reports, by superseding the redundant statement of total-float alongside each activity of a path. Now, each activity was allocated its discrete, additive, and comparable amount of total-float.

- It brought *urgency* to project execution. Since Discrete Activity Float values are typically much smaller than path float values, activities acquire a greater awareness that time is a natural resource in limited supply.

Relationship-Duration Definitions

Momentum Studies performed over a ten-year period on hundreds of failed schedules had convinced me that approximately 40 percent of all *actual* critical paths travel through the relationship-durations (start-to-start, finish-to-finish, and finish-to-start), while the other 60 percent travel through the activity-durations. I had further discovered that roughly 90 percent of delays that occur *on the relationship-durations* are due to administrative, not productive, deficiencies. (We will cover this in Chapter 10.)

As a result, I developed an understanding of what should be taken into consideration when setting relationship-durations, the term I created to represent the numeric value assigned to any relationship type. With this change, relationship-durations were put on equal footing with activity-durations.

This equality is important because, in the current practice of Scheduling, strict guidelines exist for the development of *activity*-durations, including a popular conviction among Scheduling experts that there should be an alignment between work scope and assumptions about resource commitments and performance rates.

Yet, when it comes to how relationship-durations are quantified, I found that there are no established guidelines and, as a result, relationship-duration values are entirely subjective. So, as a critical element of Momentology, though not specifically related to the Momentum unit of measure, I created the Administrative Time Gap and Productive Time Gap values, as well as a process for determining relationship-durations. (See chapter 10 for more on this topic.)

Additional Measures of Criticality

Finally, throughout my Scheduling career I have been bothered by how casually we declare something as "critical." In fact, for most of us, an activity is *critical* simply because it resides on a critical-path. But, in realty, this is quite often not the case. Using Discrete Activity Float, we quickly see that some activities are more critical than others, regardless of whether they are on the critical-path, or not. Beyond total-float, there are several other ways to judge criticality including *Density*, *Buoyancy*, *Potency*, *Activity Placement*, and *Activity Profiles*.

MOMENTUM SCIENCE, A NEW SET OF PERFORMANCE MEASURES

Momentum Management draws its strength from a complex foundation of principles, axioms, algorithms, and processes, called Momentum Science. Table 8-5 in Chapter 8 summarizes the body of work encompassing Momentum Science but is a bit misleading in that it seems to imply that all Momentum Science culminates in Dilemma Forecasting. Actually, Dilemma Forecasting is only one benefit among many that come from Momentum Science. What follows is a short explanation of the many fascinating processes and calculations that, collectively, make it possible *to actually predict dilemmas before they occur*.

Momentum Science Big Picture

In order to accurately predict dilemmas before they occur, Momentum Science employs a complex set of formulas that take into consideration three key, interrelated variables: Performance Diagnostics, Schedule Achievement Potential, and Schedule Credibility. Of course, no one variable will tell the whole story. To appreciate why this is so, you must first understand what each of these indicators reveals about the project:

- **Performance Diagnostics** refers to Momentology processes that monitor, measure, and report on overall project performance, in terms of Management Performance, Execution Performance, and Resource Performance.

- **Schedule Achievement Potential** refers to Momentology calculations that compute a schedule's probability of achieving its time-based objectives based on the cumulative measures of Schedule Vulnerability and Schedule Resiliency.

- **Schedule Credibility** refers to Momentology calculations that compute a schedule's overall believability by considering Schedule Relevancy and Volatility.

Obviously, indicators derived under these three headings cannot be interpreted in a vacuum. For instance:

- Neither Performance Diagnostics nor Schedule Achievement Potential are a trustworthy assessments if the underlying schedule lacks credibility.

- Likewise, Performance Diagnostics may indicate a well-performing execution team, but that may not be enough to overcome insurmountable obstacles, if so indicated by depressingly low Schedule Achievement Potential readings.

- Or, we may assume unwarranted optimism upon seeing highly promising Schedule Achievement Potential figures, if actual performance in the field has been abysmal, as may be indicated by unimpressive Performance Diagnostics data.

Now, let's consider each of these categories of analysis separately.

Performance Diagnostics

Performance Diagnostics refers to a suite of Momentology processes that monitor, measure, and report on overall project performance, including Management, work execution, and resources. To put these three areas of performance analysis into a memorable context, return to our earlier example of the long distance truck driver. The "project" is the timely delivery of a shipment from one end of the country to another. At any time, if we were to inquire on the overall *status* of the project, we would want to know three things:

- **About the driver (Management)** Is this an experienced truck driver? Is he familiar with the roads? Does he know how to handle the rig? Has he gotten enough sleep? Has he had any accidents on *this* trip?
- **About the trip itself (execution)** How is the trip going? Are we on schedule (pace)? Are we still on the planned route (direction)? Have we had to detour and, if so, when can we look forward to being back on the planned route? What is our average speed (Performance Intensity)?
- **About the truck (resources)** How is the engine performing? Are the tires okay? Brakes? What kind of fuel economy are we getting (i.e., EVMS)? Are we detecting any looming mechanical problems?

Management Performance Diagnostics

Management Performance Diagnostics are Momentology calculations that compute project management's overall performance in terms of *P.R.O.J.E.C.T.* performance criteria: *P*lanned *R*esources, *O*bjective *J*udgments, *E*ffective *C*ommunications, and *T*roubleshooting. This diagnostic set covers an area that traditional project management support systems completely fail to monitor, measure, or evaluate. How well does the project manager attend to administrative actions, allowances for which constitute the primary justification for Administrative Time Gaps? The project manager is not above accountability, and a meaningful and objective score card of his performance is not only appropriate, it is essential, if overall project performance is to be comprehensively monitored and reported.

Execution Performance Diagnostics

Execution Performance Diagnostics are Momentology calculations that compute a project's overall Execution Performance in terms of Performance Intensity and Performance Coordination. This diagnostic set cuts to the heart of what all of us in the project management business consider to be *real* "performance measurement." In Chapter 11, I present my arguments for why, admittedly swimming against the tide, I do *not* consider the Earned Value Management System a performance measurement system in the above sense. If you examine its underlying formulas, EVMS measures the efficiency of consumed resources—most particularly, money. Even Schedule Performance Indices are based on the consumption of labor dollars and what interpolations might be made from such data.

To my thinking, *real* performance measurement has to do with measuring the performance of the execution efforts. To derive such measurement, Momentum Science looks at the two sides of the momentum coin: pace and direction.

Performance Intensity involves Momentology calculations that monitor, evaluate, and report on an alignment of Execution Performance levels with planned pacing within the Execution Schedule. Conversely, Performance Coordination entails Momentology calculations that monitor, evaluate, and report on the alignment of execution efforts with charted sequencing and priorities within the Execution Schedule.

Resource Performance Diagnostics

Resource Performance Diagnostics refers to Momentology calculations that incorporate and summarize various Resource Performance indices, including EVMS statistics. This diagnostics set is hardly an unimportant area of study. Returning to our truck driver example, fuel economy is a big deal. Poor fuel economy not only threatens the project's budget, it also threatens the schedule. More frequent pit stops translate into lost time. On a real project, the information provided by EVMS is extremely important. But please note, EVMS is not synonymous with Resource Performance, as Momentum Science looks at other aspects of Resource Performance beyond EVMS, such as labor productivity, the effect on the schedule of cumulative impacts brought on by multiple scope changes, and so on.

Schedule Achievement Potential

Again referring to Table 8-5, the second major component of Momentum Science is Schedule Achievement Potential, a suite of Momentology calculations that compute a schedule's probability of achieving its time-based objectives, based on the cumulative determinations of Schedule Vulnerability and Schedule Resiliency.

Schedule Vulnerability Diagnostics

Schedule Vulnerability refers to Momentology calculations that compute a schedule's likelihood of incurring a time impact, based on the cumulative probabilities of its subordinate MCPs. You will find that many of the calculations used to determine schedule-level data are equally valid at subordinate levels.

For instance, Schedule Vulnerability is merely a reflection of collective MCP Vulnerability. An MCP is a Momentum Control Point, which you would recognize as a point of confluence where multiple activity paths come together in a schedule. Various momentum readings are taken at each identified MCP and, much like the way meteorologists gather wind and precipitation readings from sensors and detectors located all around town, an overall sense of schedule-level conditions can be gleaned from the readings of numerous MCPs.

In turn, *MCP* vulnerability is a reflection of collective Waterway Vulnerability. A Waterway is a Momentology term that refers to a logic-tied string of activities that, in CPM jargon, would typically be called an activity path. Waterway Vulnerability is derived from Activity Vulnerability that, in turn, examines *five* sets of criteria.

Criticality Factors Criticality Factors are Momentology variables that reflect a weighted average across Density, Buoyancy, and Potency and determine an accordant probability of time impact. Criticality is determined by carefully monitoring and analyzing the following variables:

- **Density** Momentology calculations that express the duration as a percent of composite duration plus Discrete Activity Float and determine the probability of time impact accordingly.

- **Buoyancy** Momentology calculations that express Discrete Activity Float as a percent of composite duration and determine the probability of time impact accordingly.

- **Potency** Momentology calculations that express Discrete Activity Float as a percent of worst Discrete Activity Float and determine the probability of time impact accordingly.

Relationships Aggregation   Relationships Aggregation refers to Momentology calculations that evaluate and describe an activity in terms of the number of activities upon whose performance it depends.

Confluence Aggregation   Confluence Aggregation refers to Momentology calculations that evaluate an activity in terms of the number of Waterways upon which it is influenced.

Activity Placement   Activity Placement refers to Momentology calculations that evaluate an activity's likelihood of being time-impacted by considering its location along the project timeline continuum.

Activity Profiles   Activity Profiles refer to Momentology calculations that categorize and characterize an activity according to performance timing and scope uniqueness attributes.

Schedule Resiliency Diagnostics

Schedule Resiliency is the counterbalance to Schedule Vulnerability in the assessment of Schedule Achievement Potential. Schedule Resiliency Diagnostics refer to Momentology calculations that compute a schedule's likelihood of recovering from a time impact, based on the cumulative probabilities of its subordinate MCPs. Like Schedule Vulnerability, Schedule Resiliency is a roll-up of collective MCP Resiliency data, and so on. The definitions in the following subsections apply to Schedule Resiliency.

MCP Resiliency   MCP Resiliency refers to Momentology calculations that compute a Momentum Control Point's likelihood of recovering from a time impact, based on the cumulative probabilities of its tributary Waterways.

Waterway Resiliency   Waterway Resiliency refers to Momentology calculations that compute a Waterway's likelihood of recovering from a time impact, based on the cumulative probabilities of its resident activities.

Activity Resiliency   Activity Resiliency refers to Momentology calculations that compute an activity's ability to "bounce back" from a time impact, based on various statistical factors, including criticality, relationships aggregation, confluence aggregation, and activity placement.

Criticality Factors   Criticality Factors refer to Momentology calculations that compute a weighted average across Density, Buoyancy, and Potency and determines the probability of recovery from a time impact accordingly:

- **Density** Momentology calculations that express the duration as a percent of composite duration plus Discrete Activity Float and determine the probability of recovery from a time impact accordingly.

- **Buoyancy** Momentology calculations that express Discrete Activity Float as a percent of composite duration and determine the probability of recovery from a time impact accordingly.

- **Potency** Momentology calculations that express Discrete Activity Float as a percent of worst Discrete Activity Float and determine the probability of recovery from a time impact accordingly.

Relationship Aggregation   Relationship Aggregation refers to Momentology calculations that evaluate and describe an activity in terms of the number of activities dependent upon its performance.

Confluence Aggregation   Confluence Aggregation refers to Momentology calculations that evaluate an activity in terms of the number of paths emanating from the activity.

Activity Placement   Activity Placement refers to Momentology calculations that evaluate an activity's ability to recover from a time impact by considering its location along the project timeline continuum.

Schedule Credibility

Schedule Credibility is the third major component of Momentum Science and refers to a suite of Momentology calculations that compute a schedule's overall believability by considering a schedule's Relevancy and its Volatility.

Schedule Relevancy

Schedule Relevancy refers to Momentology calculations that evaluate the ongoing relevancy of the schedule by considering the frequency and magnitude of out-of-sequence work and/or significant variances between planned and actual relationship-durations and activity-durations. Schedule Relevancy is all about monitoring the Execution Schedule to make sure that it is still a valid and relevant document in the eyes of the project participants. Are they coordinating their activities with the pace and direction specified in the schedule? Momentum Science monitors three key variables, discussed in the following subsections.

Out-of-Sequence Work   Out-of-Sequence Work refers to Momentology processes that monitor, measure, *qualify*, and report incidences of work being performed out of sequence.

Activity-Duration Variances   Activity-Duration Variances refer to Momentology processes that monitor, measure, and report variances between planned and actual activity-durations.

Relationship-Duration Variances   Relationship-Duration Variances refer to Momentology processes that monitor, measure, and report variances between planned and actual relationship-durations.

Schedule Volatility

Schedule Volatility refers to Momentology calculations that evaluate the ongoing stability of the Execution Schedule by considering changes to logic, durations, settings, date-constraints, and calendars. Meanwhile, Schedule Volatility closely monitors the integrity of the Schedule by watching for evidence of indicative changes in key schedule components.

Changes to Logic   Changes to Logic entail Momentology processes that monitor, measure, and report the extent to which original schedule logic has been modified.

Changes to Durations   Changes to Durations involve Momentology processes that monitor, measure, and report the extent to which changes have been made in the number, type, and level of detail of both relationship-durations and activity-durations.

Changes to Settings   Changes to Settings refers to Momentology processes that monitor, measure, and report the extent to which changes have been made to originally incorporated schedule software settings.

Changes to Constraints   Changes to Constraints pertains to Momentology processes that monitor, measure, and report the extent to which changes have been made to originally incorporated arbitrary date-constraints.

Changes to Calendars   Changes to Calendars refers to Momentology processes that monitor, measure, and report the extent to which changes have been made to originally-incorporated automated calendar settings.

OVERVIEW OF APPLIED MOMENTUM

Applied Momentum offers useful applications in both project management and post-project dispute resolution, although obviously Momentology is primarily intended for the project manager who wants to proactively manage project momentum. Momentum Science will provide management with early insights into performance trends, even to the point of predicting outcomes (Dilemma Forecasting) long before they occur.

However, Momentum calculations can also be useful in measuring and analyzing loss of productivity claims. For example, historically it has been nearly impossible to calculate and demonstrate the compounding effect of a multitude of change orders or Requests for Information (RFI) on the efficiency of work performance. Using Performance Intensity, the relationship between impacted variables and resultant inefficiencies can be clearly measured and depicted.

Instant Compatibility

Momentum Management, also called Management by Momentum, is a new way to manage projects, but it does *not* require any radical changes in the way schedules are developed or used. In fact, the essential principles of Momentum Science require that the underlying schedule have as much integrity as possible. For this reason, Momentum Theory strongly advocates the purity of activity-durations and relationship-durations, as well as the responsible employment of relationship ties and imposed date-constraints. Momentum Science relies upon the credibility and reasonableness of the Project Schedule, and therefore basic tenets of the Critical Path Method are essential to successful Management by Momentum. That is why a book on how to create sound schedules is the first in the anticipated set of works dedicated to Momentum Management.

Momentum Control

For the following discussion, see Chapter 8, Table 8-6. Momentum Control involves a set of processes that parallel the traditional Scheduling Practice phases of Schedule Design, Schedule Development, Schedule Maintenance, and Schedule Usage. During Schedule Design, plans for the implementation of Momentum Theory are finalized. As the Project Schedule is developed, certain additional codes and variables are introduced into the process in order to support subsequent Momentum Analyses.

During Performance Control cycles, Performance Diagnostics are produced and specific momentum-related evaluations are conducted in order to determine Performance Intensity and develop appropriate metrics. Finally, Performance Analysis is a key aspect of Schedule Usage, and important insights into the project's overall health are developed with respect to project momentum. For instance, it is during Performance Analysis that Dilemma Forecasting is supported.

Momentum Analytics

Momentum Analytics, a part of Performance Analysis, has been shown to provide more accurate and immediate feedback on true project trending patterns than either traditional CPM Analysis or Earned Value analysis (see Figure 7-2). The chief reason for the difference in effectiveness is that the latter methods assume backward-looking perspectives, whereas Momentum Analytics looks forward.

Figure 7-2 shows a ten-month project with a required completion date of August 1, 1999, which is shown by the thick horizontal line midway up the chart. Even using three different ways of calculating SPI, EVSM did not report trouble for the project until the sixth month. Similarly, total-float calculations remained positive for four months, and only reported that the end date was in jeopardy in the fifth month. In stark contrast, Performance Intensity data suggested trouble as early as the second month!

Furthermore, Momentum Analytics monitors and reports on *actual* performance as opposed to the *effects* of performance, whereas CPM analytical reports speak about gains or losses of total-float, a secondary variable that results *from* performance. Likewise, Earned Value analytical reports discuss resource consumption, which is then

Figure 7-2

Project Completion Predictions; Using Momentum, Earned Value and CPM

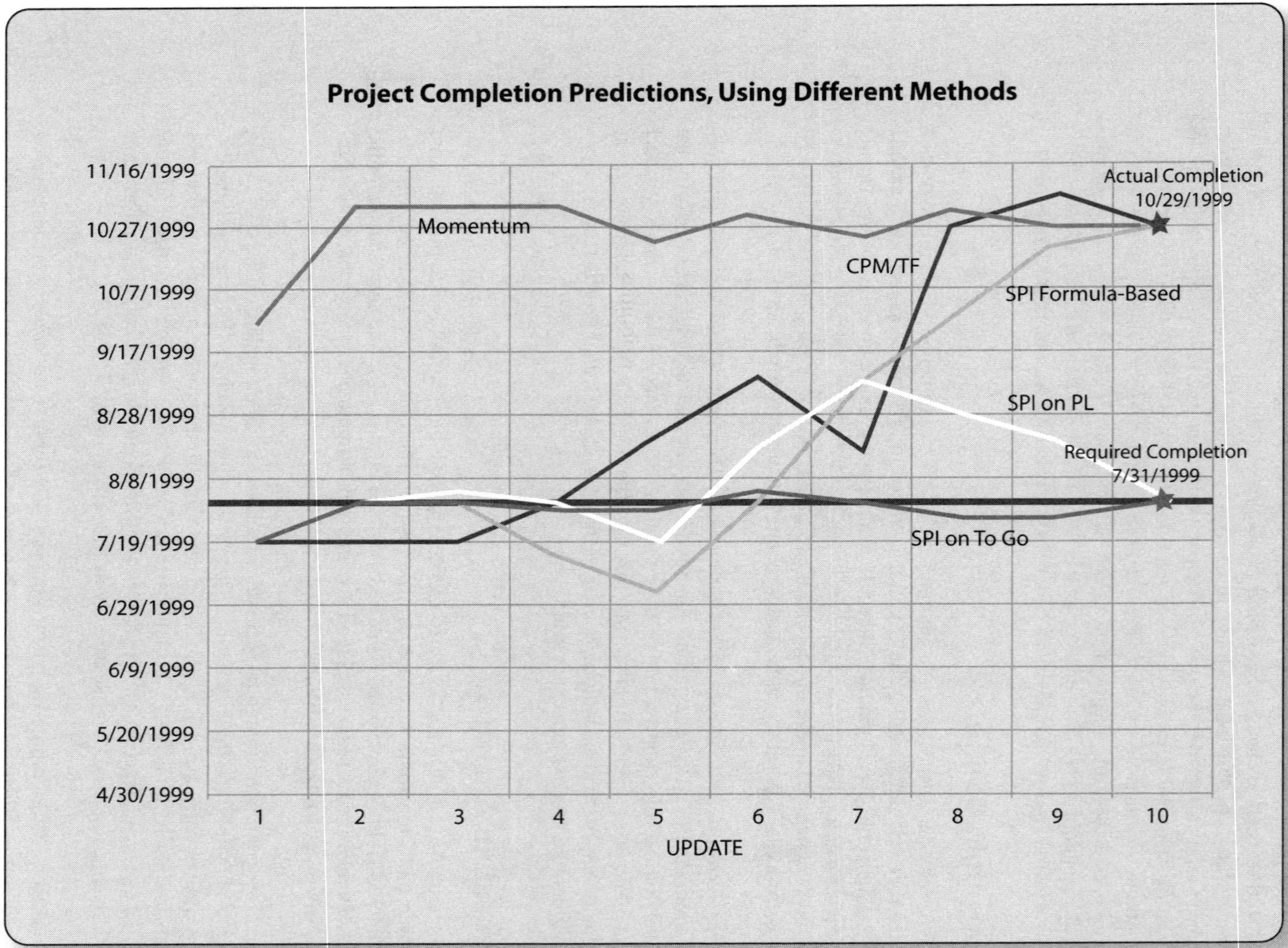

Project Completion Predictions, Using Different Methods

used to interpolate or speculate on performance. Refreshingly Momentum Analytics measure and report on performance *directly*.

Management by Momentum

The remaining puzzle piece involves the project manager's use of momentum-based information. As stated numerous times throughout this text, it is a fundamental principle of Momentology that the project's successful achievement of time-based objectives can best be insured by carefully safeguarding project momentum. Through Performance Control using Momentum Analytics, the project manager will be supplied with sufficient information to effectively manage project momentum to the betterment of the project.

Part of Momentum methodology is a set of procedures it is recommended that the project manager follow. These processes will provide him with a structured means of linking his daily activities to the true priorities of the project itself. Most important of all, timely Momentum data will allow the project manager to *proactively* influence the immediate performance of all project participants.

In the end, I achieved the original goal I set out to accomplish, as the project manager no longer needed to wait until the end of the month to learn that Subcontractor X had decelerated during the month and had squandered six days of total-float, that precious public commodity to which the subcontractor did not have exclusive consumption rights.

Management by Momentum presents a whole new world of possibilities for the project manager whose management style embraces the challenge of work performance coordination. Experienced drivers know to look a mile down the road to spot the traffic light that has just turned red. As soon as they see the change of colors, they take their foot off the gas pedal and allow the vehicle to naturally slow down as they approach the intersection. They know it makes little sense to burn fuel in order to race to a corner, only to pounce on the brake pedal and wear down brake lining and tires.

Likewise, thanks to exciting innovations like Dilemma Forecasting and Momentum Analytics, the project manager is now able to ascertain the imprudence of pushing Subcontractor X to complete a set of activities, only to have the completed work sit idle because follow-on activities are still a week or more away.

With a whole new set of Momentology data, the project manager is able to run his project using Management by Momentum principles. In doing so he is now able to perform Preventive Administrative Actions, Priority-Based Decision-Making, Momentum-Focused Coordination, Critically Oriented Problem-Solving, and Proactive Project Management.

Administrative Activities

At the practical level, Management by Momentum is completely compatible with traditional project management practice. It merely provides a more reliable and significant set of project data upon which the project manager can rely when performing his

Planned Resources, Objective Judgments, Effective Communications, and *Troubleshooting* duties.

Finally, it is worth noting that Momentum Theory addresses the single greatest oversight in the current Scheduling Practice, the administrative activity. Almost without exception, schedule activities exclusively represent productive work, while consistently ignoring administrative activities. Administrative activities are ones that the typical schedule assumes *should be* performed in advance of each productive activity, but does not incorporate into Project Schedule.

Studies have shown that the vast majority of schedule delays can be traced back to belated or incomplete performance of administrative activities. Momentum Theory, for the first time in the history of network-based scheduling, systematically encompasses administrative activities in its calculations and reporting products.

The New Look of CPM

The radical breakthrough of Momentum Theory is Performance Intensity, a unit of measure that reflects the *rate* of performance, regardless of project or activity particulars. Performance Intensity can be measured and reported across any type of project or any type of activity, and the Performance Intensity of different projects can be compared even if one is an airport project and the other is pharmaceutical product development project.

Thanks to the discovery of Performance Intensity, it is now possible for the first time to depict work progress in terms of differing paces of performance flow. Activity strings can be portrayed as Waterways of varying significance to project performance goals. The most critical Waterway through the schedule is called a River. Secondary Waterways that converge with Rivers are called Streams. Likewise, Creeks flow into Streams, and Brooks flow into Creeks. Finally, Inlets are small activity linkages that spring from and return to a single waterway.

In Figure 7-3, the River flows through Activities 2440, 2450, 2500, 2530, and 2410. There are three Streams, each flowing into the River. The upper Stream includes Activities 2310, 2320, 2330, 2350, 2360, and 2370. The lower Stream connects Activities 2510, 2570, 2580, and 2590. A third Stream, in the middle of the diagram, contains the start of Activity 2450. No Creeks or Brooks are shown, but Activities 2380 and 2390 constitute an Inlet.

Points of confluence are called Momentum Control Points (shown as ovals) and a host of momentum calculations are pitted against these MCPs. Management by Momentum entails monitoring and regulating performance so that MCP objectives are achieved.

Applied Momentum and Traditional Project Management

Applied Momentum parallels traditional project management's most common practices. Momentum Controls Development coincides with Schedule Development.

Figure 7-3
The New Look of CPM

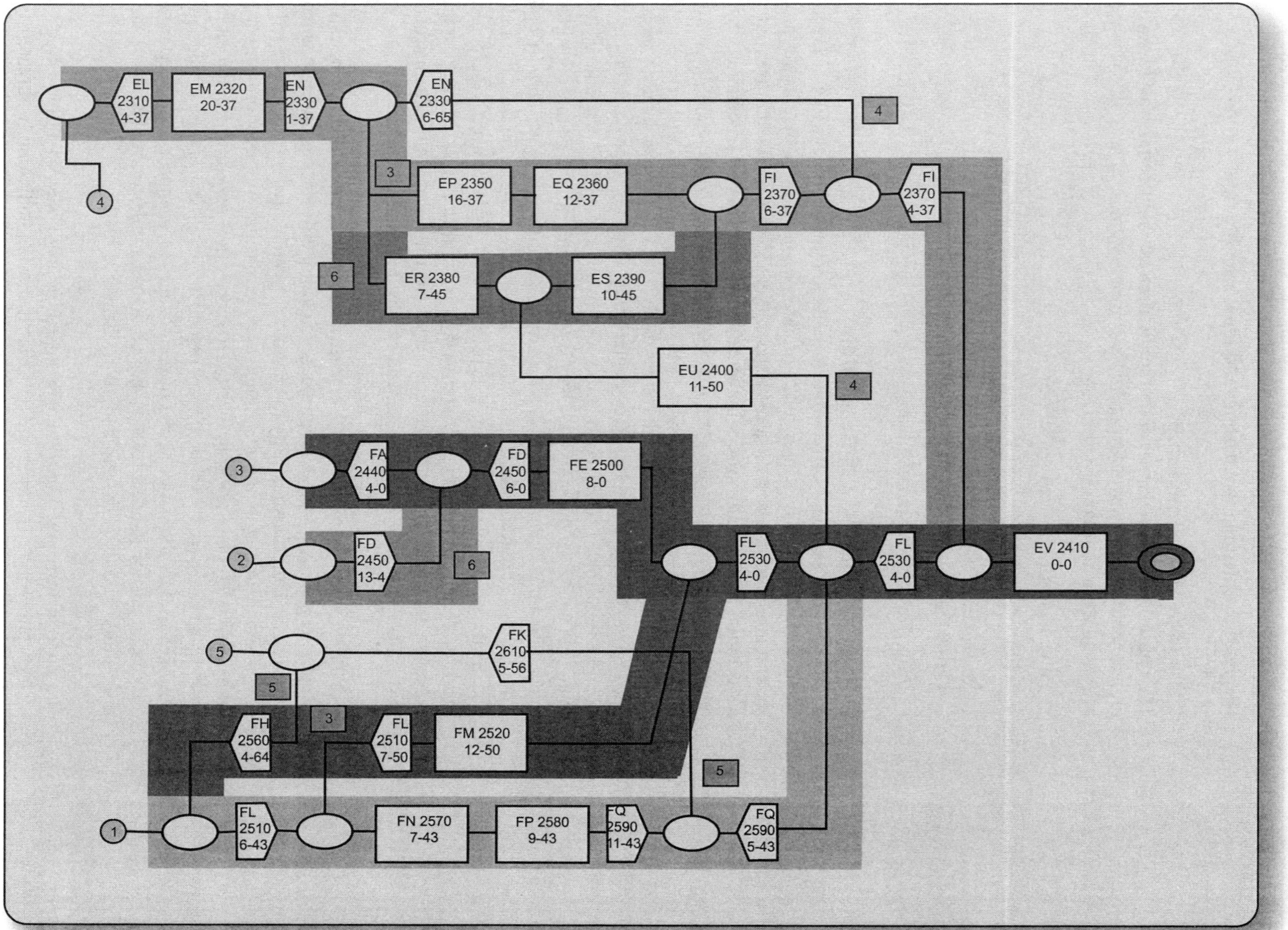

Momentum Tracking aligns with Performance Recording and chiefly includes calculations of Schedule Relevancy and Performance Intensity. Finally, Momentum Analytics corresponds with traditional Project Performance Analysis and entails Criticality Diagnostics, Dilemma Forecasting, and Flow Rate Metrics.

Management by Momentum

The phases in the preceding section yield a refreshingly better way to ensure desired project outcomes, by managing project momentum. Subsets of Management by Momentum are as follows:

- Preventive Administrative Actions
- Priority-Based Decision Making
- Momentum-Focused Coordination
- Criticality-Oriented Problem Solving
- Proactive Project Management

Momentum and Dispute Resolution

By now, you should realize that my developmental activities in the area of Momentology were never intended to produce anything other than useful products and services for our primary customer, the project manager. As it turns out, however, Momentum Science also offers immense value to the world of contract claims, when allegations involve delay, acceleration, or loss of productivity.

With respect to delay and acceleration, to be sure, there are several decades of developed methodology to handle the evidentiary requirements to prove or disprove delay or acceleration. However, those methods typically require a CPM schedule of fairly sound logic, and whenever the schedule lacks sufficient integrity the claims consultant is often faced with a true dilemma: *a choice between two options that are equally unfavorable.* If he builds his defense on a structurally unsound schedule, he runs the risk of being discredited on the witness stand. Yet, if he takes steps to "correct" the contemporaneous Project Schedule, he exposes himself to possible criticism that he manipulated the Schedule to suit his client's best interests. Here, Momentum Theory can help, as Performance Intensity does not depend on absolute logic soundness.

But the greatest contribution that Momentology provides the claims world is its ability to measure and depict losses of productivity. Labor efficiency is one area where, to date, there has been no statistical way to quantify the cumulative impact of alleged events. To take a simple and common example, suppose that the Architect presents a contractor with a proposed change order. The contractor is then asked to provide an estimate of cost and an assessment of time impact associated with the proposed change. As the contractor considers the minor scope of the change, he cannot legitimately argue that the change, in and of itself, threatens any contractual milestones. Therefore, he does not seek a time extension for this particular change.

But now, imagine this same scenario repeating itself, say, 416 times. Each individual change proposal was minor enough that it did not individually threaten contractual milestones. But collectively—and that is the operative word—the combined set of changes might cause the contractor great hardship (in the form of extended man hours, additional shifts, additional supervision, stacked trades, and so on) and a clear loss of productivity. The problem is that, from a claims perspective, there has been no way to quantitatively depict the labor inefficiency impacts of cumulative changes—until, that is, the advent of Momentology. Momentum metrics can clearly and convincingly show how cumulative scope increases did *in fact*[5] affect project momentum.

FINAL THOUGHTS ON MOMENTOLOGY

So, that's the story of how Momentology came to be what it is today. As I look back on the original objective, to improve the quality of what we tell our primary customer, the project manager, I think Momentology meets the challenge. Table 7-1 repeats the list of

Table 7-1

Twelve Reasons Why Momentum Management Makes Good Sense

1. Effective project management requires being proactive and deliberate, not reactionary and impulsive.

2. Worker productivity is most immediately measured and most dramatically influenced by changes in project momentum.

3. The function of the schedule, first and foremost, is to support the time-related aspects of project management.

4. True performance measurement must reconcile the rate of work placement with that rate's significance to time-based goals.

5. Work performers must be held accountable for gains and losses in that all-critical public asset, total-float.

6. With consistent accuracy and reliability, scheduling products should identify future obstacles to, and opportunities for, momentum gain and maintenance.

7. Project management should be alerted to changes in performance intensity, even subtle ones, just as soon as they occur. No more month-end sports casting, where the gain or loss of precious time is announced, uselessly, after the fact.

8. The single, most-important role of project management is to orchestrate the work.

9. Project management, to be most effective, should concentrate on project momentum.

10. To help project management incubate and sustain project momentum, project schedulers must be able to measure and project schedules must be able to depict the rate at which work is being performed.

11. The relationship between work performance intensity and its consequential effects on project momentum must be made apparent to project management and work performers alike, in a timely and accurate manner.

12. Schedule management should provide project management with reasonably accurate predictions of future threats to project momentum—dilemmas—long before their actual occurence.

---

[5]Currently, loss-of-productivity (inefficiency) calculations are based on tables of theoretical impacts and their effects that "one can expect" to occur. Whether those effects *actually* occurred is rarely incorporated into inefficiency claims. As a result, loss-of-productivity damages are quite often overstated. Momentum allows for a precise measure of the extent of *actual* effect of inefficiency.

requirements presented earlier under "Conclusions About How to Improve Schedule Management." It would seem that Momentology meets all required attributes.

I hope this chapter has given you a sense of what Momentology is all about. The purpose of this chapter is simply to give you a 20,000-foot view of what Momentology entails. No doubt, you will have many questions about Momentology. As noted in the Preface, this book is the first in a three-volume series designed to introduce Momentology to the project management world. The next volume, *Project Momentum Management Using Momentology*, will provide a complete coverage of all aspects of Momentology. I hope you now understand some of the basics of Momentum Theory and Momentum Science and how they are jointly and practically applied to conventional project management practice.

8 Recap of New Concepts and Terminology

BEFORE WE GO ANY FURTHER

Chapters 5, 6, and 7 were loaded with a lot of new ideas. I thought you might appreciate a concise summary of the concepts and terminology—all in one place.

THE NEW SCHEDULING PRACTICE PARADIGM

As has been amply discussed in Chapters 2 and 5, the Scheduling Practice has suffered for all of its 50-year life span without the benefit of a comprehensive set of terms. In Chapter 5, the new Scheduling Practice Paradigm defines the Scheduling discipline as three technical specialties, each with specific subspecialties, procedures, key deliverables, and functional roles. On a small project, a Scheduling Practitioner might perform all Scheduling Practice functions, whereas on a mid-sized project, Commitment Planning, Execution Scheduling, and Performance Control functions might be performed by separate specialists. See Table 8-1.

DILEMMA CONTROL

Dilemma Control is a new project management system that strengthens the project manager's ability to anticipate and respond to everyday dilemmas. It is the unending onslaught of daily dilemmas, more than the occasional large risk, which most significantly threatens project momentum. See Table 8-2.

MOMENTOLOGY

Momentology represents the entire combination of Momentum Theory, Momentum Science, and Applied Momentum. See Table 8-3.

Table 8-1

The Scheduling Practice: A New Paradigm

Specialty / Procedures	Position	Deliverables	Educator	Strategist	Interpreter	Scribe	Investigator	Analyst	Advisor	Diplomat	Communicator
Commitment Planning	Commitment Planner		✓	✓	✓	✓			✓	✓	✓
Authorization Planning	Authorization Planner	Authorization Plans	✓	✓	✓	✓			✓	✓	✓
Feasibility Planning		Feasibility Plans	✓	✓	✓	✓			✓		
Master Planning		Master Plan				✓				✓	✓
Execution Planning	Execution Planner	Execution Plans	✓	✓	✓	✓			✓	✓	✓
Strategic Planning		Strategic Plans	✓	✓	✓	✓			✓		
Consensus Planning		Consensus Plan				✓				✓	✓
Execution Scheduling	Execution Scheduler		✓		✓	✓					
Schedule Design	Schedule Designer	Schedule Performance Specs	✓		✓						
Schedule Development	Scheduler Developer	Execution Schedule	✓		✓	✓					
Performance Control	Performance Controller		✓	✓			✓	✓	✓	✓	✓
Performance Recording	Performance Recorder	Statused Schedule					✓	✓			
Performance Analysis	Performance Analyst	Performance Analyses						✓			
Schedule Performance Analysis		Analysis of Schedule Performance						✓			
Management Performance Analysis		Analysis of Management Performance						✓			
Execution Performance Analysis		Analysis of Execution Performance						✓			
Change Optimization	Change Optimizer	Scenarios*and Revisions	✓	✓			✓	✓	✓	✓	✓
Scope Optimization		Optimized Scope Scenarios		✓			✓	✓	✓	✓	
Approach Optimization		Optimized Approach Scenarios		✓			✓	✓	✓	✓	
Conditions Optimization		Optimized Conditions Scenarios		✓			✓	✓	✓	✓	
Execution Schedule Amendment		Execution Schedule Revisions	✓						✓	✓	✓
Performance Advisement	Performance Advisor	Performance Advisement Deliverables	✓						✓	✓	✓
Performance Reporting	Performance Reporter	Performance Reports & Presentations	✓						✓	✓	✓
		Execution Schedule Editions	✓						✓	✓	✓
		Execution Schedule Extractions	✓						✓	✓	✓
Performance Consulting	Performance Consultant	Performance Consultations							✓	✓	✓

Includes actual, contemplated, and approved scenarios

Table 8-2

Dilemma Control, a Project Management System

1. Extemporaneous Response Training
2. Dilemma Forecasting
3. Dilemma Response Options
   a. Dilemma Elimination
   b. Dilemma Avoidance
   c. Dilemma Mitigation
   d. Dilemma Repair
   e. Dilemma Recovery

Table 8-3

Momentology Major Components

1. Momentum Theory
2. Momentum Science
3. Applied Momentum

Table 8-4

Momentum Theory

1. Seven M's of Momentum Management (Momentology)
2. Theory of Workload Backlog
3. Theory of Aligned Emphasis
4. Momentum
   a. Pace: Expressed as Performance Intensity
   b. Direction: Expressed as Schedule Relevance
5. Duration-Day
6. Performance Intensity: Planned, Actual, Required
   a. Work Performance: Planned, Actual, Required
   b. Time Consumption: Allocated, Consumed, Available
7. Graphics
   a. Waterways: Rivers, Streams, Creeks, Brooks, Inlets
   b. Momentum Control Points (MCPs)
   c. Geography: Regions, Capitals
   d. Maps: Topographical, Atmospheric
8. Relationship Anatomy
   a. Administrative Time Gap
   b. Productive Time Gap
   c. Relationship-Durations

MOMENTUM THEORY

Momentum Theory is the theoretical component of Momentology, including the concepts and terminology that provide the academic underpinning for Momentum Science. See Table 8-4.

MOMENTUM SCIENCE

Momentum Science is the technical component of Momentology and includes a host of additional terminology, formulas, axioms, algorithms, and other aspects of Momentology. See Table 8-5.

APPLIED MOMENTUM

Applied Momentum is the practical incorporation of Momentum Theory and Science into mainstream project management. See Table 8-6.

Table 8-5

Momentum Science

I. Performance Diagnostics
  A. Management Performance
  B. Execution Performance
    1. Performance Intensity
    2. Performance Coordination
  C. Resource Performance
II. Schedule Achievement Potential
  A. Schedule Vulnerability
    1. MCP, Waterway, and Activity Vulnerability
    2. Vulnerability Variables
      a. Criticality Factor: Density, Buoyancy, Potency
      b. Relationships Aggregation
      c. Confluence Aggregation
      d. Activity Placement
      e. Activity Profiles
  B. Schedule Resiliency
    1. MCP, Waterway, and Activity Resiliency
    2. Resiliency Factors: Density, Buoyancy, Potency
      a. Criticality Factor: Density, Buoyancy, Potency
      b. Relationships Aggregation
      c. Confluence Aggregation
      d. Activity Placement
III. Schedule Credibility
  A. Schedule Relevancy
    1. Out-of-Sequence Work
    2. Activity-Duration Variances
    3. Relationship-Duration Variances
  B. Schedule Volatility
    1. Changes in Logic and Durations
    2. Changes in Settings, Constraints, and Calendars

Table 8-6

Applied Momentum

1. Momentum Controls
  a. Momentum Planning
  b. Momentum Controls Design
  c. Momentum Controls Development
  d. Momentum Tracking
2. Momentum Analytics
  a. Momentum Diagnostics
  b. Dilemma Forecasting
  c. Flow Rate Metrics
  d. Momentum Reporting
3. Momentum Management (aka, Management by Momentum)
  a. Preventive Administrative Actions
  b. Priority-based Decision-making
  c. Momentum-focused Coordination
  d. Criticality-oriented Problem Solving
  e. Proactive Project Management

9 Scheduling Practice and Faster Projects

Now that you are sufficiently familiar with the basic specialties and deliverables of the new Scheduling Practice Paradigm, let us see how, when properly performed, they can suggest proven ways to create Project Schedules that your primary customer, the project manager, will actually want to use, so that your projects finish faster.

Since Chapters 12 through 16 are devoted to Execution Scheduling and Performance Control, this short chapter will address Commitment Planning.

COMMITMENT PLANNING

Now, with an abundantly clear distinction having been made between *planning* and *scheduling* (and *plans* versus *schedules*) in Chapter 5, we can proceed to discuss ways to perform Commitment Planning so that subsequent Execution Scheduling, will be as productive and beneficial as possible.

The many benefits of Commitment Planning can be exhaustive to list, certainly for the purposes of this text. In order not to lose sight of them, let us refocus on the main reasons for performing Commitment Planning on a project: to determine feasibility, to optimize project conditions, and to forge consensus around the most promising and most achievable execution strategy.

Authorization Planning

As the heading suggests, this is a planning effort of primary interest to the owner or developer who is contemplating a capital project. This subspecialty is performed either before, or at the earliest stages of, conceptual design. Since this is essentially a time-analysis exercise, the effort is typically aimed at determining the likely length of both design and construction, as well as at fixing critical milestone points in time. Projects that rely on public funding, such as bond issues or intense political backing, are often "planned" to accommodate such pragmatic constraints.

Feasibility Planning

Logistic concerns of owners and developers are more often the reason why Feasibility Planning is performed. A perfect example of the need for Feasibility Planning is a case I briefly mentioned in an earlier chapter. The Kennedy Center for the Performing Arts was contemplating a major renovation of the Concert Hall, one of three performance halls that make up the main floor. The Concert Hall is home to the National Orchestra and host to the Kennedy Center Honors, an annual television special attended by the President.

The project management consulting firm with whom I worked was contracted by the Kennedy Center to determine whether the contemplated renovation work could be performed within a tight window of ten months—the amount of time between when the National Orchestra goes on world tour and the taping of the Kennedy Center Honors program.

Clearly this was a Feasibility Planning assignment. And while, in fact, I developed my own logic diagrams and produced a fairly detailed "schedule"—meaning that the scheduling software I utilized produced conventional schedule reports—my objective was not to schedule, nor was it to plan. It was simply to determine *whether* the project was feasible.

The goal of Feasibility Planning is a crude estimate of overall time frames for completion and achievement of critical milestones (intermediate and final), and so the level of detail need not be terribly refined. Besides, typically, Feasibility Planning takes place at an early point in the project when details regarding project design and scope are more speculative than certain.

The chief deliverable of Feasibility Planning is a variety of study results, including possible bar charts and logic diagrams. These Feasibility Plans may be either summary or detailed, or both. Of course, even if summary in presentation format, a much more detailed logic diagram that reflects major elements of the project and takes into consideration the traditionally significant schedule drivers might invisibly support this summary illustration.

The trick is to put on paper what the Feasibility Planner's gut fully expects to happen. In this vein, the feasibility model will be no better than the experience level of those tasked with creating it. Precision is not the objective; realism *is*. For instance, it is not necessary for the Planner to know *which* pieces of equipment will be long-lead—by name or even by exact duration length. Instead, it is important that he acknowledge the likelihood that there *will* or *will not* be some long-lead items. To the extent that specific details can be ascertained, their discussions may be fruitful in deciding how to package the construction contracts—that is, whether to go out for phased bids or whether to have items suspected of being critical purchased in advance by the owner.

Feasibility Planning should take into consideration the availability of critical resources including key trades, equipment, and materials. It should also account for unique constraints to the project (such as limited site availability for staging and build-up), the nature and location of the project, climatic and geographic conditions of the site, jurisdictional concerns, and so on.

Depending on the nature of the project, computerization of a feasibility model may—or may not—be necessary. If the project is fairly straightforward and the feasibility question is simply one of how long the project will take, a manually calculated logic diagram is often all that is required. On the other hand, if there is some question as to whether the project can be completed within a restricted window of opportunity, or if there are multiple execution scenarios from which one *preferred* approach must be selected, then computerization can be very helpful.

Master Planning

Master Planning is a different type of Commitment Planning, although it is similar to Feasibility Planning in that many of the same questions are asked and answered. Three major distinctions separate these Commitment Planning efforts, however.

First, the timing of Master Planning is further into the project life cycle. Keep in mind that Feasibility Planning was performed *before* the "Go/No Go" decision. Obviously, at that early stage none (or very few) of the project's key players would have been selected or employed. As a result, little of the project detail now known to the Master Planning team would have been available then.

Second, Master Planning is aimed at a different customer: the Program Management Office. The PMO is the organizational entity from where this project will be launched and overseen. The PMO will hire the project team and staff personnel. Current trends toward Enterprise Project Management directly correlate with the understanding that no project operates in a vacuum.

This leads to the third way that Master Planning is different than Feasibility Planning. The emphasis is on the organization's ability to perform the project and less on the nature of the project itself. I'm talking about emphasis here, not overall interest, so be sure you follow my point. At the time of Feasibility Planning, nothing would be known about the performing organization, as they likely would have not been picked yet. The inquiry to be answered by Feasibility Planning is one of feasibility *based almost exclusively on information related to the nature of the project.*

By contrast, at the time of Master Planning, the PMO of the organization that will have ultimate responsibility for project execution performs the optimization efforts. In construction, this could be the Construction Manager, or Owner's Representative. In a private sector, internal service project, this is probably some form of Program Management Office. Either way, the precise number and identify of project team members is still some time away.

So, when I say that during Master Planning the *emphasis* is more on the organization's ability to perform than it is on project specifics, I mean that both sets of factors are being considered, whereas earlier, during Feasibility Planning, only one set of factors was considered.

Fourth, Master Planning is performed for a different end goal. Master Planning begins by establishing the theoretical *ideal*, a scenario that all understand can never be achieved. Next, it modifies this ideal, by swallowing a lump of reality, and the result is an *optimum* scenario, meaning that the scenario is still something to shoot for.

The Master Plan is the one that is the best among all scenarios considered, and it is derived by finding that one scenario that contains the least risks and the most opportunities for success. Of course, the key to Master Planning is to be both honest and realistic when identifying risks and opportunities for success. Personally, I feel that Master Planning is best accomplished when, somewhere during the process, a seasoned Change Optimizer is brought into the room to "shoot holes" at the Master Plan. After all, the Change Optimizer is the Scheduling Practice professional most knowledgeable of what can, and probably will, go wrong on a project.

At the same time, the Master Planner has specialized expertise in working with ambiguous designs and highly speculative resource assumptions, is familiar with a variety of contract *packaging* alternatives and performance incentive programs, and more.

The deliverable of Master Planning is the Master Plan, and it will likely look very much like a Project Schedule. But since no one will be building from this "schedule," and since the actual project team has not even been heard from yet (as they have not been convened), this could hardly be used as either a Consensus Plan or Execution Schedule.

What it *is*, though, is a reasonable project implementation model that the Program Management Office can use for further internal and external planning.

How to Conduct a Master Planning Session   Here are some helpful hints on how to conduct a Master Planning session. See Table 9-1.

BE CLEAR ON OBJECTIVES   At the opening of the session, remind the group of the *Emphasis Alignment Model* (see Chapter 11 for more details on this topic) and identify the success criterion on which the owner places greatest emphasis: time, cost, or manner. Make certain that the strategic and optimization planning sessions that follow keep this focus squarely in mind.

Most projects emphasize time over cost or manner. If for no other reason, time is not controllable or variable, whereas cost and manner of performance are. Owners understand this intuitively. In practice, high visibility projects are rarely aborted once cost exceeds budget. Functional shortfalls can be rationalized, "spun," or compensated for at a later time.

EXPLAIN GENERAL PARAMETERS OF MASTER PLANNING   Assure participants that there is no *absolutely* ideal plan—but there is a *reasonably* ideal plan. Every plan component represents time/cost/quality trade-offs. Master Planning is a precursor to management decision-making, and its objective is to provide management with substantial, valuated

Table 9-1

Master Planning Session Helpful Hints

Be Clear on Objectives
Explain General Parameters
Establish Procedural Guidelines
Safeguard Realism, at All Costs

alternatives. A guide for all Master Planning exercises is to strive for maximum realism; allocate for plan failure. Finally, document everything—discussions, rationales, and assumptions.

ESTABLISH PROCEDURAL GUIDELINES Make sure you involve the right people: those most familiar with the subject matter, planning processes, and management/project objectives. Be sure to dispel all paradigms or preconceived notions that might stand in the way of creative thinking. All too often people come to these sessions already believing that the Commitment Plan cannot be tightened any further or, conversely, that it is too fat as it is!

Allow enough time for ideas to evolve and see the light of day. Different minds run at different speeds. Also, take into account different personality types. Some are shy, while others are pensive and quiet. You never know from whom that one great idea will come.

Finally, follow time-tested Master Planning techniques:

- Use a top-down approach.
- Theorize in months, strategize in weeks, validate in days.
- Use conventional Critical Path Method for determining project, relationship, and activity durations, impacts, and their compounding effects.
- Maintain detailed Assumption Lists and Risk Lists; where risk is recognized, write a short paragraph explaining it, including duration/risk tradeoffs and ranges.
- Inject pacing milestones for monitoring and sanity-check purposes.
- Test all positions against relevant/reliable historical data.

ON TIME-SENSITIVE PROJECTS, SAFEGUARD REALISM AT ALL COSTS While realism is important to the integrity of any plan, it is especially significant on projects where finishing as soon as possible is the owner's number one desire. If, *in reality,* the end date cannot be met, the sooner you break the bad news to the owner, the sooner he can deal with the problem. But, hopefully, the Master Planning sessions already eliminated the *impossible* project.

Table 9-2 lists some helpful hints that will ensure that your Master Plan is as realistic as possible:

- Balance risk with contingency. Include in both activity-durations and relationship-durations sufficient fudge (*Duration Confidence Factors* [see Chapter 15 for more details on this topic]) to compensate for *known unknowns.*
- Document activity scope and order of magnitude for each activity-duration.
- Ensure that the Master Plan contains project contingency float, which is placed at the end of the plan.
- Be reluctant to "ratchet down" (typically front-end) activities of a contemplative nature (for example, contracts, specifications, project deadline establishment) in an effort to yield a shorter project length.
- Make sure that the most aggressive durations and logic are in the middle 70 percent portion of the Master Plan.

Table 9-2

Ingredients for
Reasonable
Master Plans

1. Balance risk with contingency.
2. Document activity scope.
3. Include sufficient project float.
4. Resist "ratcheting."
5. "Center" ambitious durations.
6. Account for resource ramp-ups.
7. Account for holidays and such.
8. Watch for "durflation."
9. Allow for rework and redirection.
10. Confirm resource availability.

- Account for required resource ramp-ups.
- Recognize holidays, weekends, and other likely nonwork periods.
- Watch for "durflation"—duration inflation due to rounding or undocumented (buried) float.
- A good Master Plan should provide for rework and redirection; they are as certain to occur as the base scope performance itself.
- Confirm resource availability to meet the requirements of all desired plans.

Execution Planning

Typically, the project team that will be performing the work conducts Execution Planning. In the construction industry, Execution Planning is often in response to a Request for Proposals (RFP) or as part of the preparation of a hard bid. Either way, the contractor has a need to determine far more than merely the overall timing and sequence of work, as was determined through Commitment Planning.

Execution Planning should be performed by those who (a) are experienced in the type of work being contemplated, and (b) have had previous experience in strategic Execution Planning. Execution Planning calls for assumptions and choices to be made which, once incorporated into the Strategic Plan, subsequently become critical elements of the project's Execution Schedule. Proven historically, the decisions made during the Execution Planning phase will have a profoundly greater impact on a project's probability of success than any decisions made by project management once the project has begun. That is why the Scheduling Practice Paradigm recognizes Execution Planning as a distinct subspecialty and the Execution Planner as a distinct subspecialist.

Execution Plans Involve a Two-Step Process

Just as Authorization Planning involves a two-step process, yielding the Feasibility Plan and then the Master Plan, Execution Planning goes through two phases as well. First there is the Strategic Plan, which develops an optimum execution strategy. Then it is modified in its final hours, to become the Consensus Plan, one that pulls back from the ideal, and gives all participants as much win-win as possible.

The Execution Planning Heavily Influences the Execution Scheduling

I want to dwell on the point of this heading for a few minutes. The ultimate work products of Execution Planning become self-fulfilling prophecies of grand success or bitter failure, and it all has to do with timing. Let's look at it both ways.

At the one extreme there are Execution Plans that are artificially *long*. Not wanting to turn in a Consensus Plan that is *too short*, for fear that the project's success criteria may be too demanding, its developers artificially elongate the Consensus Plan by depicting selected critical *driving* activities (such as long lead deliveries or protracted floor finishes) as taking longer than they actually need to.

The result is a fully believable (yet nonetheless exaggerated) Consensus Plan. The most common culprits of elongated Execution Plans are construction managers or architects who benefit from a longer project length. Of course, contractors, too, may produce elongated Consensus Plans as they pursue negotiated management contracts where bonuses or penalties apply to timely completion.

These elongated Consensus Plans are self-fulfilling in that they necessarily space critical milestones over a longer-than-necessary span of time. Consider a floor finish sequence of six months per floor, versus a more realistic four months per floor. Relying on the Consensus Plan, interior finish trades (such as millwork, glazing, flooring, ceilings, furnishings, and so on) perform long-range resource planning of their own based on this elongated Plan, which calls for their involvement long after their presence could have been received and optimized.

Once plans have been set by these trades with respect to this and all other projects in their respective portfolios, your project manager will find it near to impossible to "accelerate" the subcontractor's arrival on your jobsite—at least, not without paying a premium for their "earlier" arrival on site.

The same holds true for critical long-lead equipment and materials that are prepurchased, in order to "protect the execution schedule" (which has not yet been developed, mind you). Based on an elongated Consensus Plan, production shops schedule their jobs to accommodate each project's "need dates." If the Consensus Plan understates the urgency, the products will be delivered on these later dates, and the project manager who subsequently wishes to "gain on the schedule" will have to pay a premium for an "earlier" delivery—one which would have been *expected* (not "earlier"), had the Consensus Plan been reasonable to start with.

Now look at the other extreme, an overly short Consensus Plan. Here, the planning strategy is the opposite, but the results are the same. The Execution Planner understates the scope of the work, reflecting unchecked optimism or empty promises, by using inadequate durations and/or partial logic, and the results are intermediate milestones that are unrealistically *too early*. More often than not this approach is both conscious and intentional. The strategy calls for securing the work with an aggressive schedule (and, as the approach goes, equally aggressive price proposal) and then watching for, and seizing, every opportunity during construction to secure time (and cost) "extras" from the owner.

Although this Consensus Planning tactic is fraught with technical challenges at all levels, it sadly remains the method of preference for far too many contractors. In their defense, by the time most contractors get involved in a project (even during the bidding process), the owners and designers themselves have boldly and often irreversibly understated the true length of the project anyway. With unrealistic expectations inflexibly stated in bid documents, the contractor is often *left with no choice* but to "confirm" the owner's wishful thinking—that is, if he wants a snowball's chance of being awarded the contract!

The effect of the *shortened* Consensus Plan is the same as that of the *elongated* Consensus Plan. Suppliers, subcontractors, consultants, inspectors, and others who are vital to the construction process, but who have other constraints to their performance schedules *beyond this one project*, rely on misleading and unrealistic milestone dates found in the Consensus Plan. Many months later, a panicky project manager is on the phone asking the vendor to either "hold the units" because the project isn't ready for them yet, or "accelerate" because "we need the units yesterday."

So what's the answer? Always be precise? Never pad and never be aggressive? The answer lies in one word: reasonableness. Be reasonable in artificially elongating or shortening a Consensus Plan. A certain amount of logic manipulation during Execution Planning can be both beneficial in securing the contract and in putting the fire under the toes of those upon whom you will be dependant once the job begins. Each proposal (or bid) is different, and this text can offer no single rule of thumb that will work best in all cases. The only advice worth giving is to use common sense and remember that anything beyond a modest manipulation *will become a self-fulfilling prophecy.*

The Consensus Plan and Resource Planning

Another use of the Consensus Plan is to plan for the deployment of resources, human or otherwise. Constructors already under contract are the most interested in this form of Execution Planning. By "constructors," I refer to design professionals, contractors, suppliers, owners, tenants, or others involved in the construction process. Of course, it should be apparent that, if the Consensus Plan is being used *after* the award, and we already said it was being used to *get* the award, then it must be a living, breathing, and dynamic document. And well it is.

Now, of all resources addressed by the Consensus Plan, the primary resource of concern is, of course, labor. But just as well, money, equipment, materials, and even time itself can be managed more effectively by way of a forward-looking Consensus Plan.

Execution Planning, unlike Authorization Planning, draws from the content of a well itemized, more detailed, and better-coded Strategic Plan. Since resource management is a cyclical undertaking, it may begin within the Strategic Plan and gradually migrate to the Execution Schedule. At that point, the resource plan becomes a "roll up" schedule, which shows the deployment and timing needs of critical resources.

Resource plans that are developed in advance of detailed scheduling, at the earliest stages of Execution Planning, run the risk of inherently limiting—or wasting—valuable resources. The effect on project outcomes is obvious. Unavailable manpower will kill a schedule every time, and oversupply of labor will kill a budget every time.

Resource planning is not an exact science—but it really ought to be, if a contractor has any hope of making a profit, given how thin profit margins are in today's overly competitive construction market. Long gone are the days when one could submit a *fat* bid, build it from the hip, and still come out rubbing two pennies together. Bids are now down to the gnat's eyelash, project management is a refined science using computers throughout the construction process to monitor and influence project momentum, and . . . well, no one bends down for dropped pennies anymore.

EXECUTION SCHEDULING

Execution Scheduling is what this book is mostly all about. Those who will be executing the project should create the Execution Schedule. The Execution Schedule's development should be influenced largely by the contents and supporting documentation of the Consensus Plan. For a complete treatment of the design, development, and maintenance of the Execution Schedule, see Chapters 12 through 15.

PERFORMANCE CONTROL

Performance Control is an extremely complex specialty and the subject of the anticipated third book in the Momentum Series. However, various aspects of Performance Control are covered in this text because I believe that you cannot produce a really useful Project Schedule if you don't know how to extract pertinent, vital data from it, during Performance Recording, Performance Analysis, and Performance Advisement.

Part 3 Preserving Project Schedule Integrity

W e are getting extremely close to the meat of this book: how to create great Project Schedules. But first we need to get two important topics out on the table.

Chapter 10 will provide you with a perspective on the Network Diagram that, quite likely, you have never encountered before. In "Anatomy of a Schedule," I dissect the two most basic building blocks of all Project Schedules: activities and relationships. Like any building blocks, if they are weak or compromised, so is the integrity of anything built with them. Peer reviewers of this book have said that this particular chapter was as enlightening to them as all of the rest of the book combined!

Chapter 11, "Signs of Erosion," might more properly fall under the heading "Forewarned is Forearmed." Its message is that, unless we are diligent in guarding our Project Schedules, they can easily be commandeered by "others" who, whether intentionally or not, may negatively affect the integrity of our Project Schedules.

10 Anatomy of a Schedule

In this chapter you will take an interesting journey through the anatomy of a schedule and see it in a far different light than perhaps ever before. We will start our discussion by examining the typical activity. Next, we will dissect the four basic relationship types. This chapter will conclude with the introduction of new concepts that, I promise, will forever change the way you see schedule logic.

ANATOMY OF AN ACTIVITY

What follows may seem elementary, if not unnecessary. After all, how important is it that we perceive a CPM activity or relationship as graphical shorthand? The answer to this question will become obvious to you before the end of the chapter. I assure you that several of the most significant reasons why Project Schedules fail to achieve end-user satisfaction can be related to a failure to understand the true architecture of the CPM diagram. Let's start with the anatomy of an activity.

CPM Is a Mathematical Simulation Model

The Critical Path Method was initially conceived in response to a call for tapping the power of the recently invented computer to simulate a project *before* actually embarking on it. CPM responded by providing an intricate set of symbols that a human could use to depict project strategy and that the computer could use to interpolate the collective results of that strategy. At its heart, CPM is a symbolic language.

Elements of an Activity

Each activity has four essential elements: scope, duration, start, and finish. Every activity, by definition, represents a limited, definable *scope* of work. The performance of that work consumes an estimated or actual length of time, called a *duration*. For each activity there are two conceptual *moments in time*, the moment when an activity can or does start, and the moment when an activity can or does complete.

ADM Symbolism

In the Arrow Diagramming Method (ADM), the four essential elements of an activity are represented symbolically, as follows:

- The activity's *scope* is described, albeit cryptically, using the Activity Description (sometimes called Activity Title or Activity Label).
- The activity's *duration* is depicted graphically using an arrow. The activity's duration is valuated in a numeral that is written directly below the arrow.
- The activity's *starting moment-in-time* is represented by a node (circle), which is attached to the left end (tail) of the arrow.
- The activity's *ending moment-in-time* is represented by a node (circle), which is attached to the right end (head) of the arrow.
- Activities (arrows) can never touch one another; relationships (nodes) always separate them. When a single node separates two activities, it at once represents the predecessor activity's *ending moment-in-time* as well as the successor activity's *starting moment-in-time*.
- All relationships are assumed to be *finish-to-start,* meaning that the successor's starting moment-in-time succeeds, even infinitesimally, the predecessor's ending *moment-in-time.* A single node represents the two *moments in time,* the equivalent of a PDM finish-to-start relationship with a relationship-duration of zero. This interpretation is essential to a correct understanding of the ADM methodology.

PDM Symbolism

In the Precedence Diagramming Method (PDM), the four essential elements of an activity are represented symbolically, as follows:

- The activity's *scope* is described, albeit cryptically, using the Activity Description.
- The activity's *duration* is depicted graphically by the horizontal sides of the activity box. Specifically, the upper and lower sides are tantamount to the arrow of the ADM method. The activity's duration is quantified by use of a numeral, written directly beneath the activity box.
- The activity's *starting moment-in-time* is represented by the vertical line that forms the left side of the activity box.
- The activity's *ending moment-in-time* is represented by the vertical line that forms the right side of the activity box.
- Activities (boxes) can never touch one another; relationships (arrows) always separate them.

Up to this point, ADM and PDM are virtually identical, except for their choice of symbols. But this is where the similarities end. Now come the contrasts in methods.

In ADM, the node represents both the existence of a relationship *and* the two moments-in-time, the ending moment-in-time of the predecessor, and the starting moment-in-time of the successor. In PDM, each of these three components has its own symbol. The existence of a relationship is depicted by way of an arrow. The right side (vertical line) of the activity box represents the ending moment-in-time, while the left side (vertical line) of the activity box symbolizes the starting moment-in-time.

There are multiple relationship types in PDM: start-to-start, finish-to-finish, start-to-finish, and finish-to-start, whereas in ADM there is only the finish-to-start relationship.

In ADM, the relationship-duration can only be zero, but in PDM relationships can have nonzero durations. But what do you do in the case where a gap in time needs to be interjected between two activities? In ADM, an additional activity must be created and given both an activity-duration and an activity-description. In PDM, however, the relationship may be assigned a nonzero duration. There is no place in PDM to provide a corresponding description explaining what is supposed to happen during the nonzero relationship-duration, however.

ANATOMY OF A RELATIONSHIP

This brings us to one of the most important concepts in this entire book. As noted throughout this text, Momentum Studies have shown that the preponderance of schedule slippages occur in between, as opposed to during, activities. No wonder, then, that I get passionate when I talk or write about relationship ties. When the logic is wacky, so are any predictions based on that logic. The reliability of an Execution Schedule's predictions of future project outcomes is directly correlated with the reasonableness with which its inherent activities and relationships are logically tied.

So, what can we do to improve our practices with respect to depicting what occurs in between activities? The answer to this question greatly depends on the management style on the project to which your Scheduling efforts are being applied. In other words, I have two answers for you.

If your Execution Schedule is meant to support a Collaborative manager, then the level-of-detail of the schedule will be more general, with the vast majority of activities overlapping. The average duration, for both activities and relationships, will be a larger number. Since the purpose of Collaborative Scheduling is to set "push-pin" target goals for performance of activity clusters (in Momentum jargon: *regions*), it is far less important *how* the dates are created by the software.

Conversely, if your Execution Schedule is meant to support a Command-and-Control manager, then the level-of-detail of the schedule will be more granular. As a result, there will be a larger proportion of finish-to-start relationships. The average duration, for both activities and relationships, will be a smaller number. With more focus on the relationships, the need is greater to understand the implications and practical effects of different relationship types—and their calculations.

While I hope for, anticipate, and encourage a move away from Command-and-Control-oriented Schedules toward Collaboration-intended schedule, I recognize that the latter is still the exception. Therefore, in order to keep my word and help you create Project Schedules that will actually be used in the here and now, I must provide you with techniques that will make for better Schedules in a Command-and-Control environment. The remaining comments are so intended.

As I noted earlier, the Project Schedule's ability to project into the future is directly correlated to the reasonableness with which its inherent activities and relationships are logically tied. This may well explain why I am constantly amazed at how often supposedly "seasoned" Execution Schedulers fail to make the distinction between relationship configurations or how they often appear cavalier when tying activities together.

Negative Finish-to-Start Tie

For instance, I can't tell you how many times I've found myself in a heated debate with a fellow Scheduling Practitioner who wants to use a negative finish-to-start instead of a positive start-to-start, as if the two are functionally identical. They are not—even if they yield the same earliest-dates in a steady-state situation! To explain my heartburn, consider a few helpful illustrations.

Figure 10-1 might seem to confirm my colleague's contention that the two connections yield the same results. In the upper panel, using an SS+4, Activity B cannot start until

Figure 10-1

Steady State
Condition

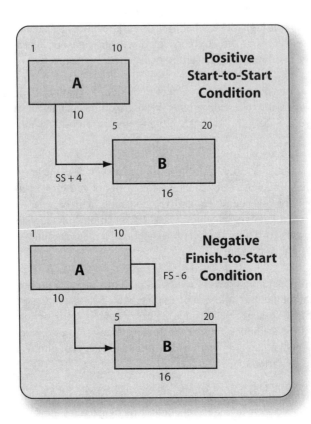

Day 5. If we change the relationship to an FS–6, as in the lower panel, we get the same results: Activity B still can't start before Day 5. So why do I see the two ties as appreciably different?

The answer should be apparent to you if you understand what each relationship type is actually depicting. A finish-to-start relationship says that there is *something* about the *end* of Activity A that controls the start of Activity B. A start-to-start relationship says that there is *something* about the *start* of Activity A that controls the start of Activity B.

Now, using Figure 10-2, let's introduce Activity X and tie it to Activity A with a finish-to-finish relationship. Let us suppose that Activity X is delayed such that it cannot finish before Day 14. With an FF+3 linking it to Activity A, Activity A cannot finish before Day 17. Okay, given this development, now tell me if the two different relationships between Activity A and Activity B say the same thing!

When Activity A is tied to Activity B with an SS+4 (lower panel), the delay to the end of Activity A by Activity X has no bearing on the start of Activity B. But when Activity

Figure 10-2
Negative Finish-to-Start with Finish Impact

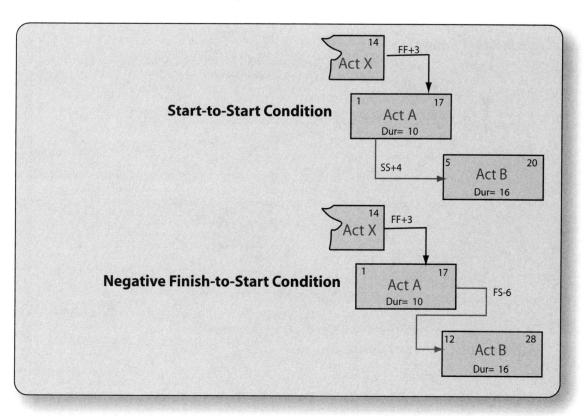

A is tied to Activity B with an FS-6 (upper panel), the delay to the end of Activity A by Activity X has a direct bearing on the start of Activity B.

The contrast is just as dramatic if the delaying activity is affecting the *start* of Activity A. Consider Figure 10-3. Here we introduce Activity Y, which is tied to the start of Activity A, with an FS+0 (implied, but not shown). We continue to assume the presence of delaying Activity X as well. If Activity X was an owner activity, and Activity Y was a contractor activity, we might have a *concurrent delay* situation—but only if we can show that the two were *each* impacting the same activity at the same time.

In Figure 10-3's upper panel, Activity A is tied to Activity B with an SS+4 relationship. In this scenario, the delay created by Activity Y transmits directly to the start of Activity A, which in turn passes to the start of Activity B. But when we switch to the other scenario, shown in the lower panel, where Activity A is tied to Activity B with an FS-6, the delay of Activity Y is not immediately felt by Activity B. Instead, Activity Y would have to impact Activity A by *more than ten days* before it would have any effect on Activity B.

Figure 10-3
Negative Finish-to-Start with Start Impact

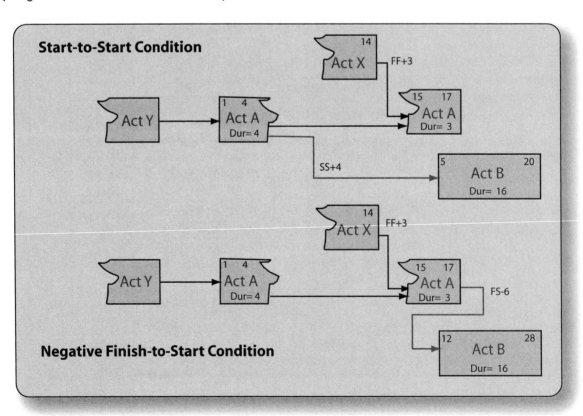

There is a bigger lesson in this discussion, however, than simply the difference between a positive start-to-start and a negative finish-to-start. Underlying this confusion is a tendency among even seasoned Schedulers to think, erroneously, that if a schedule's logic looks viable before the project starts, it will remain viable once the project is underway and is acquiring status. The use of date-constraints is another condition in which this confusion plays out. Date-constraints, also called imposed-dates, look good in the original Baseline Schedule, but once the project begins and Performance Recording commences, those date-constraints don't always perform as intended.

That is why the logic must be as realistic as possible. Use a start-to-start relationship type when there is something about the *start* of Activity A that must be completed before Activity B can *start*. A helpful way to understand this is to see Activity A as having two distinct segments; call them Activity A^1 and Activity A^2, as shown in Figure 10-4.

I'm sure you would agree with me that if Activity A^1 was a distinct activity, we would know what its scope was meant to entail, and we would have no difficulty knowing whether, or when, it was completed—and, hence, when Activity B could commence.

Figure 10-4
Productive Work Segments

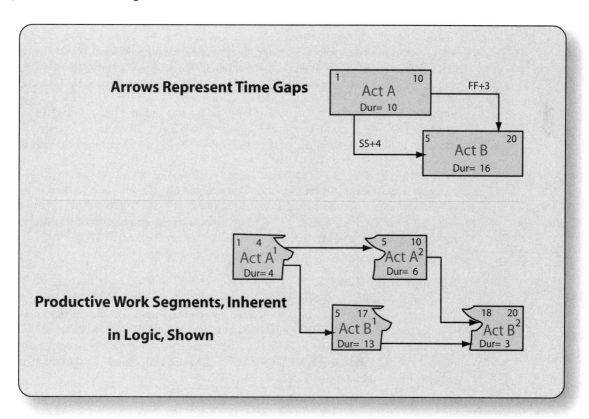

We should apply the same rigor to defining the scope to be completed within the four days of Activity A[1], when we use an SS 4.

Time Gaps and Work Segments

This provides the perfect segue into a discussion of four new terms: *Productive Work Segment, Time Gap, Productive Time Gap, and Administrative Time Gap*:

- **Productive Work Segment (PWS)** An activity portion[1] restrained at its start by a unique set of Productive Work Segments, the start of the project, or by one or more arbitrary constraints.
- **Time Gap (TG)** An imposed delay to the start of a Productive Work Segment.
- **Productive Time Gap (PTG)** A Time Gap required by the completion of a prior Productive Work Segment.
- **Administrative Time Gap (ATG)** A Time Gap required by the completion of administrative actions that are prerequisites to a Productive Work Segment.

Now let's discuss these definitions. To begin with, the expression *productive* work refers to any scope of work represented by a portion, or all, of an activity-duration. With this interpretation, I am suggesting that the activity-duration is not just a measure of time. It can also be construed as a measure of productive work to be performed. This, you may recall, is a principle important to Momentum Theory.

Productive Work Segment

A *Productive Work Segment* refers to the division of an activity's duration, by way of logic ties. Consider Figure 10-5. When activity-durations are set to the Interruptible Condition setting, an activity can have multiple Productive Work Segments, separated by Time Gaps.

Activity A has two distinct Productive Work Segments, the first being four days long (PWS:A[1]) and the second being six days long (PWS:A[2]). PWS:A[1] is restrained by whatever logic ties restrain the start of Activity A. PWS:A[2] is restrained by the completion of PWS:A[1].

Activity B has two distinct Productive Work Segments, the first being 13 days long (PWS:B[1]) and the second being 3 days long (PWS:B[2]). PWS:B[1] is restrained by the completion of PWS:A[1], while PWS:B[2] is restrained by the completion of PWS:B[1] *and* by the completion of PWS:A[2]. As you can see, each Productive Work Segment is restrained by one or more other Productive Work Segments.[2]

Concept of the Time Gap

Now, let's consider the *numeric value* assigned to a relationship that links two Productive Work Segments. In general terms, we call these *relationship-durations*. But, in order to fully understand the true dynamics at play behind the scenes, we must regard the relationship-duration as a *Time Gap*, an imposed, intentional delay to the commencement of a Productive Work Segment. We must also understand *why* the gap in time is being imposed in the first place.

---

[1] The portion may be the entire activity, or merely a part of the activity.
[2] Except for the first work segment of the schedule's first activity.

Figure 10-5

Time Gaps and Productive Work Segments

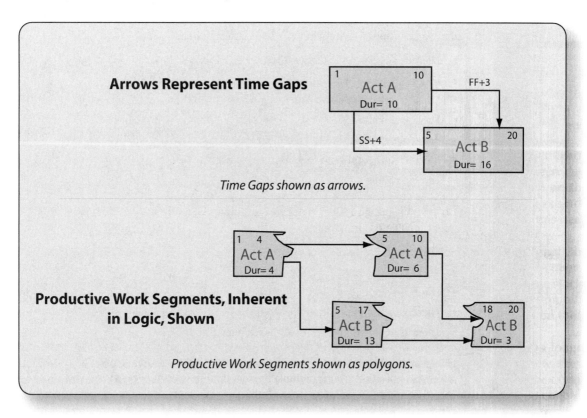

Arrows Represent Time Gaps

Time Gaps shown as arrows.

Productive Work Segments, Inherent in Logic, Shown

Productive Work Segments shown as polygons.

One further distinction needs to be made regarding Productive Work Segments, the *nature* of the Time Gap. That is, we must determine whether the Time Gap is to allow time for *productive* or *administrative* actions. It is within this distinction that we can at last find one of the most influential reasons why Project Schedules so often fail.

Productive Time Gap

As just explained, a Productive Time Gap is a planned delay in the commencement of a Productive Work Segment while waiting for completion of another Productive Work Segment. I'd like to point out that the conventional (and essentially universal) interpretation of both start-to-start and finish-to-finish relationships is consistent with the Productive Time Gap definition. For instance, Activity B cannot commence until after x days of Activity A have been performed. Likewise, Activity B cannot complete (that is, its latter Productive Work Segment cannot commence) until the completion of prior Activity A.

Administrative Actions

It might be helpful to take a simple example from your kitchen. The activity Wash Dishes has both productive and nonproductive aspects. The productive actions include holding the dish and rubbing it with a scrub pad containing dish soap while holding it beneath a stream of hot water. It also entails setting the dish into a dish drain. The activity Dry Dishes entails lifting the wet dish, rubbing it with a towel, and then setting it down on a dry surface. Examples of administrative actions that are necessary prerequisites to the Wash Dishes activity would include ensuring that:

- There is access to the dirty dishes.
- There is a scrub pad.
- There is sufficient dish soap.
- There is a dish rack.
- There is someone to wash the dishes.
- There is sufficient time to wash the dishes.
- There is water.

Concerning the Dry Dishes activity, examples of prerequisite administrative actions might include ensuring that:

- There is access to the wet dishes.
- There is a dishtowel.
- There is someone to dry the dishes.
- There is sufficient time to dry the dishes.
- There is somewhere to put the dishes once dried.

If you stop to think about it, every one of these administrative actions is critical to the *commencement* and *continuation* of the two Productive Work Segments. Failure to complete any of the first seven administrative actions could easily preclude the Wash Dishes activity from either starting or continuing to completion. Likewise, failure to perform any of the other five administrative actions could easily preclude the Dry Dishes activity from either starting or continuing to completion.

Administrative Time Gap

An *Administrative Time Gap* is a Time Gap required for the completion of administrative actions that are prerequisites to a Productive Work Segment. The tremendous importance of the Administrative Time Gap cannot be overstated. I believe the root of most schedule delays can be traced back to failure to perform administrative actions in a timely manner, as well as in how conventional CPM practice treats (ignore) the Administrative Time Gap.

Finish-to-Finish Relationship   Let's understand where the Administrative Time Gap occurs in a typical PDM schedule. Table 10-1 shows where both productive and administrative Time Gaps appear in the PDM anatomy. As noted earlier, a finish-to-finish relationship is an excellent example of a pure Productive Time Gap, because PWS:B^2 is *only* restrained by *Productive* Work Segments, and *not* by administrative actions. Both PWS:B^1 and PWS:A^2 restrain it. Any administrative actions required for PWS:B^2 were already contained in the Administrative Time Gap preceding PWS:B^1.

	Productive Time Gap	Administrative Time Gap
Start-to-Start	Yes	Yes
Finish-to-Finish	Yes	No
Finish-to-Start	No	Yes

Table 10-1

Correlation Between *Time Gap* Types and PDM Relationship Types

Finish-to-Start Relationship   A finish-to-start relationship exemplifies the exact opposite condition. Assuming that the finish-to-start relationship has a relationship-duration of zero, then Activity B is restrained *only* by the prior completion of Activity A. Now you begin to see the importance of the distinction between administrative and productive Time Gaps, for if there is one or more administrative prerequisites to the commencement of Activity B, then the finish-to-start relationship duration, *in theory*, ought to be greater than zero,[3] or these actions must be performed at the same time as other predecessor Productive Work Segments.

Start-to-Start Relationship   Now hold on—if you have heartburn over my suggestion that the finish-to-start should have a duration to represent work that is *not* also represented by an activity description or other clarification of work scope, then consider the start-to-start relationship. For with the start-to-start relationship, we almost *always* have a Time Gap with *both* administrative and productive elements (and yet no accompanying description).

Surely, Activity B cannot start until some amount of productive work is performed on Activity A. This, of course, is the conventional interpretation of a start-to-start. But what is *not* conventional is realizing that virtually every activity in a Project Schedule has administrative prerequisites to its commencement, and those administrative actions are rarely delineated or their performance durations quantified. Here's why I say this. I challenge you to find an industry where these project management basics do not apply:

- Before an activity can start you need *people* to perform the work of that activity.
- You likely need *materials* and *equipment*.
- You need a *place* for the work to occur.
- You almost always need *vital information*.

Ah, now there's the rub: making sure that these required elements are in place in time for the activity to begin is a management task *that is not included in the Project Schedule.* Do you get that? It is the rare Project Schedule that includes or allows time for administrative activities. It is just *assumed* that management will do its job and see to it that the people, materials, equipment, logistics, and information will be in place *in time* for the activity to start. And management will do all of this in sufficient time so as not to hold up the work (yeah, right!).

---

[3]Or, those Administrative Actions must be performed and completed by the time PWS:A^2 is completed.

According to the Momentum Studies, the cold truth is that—more often than not (to the tune of about 60 percent)—administrative actions are *not* completed in time, and so the successor activity's start *is* delayed accordingly. In the end, so is the project, if such a delay affects activities on the critical-path. Can you think of a single construction activity on any project that does not require the prerequisite availability of material, equipment, labor, logistics, or information? Of course not, and that is why I contend that, "virtually every activity in a construction Schedule has administrative prerequisites."

The other side of the coin is that start-to-start relationships are hardly ever developed with administrative actions in mind. Instead, as the conventional wisdom goes, a start-to-start duration limitedly refers to the prior completion of a preceding Productive Work Segment. In fact, the very term "start-to-start" suggests that the successor's start is dependent on the predecessor's start—*and nothing else.*

Momentum Studies have shown beyond doubt that most project delays trace back to administrative failures. This is because, as I noted earlier in the book, "around 90 percent of *all* activities finish within 5 percent of the original estimated duration." It is not the untimely performance of Productive Work Segments that causes the majority of delays. It is the untimely, slow, or omitted performance of administrative actions that causes projects to slip.

So now you know why Execution Schedules, especially PDM varieties, so often fall short of meeting implicitly or explicitly assumed objectives. The vast majority of project delays occur because:

- Administrative actions are either not performed, or performed slowly or incompletely

and

- The Execution Schedule fails to allocate time for their performance in any regard.

So, in a real example involving Erect Studs and Hang Drywall, a planned start-to-start duration of three days became an actual start-to-start duration of seven. Yet, when we examined the performance of Erect Studs, we saw that it had a planned continuous-duration of ten days and an actual continuous-duration of ten days. In other words, Erect Studs was performed at a productivity rate exactly equivalent to what had been estimated. Reason would suggest, therefore, that Erect Studs was not responsible for the Hang Drywall activity starting late. That is, at the end of the third day of consecutive work, Erect Studs was 30 percent complete, and at that point it no longer represented a restraint to the start of Hang Drywall.

We then reviewed project documentation, including submittal logs, personal diaries, meeting minutes, and correspondence, and found that Hang Drywall did not start for the following reasons, all of which were the result of administrative actions that were either not performed, or were performed incompletely, inadequately, or untimely.

- The intended work area was cluttered with materials of another subcontractor.
- Design questions, posed to the engineer only the day before work was scheduled to commence, had not yet been answered.

- The labor crew was short by two men.
- The material hoist was broken and there was no way to get the compressor to the floor.

It was only after these items were resolved, *which collectively consumed seven days*, that Hang Drywall was able to commence.

THE ADM-PDM BATTLEGROUND

For many years, the most heated debates among Scheduling Practitioners have been on the comparative merits and drawbacks of PDM or ADM. To be sure, over the last 15 years or so, PDM has achieved CPM legitimacy, even supremacy. While in the mid-1980s it represented maybe 20 percent of all CPM schedules, I would estimate that, today, 85 out of 100 CPM schedules are in the PDM format, if not more. The rate would be even higher if it weren't for outdated government specifications still requiring that Critical Path Method schedules be developed in "activity on arrow" format. As hard as this is to believe, I still encounter specifications requiring activity numbers to be sequential and in ascending order only—a clear fallback to the late '70s when early CPM software algorithms had such computational requirements.

In my recent leadership role at the College of Scheduling, heading up the Schedule Excellence Initiative, I had the opportunity to dialogue with literally hundreds of Scheduling Practitioners from all around the world and from all industries that employ CPM Scheduling. I believe I have heard every argument for or against either diagramming method. I have reached my conclusion: you will have to make up your own mind. To help you do so, allow me to present a summary of the main arguments made by each camp.

From the PDM Camp

Those who favor PDM insist that it is easier to interpret, it handles logic changes more easily, it reduces a Schedule's activity count, and it achieves broad acceptance more readily. By contrast, they insist that ADM draws more participant resistance, it is not as intuitive to read diagrammatically, the use of dummies seems artificial (if not also offensive), and the ADM method, with its many "rules," ties the Scheduler's hands more.

PDM Is Easier to Interpret

Draw a PDM chart on the board and it looks like a flow chart. Even constructors with absolutely no formal training in CPM scheduling can follow the direction of the arrows. By contrast, draw an ADM chart with its paired nodes and dashed-line "dummies," and in a very short time people start scratching their heads. (They also joke about the dummies!). See Figure 10-6.

PDM Handles Corrections More Easily

During logic development sessions, especially on renovation projects, there is a lot of mind changing. As the members of the Schedule Development team sit around the table watching the Scheduler slowly add activity after activity to the diagram taking shape on the wipe-off board, they frequently disagree with and override one another. Some logic

Figure 10-6

ADM versus PDM; No Overlaps

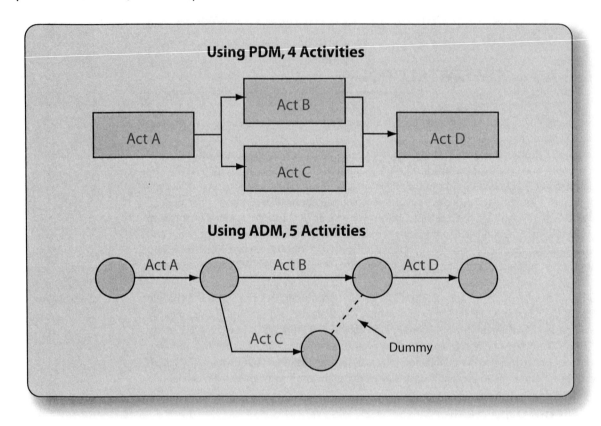

ties are removed while others are inserted. In PDM, this is easily accomplished with the swipe of the thumb (to erase) and a pen (to draw in the new line). In ADM, complete sections of the logic need to be erased and redrawn, since ADM diagrams are necessarily scaled.

PDM Reduces Activity Count

ADM prohibits the connection of activities midlength; activities can only be connected at their start or end. This is perhaps the biggest difference between ADM and PDM. In our earlier example of overlapping Activities A and B, in ADM Activity A would have to be divided into two activities: Start Activity A and Finish Activity A. Activity B would then *start* at the *end* of Start Activity A and run parallel to Finish Activity A. Because of this limitation, ADM schedules are inundated with what I call *stuttering* activities. It is not at all uncommon to see three, four, and even five or more similarly worded activities in a row: Start Excavation, Continue Excavation, Continue Excavation, Continue Excavation, and Complete Excavation. In PDM, these five activities would still be *one* activity, Excavation. It is no wonder that ADM schedules are, on average, 35 percent larger in terms of activity count!

Fourth, ADM requires the use of "dummies," bogus activities of zero duration and zero scope, needed to accommodate ADM's inflexible demand that no two activities have the same head-tail node pair. Between the proliferation of dummies and the overwhelming presence of "stuttering activities," ADM schedules are typically 30–40 percent larger in number of activities than their PDM counterparts.

Figure 10-7 illustrates the point that ADM generates far more activities than PDM.

PDM Earns Contractor Buy-In More Easily

Many PDM proponents insist that ADM schedules tend to enjoy less contractor *buy-in* than PDM schedules. Project Schedules aren't worth producing in the first place if they aren't going to be used, and contractors, like most human beings, have this bad habit of avoiding things they don't understand. By contrast, when a contractor enjoyably participates in a schedule's Logic Development Sessions *and* when he understands how to interpret the resultant Execution Schedule, he is far more inclined to incorporate the Project Schedule into his implementation plan.

The opposite is just as true. Contractors have a hard time understanding ADM diagrams. The logic sessions are less "friendly," to borrow a term from the software world. They sit through the logic sessions watching the Scheduler slowly paint on the board what looks like an electrical circuitry schematic you'd find on the back of a television set.

But here's the real kicker! When it comes to assigning activity-durations, the contractor's input is vital—indeed, indispensable. Durations from any other source can never be as valid or as meaningful as the ones coming from the guy who is going to do the work. First, he probably has the most experience in that specific field of construction. Second, and more importantly, if it is *his* duration, he's more apt to achieve it. If it's a duration being imposed upon him, he'll remind you of that little tidbit when the dates start slipping.

ADM Draws More Contractor Resistance

Now let me tell you why ADM schedules get less buy-in from contractors. It has to do with those stuttering activities. Try asking a contractor to tell you how much time he requires to perform his activities. He'll answer in the most general numbers he can get away with and work his way down from there. He'll start with something like, "Give me three months and I'll be out of here."

So you push him to be a bit more specific—say, how long on each floor? He mumbles something under his breath, not wanting to be pinned down, and finally says, "I'll need five weeks per floor." But you're not satisfied because his work involves at least seven distinctly different activities. Let's say that he is the plumber, and he has toilet fixtures, water fountains, boilers, and vertical lines in the pipe chase to perform, just to name a few. You want separate durations for each separate activity and you *need* this level of detail, because each item fits at a different place in the schedule.

Again he grumbles, but essentially holds his ground: "Give me three weeks for each activity." Now you know he doesn't need three weeks to install toilet fixtures, but he

Figure 10-7

ADM versus PDM; with Overlapped Logic

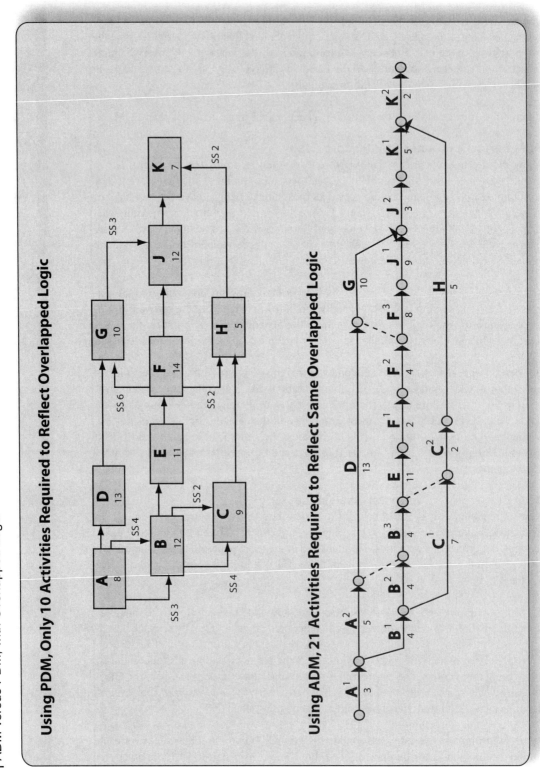

Using PDM, Only 10 Activities Required to Reflect Overlapped Logic

Using ADM, 21 Activities Required to Reflect Same Overlapped Logic

may need more than three weeks to install the pipe chase. You decide not to squabble (for the moment), recognizing when it is prudent to *take what you can get and be grateful*. What you think to yourself is that you'll show his Toilet Fixtures activity at three weeks and simply overlap predecessor and successor activities accordingly. Prior to Toilet Fixtures there is Ceramic Tile work, afterward Toilet Partitions. No problem—if you're in PDM, that is. But the story would be much different if you were using ADM.

In ADM, you have a problem. There is no capacity for overlapping of activities—that is, not without stuttering the activity. And so, you grit your teeth, wince your eyes, and return to confront the now clearly defensive (and impatient) contractor.

"Mack, there are three clusters of bathrooms per floor. In order for me to overlap your work with the others, I need to establish a duration for *each bathroom*." You take a deep breath—and wait. Quietly the man stands up, closes his book, adjusts the cell phone hanging from his belt, and heads for the door. Over his shoulder, he informs you that he has a field problem to attend to, after mumbling something about pounding sand. And with that, your audience and his cooperation are lost forever. Whatever else you may choose to do with his activities matters not to him; he'll neither understand it nor agree to it. From this point on, it'll be "that damned Scheduler's pipe dream."

The preceding story may seem far-fetched. It is not! That same storyline has played out on, easily, half of all the ADM logic sessions in which I have ever participated. At the core, ADM diagrams just don't *look* like construction; they look like computers. PDM logic is nonoffensive; there is nothing to distract the participant from reading the activity's description, duration, and logic, and *going on from there*.

From the ADM Camp

Those who favor ADM take issue with what they perceive as PDM's more lax approach to logic depiction. They contend that "Precedence" (PDM's nickname) encourages schedule abuses. Specifically, they register the following complaints.

Objection to Non-Specific Start-to-Start

Surely the most often cited criticism of PDM is the concept of the start-to-start relationship. To these critics, the start-to-start relationship provides for a numeric "delay" between the start of one activity and the start of a successor, yet it does not require any corresponding declaration of associated scope to "explain" why the delay is necessary. This failure to require corresponding scope definition is seen as an excellent breeding ground for schedule distortion and manipulation. To be sure, ask any claims consultant whether this argument has merit, and you will receive an earful about how shady Schedulers and project managers use the start-to-start values to artificially shorten or lengthen paths at will.

Objection to Negative Lags

Another popular criticism attacks the practice of assigning negative relationship-durations, also called negative leads and lags. Critics contend that negative values are counter-intuitive, and thus just another opportunity for schedule abuse. To be sure, some negative values and relationship type combinations truly do defy commonsense inter-pretation. Consider a negative finish-to-start of 12. In this case, Activity B cannot start until 12 days before Activity A finishes. But, unless one is either God or has a crystal ball, how does one know *when* Activity A will finish? Since we cannot know Activity B's planned finish date, we cannot know Activity A's planned start date.

Objection to Overlapping Activities

As an extension of the first argument, ADM proponents criticize the use of any rela-tionship type other than the straightforward finish-to-start. They insist that overlapping activities with the start-to-start and finish-to-finish ties is just the lazy Scheduler's way of avoiding the more meticulous level of precision possible with ADM. The start-to-start and finish-to-finish numeric values represent elements of work for which the PDM method requires no corresponding descriptive clarification of scope.

Guilty by Association

Several other arguments have been lodged against PDM, which I will list here. While I list them under the general heading of complaints from the ADM camp, I wish to quickly point out that the following items are actually not unique to PDM, and could/would just as easily appear in ADM schedules, if present-day scheduling soft-ware offered the ADM format.

- **Too Many Constraints**   Project Schedules that include an excessive amount of arbitrary date-constraints have the undesired effect of over-complicating the logic and distorting total-float readings and critical-path mapping.
- **Too Many Calendars**   The use of numerous automated calendars can have an equally debilitating effect on the integrity of the Project Schedule.
- **Absence of Resource Planning**   A common criticism of PDM is that Project Schedules developed without adequate consideration of resource availability or deployment create unrealistic and misleading Execution Schedules.

As already noted, whether or not these are legitimate criticisms in any context, their attribution specifically and exclusively to PDM is both unfair and unfounded, in my opinion. The reason PDM has become the target for the above complaints is because the software features to which these practices apply evolved at the same time PDM overtook ADM as the dominant diagramming method. One would be hard-pressed to find, in any of today's scheduling software, the option to schedule in ADM. Thus, when abuses do occur—whether with excessive date-constraints, excessive calendars, or defi-cient resource planning—they occur in PDM schedules mostly.

11 Working at Cross-Purposes

The purpose of this chapter is to identify and acknowledge the influence of unseen forces that may subtly eat away at the fabric of the scheduling process and, as a result, *your* Project Schedules. Little by little, and rarely intentionally, certain encroaching forces gradually erode the Project Schedule's potency as a time management tool. In this chapter we will look at three seemingly unrelated topics. What they have in common is an equal ability to invalidate Project Schedules, destroy the Scheduling processes on the project, and undermine the integrity of our Scheduling Practice altogether.

- **Harmful Scheduling Practices**   Throughout the course of this book, various problems with the CPM methodology have been identified, a few inherent in the Method itself, but many others created by the manner in which the methodology is applied in common practice. The focus of this section will be on the most common and popular techniques by which Execution Schedules are employed in the project management world. This discussion will alert you to how, as you innocently operate according to the conventional wisdom you have been taught, you may unwittingly be weakening the overall usefulness of the Scheduling effort on your projects.

- **Competing Project Controls**   Next, we will look at how the integrity of a Project Schedule can be compromised by well-intentioned, yet nevertheless imposing, requirements of project controls interests that hope to use the Project Schedule to achieve project objectives other than deadline achievement. Good intentions notwithstanding, the net effect of a constant pulling and tugging on the fabric of the Scheduling cloth can be seen in the irrefutable chaos that now ensues within the Scheduling community. As a tangible example of this chaos, consider the state of Scheduling terminology.

- **Flawed Definitions**   Our Practice is suffering from what I call the "Tower of Babel effect," where, among project management team members, there can be an undeniable language barrier. In practice, we use terms that have different meanings to different people. Elsewhere in this book I have identified two separate disconnects, as relate to the technical words we use. First, there are certain expressions that have more than one meaning. Second, there are certain intended meanings for which we have more than one expression.

These inconsistencies manifest themselves in the form of two distinct problems with the preponderance of today's definitions: most are simply incorrect, and collectively they are inconsistent with one another. I'm not sure which is worse; that the newcomer to the world of construction project Scheduling can find so many different definitions for the same terms, or that (in certain cases), not one of the definitions is correct!

But let's save this hot topic for last, and instead begin this chapter with an examination of how, in the ways we *use* the Project Schedule, we can actually cause measurable erosion of its time-relative potency.

HARMFUL SCHEDULING PRACTICES

However you categorize it, the CPM methodology has both deficiencies and limitations that, if operative, can bring into question the accuracy, reliability, potency, and overall value of the schedules it produces. To be sure, the Critical Path Method in its purest theoretical version is fundamentally sound. My only major criticism concerning the methodology itself is that its inventors stopped short of identifying *activity* total-float, instead choosing to attribute *path* total-float to the activities that reside on that path. As a result, standard schedule reports are often potentially misleading in their redundant citation of total-float and are problematic in their willing allocation of total-float on a first-come-first-served basis.

Turning to an examination of *how* the Methodology is applied in the real world, we will explore four major deficiencies and limitations in particular. See Figure 11-1. In this sense, CPM (and the software that drives it) doesn't fail projects, the people who employ them do. Also, notice that there is a compounding effect to the more glaring of these deficiencies.

Total-Float: The Only Statement of Criticality

We use total-float as the *only* statement of criticality, but total-float is not the only way to determine relative criticality. Other methods of defining criticality (pertaining to activity, path, or schedule components) are noticeably absent from the CPM methodology. See my comments on "Criticality" in Chapter 16.

But even setting aside the existence of other measures of criticality, though, we would still be prudent to temper our sole dependence on total-float, given its imprecise nature. Total-float is nothing more than the difference between earliest-dates and latest-dates, and those "dates" are nothing more than the arithmetic effect of activity-durations and relationship-durations. Since we typically give little serious thought to the start-to-start values we assign in the first place for Productive Time Gaps, relationship-durations are derived rather unscientifically, with little underlying basis or historical documentation of assumptions. Furthermore, the Administrative Time Gap is not acknowledged at all as a discrete value in its own right!

Certainly, there may be Practitioners who inflate the activity-duration to provide time for the performance of administrative tasks, but in doing so they compromise the integrity of the activity-duration as a pure representation of *productive* work. I am opposed to this practice of including time for administrative tasks in the activity-duration. Besides, many

Figure 11-1
Harmful
Scheduling
Practices

Harmful Scheduling Practices

Total-Float as the
Only Measure of Criticality

Not Perceiving Activity and
Relationship Durations
as of Equal Importance

Total-Float Obession
Ignores Nearby Smoke

Pervasive Practice of
Incomplete Logic

administrative tasks are prerequisites to multiple activities. Should all affected tasks be reflected by redundantly increasing numerous activity-durations by the same padded amount?

Relationship-Durations and Activity-Durations Equally Important

The relationship-duration and the activity-duration are of equal importance to the determination of earliest-dates, latest-dates, total-float, and critical-paths. This is not only arithemtically true, but statistically true as well. According to the Momentum Studies, 40 percent of the critical path typically travels through relationships rather than through activities. If 40 percent of the collective project length of any Project Schedule is based on unsupported relationship-durations, how reliable can that Execution Schedule be in projecting critical start and finish dates, speculating on schedule slippage or gains, or in any of its many other uses?

The compounding effect of inaccurate or unrealistic relationship-durations can be seen in the example of high-rise construction. Imagine a 41-story building, and a floor-to-floor stagger of 10 days. There are *40* such overlaps. Now if we simply change the 10-day stagger to an 11-day stagger, we add 2 months to the project schedule—40 workdays!

This same phenomenon occurs throughout the logic of *every* Execution Schedule, whether the logic string is repetitious or not. For instance, if the longest path through the Project Schedule contains 41 activities, then there are 40 relationships, right? Now, if 60 percent of those are through start-to-start ties, and if we reduce these 24 relationship-durations, by 1 day each, our total-float value is decreased by 24 workdays, or nearly 5 weeks! If we increased the average relationship-duration by 3 days, total-float would be extended by over 3.5 months! The point is that total-float, at its core, is based in large part on unsubstantiated relationship-durations.

Ignoring Nearby Smoke

The Total-Float Report, the second most frequently used Schedule Extraction format (after the Earliest-Start Report), encourages project managers to stare obsessively at the scattered fires (those first few pages of activities with negative total-float) while simultaneously ignoring nearby smoke (latter pages with quickly disappearing positive total-float). Tomorrow's surprises are rarely on today's radar screen.

Incomplete Logic

Add to this practice the equally frequent occurrence of incomplete logic, and the Project Schedule becomes even more suspicious. Dangling activities and missing logic ties are the more apparent signs of incomplete logic, but unpaired start and finish ties are another. Excessive or inappropriate use of date-constraints is still another cause of distorted Execution Schedules.

The purpose of this section is not to list *every* pitfall and shortcoming of CPM, but rather the more egregious. Some may quarrel with my choices for inclusion, but here is my reasoning. As noted earlier, unless you are building a cookie-cutter project, each project is unique. The more unique the project, the less predictable a project is from day to day. And the more unpredictable a project, the more likely it is to incur schedule slippage that results from failing to anticipate or not responding to those surprises in a timely and adequate manner.

This places a very real burden and expectation on Project Schedules, and the methodologies that produce and maintain them, to help project management anticipate, manage, and overcome those surprises. But how can they help us anticipate problems when we only use them in a *reactive* mode? How can they help us when they are based on spurious relationship-durations, incomplete logic, and redundantly stated total-float?

COMPETING PROJECT CONTROLS

Elsewhere in this book I have talked about the mutual exclusivity relationship between many of the project management support systems that commandeer the Execution Schedule in support of well-intended, yet nevertheless competing, purposes. Specifically yet collectively, as the number of functional demands upon the Schedule increases, mandated by the mechanics of various project management support technologies, the value of the Project Schedule as a strictly *time management* tool decreases.

Principally this diminished utility is because each technology imposes certain requirements that the Project Schedule must incorporate during design, development, maintenance, or usage phases.

For this reason, I encourage extreme discretion when deciding which, if any, project management support systems to impose on the Execution Schedule. Surely, consideration of the Emphasis Alignment Model should guide such decisions (see Chapter 12). Additionally, though, the independent potential usefulness of any given system of project management support should be evaluated as part of the decision to:

• Employ that project control system at all

and

• Burden the Project Schedule with its structural and functional design criteria

With the latter advice in mind, I offer thoughts on two popular project management methodologies, both of which impose, through their implementation, *significant* modifications to the design, development, content, maintenance, and usage of conventional CPM schedules. The reader is asked to infer an overall message from these two examples: be smart about what you allow to weaken the integrity of the Project Schedule as a pure *time management* tool.

THE BENEFITS AND LIMITATIONS OF EARNED VALUE MANAGEMENT SYSTEM (EVMS)

The reason for discussing Earned Value in a book dedicated to improving CPM schedules is that proper application of Earned Value requires a viable Execution Schedule[1], with "viability" defined by Earned Value performance standards, thereby creating yet another opportunity for project management disappointment, should Earned Value—or the Execution Schedule that underpins it—fail to contribute their expected advantages to the project.

While Earned Value is a most worthwhile and powerful cost management tool, it has limitations as to what it can tell us about the project from a time perspective. It also comes at a significant risk: a potential weakening of the Project Schedule's *time*-management muscle. We will look at each of these issues separately: Earned Value's advantages, its limitations, and its tendency to weaken the schedule as a time management tool.

Advantages of Earned Value

Earned Value is a fascinating improvement in project management, providing the project with many real benefits, principally through its ability to evaluate performance trends and speculate on project outcomes, accordingly. More than anything, Earned Value provides

---

[1]Technically, this is not true since Earned Value principles can be applied to a manual bar chart, but, in practice, virtually all Earned Value applications are within CPM schedules.

an "early warning" to management about the efficiency of resource performance in terms of cost and schedule variables.

Earned Value also makes good use of the concept of *trending*; something conventional CPM fails to do very well. CPM's total-float reporting argues (rather ridiculously) that if a project has lost 2 days each month for the first 4 months of a project, then at the end of the project's 2-year length, it will complete 8 days late and not 24 days late (if trending had been taken into consideration). By contrast, Earned Value looks at the performance of work, calculates performance trends, and then speculates on a more realistic cost-at-completion.

Limitations of Earned Value

For the many benefits that Earned Value yields to project management, it also has inherent limitations that I suggest are the source of some of the disappointment expressed within the Scheduling Practice. I say this because Earned Value's popularity brings with it high expectations that the project manager's number one adversary, *surprise*, will be arrested. That is, with Earned Value up and running, the project will have ample warning about performance deficiencies in sufficient time to make a difference. In reality, though, it all too often does not provide adequate early warning—or it provides misleading information. Either way, when Earned Value fails to deliver, the Project Schedule, and not Earned Value itself, is typically blamed, and therein lies my motivation for warning about applying Earned Value on a time-sensitive project.

Proper Earned Value application requires a rigorous scope definition process, including complex structures of organizational and work breakdown. These requirements quite often drive the Execution Schedule to a work package level that is more detailed than what would be needed to support effective time management processes. In other words, Earned Value can, and often does, make the Project Schedule more convoluted than it would be otherwise.

Further, it forces the Schedule Development exercise to follow a thinking process that is sometimes counterintuitive. In the next section, I will discuss the Critical Chain scheduling variant, which argues, as I do, that the proper way to think through a project scope is *backward*, from that one Ultimate Deliverable, back to the subordinate deliverables of predecessor phases of work that yield the Ultimate Deliverable, and so forth. Critical Chain proponents argue that the Newtonian structure mandated by Earned Value serves to fragment the work into detached "legs" that one must mentally span in order to envision (and plan) the continuity and interdependence of workflow. This is especially true when it requires that each separate work package have no more than one Work Breakdown Structure (WBS) element and one Organizational Breakdown Structure (OBS) element.

It is my contention that Earned Value is not appropriate for every project type. In fact, it is most appropriate for projects on which the scope of work is highly repetitive and extensively familiar to those performing the work. The reason I say this is because Earned Value is, at its heart, a baseline comparison method. It is a set of comparative formulas—contrasting estimated values to actual values. Cost variance analyses compare resources actually consumed with those estimated (budgeted) to be consumed. Schedule Variance analyses compare the estimated resources of planned activities to the estimated resources of performed activities.

Least Reliable on One-Of-A-Kind or Unfamiliar Project Types

If the underlying estimates were spurious, wouldn't the calculations based on those estimates be equally questionable? If a project entails a one-of-a-kind design that has never been performed in the history of the world, how good could be initial estimates of resource requirements? Ask the same question about a project entailing a design with which not one member of the project team has ever had experience.

Best When Extensively Familiar Only a few years ago, a world-class telecommunications giant embarked on building, launching, and operating a constellation of over 100 satellites, in support of a worldwide wireless voice and data communication system. The cost was in excess of $14 billion. Everything about this project was one-of-a-kind:

- It was one of the largest commercial projects in history.
- It involved contractors from all around the world, who would collaborate via the Internet.
- The satellite design was entirely unique in terms of the payloads it would carry.
- The software design was groundbreaking, as was the chip technology to support it.
- Over 3,000 engineers were assigned to the project, few having much more than *partial* prior experience to draw upon.

Given these conditions, is this the kind of project on which to employ a performance measurement method that evaluates current performance and speculates on future performance *based on estimates of what "reasonable" performance ought to be?* You can think of other examples of your own, where the nature of the work is essentially new or uncharted. Virtually all research and development (R&D) projects fall into this category. Can you estimate how long it will take (or how many labor hours will be required) to find a cure for cancer?

Best When Highly Repetitive Likewise, if the project involves numerous distinct phases, each containing different predominant work activities, such that performance during one phase provides few insights on the likely performance of subsequent phases, how rational would such speculation be?

Imagine a typical construction project that moves from one discipline to another. Most projects have a heavy civil concentration at the outset (earthwork, concrete, steel) followed by specialty trades (electrical, mechanical, controls). In corrections facilities, civil is followed by security equipment. In healthcare, civil is followed by utilities, just as is the case with most large process plants. In roadwork, civil is followed by signalization.

The question I am posing is this one: if performance during civil construction is appreciably good (or bad), and we generate Earned Value metrics for the civil work, does that tell us anything useful about how the project will be doing during subsequent and distinctly unique (in terms of discipline) phases of construction? If earthwork's Schedule

Variance is negative, will the 13,000 electrical cable terminations, yet to be performed, also be negative?

For these two reasons, I am reluctant to encourage the application of Earned Value on most commercial, private sector projects. The vast majority of commercial, private sector projects are performed by an assortment of independent contractors, giving life to a project execution plan that moves from one distinct work type to the next. On projects where the work is not highly repetitive or extremely familiar, rather than a baseline-based method, I would recommend any form of *To-Go*–based trending system.

Earned Value as a Schedule Performance Measurement Device

I admit that I am bugged when I hear people referring to Earned Value as a *performance measurement* methodology. While it may measure the performance of resources, it does not measure productivity of the worker. It doesn't measure time. It doesn't consider whether the work that *was* performed was the *right* work, added work scope, rework, or—even more importantly—whether the performed work was critical or not critical.

Whereas Cost Variance analyses deal with cost values, Schedule Variance analyses do not deal with schedule values. Rather, they too deal with cost values. Schedule Variance analyses typically compare planned and performed work *in terms of labor dollars or labor hours*, but not in terms of productive work performed. Both money and labor are resources, and project progress is derived by comparing the resource consumption estimates of work *scheduled* for performance versus the resource consumption estimates of work *actually* set in place.

Surely, using money as a basis for comparison is unreliable because it is two steps away from true work productivity, or even time consumption. If the "dollars" being compared are direct cost dollars, large equipment or materials costs could skew the ratio of dollars expended to work performed or time consumed. But even if just labor dollars are used, differences in pay rates, crew configurations, composite crew sizes, and work types—from one activity to the next—still distort the results.

Even labor hours themselves cannot be used to reflect performance because there is no direct correlation between labor consumption and time consumption. Remember that we are talking about (what EVMS calls) *schedule* performance, specifically. We want this methodology to opine on whether the project is behind, ahead of, or essentially on schedule.

To demonstrate this point in an admittedly extreme example, consider a two-activity longest path: Activity A requires two workers for 20 days, while Activity B requires 20 workers for 2 days. Combined, the project is expected to consume 80 worker-days and take 22 days to complete. Now here's what happens: for the first 18 days no work takes place whatsoever. The contractor, fearing that he'll look bad, decides that he will perform Activity B (out of sequence) during the last two days of the reporting period. He does so, and he earns a 1.00 SPI. According to Earned Value, he was supposed to burn 40 worker-days and he *did* burn 40 worker-days.

The point of this example is not that the work performed wasn't critical; it was. Nor is the point that the work was performed out of sequence, even though it was. Instead, the point is that the particular work performed was *not* the work *scheduled* to be performed. It was some other work that ultimately had to be done and that, if done ahead of schedule, would make the contractor look good.

And just how well is the project doing, *in terms of schedule performance?* Lousy. With only 2 days of the 22-day project length remaining, the length of the longest path of unfinished work is still 20 days long. The project is running 18 days behind schedule, yet according to Earned Value calculations, based on resource consumption comparisons, the project is on schedule!

Finally, we need only change our example slightly (making the two activities parallel) to create a circumstance where the work performed was *not* on the critical path, yet such performance offsets parallel deficiencies *on* the critical path. Earned Value's Schedule Variance analyses fail to take into account either the criticality of activities or whether those activities were the particular ones scheduled for accomplishment during the reporting period in the first place.

Emphasis-Aligned Management

We have to return to basics: focusing on that which the owner considers of greatest importance. If the owner wants the project done as quickly as possible, then the Schedule should be tailored to be the best *time* management tool possible. In any event, I am fundamentally opposed to Earned Value being permitted to opine on *schedule* performance since it is weak in that area.

If, on the other hand, the owner considers the project *cost*-sensitive, then Earned Value might be appropriate, if the project type supports the Earned Value method (scope is repetitive and historically familiar). Even then, the imposition of Earned Value requirements on the Execution Schedule should be restricted so that the Project Schedule's ability to manage time is not reduced below the level needed to meet owner time concerns.[2]

How Earned Value Weakens a Schedule as a Momentum-Management Tool

Traditional Earned Value methodology requires that the project scope be decomposed into *work packages*. A rather universal characteristic of the work package is that it is limited to a specific control account, which in turn is limited to a single OBS element. Additionally, the work package typically is limited to a single WBS element. These limitations can have the effect of driving the Execution Schedule's detail down to a level greater than what is either wanted or needed for time management purposes.

---

[2]Remember that, according to the Emphasis Alignment Model (see Chapter 12), while every project has one outcome that is more important to the owner than the other two, the owner is still concerned about all three. So, even though cost is the highest priority, the owner still expects the project to be done in a timely manner, and he will still insist on periodic predictions of when project completion will occur. The Schedule must remain viable as a time management tool, given this owner need, along with all the other legitimate uses of the Schedule, that no other project controls tool can provide.

Mandating the use of WBS and, quite often, OBS, also dictates the manner in which the Project Schedule is developed in the first place. Where Schedule developers might prefer to use a bottom-up, or end-backward approach to logic development, WBS (an EVMS mandate) demands that the process *must* be top-down.

Finally, Earned Value yields performance metrics that, for whatever the political reasons, have acquired an authenticity in the project management world that is not entirely supported at the foundational level. Even though these reports have the potential to be misleading, unfounded, or contradictory to CPM conclusions and projections, Earned Value's popularity is so great that pressure is often brought upon the Execution Schedule to make its conclusions agree with those of Earned Value. As a Scheduling Practice loyalist, I find this tantamount to the tail wagging the dog!

Surely Earned Value is valuable in quantifying and opining on the performance of project resources, principally money and labor hours. However, because it fails as a time-performance metric, and because in the course of posing as one it often has the effect of weakening the Project Schedule's ability to provide vital time-management information, I recommend that it be used *only* on projects where the owner values cost savings over time or quality, and where the project type supports Earned Value application.

THE BENEFITS AND LIMITATIONS OF CRITICAL CHAIN PROJECT MANAGEMENT (CCPM)

Critical Chain Project Management (CCPM) is a relatively recent arrival on the project management scene, a CPM aberration with strong emphasis on risk management. CCPM has gained an quick foothold in the IT world and has earned the acclaim of many IT managers for having shortened project lengths, and project managers seem more content.

To be sure, excluding the high acclaim by those who market CCPM products and services, to this mind the jury is still out on just how valuable or practical the methodology truly is, at least for construction projects. The sole reason I include it in this book is because a discussion of CCPM's strengths and weaknesses may help to further illustrate and emphasize some of the primary concerns I have been trying to drive home about the diluting effect of competing technologies on the Project Schedule.

Much like Earned Value, CCPM requires the presence of a viable CPM schedule, but with "viability" defined in accordance with CCPM's particular scheduling philosophy.[3] Also like Earned Value, this mandate places specific performance expectations on the CPM schedule. High hopes associated with the use of CCPM can easily lead to finger pointing in both directions, when either CCPM or the Project Schedule itself fails to deliver expected benefits to the project.

---

[3] In particular, CCPM has peculiar ideas about how the activity-duration is to be developed.

Please don't misinterpret my opening remarks concerning CCPM as being overly harsh. I happen to think CCPM is on the right track as it seeks to improve the way we manage projects, especially in its recognition of key limitations inherent in the conventional application of CPM. Where I remain skeptical, however, is with *how* it proposes to correct the problems it has so rightly identified. I admit that I have more research to do on this technology, but based on what I currently understand, several of its core assumptions seem unfounded—or, at least, inconsistent with the unique reality of the typical commercial, private sector construction projects I have run across. Perhaps one day I will change my mind, but for now I am skeptical about CCPM.

Both CCPM and Earned Value demand changes in how Execution Schedules are developed and used. To be sure, the CCPM requirements are fairly extreme and controversial (at least to me). Whether it will prove its overall worth in the construction industry at some point in the future, one thing is for sure: CCPM requires that we radically alter the way in which we construct and use CPM scheduling in the present. It demands that we abandon some of the basic tenets of traditional CPM methodology.

Since I have not thrown in the towel on long-established CPM scheduling processes and principles, I am reluctant to hop on this bandwagon just yet. While I share frustration with many of the problems inherent in traditional CPM methodology that CCPM literature has identified, I just happen to have different ideas on the appropriate *fix* for those problems.

What's Right About CCPM

A number of underlying principles of CCPM are to be applauded. Here are some of the more significant ones.

CCPM Questions Schedule Efficacy
At the top of the list, CCPM is correct when it questions the overall efficacy of CPM as a project management tool. At the highest level, CCPM advocates challenge a number of shortcomings inherent in the CPM methodology, in particular the credibility of the duration itself. They question the common approach to logic development and the essentially mandatory use of WBS.

CCPM Argues for Better Logic
When it comes to logic development, CCPM advocates a multipass approach that is intended to ensure that all of the key interdependencies of the project are captured in the Execution Schedule. CCPM also advocates for a consensus on project objectives, a complete listing of project deliverables, and most important of all, agreement on what will constitute project success. CCPM also views logic errors, in particular missed dependencies, as critical sources of risk.

CCPM Argues Against Compulsory WBS Approach
to Logic Development
CCPM training materials acknowledge the highly interdependent nature of projects, and questions the practicality of forcing logic development through WBS's Newtonian top-down structure, where one is required to envision logical *relationships* across otherwise

independent responsibility silos. This is the same point I was trying to make earlier. WBS is excellent when the project conforms to the Newtonian Model, but some project execution strategies are more driven by the *means and methods* to be applied on the project than by the layered and evolving production of deliverables.

CCPM Argues for Use of Buffers

While I have some heartburn with the buffer management concept, one thing I really like about it is that it provides a central collection point for *project* total-float and a meaningful measure of schedule resilience that is easy to track and report. Routinely neglected in traditional CPM since its inception is a quick way to measure the ability of the project to bounce back from an incurred delay. As commonly practiced, CPM merely yields a cyclical report on total-float, gained or lost. Undetected are the shifts, ebbs, and flows of dynamic forces that lead up to those gains or losses. By centralizing float, *and monitoring its dissipation*, CCPM's "project buffer" provides a convenient way to measure and report schedule dehydration.

What's Wrong About CCPM

I take issue with a number of foundational premises that CCPM assumes. Here are some of the more significant ones.

Flawed Success Criteria Assumption

CCPM assumes that on every project, getting finished quickly is the *only*, or the *most important*, success criterion. In fact, a metaphor adopted by CCPM proponents is that a project is tantamount to a relay race. I agree that, in a project where finishing on or ahead of schedule is more important than performing the work flawlessly or as inexpensively as possible, this may be the correct image. But even on time-sensitive projects, the relay race comparison ignores the competing interests of the project players, assuming instead that everyone amassed on the project has willingly adopted one, and only one, internal objective: completing the project by the owner's contract date.

To be sure, contractors may initially sign up for the *project's* primary objective, finishing as soon as possible. But that doesn't mean that they do not have other objectives of their own, such as: making a profit; looking for "extras;" exploiting scope changes; maximizing worker efficiency; keeping a loyal workforce *employed* while waiting for the next job to come along; getting by with overstretched supervision, equipment, supplies or materials; and so on. In each of these cases, the subcontractor might well want to drag things out, not speed them up. It is up to the project manager to spot foot-dragging and respond accordingly.

Incorrect Assumption about Activity-Duration Estimates

A key belief within the CCPM canons is that the typical activity-duration is inherently puffed, as much as two or three times the amount of time truly required for work completion. The notion is that such durations reflect an 85–90 percent confidence that the work can be performed in the stated amount of time. Feeder and project buffers, pools of otherwise hidden total-float, are funded by arbitrarily reducing the activity-durations to where there is only 50 percent confidence in the duration being achieved. It is this difference, between 50 percent and 90 percent confidence in duration achievement, that constitutes the "safety" that can be removed from these activities and reassigned to the buffers.

Perhaps in some industries one has the luxury of initially padding durations by a factor of two or three, but that is certainly not the case on commercial, private sector construction projects. I also think it is *not* the case in public sector work, either. Nowadays a contractor is hard-pressed to bid on a project that doesn't already have an unrealistically short project length. If the bidder is entertaining any serious hope of being awarded the job, he can kiss that hope goodbye if he starts increasing the project length two or threefold (the logical effect of increasing the individual activities of the critical path by a factor of two or three).

The point is that grossly padded durations are simply not the norm in the construction world—and yet, this is what CCPM uses as a starting point for the creation of buffers. If over-stated durations are the source of feeder and project buffers, I can't see how CCPM has any reasonable foundation in the construction industry.

Removal of Due Dates

CCPM rejects the use of early and late dates, because it believes in Parkinson's Law, which says that workers will take as long to finish a task as they can get away with. By removing what CCPM calls "due date distractions," the tendency to take as much time as "allowed" will be removed and activities will finish sooner, or so their argument goes. Then, in order to take advantage of the predecessor's early completion, the CCPM methodology includes "work alerts," intended to give the successor activity a heads-up that it can start its activity earlier as well.

I have two problems with this concept, one of which is that it assumes that the resources that are assigned to the successor activity, that are now elsewhere on the project, will drop whatever they are doing and come running to the location of the successor activity and immediately get it underway. On the one hand, I appreciate the spirit of the concept, to be flexible enough to take advantage of windfall opportunities to gain on the schedule.

On the other hand, if this impulsive reaction to a momentary premium is formalized as a management strategy, then it is tantamount to saying, "To hell with the plan, let's just wing it!" It stands in stark contrast to the idea of planning the work by systematically considering alternatives, performing feasibility analyses on those alternatives, agreeing on an optimum plan, communicating that plan to all involved parties, and using that plan as the guide to Execution Scheduling. Instead, it says that no matter what we may have thought was "the plan," if an opportunity presents itself, we'll abandon the plan and seize the moment.

It has taken the field of project management more than 30 years to change the culture from one of shooting from the hip to one of acting deliberately—and doing that only after development of and consultation with a Consensus Plan and Execution Schedule upon which all parties have reached agreement. We are now being asked to forget the due dates on activities and be ready to override schedule logic if an opportunity for momentary gain confronts us.

Finally, I can't begin to imagine what inefficiency this approach would create on the project. It has been known for many decades that the more times an object is handled, just as the more times a worker is required to relocate, the less efficient the operation. So, rather than working in one location for three weeks straight, a crew is being asked to hop around, from place to place, in order to take advantage of a few days here or there. I'd have to see a whole lot of corroborating evidence confirming that this approach would yield a shorter schedule before I'd sign up for this idea.

My second problem with the removal of due dates is that it ignores the *positive* effect of having commitment dates staring the contractor in the face. It may be that *some* workers may exemplify the negative side of Parkinson's Law, taking longer to do a task than is necessary simply because excess time has been granted. But let us not fail to note that the opposite situation is also described by Parkinson's Law: that workers will complete the work in less time if the time allowed is less.

As already noted, most Execution Schedules are tight from the get-go, and most activity-durations are fairly stretched as well. Far more often than not, durations have little or no padding in them. Workers have all they can do to get the work done in a short period of time, but because they are true professionals, if the Project Schedule calls for work to be completed in four days, they will kill themselves to get it done in four days.

With the preponderance of construction Schedules being taut, the opportunities for padded durations are limited at best, and the propensity for work slowdowns in accordance with the negative side of Parkinson's is equally limited. If we remove due dates, and thereby eliminate Parkinson's Law, we lose the positive benefits of Parkinson's Law as well.

What Does 50 Percent Confidence Mean?

The CCPM methodology creates buffers from the difference in two activity-durations: the 90 percent confidence duration and the 50 percent confidence duration. I take issue with CCPM's given interpretation of the latter, that 50 percent of the time the actual duration will be less, and 50 percent of the time it will be more.

If we were flipping coins, then 50 percent of the time we would see heads, and 50 percent of the time we would see tails. This is because the conditions and effort required to achieve heads are precisely the same as they are to achieve tails. But if one were to graph the *effort* required to perform an activity, the shape of the line would not look like a bell (bell curve), it would appear from left to right as a downward sloping curve, with 50 percent as the midpoint. The *effort* required to finish earlier than (to the left of) the midpoint is *greater* than what would be required to finish later. My definition of a 50 percent-confidence duration is that there is a 50 percent chance of achieving it and a 50 percent chance of not achieving it (meaning that it will take longer than the duration).

From the CCPM method, the duration has been reduced to the minimal amount of time to perform the work. Murphy's Law reminds us that the odds are greater that something will happen to delay the work than that something will happen to accelerate the work. The odds are greater that the activity will slip than that it will be improved beyond the tight duration.

The CCPM methodology, then, virtually insures that the schedule will slip and that the buffers will need to be tapped in order to offset to these instigated slippages.

Activity-Durations Overly Padded

The CCPM process does not merely aggregate the "safety" portion of the durations (90 percent–50 percent) and dump them into a buffer. Instead, they create the buffer with a duration value approximately 33–50 percent of the aggregate safety. This is in accordance with the idea that the activities were *overly* padded. If we accept that the 90 percent duration is only twice (and not thrice) the 50 percent duration, and we discard half of the aggregate of such safety padding, then this would suggest that 25 percent of all activity-durations are completely unnecessary. I find this assumption hard to fathom, in a world where activities, durations, logic, and strategy are conceived in a group environment of essentially independent (and inherently distrusting and self-serving) project partners.

Unplanned Progress Gains Are Rarely Exploited

A key argument for the radical innovations of CCPM is that, under traditional CPM usage, if a predecessor activity finishes ahead of the earliest-finish date, the successor activity is not *willing or able* to advance its start. They say that the successor activity is not *able* to respond because it is planned to start at the earliest-start date, and its resources may be committed elsewhere. They say that the successor activity is not *willing* to respond because there is no urgency to do so.

In response to these assumptions, CCPM employs "work alerts," a concept whereby the successor activity is given a heads-up that the predecessor looks like it will be wrapping up a few days ahead of its previously expected finish.

The problem with CCPM's assumption that a contractor would be unwilling to move up its start date on a successor activity is that it is simply unfounded. First, the idea of "work alerts" is hardly innovative. Advance notices are already implemented in most project management circles where the project manager, through weekly progress meetings, alerts others of work that is about to finish earlier than expected.[4]

Second, when an activity completes three days sooner than planned, something I call *spontaneous float* suddenly appears. This spontaneous float provides two opportunities for schedule gain, not just one. The resources on the completing activity now have three days available to them during which to make a difference elsewhere. (Perhaps they can bolster another activity that is behind schedule.) Also, the follow-on activity can start its work three days earlier.

Whether either or both of these opportunities can be exploited is within the realm of the project management team to explore. CCPM pays no homage to the project team when it insists, as a major justification for its alternative methods, that the gains will be squandered through apathy or lethargy.

---

[4]Never mind that the CPM printout will also reflect gains on the early dates and adjust successor start times accordingly.

Finally, I am compelled by common sense to note that most contractors *are* driven to complete their assigned tasks as quickly as possible. The sooner they finish their job, the sooner they get paid, and the sooner they can move on to the next project. More completed projects per year means higher gross revenues per year, and finishing earlier than expected translates into satisfied owners and, hopefully, repeat business.

Earlier activity completion also allows the completing resource to "catch up" in another area where work was behind schedule. This often reveals itself as out-of-sequence work, or skipping to an activity not logically tied, but it still represents opportunity exploitation for schedule gain. Finally, CCPM methodology ignores the tremendous pressure or urgency created by getting paid for what is done. The sooner one gets done, the sooner he makes a profit.

How CCPM Weakens a Schedule as a Time-Management Tool

CCPM also weakens the Project Schedule, as a time-management tool, by violating the purity of the activity-duration, ignoring the context and environment of the project itself, creating project delay, and failng to address the root causes of project delay.

It Demeans The Importance of Activity-Duration Purity

First, the CCPM methodology requires us to abandon a universally accepted tenet of the Scheduling Practice, that the activity-duration is traceable back to core assumptions about work scope, productivity rates, and resource allocations. Instead, it asks us to assign durations that carry only a 50 percent probability of achievement. If the activity-duration was derived after considering scope, productivity, and resources, why would the confidence be as low as 50 percent? If a portion of the activity-duration is arbitrarily reassigned from an activity to a buffer, but the scope of the activity remains the same, haven't we violated the scope/duration balance inherent in the basic theory of CPM?

It Ignores the Project's Operating Context and Environment

Second, the CCPM methodology asks us to dispense with due dates, earliest-dates in particular. It argues that workers are "distracted" by such dates and only tend to procrastinate when given more time than they truly need to perform a given task. Besides disagreeing with the underlying premise, I question the implementation of this counterapproach in a world where dates drive everything. Even if the entire project adopted the CCPM approach, the owner is interested in dates, the contract speaks in terms of dates, vendors care about dates, and the subcontractors themselves work to commitment dates on other projects, and so forth.

It Assumes, and Even Creates, Project Delay

Third, the CCPM methodology goes out of its way to create activity delay, virtually guaranteeing schedule (though perhaps not end date) slippage by reducing each activity's duration to one having only a 50 percent chance of achievement. It then graciously provides a mechanism for managing the slippage (that it alone caused to occur) through centralized pools of time reserve, called *buffers*. This approach not only forces project management to operate in a reactive, rather than preventive, mode, it denies the resources control over their own destiny—by wrestling the duration away for the work performer and handing it over to management.

I am opposed to any methodology that makes matters worse. Construction projects already have so much stacked against them; they don't need a methodology forcing them into a worse situation. We already know, from Momentum Studies, that the main source of project delay comes from management's failure to perform timely administrative tasks in advance of Productive Work Segments. These tasks are performed *between* activities, during Administrative Time Gaps reflected in start-to-start and finish-to-start relationships. The CCPM approach offers *nothing* to improve this area of vulnerability.

Needed, instead, are systems that will assist the project manager in identifying, prioritizing, tracking, and completing administrative tasks that, if not performed at all or performed too slowly, will only delay a project. By artificially draining the Execution Schedule's activities of any spontaneous float that might have resulted from modest activity padding, thanks to CCPM the Project Schedule is merely rendered *more* volatile. As an extension, this methodology increases the likelihood that the Execution Schedule will require a wholesale revision, as work is performed seemingly without "a method to the madness."

It Is Only Applicable to Time-Sensitive Projects; Its Contribution Is Questionable

Fourth, the CCPM approach, if beneficial at all, is only helpful when the project is time-sensitive. On cost-critical or manner-critical projects, CCPM is guarding the wrong door. As a time management tool, the jury must remain undecided on this methodology. Further field tests are necessary to demonstrate how the process overcomes many inherent limitations that it possesses, as well as other logically questionable assumptions and premises that it makes.

It Fails to Address Main Causes of Project Delay

Fifth, and finally, because of the sweeping claims made within its promotional material, CCPM has the potential to lull the less diligent, more naïve supporter into a false sense of comfort that the project has been effectively insulated against slippage. To be sure, CCPM literature practically *guarantees* that, between resource, feeder, and project buffers, the end date is safe from slippage. But there is a fundamental flaw in the rationale underlying its dogma, and that flaw stems from a misunderstanding of what causes the preponderance of project delay in the first place.

As will be covered in Chapter 16 in the section, "The Element of Surprise," sources of delay are at two levels, one specific to the activity or relationship, and the other at the project level. Concerning the former, we learn that activity-tenure surprises might be offset by adding a *DCF* (*Duration Confidence Factor*; see Chapter 16) to the Scope-Limited Duration estimate. Similarly, relationship-tenure surprises could be offset by adding a DCF to Administrative Time Gaps, as appropriate. Next, we would add a project-level time contingency to safeguard against the impact of any *Unknown-Unknown*, if the contractual project length makes it possible to do so.

The preceding process is based on a few key assumptions:

- Scope-limited durations, properly derived and documented, typically earn a 90–95 percent confidence rating from those who develop them.
- Activity-tenure surprises can be estimated and insured against, via DCFs, resulting in a Composite Activity Duration with a near-100 percent confidence.

- The majority of schedule slippage occurs during *relationship-tenure*, not *activity-tenure.*
- Relationship-tenure surprises, though more obscure and more frequent, can also be insured against, via DCFs, resulting in a Composite Relationship Duration with a near-100 percent confidence.
- Project-level surprises of the known-unknown variety can be acknowledged with the use of calendar blockouts.
- Project-level surprises of the unknown-unknown variety can be buffered by a single time-contingency activity at the end of the schedule.

While there are many differences between the preceding assumptions and what CCPM believes, these two are most noteworthy:

- According to CCPM, activity-durations, as commonly derived, are *twice* (200 percent) what they need to be, given the activity's scope and reasonable resource assignments. Accordingly, CCPM feels that most activity-durations can be cut in half, or at least by a third. CCPM claims these puffed durations earn an 80–90 percent confidence rating from those who derived them. By contrast, Momentum Studies show that time should be *added* to [relationship-]durations in the form of DCFs.
- CCPM fails to acknowledge that *any* schedule delay occurs on the relationship, only on the activity. Therefore, the entire CCPM methodology fails to address the primary location/source of schedule delay[5] and instead focuses *only* on activity slippage.

Not wanting to throw out the baby with the bath water, perhaps we can *borrow* from CCPM some sensitivity to duration variability when we are creating our Project Schedules in the first place. To its credit, CCPM highlights a few key common-sense elements that are often overlooked during Schedule Development.

For instance, one good benefit of CCPM is that it helps to focus the Schedule Development on the problem of excessively multitasking resources. In many of the projects I see now, it is not uncommon to have a single resource spread so thinly, due to multitasking, that there is simply no way to achieve all of the work slated for that resource in the time period due to the diversity of assignments.

Overall, though, CCPM fails to acknowledge, address, or resolve delays caused during relationship tenure, and with respect to activity-tenure delays, it exacerbates the problem by taking well-defined, well-documented, and properly derived scope-based activity-durations and arbitrarily reducing them.

FLAWED DEFINITIONS

In Chapter 3, I complained that virtually every significant term related to the practice of planning and scheduling suffers from multiple and different definitions that are not just conflicting, they are confusing as well. Then, at the start of this chapter, I went further

---

[5]This was confirmed in the Momentum Studies.

by suggesting that many of these definitions are factually incorrect as well. In this subsection I will support my allegations, beginning with a brief recounting of two significant trends in the Scheduling Practice over the last twenty or so years. It is my contention that a majority of today's inaccurate definitions can be traced back to authors and other definition originators who have remained stuck in the '60s while the Scheduling Practice has moved on, around them, like water maneuvering around large boulders in a river.

Two Important Trends in Scheduling Practice

In two significant ways, the manner in which we practice Scheduling today is *much* different than how it was 30 or more years ago. Unfortunately, many technical definitions betray an otherwise hidden truth: some Scheduling authorities are stuck in the '60s.

Precedence Overtook Arrow

Sometime in the late 1980s or early 1990s, the Scheduling Practice reached an invisible milestone that went virtually unnoticed. Up until that point, the majority of CPM schedules were drawn using the Arrow Diagramming Method (ADM). After that magical moment—whenever it was—the dominance went to Precedence Diagramming Method (PDM). Perhaps the biggest difference in the methods was the introduction of three new relationship types beyond the old standard: finish-to-start.

We are all familiar with the different relationship types and how they work, but here I would like to discuss some of the less obvious implications of these additional relationship types regarding basic total-float and critical-path calculations.

Start Float and Finish Float Are Not Always the Same   Back in the days of ADM, every activity had only *one* total-float value, and this was because once an activity started, nothing could interrupt it. A nonnegotiable rule of ADM was that activities could only connect at the nodes (the circles at the juncture of arrows). If you wanted to start a successor activity midway through a predecessor, you would have to divide the predecessor activity into two parts. Figure 11-2 shows a condition where Activity B is to start at some point after Activity A has commenced (but not yet finished). To depict this in ADM, we would divide Activity A into two distinct activities: Activity A^1 and Activity A^2.

Now let's do forward and backward pass calculations to determine earliest and latest dates and total-float values. In Figure 11-3, we see that the total-float value at the start of any activity is the same as it is for the end of that same activity. This is because nothing intervenes in the middle of the activity.

Now let us consider the same logic segment using PDM. While there are only two activities, instead of the four required by ADM, each activity has two separate total-float calculations: one for the *start* of the activity, and one for the *end* of the activity. A visual comparison of Figure 11-4 to Figure 11-3 shows that the two methods yield the same diagrammatical and mathematical results. In ADM, there are four activities with one

Figure 11-2

Overlapping
Activities in ADM

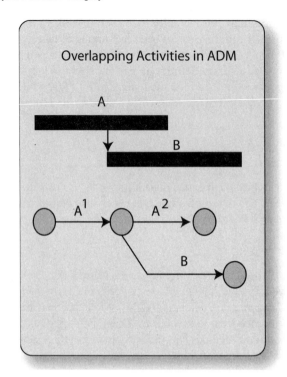

Figure 11-3

One Float Value per Activity in ADM

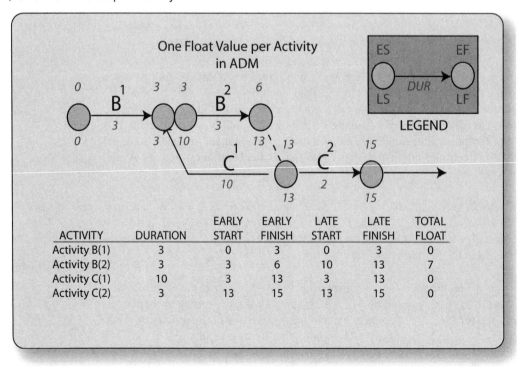

ACTIVITY	DURATION	EARLY START	EARLY FINISH	LATE START	LATE FINISH	TOTAL FLOAT
Activity B(1)	3	0	3	0	3	0
Activity B(2)	3	3	6	10	13	7
Activity C(1)	10	3	13	3	13	0
Activity C(2)	3	13	15	13	15	0

Figure 11-4

Two Float Values per Activity in PDM

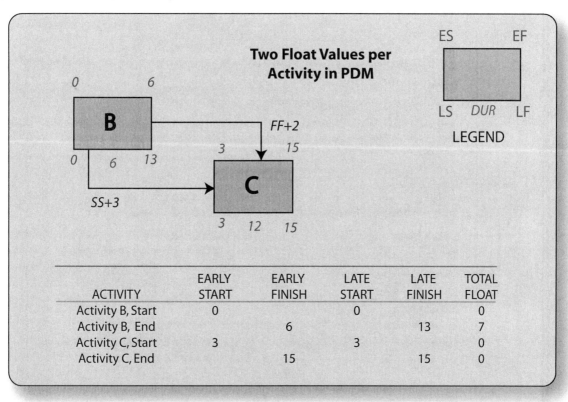

ACTIVITY	EARLY START	EARLY FINISH	LATE START	LATE FINISH	TOTAL FLOAT
Activity B, Start	0		0		0
Activity B, End		6		13	7
Activity C, Start	3		3		0
Activity C, End		15		15	0

total-float value each (therefore, four total-float values), while in PDM there are two activities with two total-float values each (therefore, also four total-float values).

Armed with the clarity of this distinction, we are now able to see *why* certain definitions are simply wrong. Before we visit them, however, let's agree on a few conclusions, based on the preceding distinction between ADM and PDM diagramming methods.

Total-Float Paths Need Not Pass Entirely Through an Activity   In ADM, any consistent total-float path *must* pass *entirely* through an activity. This is true because there is no way, with ADM, to intersect an activity midway through it. This truth manifests itself mathematically with the behavior we just noted, that there is only *one* total-float value per activity.

In PDM, however, the situation is exactly the opposite. Activities can be intersected *after* they commence (but before they complete), and this creates the possibility that an activity's *start-float* may be different than its *finish-float*. As a result, it is entirely possible for a total-float path to pass through a *portion* of an activity without passing all the way

Figure 11-5

A Single Activity Can Be Both Critical and Non-Critical

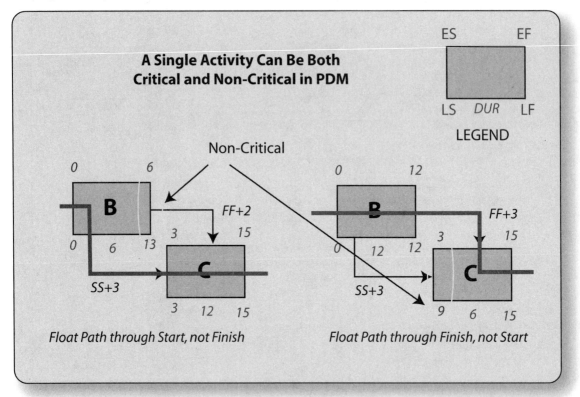

through it. Figure 11-5 shows two examples of this phenomenon. In the left panel, we see a situation where Activity B's start-float is zero (critical), while its finish-float is +7 (noncritical). In the right panel, we see an opposite condition, where Activity C's start-float is +6 (noncritical), while its finish-float is zero (critical).

New Understanding of Total-Float and Free-Float From the previous discussion it should be obvious that any understanding of total-float or free-float must take into account the possibility that, in PDM, only a portion of an activity may be critical. In the next part of this subsection, we will examine some rather popular definitions of total-float and free-float and see that they fail to take into consideration these PDM scenarios. My suspicion is that the authors of these definitions are still thinking of ADM (only) when they write about Critical Path Method.

Use of Date-Constraints Dramatically Increased

Old-time Practitioners will confirm that the ability to inject a date-constraint into a network diagram existed in the earliest CPM software programs, so the use of date-constraints is really nothing new. What *is* new, so to speak, is the proliferation of their use, and this change has dramatically and sweepingly affected the quality and functionality of Project Schedules. Elsewhere in this text, I caution against the unbridled use of date-constraints.

Here, I wish to discuss the practical effect of responsible multiconstraint usage. Again, in the early days, we did use date-constraints, but only minimally. The first activity in the Project Schedule might have a Start-No-Earlier-Than date-constraint, and the final activity in the Schedule would be restricted with a Finish-No-Later-Than date-constraint. This solitary finish constraint was sufficient to force a critical-path terminating at this completion milestone.

Over the years, it became common practice to employ numerous date-constraints into a Project Schedule. Often, the underlying motivator was the increasingly complex construction contract in which could be found an assortment of intermediate contractual milestones. Elsewhere, as in the IT industry, date-constraints were used to formalize the handoff of deliverables from one internal department to another. For whatever the reason(s) and legitimacy, the gross percent of a Schedule's activities encumbered by date-constraints seemed to be climbing with each passing year. The net effect is that, today, it is not uncommon at all to find schedules with 10 percent or more of the activities loaded with date-constraints. Most claims consultants have even encountered Project Schedules having as many as 80 percent of the activities driven by date-constraints.

Here are some of the more important effects of this proliferation of date-constraint usage on basic total-float and critical-path calculations.

The Critical-Path Can Have Positive Total-Float   Let us start with a rather conventional logic diagram, as shown in Figure 11-6. In this case, the project had a contractual completion date of Day 72. Notice that the logic, as initially developed by the project team, shows that the work will take 60 days, and thus the initial Project Schedule has 12 days of positive total-float. This diagram immediately disproves the position held by some, that the critical-path's total-float value cannot be a positive number, but only one with zero or negative total-float. Notice also from this example that the critical-path happens to be the longest path, as well as the path with the least total-float.

The Critical-Path May Not Terminate at Project End   In Figure 11-7, we will modify our logic, by introducing an intermediate completion milestone. Suppose, according to the contract, Activity L must be completed by Day 30. Suddenly, the critical-path has only one day of positive total-float and runs to the intermediate completion milestone, not to the project's completion milestone. This clarifies another important point. Definitions that make sole reference to impacts to "project completion" are incorrect, because they ignore the equally common condition that a critical-path can terminate at another (not project end) completion milestone.

The point of this heading is that, if we define a critical-path as either the longest path or the path with the least float, the critical-path may not be one that terminates at project completion.

The Critical-Path Need Not Be the Path with the Least Total-Float   Of course, since there is no recognized authority within the Scheduling Practice to resolve disputes among its Practitioners, it remains a matter of personal opinion as to whether the critical-path is *always* expressed in terms of project completion. If this were to be the rule, then

Figure 11-6
Sample Logic; One Finish-No-Later-Than Constraint

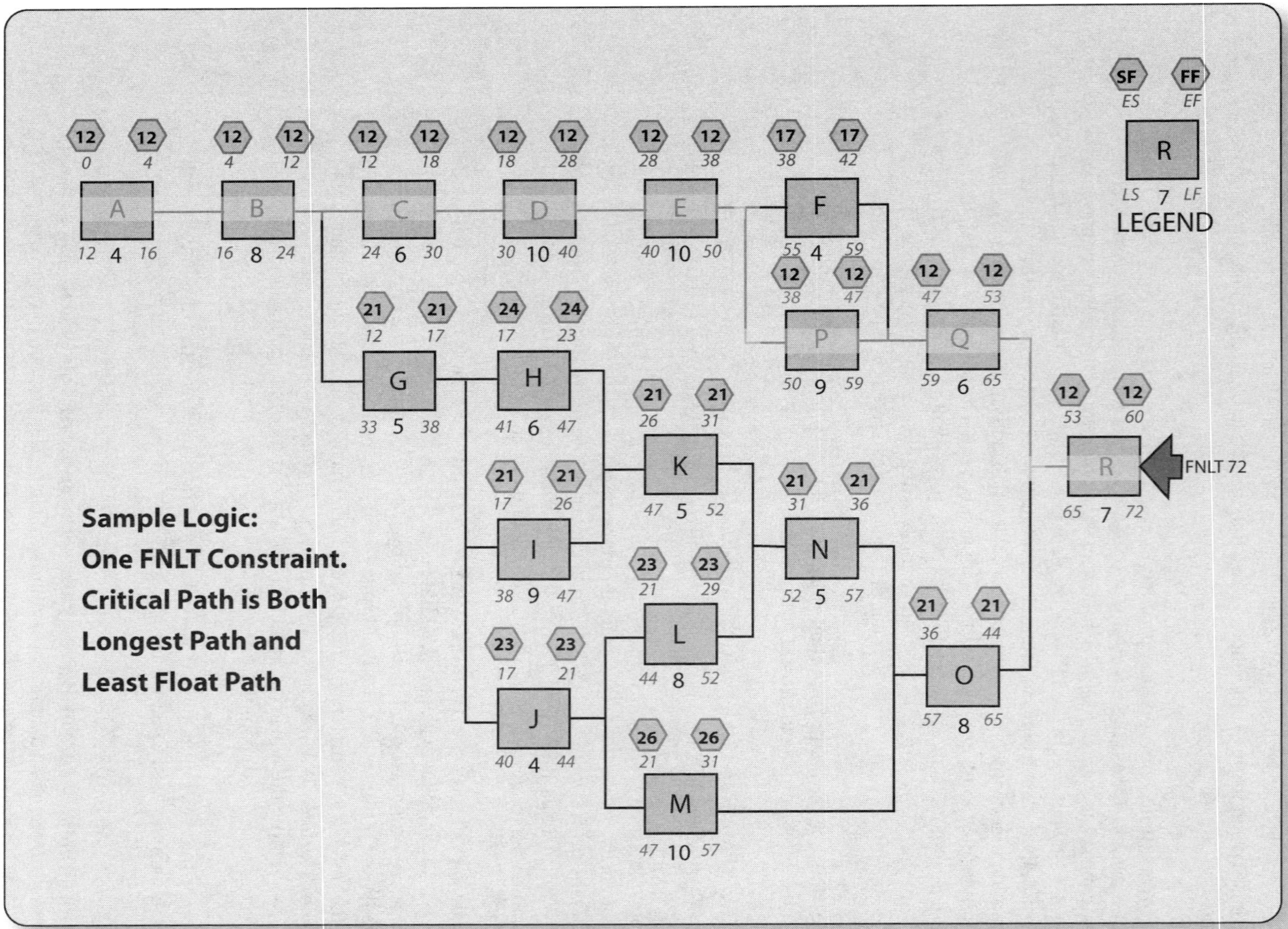
Sample Logic:
One FNLT Constraint.
Critical Path is Both
Longest Path and
Least Float Path
A
B
C
D
E
F
G
H
I
J
K
L
M
N
O
P
Q
R
FNLT 72
SF
FF
ES
EF
LS
7
LF
LEGEND

Figure 11-7

Sample Logic; Two Finish-No-Later-Than Constraints

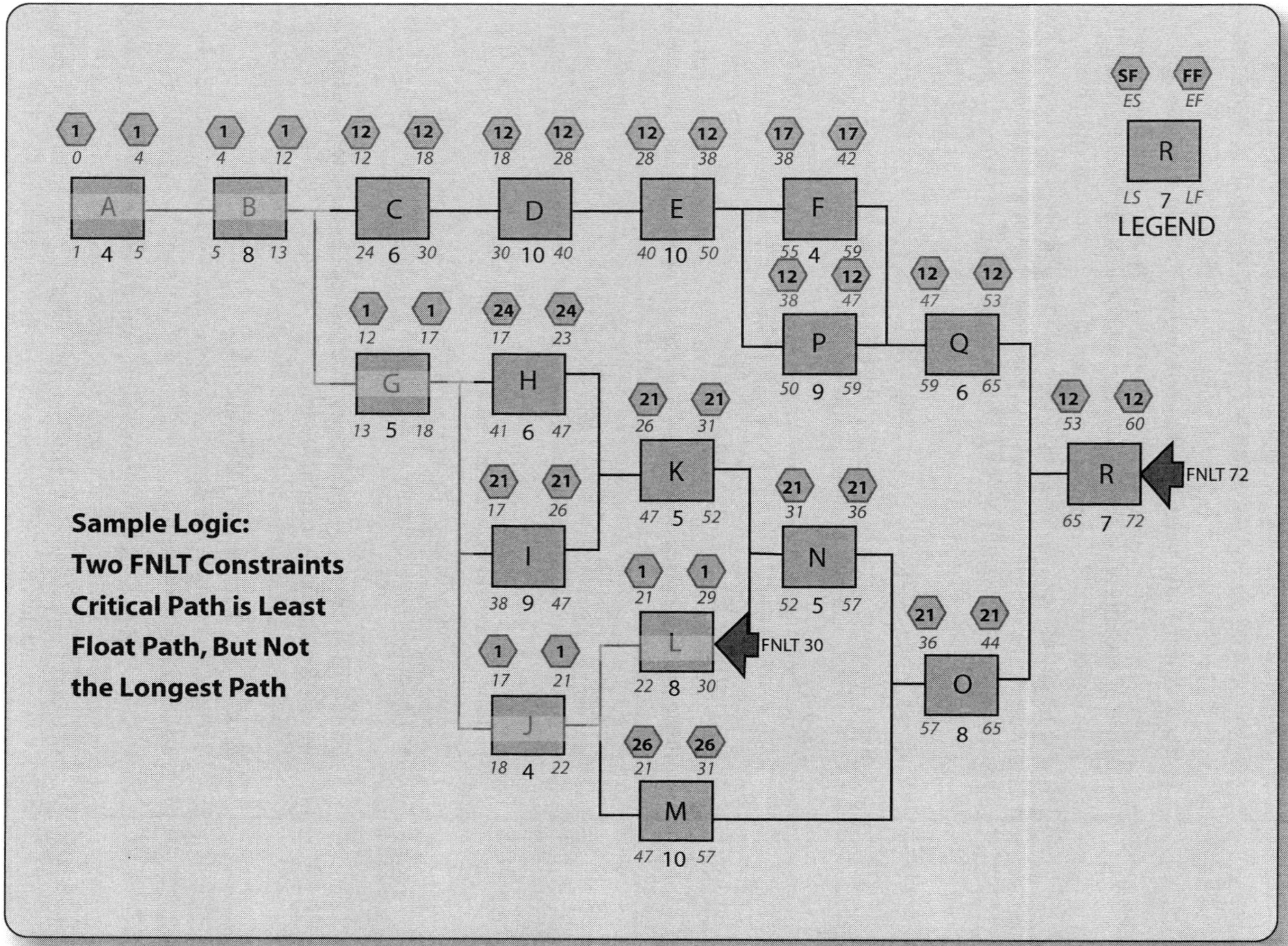

Sample Logic:
Two FNLT Constraints
Critical Path is Least
Float Path, But Not
the Longest Path

in Figure 11-7, the critical-path would be the one we saw in Figure 11-6, with 12 days of positive total-float. How do you feel about giving the answer, "We're twelve days ahead of schedule," to a Management question, "How are we doing?"? If everyone *assumes* that we are strictly and only speaking about the project completion, then we shouldn't mention the one day of total-float on the "least float" path, should we?

The Critical-Path Need Not Be the Longest Path in the Schedule   Now take a look at Figure 11-8. Imagine that we have just discovered, embarrassingly, that a key piece of equipment and its installation work had been innocently omitted from the Project Schedule. Additionally, we learn that this piece of equipment will be arriving toward the end of the project but will only require a few days to install. So, in Figure 11-8, we will add the delivery activity (shown as a diamond) and the subsequent installation activity. We'll tie these new activities into the project's last few closeout items.

In Figure 11-8 we have a clear example of a project completion critical-path that is not the longest path in the Project Schedule. In fact, it may well be one of the shortest paths! Yet, it is the path that precludes the project from completing any earlier than its earliest-finish date.

Critiquing Existing Definitions

In the preceding discussion, we have uncovered several truisms that need to be incorporated into any reliable Scheduling Practice lexicon. To recap:

- Start-float and finish-float are not always equal, per activity.
- Total-loat paths need not pass entirely through an activity.
- The critical-path can have positive total-float.
- The critical-path may not terminate at the project's end.
- The critical-path need not be the path with the least total-float.
- The critical-path need not be the longest path in the schedule.

So now let us take a look at some of those definitions we cited in Chapter 3 and see if we can spot the flaws in their wording.

Erroneous Critical Path Definitions

We'll start with some definitions of *critical-path*. I will italicize the problematic wording in each definition.

- The series of tasks that must finish on time for the *entire project* to finish on time.
  - **Flaw** Limits the critical-path to project completion only.
- In a network diagram, the *longest path* from start to finish or the path *without any slack*, and thus the path corresponding to the shortest time in which *the project* can be completed.
  - **Flaw** Limits the critical-path to project completion only.

Figure 11-8
Sample Logic; One Start-No-Earlier-Than Constraint

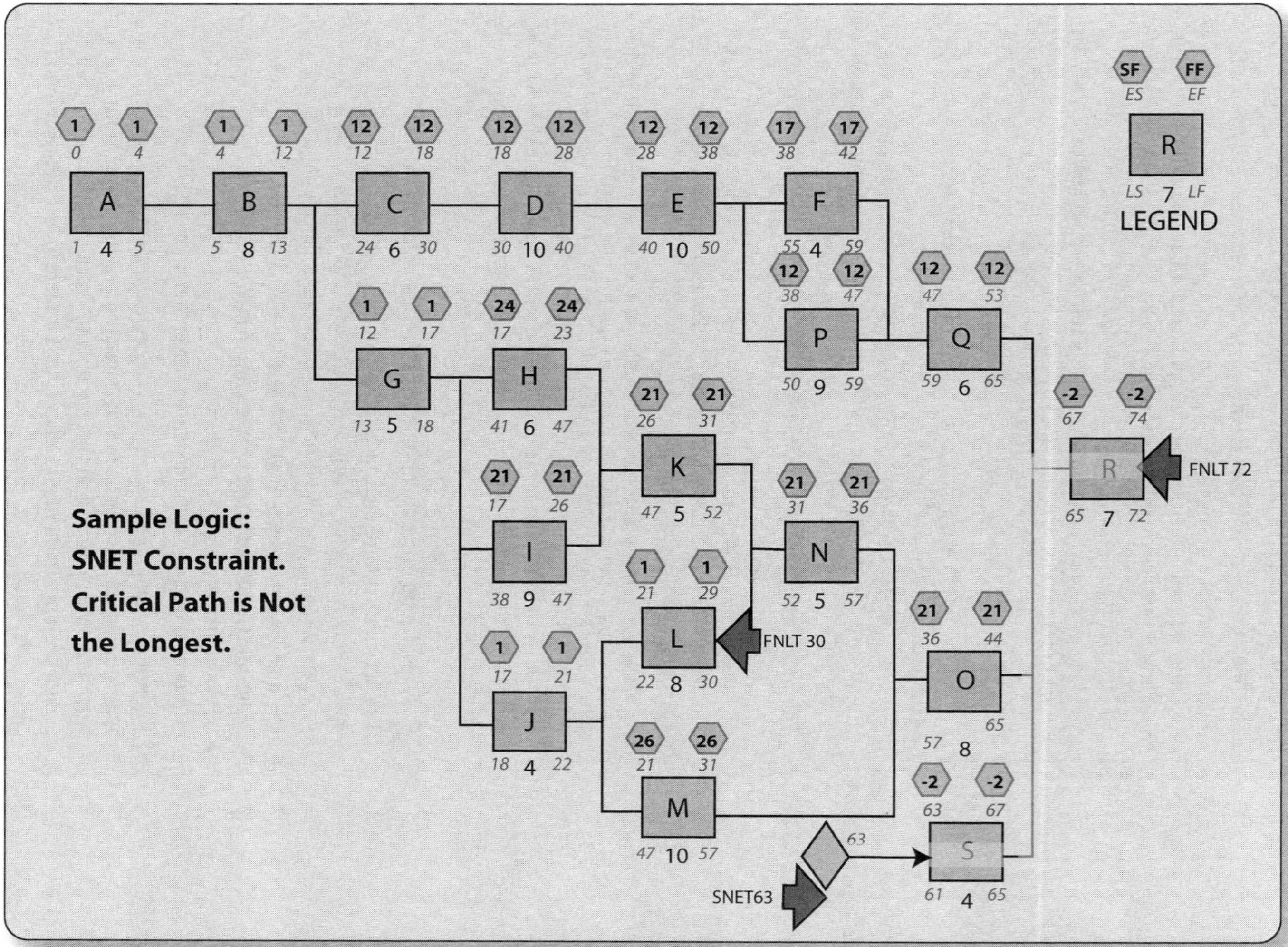

Sample Logic:
SNET Constraint.
Critical Path is Not
the Longest.

- **Flaw** Assumes that the critical-path cannot have positive total float.
- **Flaw** Assumes that the critical-path must be the longest path in the schedule.

- In a network diagram, the path with *the longest duration.*
  - **Flaw** Assumes that the critical-path must be the longest path in the schedule.

- The line of project activities having *the least float*, especially when float is *close to, or below, zero.*
  - **Flaw** Assumes that the critical-path cannot have positive total float.
  - **Flaw** Assumes that the critical-path must have the least total float.

- The route through the network that has *only critical activities.*
  - **Flaw** This one is just plain weird. It employs circular reasoning. Since the overwhelming understanding in the project management world is that an activity is "critical" if it lies on a critical-path, it is completely circular to define the critical-path as the path being the one with critical activities.

- The series of interdependent activities of a project *connected end-to-end*, which determines the shortest total length of the project.
  - **Flaw** This one was on its way to being a decent critical-path definition, except that it overlooked the three additional PDM relationships, instead assuming that the only relationship type is finish-to-start ("end-to-end").

- The path (sequence) of activities which represent the longest total time required to complete the project.
  - **Acceptable** While this definition doesn't acknowledge the role of date-constraints (in addition to durations and logic), at least it doesn't contain any glaring errors.

- The *longest connected route* through the CPM network.
  - **Flaw** Assumes that the critical-path must be the longest path in the schedule.

- The sequence of activities through a project network *from start to finish*, the sum of whose durations determines the overall *project duration.* There may be more than one critical path depending on workflow logic. A delay to progress of any activity on the critical path will, without acceleration or re-resequencing, cause the *overall project* duration to be extended, and is therefore referred to as a critical delay.
  - **Flaw** Limits the critical-path to project completion only.

- The series of interrelated tasks that comprises the longest duration to complete *a project*, where a delay in any task will extend the *overall schedule.*
  - **Flaw** Limits the critical-path to project completion only.

- An analysis technique used to *predict project duration.* Analysis of activities, sequencing, and paths and determining which path has the least amount of schedule flexibility (float).
  - **Flaw** Limits the critical-path to project completion only.

- In project management, a critical path is the sequence of project network activities with *the longest overall duration*, determining the shortest time possible to *complete the project.* Any delay of an activity on the critical path directly impacts the *planned project completion* date (that is, there is no float on the critical path). A project can have several parallel critical paths. An additional parallel path through the network with the total durations shorter than the critical path is called a sub-critical or noncritical path.

- **Flaw** Limits the critical-path to project completion only.
- **Flaw** Assumes that the critical-path must be the longest path in the schedule.

Erroneous Total Float Definitions

The following are some erroneous definitions of *total-float*. Again, I will italicize the problematic wording in each definition.

- The maximum number of work periods by which an activity can be delayed without delaying project completion or violating a target finish date.
  - **Acceptable** This definition fails to note the precise formula that derives total-float, yet it correctly acknowledges both the project end date *and* any other completion milestones against which a backward pass might be performed and a critical-path generated.

- The amount that an *activity can be lengthened* without *delaying the project completion*, assuming that all other activities are done in their normal time.
  - **Flaw** While lengthening an activity is one way that its earliest finish can be delayed, another means is to start the activity later than planned. This definition fails to account for delayed start.
  - **Flaw** Limits the critical-path to project completion only.

- The amount of time (in work units) that an activity may be *delayed from its early start* without delaying the *project finish date*.
  - **Flaw** Limits calculations to start dates; ignores finish date delays.
  - **Flaw** Limits the critical-path to project completion only.

- The excess time available for an activity to be expanded or delayed without affecting the *rest of the project*, assuming it begins at its earliest time.
  - **Flaw** Limits the critical-path to project completion only.

- Measure of scheduling flexibility available on a network path.
  - **Flaw** Simply too vague: Doesn't explain how total-float is calculated or what components of the Project Schedule are involved.

- The amount of time that an activity may be delayed beyond its early start/early finish dates without delaying the *contract completion date*.
  - **Flaw** Limits the critical-path to project completion only.

Arcane Term Meaning Clarifications

It is poor form to issue criticisms without also offering constructive suggestions in their place. Accordingly, I would like to propose a set of Meaning Clarifications that I think could clear up much of the confusion we have uncovered on the previous pages. My approach, however, is first to discuss a few "building block" terms before attempting the wording of Meaning Clarifications for *major* terms.

If this were Day One in the history of the Scheduling Practice, every fresh word would be up for grabs. But today, 50 years later, all of the common terms have been grossly over-worked, misused, and convoluted through sloppy linguistics.

Some Terms Are Set in Concrete

If I had my druthers, I would do away with all worn out terms and create, in their place, an entirely new set of expressions. But the political and practical reality is that CPM will always be called Critical Path Method, and that means that the words "critical" and "path" cannot be disowned. Pardon the pun, but we must come to *terms* with them!

Path   The term *path* mildly troubles me because I think of a path as a route that has been previously traveled. The first explorer to cross the Great Plains surely found (or followed) no path, per se; he simply made his way. Only subsequent travelers would have found the physical indentations of a well-worn path. To me, the word "path" implies an established or preferred route. For those who view the Project Schedule as a prescription rather than an objective game plan (which can be altered as the game progresses), the word "path" is no doubt acceptable to them—but not to me.

Another objection I have to the word "path" is that it implies a route *upon* which one progresses. To be sure, the Scheduling Practice is rather insistent that there *is* a progression to be made from here to there (even graphically, from left to right). But "path" or route also implies a level of certainty that I am not so confident we possess at the time we create our logic, or even later as we struggle to carry out the strategies. Overturn a storage tank and watch the water run free. The rushing current will appear to have a mind of its own, meandering through the open field, finding its way from high ground to eventual pond. Along the way, it will twist and turn. It does not follow a predescribed path or route; rather it creates its own route.

On a more literal level, I don't like the word "path" because it conveys the image of something physical—like a sidewalk. Such a path is *not* interactive. If we, instead, used the expression "obstacle course," that would surely come closer to describing the reality on any project. The route across the project's terrain is marred with obstructions, crosswinds, attacking animals, rivers to forge, grades to climb, and overhead predators to avoid.

In Scheduling, it is not just a sequential set of activities that we pass *through* as we move from project inception to project completion. Rather, in between all of those activities are decisions to be made, obscured actions to be taken, and active dynamics at play that can (and most certainly do) affect the flow of work that is progressing down any loosely defined "path."

If I could change our culture, I would suggest the words "circuit" and "circuitry," in lieu of path and network, respectively. Circuitry, although mainly use in the field of electronics, is also used in neurology as "the network of interconnected neurons in the nervous system and especially the brain *also*: the neuronal pathways of the brain along which electrical and chemical signals travel." What I like about circuitry is that it invites inclusion of operators that can, and do, influence the flow of whatever is traveling through the circuit. There is an implied interactive, dynamic aspect to the circuit. But "path" is here to stay, and so it is one of those irreplaceable terms.

Critical   I could write a chapter on the term *critical* alone. If ever there was an overworked word in the project management jargon, it is "critical." Activities are considered *critical* if they reside on the critical-path. But they are also considered "near critical" if their total-float values are "close to" the critical-path—whatever *that* is supposed to mean!

I wish we could do away with the word "critical" altogether. It sounds like someone is dying. The word "critical" has such an ominous tone to it. Besides, there is little factual or formulaic evidence to support the notion that activities on the critical-path are necessarily the ones whose performance is *most critical* to the achievement of project time goals. To make my point, how can an activity that cannot be performed for another two years be considered "critical" *today*, just because it has a total-float value of zero? For all practical purposes, it is *not* critical, because it cannot be performed today. And two years from now, Lord only knows what its total-float value will be. So is this activity really "critical," in the truest meaning of the word, or is it merely "*technically* critical" based on some formula?

But the word "critical" is here to stay, and so I think we should give thorough consideration to its responsible use. I see two separate questions that need to be discussed. One has to do with criticality in terms of a single activity, and the other deals with path criticality.

First, is activity criticality as simple as "an activity is critical if it resides on a critical-path?" Is it as simple as "Only activities on a critical-path are critical?" I don't think so. In Chapter 16, I identify numerous other ways of determining activity criticality, with new concepts like: Activity Placement, Relationships Aggregation, Confluence Aggregation, Schedule Resiliency, and Discrete Activity Float, just to name a few. My point, here, is that it serves the project poorly for us to tightly limit activity criticality to critical-path residence alone.

   Conclusion: Stop exclusively correlating activity criticality to critical-path residence.

Second, with path criticality, according to conventional treatment, the question is one of degree. The usual definition of a critical-path *always* speak about total-float, which, you will recall, is the mathematical difference between earliest and latest start or finish dates. But the ambiguity in this term's application is in the established total-float range that will constitute criticality. Few disagree that an activity with negative total-float is critical, and even a zero total-float activity is critical. That leaves us with what to say about paths having positive total-float. Can positive total-float paths ever be considered critical?

To answer this question, we need to distinguish between two different situations. In the first scenario, the positive total-float path is also the one with the least total-float. Refer back to Figure 11-6. In this example, the path with the least float (+12) is also the longest path, and the path that determines the earliest finish date for the project completion milestone. According to most critical-path definitions (for example, longest path, least float, affecting project completion), this positive total-float path is the critical-path.

The other scenario is one in which the positive total-float path is *not* the least float path. Consider the network diagram shown in Figure 11-7. Here we see two significant paths. Which one(s) should be considered "critical?" The path with the least float (A-B-G-J-L) drives an intermediate completion milestone (Activity L), and has a total-float value of +1. But then there is the other significant path (A-B-C-D-E-P-Q-R) bearing a total-float value of +12. This is the same path as in Figure 11-6 that we just agreed *was* critical. Now, just because there is another path with a lower total-float value, a previously "critical" path is no longer critical.

This phenomenon introduces a concept I call "relative criticality." By this term I mean that whether a path is declared "critical" depends on whether some other path is "more critical." Our current scheduling lexicon does not include the expression "more critical" (even though, ironically, it includes the term "near critical"). In other words, there can only be one Miss America at a time. Like Musical Chairs, as soon as one path becomes *the* "critical path" it at once displaces the outgoing critical-path, without any fanfare.

The reason this problem exists is because we have too many different conditions that can yield criticality (using any of the popular predications: for example, longest path, least float). The standoff between "longest path" and "least float path" is only part of the problem. The greater complication comes from multiple completion milestones. Each completion date-constraint creates a different associated path.

Later in this chapter when I offer Meaning Clarifications for key Scheduling terms, I will advocate for the required use of modifiers in front of the term "critical-path." I contend that there is a separate critical-path for each date-constrained completion milestone. Therefore, there is a "Project Completion Critical Path," a "Building Dry-In Critical Path," a "Permanent Power Critical Path," and so forth.

With this simple innovation, we need only resolve the total-float range question in order to have an objective way to determine *when* a path is critical or not. I will leave for elsewhere the discussion of relative criticality. For now, let us agree that the words "critical path" are to be used only to describe the predetermined requirements for path criticality. In other words, "on this project, a path will be considered critical if its total-float value is *blank*," where "*blank* can be a numeric range or a percent of project length or some other formulaic basis.

> Conclusion: Use the term *critical path* only with a modifier that relates the path to a specific completion milestone.

Some Terms Can Be Retired or Chosen from Among Many

There are other terms that are among a set of synonymous terms, from which we can select one and eliminate all others. Let's see if we can identify terms under this heading.

Logical Diagram   Let's start with the words "logic" and "logical." First of all, they are *not* interchangeable, even though they are so often used synonymously. The word "logic" has to do with *reasoning*, which is "the basis or motive for an action, decision, or conviction." "Logical" implies that something is "capable of, or reflecting the capability for, correct and valid reasoning." The expression "logical diagram," therefore is semantically inappropriate.

Conclusion: Stop using the term *logical diagram*.

Logic Diagram   From the previous point it seems that "logic diagram" is preferable to "logical diagram," and it is—but it is still not my first choice. I prefer the expression "network diagram," because the emphasis is on the characterization of the diagram ("network") rather than on the wisdom inherent in it ("logic"). "Logic" implies reasoning, and not all stipulated linkages between and among activities are founded on great deliberation and thought. Some are just linkages of convenience or practicality or expedience.

Conclusion: *logic diagram* is preferable to *logical diagram*, but still a second choice after *network diagram*.

Network Diagram   The word "logic" gives the resultant diagram too much credit. I think it would be safer, and we would be more honest, simply calling it a "network" diagram because, after all, the activities are weaved into a network. At least three popular definitions of the word "network" seem to come close to describing the structure and intent of the Project Schedule:

a. A system of lines or channels that cross or interconnect.

b. A complex, interconnected group or system.

c. An extended group of people with similar interests or concerns who interact and remain in informal contact for mutual assistance or support.

Conclusion: The term *network diagram* is the preferred label for the mass of activities, relationships, date-constraints, and software settings that constitute a project simulation model (schedule).

PERT Diagram or PERT Chart   You want an example of an oxymoron? How about referring to a CPM diagram as a PERT chart? PERT and CPM are two different nationalities, like Italian and Greek. They may both be human, European, and ethnic, but lasagna is not a Greek food; it's an Italian food! And a CPM network diagram is *not* a PERT chart.

So how did this blunder get started in the first place? Again, the error can be traced back to   Venerables who are still living in the golden years of CPM when Arrow Diagramming ruled. In the early days, before PDM, *all* CPM schedules were drawn with activities shown as arrows. Contemporaneously, PERT diagrams depicted activities as boxes. When PDM came around, with its diagramming convention depicting the activity as a box, to the old-timers it looked an awful lot like PERT. Even to this day, many texts still refer to ADM as "activity-on-arrow" and PDM as "activity-on-node." (And another thing: shouldn't the latter be called "activity in box" rather than "activity-on-node?" Why are we still using the term "node," another ADM throwback, that went out of vogue 25 years ago!)

Conclusion: Stop using the term *PERT diagram.*

Dependency   The meaning we seek to capture for a continuous string of activities, logic, and date-constraints that course through a schedule is neither as simple as a sidewalk, nor as chaotic as a labyrinth where any direction is acceptable. Indeed, we anticipate that progress will be shown graphically from left to right, from inception to completion. We understand the meaning of dependency, but that takes us to another oversimplification of the existing lexicon; dependency.

I have long objected to the term "dependency," because it too implies a linear, unidirectional association. For instance, we explain a finish-to-start relationship to a scheduling newcomer as, "Activity B cannot begin until Activity A has finished." We then add: "Activity B is dependent on Activity A." Implied, and sometimes even stated, is that Activity B is the *dependent* activity, whereas Activity A is the *independent* activity. But I feel that this oversimplifies the true relationship between these two activities.

To be sure, it seems that Activity B is pushing Activity A to complete. Activity B is standing in the wings, tools in hand, just waiting for Activity A to get the heck out of the way. Activity A feels the heat, knows Activity B is waiting, and rushes to finish.

All of this may be true, but is Activity A in any manner dependent on Activity B, as well? Does Activity A need Activity B? At some level of meaning, each activity in a project *needs* the other activities, much like each musician in an orchestra needs the other musicians in order for there to *be* an orchestra at all. This may be a bit abstruse for this discussion, so let me offer a more germane answer to the question. I must warn you, however, that this explanation emphasizes an important human, psychological underpinning. That is, this explanation is not just rhetorical; it is important to your understanding of how projects really work.

Project management is essentially people management, and the primary goal of project management is to positively influence project momentum. Momentum is the manifestation of human commitment and effort. Human commitment and effort are the result of *will.* Now take that to the activity level.

A small crew of three workers are hanging drywall. They hear, through the grapevine, that there has been a breakdown in contract negotiations between the general contractor and the painting low bidder. As of right now, there is no painting subcontractor on the job and, judging by the state of stalled discussions, there won't be a painting contractor on the job for at least another few weeks. Meanwhile, the drywall contractor is being beaten down by the general contractor on another project, so he decides to pull some of his men from this project and move them elsewhere.

What we see from this example is that influences from one activity to another travel in both directions, not just in the single direction shown with arrowheads. The idea that between any two activities one is dependent while the other is independent is a misrepresentation that entirely misses the way things really work on every project.

Conclusion: Stop using the term *dependency.*

Interdependency   From the previous discussion, I contend that each activity needs the other. Activity B needs Activity A to finish, so it can start. But Activity A needs Activity B to provide the motivation to do its work *now*, and do it *well*. For this reason, I am more comfortable with the term *interdependency* than *dependency*. Let me offer one additional reason for this word preference. Projects are (or should be) fluid. By that I mean that, while the Execution Shedule lays out a plan of attack, it should be viewed as a goal, rather than a hard-and-fast directive.

As noted numerous times throughout this book, but especially in Chapter 4 where we discussed changing attitudes in project management circles, projects are increasingly being seen as dynamic, and decision-making and problem solving powers are more often being vested in the folks on the front line. Under this new paradigm, as solutions to daily problems are conceived, they can, and quite often do, result in a change of sequencing, such that what used to be the predecessor is now the successor.

Before you hastily blurt out that the reversed order of activities can still be expressed as independent and dependent, respectively, try to imagine the team discussions that would have led up to that change in order. The project participants responsible for performing these two activities would have met to discuss alternative ways to get the project done. By objectively exploring the advantages and disadvantages of each order, they eventually settled on a new sequence of events. This collaborative effort is the best argument I can give for why I see the activities as equal partners, and not superior and subordinate.

> Conclusion: Use the term *interdependency* when, at the conceptual level, referring to the nature of the relationship between activities.

Logic Tie   The logic tie is an acceptable nickname for interdependency and is appropriate when speaking tangibly about the physical arrows that are drawn to connect to activities.

> Conclusion: Use the term *logic tie* when referring to the graphical representation of the relationship between activities.

Relationship   I like this term best of all, because it hints at the human dynamics that breathe life into the inert linkages between tangible activities. The word *relationship* transcends schedule mechanics and speaks to the human element on the project, which, more than any others factors, converts into project momentum. The relationship between activities implies so much more than just the interdependency of physical actions. In this book, I elevate the relationship, as a primary Project Schedule component, to equal status with the activity itself. Just as the Project Schedule has activities and activity-durations, it also has relationships and relationship-durations.

> Conclusion: Use the term *relationship* to refer to the truest essence of the functional and practical bond between activities.

Leads and Lags   After much research of current literature, I can find no consistent use of these terms. For some, the terms are bookends, each meaning the opposite of the other. For others, the terms are synonymous. Between conflicting definitions, the terms can actually mean the opposite from one person to the next. Since there is no consistency, and since the terms are not intuitive (having an understood general meaning) I strongly urge that their use be discontinued.

Conclusion: Retire the terms *leads* and *lags*.

Proposed Terminology Meaning Clarifications

The following Meaning Clarifications have, as their underlying rationale, the collective reasoning discussed in the previous subsection. If you find yourself not understanding the justification for a particular choice of words, please re-read the last subsection. Here, I will concisely state the Clarifications that I propose for adoption by the Scheduling and project management communities. Please note that these are not *definitions*, per se, as I have not taken the time to wordsmith each Clarification with focused attention on the many possible nuances of meaning in each combination or choice of words. Rather, I call these Meaning Clarifications simply because I wish to convey the *spirit* of the meaning, rather than the linguistic construction of a carefully worded definition. Put in laymen's terms: don't get too literal as you read the following! (Words in *italics* indicate key terms.)

- **Task** A project work element that comprises a portion of an *activity*. Not all activities need to, or will, be subdivided into tasks. Typically, tasks are useful in breaking down the work for Execution Planning and Performance Recording but are not necessary for coordination or reporting level efforts.

- **Activity** This is the basic project work element. The *activity description* should define the portion of project work scope represented by the activity.

- **Activity Description** A short description of the general scope of work to be accomplished by the *activity*.

- **Activity-Duration** Each activity is assigned a duration that reflects the underlying assumptions of activity work scope, workforce configuration, worker and team productivity, resource availability, and so on. The bases for duration estimates should be documented separately for reference.

- **Relationship** The graphical and *agreed upon* basis of interaction between *activities*. The term "relationship" should replace confusing terms like *leads*, *lags*, and *dependencies*.

- **Relationship-Duration** A numerical value assigned to a relationship meant to simulate a time gap between the start and/or finish of one *activity* and the start and/or finish of another *activity*. This term should replace the confusing *lead value* or *lag value* terms.

- **Relationship Type** CPM uses four different relationship types: finish-to-start, start-to-start, start-to-finish, and finish-to-finish. All four relationship types are possible using PDM, whereas ADM only employs the finish-to-start relationship type.

- **Interdependency** A term that reflects the nature of the *relationship* between *activities*, that no one *activity* is superior or subordinate to the other. Use of the terms *dependency*, *lead*, and *lag* should be discontinued.

- **Lead Value** Discontinue using this term. Instead, use *relationship-duration*.

- **Lead** Discontinue using this term. Instead, use *relationship*.

- **Lag Value** Discontinue using this term. Instead, use *relationship-duration*.

- **Lag** Discontinue using this term. Instead, use *relationship*.

- **Dependency** Discontinue using this term. Instead, use *interdependency*.

- **Date-Constraint** Any arbitrarily imposed date on, before, or after which an *activity* may or may not start or finish. Date-constraints should be given equal weight in your mind, and are of equal effect, to *relationships* and *activities* (including their respective durations), in determining the calculated early and late dates of *activities*. Date-constraints have the power to override logic in forward and backward pass calculations.

- **Software Settings** All scheduling software programs provide a host of optional settings, applicable globally or per activity, which can affect the results of basic CPM calculations of earliest and latest dates, as well as *total-float* and *free-float*. Examples of such settings include: zero-free-float, zero-total-float, retained-logic, progress-override, contiguous-durations, interruptible-durations, start-float, finish-float, least-float, calendars, and so on.

- **Path** Any combination of associated, sequential, and proximate *activities*, *relationships*, durations, *date-constraints*, and *software settings* that form a cohesive work execution stratagem. This explanation goes well beyond most definitions, by including *relationships*, date-*constraints*, and *settings*, in addition to the *activity* itself. In order to form a "cohesive stratagem," these components must be associated, sequential, and proximate—the latter term meaning, "very near or next, as in space, time, or order."

- **Critical** With Criticality based on one or more criteria (not just total-float), the word "critical" should not be used in isolation but only as a modifier, such as critical-activity or critical-path. Of course, alternative sentence wording may yield, "the activity is critical . . ." or "the path is critical . . ." Other measures of criticality include: Activity Placement, Relationships Aggregation, Confluence Aggregation, Schedule Resiliency, Discrete Activity Float, to name a few.

- **Critical Activity** An activity that is deemed critical, according to one or more measures of Criticality, including but not limited to *total-float*. When used as a modifier to an *activity*, as in this term, the word "critical" implies importance or significance to one or more declared time goals of the project. Hence, an *activity* might be *critical* if the project team deems it important that an *activity* be achieved quickly, or "perfectly the first time," or silently, or with Zero Inconvenience to the owner, or with minimal resources, or flawlessly, and so on. Note: There is no direct correlation between *activity* Criticality and an activity's residence on a *critical path*. That is, an *activity* may be *critical* whether it resides on a *critical path* or not. Likewise, an *activity* that resides on a *critical path* may or may not be critical, in the broader sense of the word *critical*.

- **Completion Milestone** Any activity whose timely completion is defined by an imposed date-constraint is a completion milestone, regardless of the activity's duration value. For example, if a Project Schedule has a Project Complete *activity* bearing a Finish-No-Later-Than *date-constraint*, then this would be a Completion Milestone. Likewise, if the Project Schedule contains a Building Dry-In *activity*, with an accordant Finish-No-Later-Than *date-constraint*, then this would be a separate Completion Milestone.

- **Critical Path** As a major improvement in Scheduling Practice terminology, through this Meaning Clarification I propose a requirement that the term "critical-path" *always* be associated with a specific *completion milestone* and, therefore, accompanied by a modifier—in all cases. For example, if a Project Schedule has a Project Complete *completion milestone*, then there would be an associated Project Critical-Path. Similarly, if the Project Schedule contains a Building Dry-In *completion milestone*, then there would be a separate Dry-In Critical-Path. Note: The wording of the modifier need not be precisely the same as the wording of the *activity* to which it is linked. As for the formulaic determination of what constitutes a *critical-path*, use this definition: "That combination of associated, sequential, and proximate *activities*, *relationships*, *durations*, *date constraints*, calendars, and *software settings* that establishes a *completion milestone's* earliest possible completion date." This definition disregards whether the *path* happens to be the longest one in the Project Schedule or the one having the least float. Instead, it looks to the *effect* that each *path* has on its associated completion milestone. One (or sometimes more than one) *path* will mathematically generate the *chronologically latest* of the earliest-finishes for a completion milestone, and this will be considered it critical-path.

- **Total-Float** As revealed earlier in this chapter, the majority of published definitions of total-float fail to take into account the additional *relationship types* provided by PDM and, as a result, their definitions mostly prove inadequate by not considering that activities can have different start-float and finish-float values. Accordingly, each *activity* has three total-float values: *start-float, finish float, and least-float* (which is derived as the lesser of the other two). For example, if an start-float is –4 and the finish-float is +3, then the least-float is –4. The expression "total float," when not preceded by a modifier is understood by this Meaning Clarification to be synonymous with least-float.

- **Start-Float** The numeric difference between an activity's earliest-start and latest-start values.

- **Finish-Float** The numeric difference between an activity's earliest-finish and latest-finish values.

Part 4 Execution Scheduling and Performance Control

At last we have made it to the proverbial *meat on the bone*. In the following five chapters, I cover a number of subjects, all having something to do with Execution Scheduling or Performance Control. Execution Control entails Schedule Design and Schedule Development. Performance Control deals with Performance Recording, Performance Analysis, Change Optimization, and Performance Advisement. A constant theme throughout this book is that the project is never static. To be sure, the project is a living, breathing animal, with a mind of its own. Driving the project are infinite dynamic forces. The challenge of every project manager is to recognize these forces, anticipate their impact, and respond to their energy. The adroit sailor cannot control the wind, but he can surely control his sails. By tacking, he can actually sail in a direction *opposite* the flow of the wind. Imagine that!

In this fourth section of the book, you may find some ideas easy to comprehend and accept, while others may require you to stop and think how they affect the ebbs and flows on the project jobsite. I hope you will enjoy reading about these invisible forces as much as I have enjoyed writing about them.

12 Concerning Schedule Design

This chapter, divided into three subsections, will discuss one of the least understood or practiced aspects of what we loosely call *scheduling:* Schedule Design. The first subsection addresses the purpose and overall processes of Schedule Design. The middle subsection provides a complete description of the Schedule Design Summit, where key program leaders (and their staffers, –among whom is the Strategic Planner) gather to shape the upcoming project's management strategy. The third subsection contains individual treatments of special topics, including:

- Understanding project Priorities and Emphasis
- Project management styles and level-of-detail
- Schedule granularity
- Schedule Performance Specification

PURPOSE AND OVERALL PROCESS OF SCHEDULE DESIGN

Schedule design is an often-omitted *phase* that precedes Schedule Development.

Purpose of Schedule Design

Working backward, Schedule *Development* involves a number of meticulous and inter-related steps that lead to the creation of a Project Schedule. To be ultimately successful, the Project Schedule's architecture and content must coalesce to support its expected and required uses, which often include: field coordination, communication, work organization, resource management, performance measurement, contract support, cost control, marketing, public relations, financial planning, and extra-contractual participant coordination. Each of these intended uses of the Execution Schedule carries with it various expectations on the part of the Schedule's ultimate users.

Schedule Design is a set of preliminary processes that culminate in the creation of a Schedule Performance Specification, the purpose of which is to guide subsequent Schedule Development, thereby ensuring that the final product, the Execution Schedule, will be the best it can be.

Process of Schedule Design

Schedule Design involves three overlapping steps:

- Intelligence gathering
- Schedule Design Summit
- Creation and adoption of Schedule Performance Specifications

Intelligence Gathering

A Project Schedule is as multidimensional as the project it seeks to support. A project has many participants; each with different goals and priorities, and the Project Schedule must reflect those differences. A project has multiple deadlines and constraints, and the Project Schedule must recognize and reflect each one in some manner. Of all the variables that define the project, none is more significant to the design and integrity of the Project Schedule than the informational needs and wants of the Execution Schedule's stakeholders.

I cannot overstate the importance of conducting adequate intelligence gathering as the first step in the Schedule Design process. Understanding the informational needs and wants of the project's end users requires tireless interviews, diligent note taking, skillful coalescence, and intense attention to detail. Helpful techniques include: interviewing the key players in *their* offices; asking what *they* expect of the project execution effort; getting a sense of their concerns about the project schedule's design, construction, and use; listening for hints of doubt, discord, skepticism; and, then incorporating into the Project Schedule's design strategy reasonable responses to these concerns.

Perhaps you are thinking that intelligence gathering can be performed *at* the Schedule Design Summit. If so, then your instinct is *near* the target's center, for a critical aspect of the Summit is an open exchange and sharing of individual needs and wants. It is important for each project participant to offer their concerns, while also hearing the concerns and expectations of all other project members. However, a one-day session (the time usually allotted for the Summit) is rarely long enough for all concerns to be brought to the forefront, and for this reason a certain amount of prior legwork is needed. Thus, intelligence gathering begins in the days and weeks leading up to and continues into the Summit itself.

Schedule Design Summit

As a general overview of the Summit, it is convened quite early in the overall project Execution Planning process, it is attended by all key decision makers, and it focuses on *how* the project will be managed. To be effective, the Summit should be highly structured and follow a guiding script, and all decisions should be formalized with votes and meticulous minutes. The central byproduct of the Summit, at least in terms of Execution

Scheduling, is the Schedule Performance Specifications. For a detailed discussion of the Summit, see the section "Schedule Design Summit," later in this chapter.

Schedule Performance Specifications

The point of Schedule *Design* is to come to a consensus on what are reasonable expectations with respect to the Project Schedule's ultimate performance. The end product of the Schedule Design Summit is a set of *Schedule Performance* Specifications that becomes the springboard for Schedule Development. You can imagine the importance of this document in clarifying what the Project Schedule will do or not do. To the point, Schedule Performance Specifications are to Schedule Development what plans and drawings are to field construction.

Keep in mind that this book is all about creating Project Schedules that end users will *want* to use. That's just another way of saying that the end users of the Execution Schedule will be satisfied with its performance. Dissatisfaction comes from unrealized expectations, and the gap between what was expected and what was delivered can be short on one end or the other—of both. That is, it is often the case that end users expect too much from the Project Schedule or are unclear at the outset as to what a good Project Schedule is capable of doing. The third possibility, of course, is that all parties maintain reasonable expectations but that the Project Schedule simply fails to deliver the goods. Schedule Performance Specifications serve as a barometer against which to measure the Project Schedule's ultimate utility and quality.

The best way to close this gap is by having *all* involved parties participate in a brainstorming and decision-making meeting in which the Project Schedule's intended uses are fully described, its functionality clarified, and its architecture understood. At this meeting, it is the responsibility of the end users to ask for what they want and of the Schedule Developers to promise only what they can deliver and no more.

Without such a meeting of the minds, the door is flung wide open for the entry of all kinds of disparities between what the project needs and what the end users want, between what the end users want and what the Schedule Developers can create, and between what is created and what the end users elect to use.

As this last point suggests, the odds of disappointing rest on both sides of the coin. Plus, those who develop the Project Schedule are most often also the ones to *maintain* the schedule. This means that, for those involved in producing and maintaining the schedule, there is understandable frustration when the customers, for whom the Execution Schedule was created in the first place, fail to use the Project Schedule as it was designed or fail to ask for their "schedule wish list" up front but whine later, once the Execution Schedule is already formalized and in play.

SCHEDULE DESIGN SUMMIT

Before any other Schedule Development activities take place, Management needs to hold the Schedule Design Summit, during which many joint decisions important to subsequent Execution Scheduling activities are to be made.

Purpose of Summit

The sole purpose of the Summit is to provide an opportunity for all key project leaders to forge a consensus on how the project will be managed, as well as how the overall Execution Scheduling effort, including the Execution Schedule itself, will support that management approach.

The rationale underlying this session is both simple and logical. Since a Project Schedule is a tool for project management, then before the tool is crafted it is important to establish a solid understanding of the *project*, as well as the *organization* that will manage that project. Further, because Project Scheduling drives so many significant project management functions, it is essential that all scheduling performance requirements be understood *before* Schedule Development commences.

Finally, the Project Schedule is the hub in the Scheduling Practice Paradigm, and therefore it is vital that all parties agree on the intended relationship between the Project Schedule and the other functional concerns of management—such as budget, contracts, change management, communications, quality control, risk management, procurement, and the like.

Specifically, every project is unique, and thus, out of necessity, so should every Project Schedule be. One size does not fit all! While most reasonable minds intuitively understand this point, with respect to the content of the Execution Schedule, the common practice in most constructor organizations is to establish and enforce *standardized* scheduling procedures, and the net effect is a cookie-cutter approach to Project Schedule architecture and functionality. Later, they wonder why the Execution Schedule was not more warmly embraced.

To be sure, there are many variables that affect the look and feel of the Project Schedule, but no one factor is more influential than the Execution Schedule's *level-of-detail*. I have provided full coverage of this topic in this chapter's final section, "Special Considerations," but for now, know that this and other Project Schedule characteristics should be topics of lively discussion during the Schedule Design Summit.

Who Should Attend

It is essential that the highest levels of management from each performing organization participate in the all-day session. For some executives, this may be the first and last time they will pay personal attention to *this* project. An important expression of commitment is conveyed when principals of the design firms, contractors, owners, and major vendors are willing to participate in making critical decisions that will influence how the project will be managed, how project dynamics will be controlled, how the players will interact, and how success will ultimately be determined.

Summit Proceedings

There are as many different ways to organize and conduct a Schedule Design Summit as there are project leaders.

However you do it, the Summit should address these essential issues: project description (in terms of type, length, cost, and current scope level); management strategy (in terms of relationship with schedule, cost, resources, risk, and information flow); and, subsequent and necessary roles, tools, methodologies, and technologies.

SmartStart

Again, how you accomplish this is typically a matter of personal preference and/or corporate culture. To give you an idea of how the Schedule Design Summit can work, here is what I routinely propose to my clients. For mnemonic effect, I call it *SmartStart*®.

Overview I recommend guiding your Schedule Design Summit using the SmartStart approach. SmartStart begins by gathering a team of key leadership figures subject who jointly make their way through the maze of decisions, options, and deadlines that characterize the "front end" of any project. But SmartStart goes beyond getting the players in the room and handing out an agenda. It is also a structured process that ensures that all essential questions are asked, sufficiently understood, and adequately answered.

Smart stands for Synchronized Methods, Attitudes, Roles, and Tools. In order for a project to be effectively managed during its life cycle, it is imperative that, at the outset, all Project Management and Scheduling Practice methods, approaches, roles, and tools are fully defined and closely integrated so that their collective synergy yields maximum value to the project.

At the core of the SmartStart approach to project strategic planning are SmartMaps, SmartGrids, and SmartSpecs.

The SmartMap More than anything else, the Schedule Design process is a series of decisions that, whether made well, poorly, or not at all, will profoundly affect the overall success of the project. Sound decisions are those made after careful review of all pertinent facts and with full consideration of all significant variables, such as priorities, assumptions, objectives, political and logistic realities, and so on.

It has been found that the best decisions are those made following energized, structured and yet open exchanges of ideas. The Smart*Map*®, which stands for Methodological Approach to Planning, is the primary tool for the Schedule Design Summit. See Figure 12-1. For your easy adoption, see Figure 12-2 where I have included a version of the SmartMap devoid of any notations.

The SmartGrid Accompanying the SmartMap are supporting SmartGrids®, which provide Schedule Design participants with generic recommendations for integrated deliverables, assuming "typical" conditions. These grids are intended to provide "starting points" for subsequent discussion and decision-making. SmartGrids provide a cursory depiction of deliverables at different levels of detail. Used in conjunction with the SmartMap, the Smart*Grid*, which stands for Generic Recommendations for Integrated Deliverables, can "suggest" appropriate levels of detail, based on other projects of similar description. Figure 12-3 provides an example.

Figure 12-1
SmartMap Example

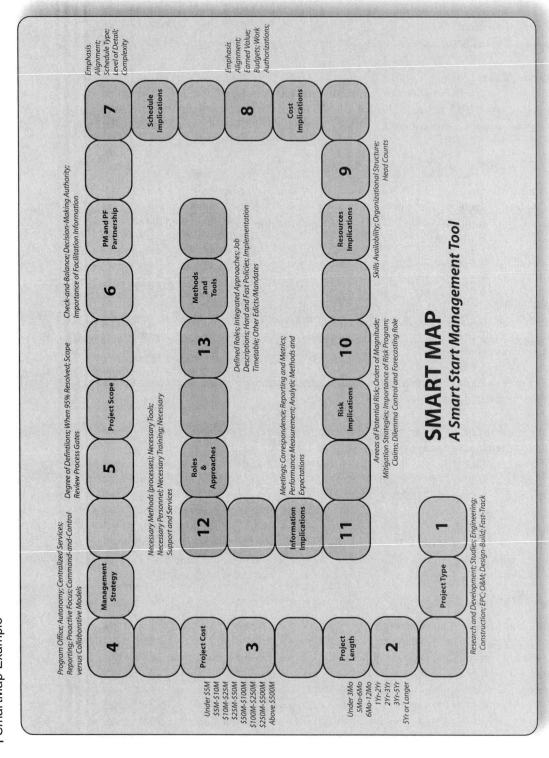

Figure 12-2
SmartMap Template; without Annotation

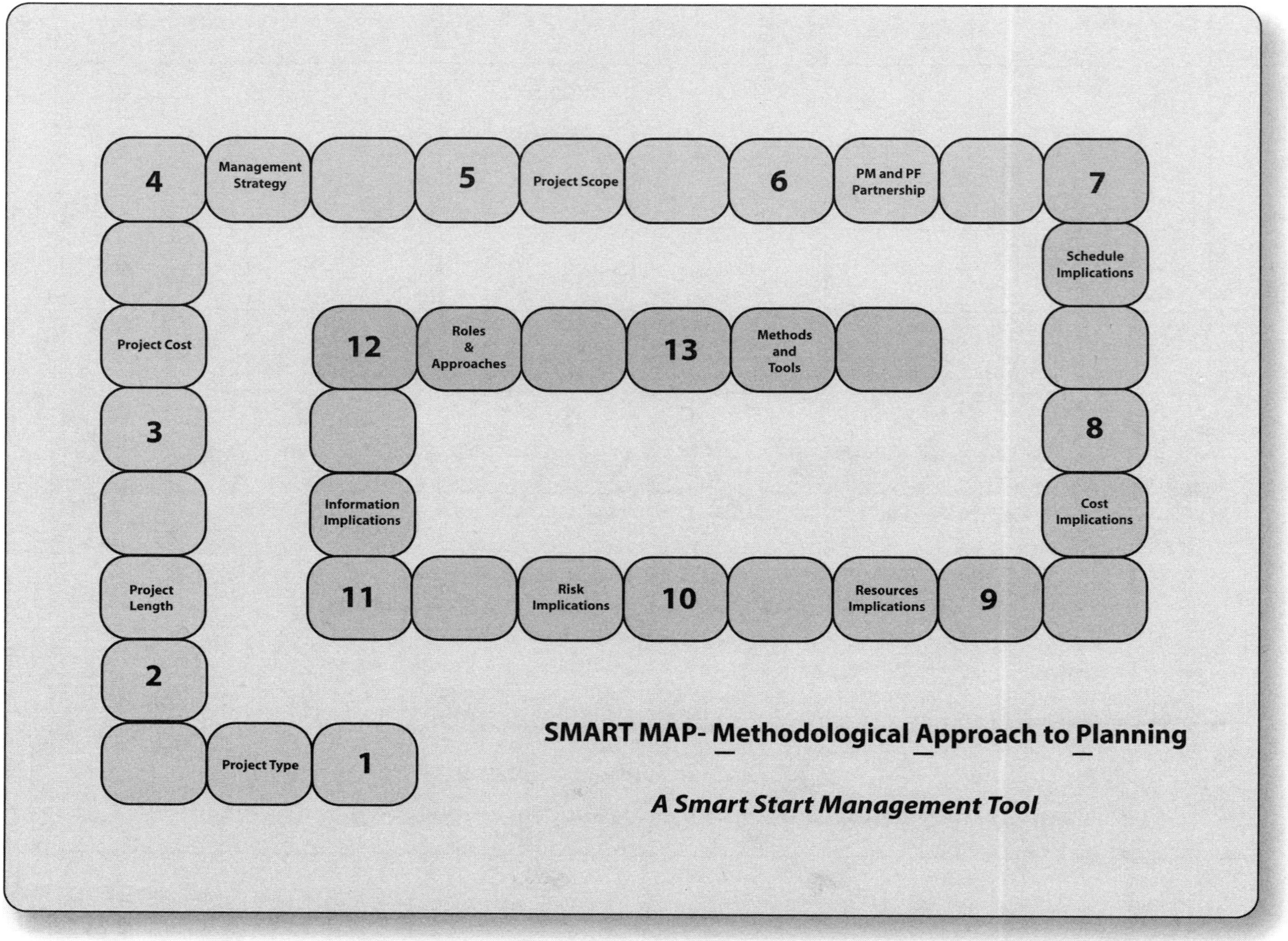

SMART MAP- Methodological Approach to Planning

A Smart Start Management Tool

Figure 12-3
SmartGrid Example

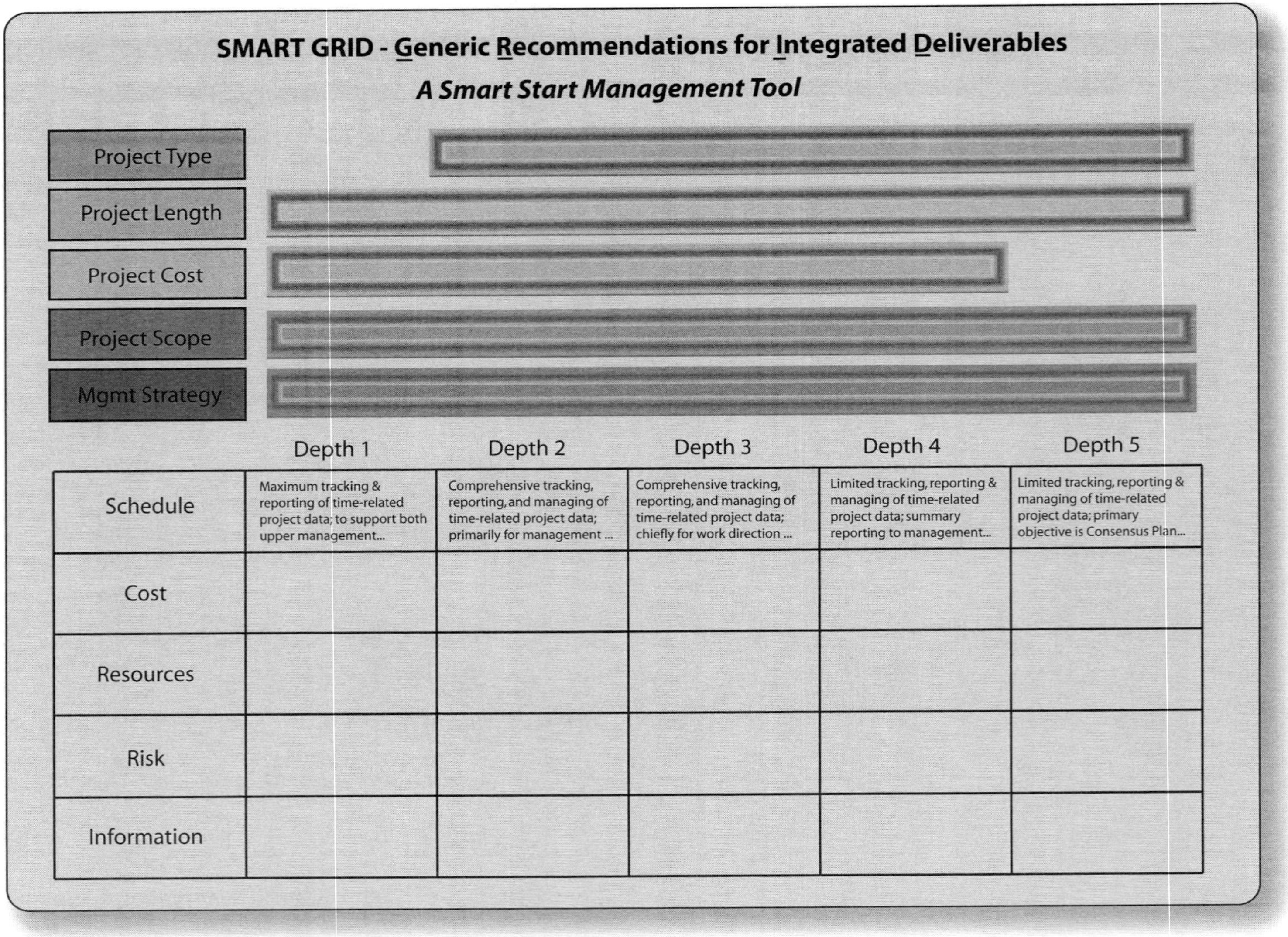

SMART GRID - Generic Recommendations for Integrated Deliverables
A Smart Start Management Tool

	Depth 1	Depth 2	Depth 3	Depth 4	Depth 5
Schedule	Maximum tracking & reporting of time-related project data; to support both upper management...	Comprehensive tracking, reporting, and managing of time-related project data; primarily for management ...	Comprehensive tracking, reporting, and managing of time-related project data; chiefly for work direction ...	Limited tracking, reporting & managing of time-related project data; summary reporting to management ...	Limited tracking, reporting & managing of time-related project data; primary objective is Consensus Plan...
Cost					
Resources					
Risk					
Information					

Project Type

Project Length

Project Cost

Project Scope

Mgmt Strategy

The SmartSpecs   The SmartGrid, however, may not provide information specific enough as to what one can expect to find in a given deliverable. For a more detailed explanation of what a deliverable will likely contain, one can study SmartSpecs associated with one of the major project controls disciplines, such as Schedule, Cost, Resources, Risk, or Communications. Figure 12-4 shows a SmartSpecs® for the Scheduling category, partially filled out. Smart*Specs* stands for Specific Product Expectations Clearly Stated. Again, the intent of this and the other two SmartStart components is to assist the Schedule Design Summit in its goal of achieving consensus on what the Scheduling Practice work products will look like, how they will function, and what their limitations will be.

Procedural Guidelines

In the event that you are not interested in the SmartStart approach, here are some guidelines to ensure that, no matter how you conduct it, your Schedule Design Summit is as successful as possible.

Project Description   Describe the project in terms of what it entails. Is this new construction, renovation of existing construction, or both? Is this a virgin (green field) site, or is demolition work required? Is it a congested area? Are there unique obstacles to construction? Will the owner occupy all or some portion of the premises during construction?

What are any unique aspects of the design? Is this a skyscraper or an especially large building? Does it employ a relatively new or untested technology (for example, a unique roofing system)? Are there any one-of-a-kind materials or any long lead items? Are they owner-supplied?

What about contractual characteristics? What is the project delivery method? Is this a fast-tracked project? Is this a design-build contract? Is it an Engineer-Procure-Construct (EPC) contract, or a Build-Operate-Transfer (BOT) contract? What is the contractor's relationship to the owner? Is there a construction manager sandwiched between the owner and the contractor? What are the contractual requirements for Execution Scheduling? What exculpatory contract language pertains to Execution Scheduling? Who owns the float? How will scope changes be handled? What constitutes a schedule revision?

What about any bid information, including context of the contractor's bid or proposal? Did the contractor already commit to a certain project length? Does the owner expect a certain project execution plan? Are there milestones that must be contractually met? Are there limitations that would prevent certain work from being performed at certain times (for example, shutdowns on rail projects, weather restrictions, or noise abatement).

You get the idea. The point is to have an open, robust, roundtable discussion among the participants. Not only will a wealth of important information be imparted to all concerned, this opening session makes for a great icebreaker for the project itself.

Emphasis-Aligned Management   Emphasis-aligned management simply means that all management processes and actions are performed in alignment with the owner's success criteria. (See Figure 12-5, later in this chapter.) To accomplish this, use the bid documents

Figure 12-4
SmartSpecs Example

SMART SPECS- Specific Product Expectations Clearly Stated
A Smart Start Management Tool

Schedule

	Objectives	Products & Methods	Infrastructure/ Environment/Comments
Depth 1	Maximum tracking & reporting of time-related project data; to support both upper management and lowest levels of work performance.	Format: Integrated CPM Network Level of Detail: Work package; 2-4 week duration Data Source: PM and PF Personnel Documentation: Durations, logic, resource assumptions Usage: Integral to management process Commitment: Sign-off; interdependency management	Infrastructure: Comprehensive WBS, OBS, and RAM Environment: All but mega-projects and mini-projects Comments: Activity-duration level-of-detail should correlate with reporting level-of-detail
Depth 2	Comprehensive tracking, reporting, and managing of time-related project data; primarily for management edification.	Format: Selective CPM Network Level of Detail: Planning package; 1-3 month duration Data Source: PM and PF Personnel Documentation: Assumptions, concerns Usage: Integral to management process Commitment: Sign-off	
Depth 3	Comprehensive tracking, reporting, and managing of time-related project data; primarily for work direction and implementation.		
Depth 4	Limited tracking, reporting, and managing of time-related project data; summary reporting to management but detailed work tracking.		
Depth 5	Limited tracking, reporting, and managing of time-related project data; primary objective is feasibility analysis, scenario optimization, or strategic planning.		

and any other relevant sources and jointly determine the correct balance between owner success criteria and appropriate contractor performance emphasis. Put the red dot where it belongs on the Emphasis Alignment Model.

Organizational Structure Have Management share its vision of project staffing and organization. Which project management functions will be handled from the home office, and which ones will be situated at the jobsite? Specifically, who will be the project team members? How will critical cost, schedule, and quality control functions be handled, centrally or remotely?

Project Schedules, once running at full capacity, are expected to provide meaningful value to all levels and all aspects of the project. This means that at the highest level a Project Schedule might be focused on reporting, at the midmanagement level on prevention and at the grass roots level on facilitating. Depending on the level of focus, Schedule Design criteria can change dramatically. Earned Value, for example, is of little use at the facilitation level, no matter what the project size.

Any attempt to design (or even recommend) schedule architecture must allow for the reality of delegation. As projects increase in size and complexity, so does the underlying administrative organization. Collectively, the largest management organization performs the same steps that a few individuals, wearing multiple hats, might do on a much smaller project. But while projects and personnel expand and contract in parallel, the scheduling tool remains constant.

Resources What are the availabilities of key resources, including labor, materials, equipment, office facilities, and capital? Are material shortages expected by the prime contractor, its major subcontractors, or vendors? Will this project be competing with other projects in the area, or even nationally, for limited resources?

Schedule How will Execution Scheduling be used on the project? Will the project be run from the Execution Schedule as a chief coordination tool, or will it simply be a record keeping device? Will it be used to justify/validate progress payments? How often will it be statused? Under what conditions will a Project Schedule revision be mandated? Who will participate in Schedule Development? Who will be the likely end users of Scheduling products? How will scope changes be handled in the Execution Schedule? How will basic scheduling information be generated? What will be the basis for defining project scope? Will a Work Breakdown Structure be utilized to align the construction documents and the Project Schedule?

Cost How extensively will cost accounting be performed? If a substantial amount of the project work is to be subcontracted, will there be enough self-performed work to justify sophisticated performance measurement efforts, such as Earned Value? Will the contractor have access to sufficient *subcontractor* costing information to support such monitoring? Will there be a formal work authorization process, whereby criteria must be met before work will be authorized?

Risk Management and Dilemma Control Will a formal risk identification and avoidance program be implemented? Will it be performed by a simpler approach, or will Monte Carlo simulations be performed on the Project Schedule—at the outset and during routine updates? Will contingencies be built into the project budget or the Project Schedule? If so, what will be the allocation strategy? During construction, will trending be used to detect *smoke* before blazing fires break out? Will a Dilemma Control program be implemented on the project? If so, how will dilemma forecasting be incorporated into the project manager's strategy for project communications, direction, and problem solving?

Procurement Will the purchasing effort be handled from the jobsite or remotely? Will contractual commitment dates be related to the Project Schedule and, if so, how? In what order should the project be bought out? Against what criteria will subcontractors be selected? Will more than price dictate their selection? Will the selected contractors adopt the owner's project success criteria? To what extent will the subcontractors be required to provide information to, and comply with, the contractor's project management support system efforts? For instance, will subcontractors be required to submit CPM schedules, and must those Execution Schedules contributions be resource-loaded? Who will review the subcontractor's Execution Schedule and how will their information be coordinated with the input of others? Who resolves any discrepancies or conflicts between different subcontractor schedules? Will the subcontractor be required to provide confidential job costing information necessary for Earned Value calculations?

Communications What will be the project's communication protocols? Who are the key contacts for each project organization? What will be the formal communication channels between the owner, the construction manager, the design professionals, the general contractor, other prime contractors, any subcontractors, suppliers, vendors, and so on? Will there be a project-wide document control system and, if so, how will it be described and by whom? How will verbal communications be captured or formalized? What will agendas and rosters of routine meetings include? How and by whom will meeting agendas be created and formatted? How will agenda items correlate to the Project Schedule? Who will attend these meetings?

Management Style What will be the prevalent management style: Command-and-Control, Collaborative, or other? Is the project manager's style one of micromanagement or extensive delegation? If delegation is the project manager's style, how will accountability be maintained, and how will he resolve differences among staffers? How involved will the project manager be in schedule and cost procedures? Are key leadership roles (project manager, chief superintendent, and so on) staffed by individuals whose personal performance styles are compatible with the owner's success criteria?

Outputs Based on decisions reached during discussion to this point, decide on the type, frequency, format, and distribution of key management reports. Specifically, in light of the preceding, which Schedule Extraction Reports make sense and which do not?

Other Project Controls Pursuant to decisions reached up to this point, and especially considering the Emphasis Alignment Model, what other project control efforts, beyond Execution Scheduling, make sense? For instance, is Earned Value an appropriate management tool? If so, is its contribution sufficient to justify the erosion of schedule integrity that might result? Quite often, the implementation of Earned Value forces the Execution Schedule's level-of-detail to be decomposed below a point that would either be necessary or desirable for time-management purposes alone. Earned Value is principally a cost-side technology and, on a project that is *time*-sensitive, it might not be an appropriate choice.

SPECIAL CONSIDERATIONS

A number of technical issues are discussed next. Each is an important topic in its own right and should be fully understood by all who will participate in the Schedule Design Summit.

Understanding Project Priorities and Emphasis

A major reason construction projects fail to meet stated goals is that, all too often, there is a misalignment between what the owner calls for (success criteria) and what the contractor supplies (performance). I'll explain this in a moment. But before I do, let us agree that, if true, this condition suggests an opportunity for improvement in project management support systems suite design[1] whenever the Schedule somehow accommodates this misalignment—possibly exacerbating the effects of any disparity between owner priorities and contractor emphasis.

Theory of Aligned Emphasis
"I want the job done _____."

There's always a qualifier involved. By that, I mean that owners never just want the project *completed*, they wanted it completed *quickly*, or they want it completed *inexpensively*, or they want it completed *in a certain manner*. Since disappointment results from unmet expectations, owner disappointment can almost always be traced back to how they completed this sentence at the outset of the project.

If the owner wants the project finished *quickly*, he will be disappointed if the project comes in *under budget*, yet still *behind schedule*. If the owner wants a *top quality* project, he will be disappointed with a final product that is overrun with quality deficiencies, even if it was completed *ahead of schedule* and *under budget*.

To illustrate this point, consider Figure 12-5, called the *Emphasis Alignment Model*, which depicts the precise balance between three success criteria against which management must align its people and processes.

This brings us to the Theory of Aligned Emphasis, which states: "No matter what the project type, location, size, design, function, or purpose, on every project, one of these

---

[1]In particular, the Project Schedule itself.

Figure 12-5

Emphasis
Alignment Model

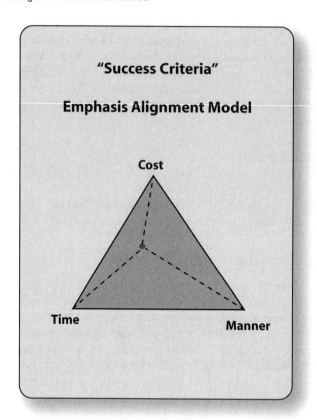

qualifiers is of a greater priority to the owner than the other two." You may question the veracity of this statement, but extensive research on hundreds of completed projects has confirmed it: the owner is almost always willing to de-emphasize two of these variables for the sake of the third.

Please don't misconstrue the point. I am not saying that the owner favors one success criterion to the *exclusion* of the other two. All three criteria are almost always important to the owner at some level. But it is indeed rare that *one* qualification is not more important to the owner than the other two. Using the Emphasis Alignment Model, it is possible to place a red dot at a point that realistically identifies and reflects the relative importance of the three success criteria to each other.

For example, some projects are extremely cost-critical to an owner. Faced with a choice of a more costly project that would complete earlier and with higher quality, versus, a less costly project that would complete later and with lesser quality, in this scenario the *cost* variable would drive the owner's decisions.

On another project the owner might place greatest emphasis on the *manner* in which the project is performed. To understand what I mean by manner, think of the three success criteria as answering these basic questions:

- **Cost** Answers the question *"how much?"*
- **Time** Answers the question *"when?"*
- **Manner** Answers the question *"how?"*

Any conditions that characterize or modify *how* the work is to be performed fall under the heading of *manner*. The owner may want the project performed quietly or with minimum disruption to ongoing activities of occupants or only during certain hours or with restricted access or with minimal dust and debris or with no objectionable smells, and on. You get the point. *How* the project is prosecuted may be more important to an owner than *when* it will complete or *how much* it will cost.

But of all the conditions falling under the *manner* label, the most frequently cited is *quality*. Here, the owner wants a top-quality project in the end, and that means that each activity must be performed with quality squarely in mind at all times. Aerospace construction offers examples of projects where the client is more concerned with manner than schedule. What good is a satellite floating in space with a faulty mechanical part? The owner will pay premium dollars to secure a top-drawer product, even at the expense of a slipped schedule, because quality is where he places greatest emphasis.

The bulk of projects, however, are of the third type, time-critical, where the owner emphasizes project completion *on* or *ahead of* schedule. Perhaps the project is a manufacturing plant that will produce a new product, which *must* get to market ahead of the competition. If the planned release date is not met, and the competitive advantage of pre-emptive marketing is missed, the entire cost of the new plant may end up as a bottom line liability to the owner. In such a case, the owner is willing to sacrifice a certain amount of quality and cost—in order to make the end date.

Selecting a Compatible Project Manager
The message to the contractor, then, is to clarify the owner's emphasis and align project performance accordingly. The owner's success criteria should influence and permeate all project management decision-making. The first decision, of course, is the selection of a specific project manager. But what are the effects of priority-emphasis misalignment?

Misalignment: Time-Focused Owner vs. Cost-Focused Project Manager In this alignment, the project manager takes pride in completing his projects under budget. He does this by taking cost-cutting measures wherever he can. He looks for substitute products that cost less. Of course, substitutions, while commonly allowed under the contract, require additional review cycles by the architect and owner. These reviews *take time* and can delay the delivery of the involved materials to site.

He tries to nickel-and-dime his subcontractors who, in turn, become defensive in their dealings with the project manager. They resort to dotting their "i'"s and crossing their "t'"s. They refuse to perform out-of-scope work, even the most miniscule, without something in writing first. The injection of a prerequisite paper process *takes time* and thwarts the spontaneity of the collective project team.

He looks for ways to use mass labor in lieu of more efficient (meaning, more costly) automated approaches. The project takes longer but it comes in under budget. He is proud. The owner is disappointed.

Misalignment: A Cost-Focused Owner vs. a Quality-Focused Subcontractor Here is another example of how misaligned owner emphasis and contractor performance can easily result in a project outcome that the owner might label "disappointing." Subcontractor X, known by reputation for his high quality work products, refuses to release any work element for owner inspection until it meets his stringent performance standards. As work-in-place materializes and deficiencies begin to naturally appear (as they unavoidably will), the subcontractor commences rework efforts at his own discretion and insistence.

Nothing the general contractor or owner can say will dissuade the subcontractor from "correcting" his own work. The schedule suffers. Downstream subcontractors, held up by Subcontractor X's snail's pace, begin diverting their work efforts around this "boulder in the river." Costs accrue all around the subcontractor, and a legally defensive prime contractor and an equally irritated owner turn adversarial. They begin to document the subcontractor's refusal to perform work in an "expeditious manner." The subcontractor is devastated—and equally defensive.

I could provide countless other combinations to make the same basic point. In selecting project team members, it is important to match performance attitudes with owner priorities. You may wonder why I am including this observation in a book on project scheduling. A Project Schedule, at any stage, that misaligns the owner's priorities and the contractor's emphasis virtually guarantees project failure, *as defined by those priorities*.

Theory of Aligned Emphasis Applied to Project Controls

Now, let's turn to the relevance of the Theory of Aligned Emphasis on the choice, design, and implementation of various project management support systems—starting with the Project Schedule itself. A simple example of project management support systems misalignment would be an Execution Schedule that does not allow for more than *one* submittal-review-approval cycle for critical submissions on a project where the owner most values quality (manner), and the contractor's upper management emphasis is on schedule. Delays resulting from a second or third iteration on a critical submittal would create frustration and anger with both the owner *and* the project manager's superiors!

What I've just said about the Project Schedule is equally true for any project management support methodology, process, or tool. You should balance the component's choice, design, and implementation against the project success criteria defined by the owner. For instance, if the owner is not overly concerned about project cost but is desperate for the project to finish as soon as possible, perhaps even ahead of schedule, then why invest in processes and tools that are designed for aggressive cost control?[2]

---

[2]This question is even more significant if the implementation of those cost controls serves to weaken the Project Schedule's ability to provide especially vital time management information.

Schedule Use	Under Command-and-Control	Under Collaborative
Planning	Minor	Major
Coordination	Minor	Major
Direction	Major	None
Communication	Major	Major
Work Organization	Major	None
Resource Management	Major	None
Performance Measurement	Major	Major
Compliance Measurement	Major	None
Forecasting	Major	Major
Reporting	Major	Major
Contract Management	Major	Minor
Cost Control	Major	None
Marketing	Minor	Minor
Financial Planning	Minor	Minor
Record Keeping	Major	Minor
Dispute Resolution	Major	None

Table 12-1

Command-and-Control versus Collaborative Schedule Uses

Project Management Styles and Level-of-Detail

Table 12-1 draws from material covered in Chapters 2 and 4. In Chapter 2 we listed numerous possible uses of Project Schedules, and in Chapter 4 we noted two different management styles, one aimed at control and the other aimed at collaboration. By correlating the two categorizations, we find that certain Project Schedule uses are exclusive to a single project management style, while others are important to both. This correlation is essential to an appropriate determination of the Project Schedule's ultimate level-of-detail.

What we see from Table 12-1 is that, under the Command-and-Control Management style, the Project Schedule must be far more detailed that under the Collaborative Model, in order to meet its intended objectives. Setting aside those uses that apply equally to both management styles, we find the following exceptions:

Planning
Planning is typically a downplayed process among Command-and-Control managers, and this tendency explains why so few projects have formalized Execution Plans, even when they have formalized Execution Schedules. When planning *is* done, it is contained in a separate document, what I would call the Strategic Plan or Consensus Plan. By default, then, planning is done in this other document and *not* in the Execution Schedule. Since one of the main uses of Execution Schedules is to coordinate and foster efficient collaboration among the project participants, the level-of-detail is more general, thus more conducive to impromptu and frequent strategy sessions during construction.

Coordination
I use the term "coordination" to refer to the planned interaction between multiple project participants. Under this definition, the logic ties linking two activities being performed

by the same party do not represent an effort to coordinate but instead simply to direct or control. A key attribute of the Execution Schedule under Collaborative Management is that activities tend to be only as specific as necessary, such that the *only* logic ties are those that depict relationships *between different* participants. In this way, such Execution Schedules are highly collaborative in intent. It's quite the opposite from Execution Schedules under Command-and-Control, where an individual participant's scope is broken into the most specific (and, I would add, *obvious*) steps. Of course, quite often this much detail is necessary to support other Execution Schedule uses, such as cost control, resource planning, claims, and the like.

Direction

Collaborative Management's philosophy is that the individual performer on the project is assumed to be competent, and therefore the Execution Schedule is not needed to instruct the performer as to what he should do from one day to the next. Command-and-Control Management adopts a different view, contending that every single action that takes place on the jobsite must be accounted for in the Execution Schedule, and the more detailed the better.

Work Organization

Command-and-Control managers see the Schedule Development process as an ideal opportunity for comprehensively capturing the total scope of the project. Collaborative managers also agree that the Execution Schedule must contain all of the project's scope. But the Command-and-Control manager sees an intrinsic value in the Execution Schedule as a work organization tool and expands upon that feature such that the level-of-detail is driven downward.

WBS begins this drive by requiring an iterative process of decomposing the scope into smaller and smaller deliverables. Enterprise Project Management introduces the need for parallel fragmentation of the organizational structure with the ultimate objective being the cross-referencing of OBS and WBS. Earned Value and Cost Engineering principles reinforce this approach, since both prefer or require that each activity's accountability be limited to *one* performer.

Collaborative Model managers adopt a different view, on several different fronts. First, they contend that the Execution Schedule is not the best place to perform cost engineering, Earned Value, and other nontime computations. Second, they do not agree that a deliverable-oriented approach to scope definition is always the best way to go. Third, they don't share the need to have each activity reduced to a single point of accountability. In fact, just the opposite philosophy prevails. Collaborative Model managers believe in the power and wisdom of synergistic problem solving and look for ways to encourage cooperation and brainstorming. One way is to group the scope of several performers into a single activity. This is the equivalent of the popular negotiation tactic of "throwing them all in the room and not letting them out until they reach consensus." A popular technique for team building follows the Forming-Storming-Norming-Performing model. These stages are defined as:

- **Forming** Team members are introduced. This is a congenial stage during which the team is trying to determine the overall concept. During this stage, certain individuals emerge as leaders, others as followers.

- **Storming** Tensions begin to rise as the stronger players begin to jockey for control of the team. Negativism and pessimism surfaces at this point. Frustration may transfer to the underlying concept as well as toward individuals. Messengers start taking arrows for their messages. But like birth pains, out come great solutions, despite all the yelling and screaming.

- **Norming** Now encouraged by the prospects of a workable concept and with fights for leadership won and lost, the team settles into a productive working relationship. The general concept derived during the Storming stage is now given the practical details to make it work.

- **Performing** With all parties on board, the strategy is implemented, each individual knowing both their role in the scheme as well as in the Big Picture.

For Collaborative Model managers, the real value of Schedule Development is this forging of team spirit and collective ownership of, and commitment to, Execution Schedule achievement. Such achievement, however, is not measured in terms of absolute compliance with each and every activity's start and finish dates or absolute adherence to the precise sequencing of the work, as denoted by the relationship ties. Rather, it is focused on achieving key "push pin" dates. This style of management doesn't require the minute detailing of sequence and duration found in Command-and-Control Execution Schedules.

Resource Management

Notwithstanding the increasing call for resource-loaded Execution Schedules in certain Scheduling Practice circles, the construction industry continues to reject this method as unnecessary overkill. As a result, only a very small percent of construction Execution Schedules are manpower-loaded or cost-loaded. And the reason should be obvious: users don't think it is necessary!

In construction, those who create and maintain the Project Schedule (the owner, the owner's representative, the construction manager, or the general contractor) are *not* the ones doing the actual work—at least, not the vast majority of the work. Oh, the owner may have a handful of activities in the Project Schedule for which he is responsible, and the General Contractor may self-perform the civil work. But, by and large, the work is brokered to the subcontractors and vendors. And such brokering occurs under the protective structure of a contract. Given the contractual context, enforced by the courts, there is little concern on the part of a Project Schedule's developers just how many workers will be performing on a given activity: that's the sub's problem! The same argument applies to cost loading; the subcontractor bid the work, was awarded the contract, and what it costs him is his problem!

But those arguments are separate from the main one, the point of this subsection. Collaborative Model managers view the Project Schedule as a tool for team building, team-oriented problem solving, and Improvisational Management. They do *not* see it as a cost control tool, a resource management tool, or a claims tool. Remember the business trip example from Chapter 4. There is no need to subdivide "Get Dressed" into seven smaller activities, if the primary objective is general coordination among participants. Viewed from this perspective, it is easy to see why cost, labor, and claims factoring are essentially irrelevant to most Collaborative Model managers. And this view may well explain why, in practice, resource loading is not at all popular in construction schedules (but, by comparison, is common in IT projects, where the majority of work is self-performed).

Compliance Measurement

The need for performance monitoring is common to both Command-and-Control and Collaborative Management. What differs is how that information is used, and that tends to influence the type and manner of performance data collection. Among Command-and-Control managers, where the emphasis is on compliance with pre-established standards, Performance Control is concerned with measuring performance at the same level that the Baseline Schedule captured the initial commitments. Hence, if the initial Project Schedule is developed with a high level-of-detail, then Performance Recording data will be collected at that same level (or greater).

Data collection is accomplished through two different processes: by observation, and by computation. Through observation, the amount of work completed during the reporting period is determined. Let us call this the *raw* data. But then, this raw data is further analyzed and additional derivative statistics are developed. This is what I call computed data. When the emphasis is on compliance, types of computed data might include: activity duration variance statistics (planned versus actual activity-durations), relationship variance statistics (planned versus actual relationship-durations), completed activity statistics (planned versus actual completed activities), and so on.

Collaborative Model managers have a certain interest in the raw data but only modest interest in the computed data. They understand that there can be a wide variety of reasons for discovered variances between what was planned and what occurred. And while speculation of the cause(s) of such deviations might satisfy a curiosity and be informative and even helpful, they consider a strong focus on remaining work performance more beneficial to the project than a fixation on what did or did not occur in the past.

Compliance measurement is, of course, a vital component of any legal or contractual campaign for equitable treatment on the project. Concern over the impact of changing conditions tempers most interpretations of Execution Scheduling deliverables. When the primary use of Execution Scheduling products is legal or contractual, the emphasis on accuracy mandates methods that yield greater precision (or, more rightly, what is perceived as yielding greater precision): *more detail.*

Contract Management

Collaborative Model managers consider it unfortunate that the Project Schedule has become the key tool in all contractual and legal fights over time allotment, float ownership, and production efficiency. Any modifications to the Project Schedule, even those intended to improve its ability to support project management, are immediately evaluated from the context of their positive or negative effects on legal/contractual standing.

Command-and-Control Model managers accept the dual role of the Project Schedule far more easily, and that may have a lot to do with personality. Command-and-Control managers tend to be more process- than people-oriented. They find comfort and even protection in the absolute boundaries of the contract, and the Execution Schedule, perceived and employed as an extension of the contract, bestows additional authority to the manager. Teamwork, by contrast, cannot take place if members of the team are distracted (even inhibited) by the ever-present walls erected as jurisdictional "boundaries."

Cost Control

The point here is the same one made under Resource Management. In construction, unless the contract type is a form of Time and Materials, Cost Plus, or some other arrangement where the costs are not locked in, the owner doesn't have much interest in how much money is budgeted or spent per activity. The obvious exception to this is the desire to correlate work progress with approval of progress payments. A responsible owner does not want to pay for products or services *not* received. But here, as with resource loading, it boils down to a matter of degree. Activities with a more general level-of-detail can be cost loaded and, coupled with reasonable performance measurement, *earned budget* amounts can be determined. It is only when the Project Schedule is adopted by cost control practitioners that schedule detail is driven to a level far below what is needed to protect the time-goals of the project.

Record Keeping

Once again, the temptation to use the Project Schedule for purposes other than controlling performance of the work has proved too great for Command-and-Control Model managers, who have delighted in its ability to track all sorts of information that relate, in one form or another, back to the scope of work. The expanded role of the Project Schedule database, to house and host information not directly related to time management, was recognized long ago by scheduling software developers. As they added more and more features not directly related to time management, they changed the name of the software genre from scheduling software to project management software.

Dispute Resolution

Of all of the uses of schedules *beyond* time management, dispute resolution bears the lion's share of responsibility for the erosion of schedule reliability, at least within the construction industry. While the other nontime uses may have an unwanted effect of forcing more detail into the Project Schedule than would otherwise be included, the dispute resolution influence is so much more damaging.

Execution Schedulers and project managers who are concerned with the legal and contractual implications of Schedule Extraction Reports often (perhaps even *routinely*) find it necessary to alter Project Schedule content (durations, logic, settings, and more) in order to "protect" their business interests. These "adjustments" have nothing to do with finding the best way to manage the project and often times work at cross-purposes with that goal. More and more, the entire Execution Scheduling process, from initial design through cyclical updates, is being driven by an interest in maximizing revenues through allegations of delay, acceleration, and labor/production inefficiency.

Ever since the contract achieved its current role as a dominant influence on the construction project, the battleground for profits (on both sides of the equation) has been the "extra," or the change order. Contractors diligently look for opportunities to parlay design deficiencies and owner last-minute wishes into "extras," but owners exploit the changes, too. They continue to grow the scope, all along arguing that the changes are "in the base contract."

About 15 or 20 years ago, it began to occur to contractors and owners that *time* itself could factor into the fight for extras. Owners began including penalty clauses in contracts in an effort to convert time into money. Responding, contractors started turning time impacts into money by alleging delay, acceleration, and loss of productivity. Seen this way, construction claims are just an inevitable extension of the "extras" game.

Saddest of all, in the course of twisting and turning the Project Schedule to support claims posturing, the Project Schedule often becomes so convoluted that it ends up causing the very impacts it was re-engineered to measure and depict. I can think of no escape or reversal from this quagmire except to propose two different schedules for each project: one used to compare the Baseline Schedule to actual performance in support of claims; and the other used to actually *run* the project.

Schedule Granularity

During Schedule Design, the project team must decide the appropriate level-of-detail for the project's Execution Schedule. This is an extremely important decision because it relates directly to the frequency of Performance Control. Determining the appropriate level-of-detail for any Project Schedule is a two-step process depending first on the project management style and second on specific project variables.

As we just determined, Project Schedules in support of the Command-and-Control Model tend to be more detailed than schedules used by Collaborative Model managers. Beyond management style, however, other considerations affecting the choice of a Project Schedule's level-of-detail include project size, project length, project type, project controls use of the schedule, claims/legal environment, Performance Control frequency, performer competence and need for supervision, and the nature of the work scope. These factors are discussed at length during the Schedule Design Summit.

Most seasoned Execution Schedulers have some *duration range* in the back of their heads that they will quickly recite when asked about level-of-detail. One technique involves the project's length, with the duration range expressed as a percent of project length; say, 1–3 percent. Thus, on a 36-month project, the duration range would be between 7 to 21 days; on a two-year project, they prefer to see durations between 5 to 15 days; and on a one-year project, durations would range between 3 to 7 days. Again, this is using a generalized Project Length/Activity Duration ratio.

Other Execution Schedulers will insist that the level-of-detail is directly related to the Performance Control frequency and that it makes little practical sense to have durations less than X percent of the Performance Control cycle, with X, of course, varying with each different Execution Scheduler. For instance, if the Performance Control cycle is monthly (assume 20 workdays), and using 50 percent as the rule of thumb, average activity durations shouldn't be less than ten. The rationale for this approach is that activity-durations below the percent threshold are more likely to "come and go" in one cycle, thus constituting an administrative "buck" with comparatively little "bang." Imagine an activity that you *carry* for eight months in your Project Schedule and then, suddenly, in one month it is statused 100 percent complete! Proponents of this level-of-detail approach prefer to see more than 75 percent of the activities "split" by a Performance Control cycle. On the other end of the spectrum, these same Execution Schedulers would not want an activity to span more than two or three cycles, and so a maximum duration recommendation would be something in the order of 40 workdays, 60 at worst!

I agree with all of this advice—and then some! In other words, I think the project length, as well as the Performance Control cycle, have profound influence on the ideal activity duration range. But I consider the intended Project Schedule use(s) to be the more significant consideration. And that takes us back to Chapter 4's discussion of project management style, where we noted that the Command-and-Control Model manager tends to use the Project Schedule to direct, monitor, and control the project at a detailed level, whereas the Collaborative Model manager uses it to set goals and parameters, at a less detailed level.

To convert these generalizations into rules of thumb when deciding an Execution Schedule's level-of-detail, I recommend revisiting the list of Project Schedule uses itemized in Chapter 2 and seeing how they align with the two prominent management approaches.

Schedule Performance Specifications

Schedule Performance Specifications can vary greatly in content, format, scope, and detail. You should be guided by a constant recollection that Schedule Performance Specifications are intended to eliminate disappointment later on. That is why they are called *performance* specifications and not design specifications. To this end, it is not as important that the specifications describe the content or format of the Execution Schedule (the design), as much as *how* the Execution Schedule is to be used (the performance)—that is, its functionality.

Accordingly, the Schedule Performance Specifications should answer the following performance questions, at a minimum. Notice how I work backward from end use to initial development (see Figure 12-6).

- **End Use** Who will use the Execution Schedule, how often, and how will it be distributed? Work out the details by literally listing the reports by name and agreeing on their content, format and organization, and level-of-detail. How will user feedback be acquired and incorporated?

- **Maintenance** How often will the Execution Schedule be maintained, by whom, and how precisely? Under what conditions will Execution Schedule revisions be required? How will scope changes be incorporated into the Execution Schedule?

Figure 12-6
Why Schedule
Design Makes
Good Sense

**Why Schedule Design
Makes Good Sense**

How the Schedule Will Be Used
determines

▼

What Happens Monthly
which, in turn, dictates

▼

**Which Project Controls to Build
into the Schedule Initially**
which establishes criteria for

▼

Schedule Architecture
which influences

▼

Schedule Development

- **Project Controls** How will cost control be achieved on the project: *in* the Execution Schedule, jointly with a cost control system and in the Execution Schedule, or in a cost control system only? Will EVMS be employed on this project? Will the Execution Schedule be used for risk management? What is the plan for information flow to and from risk management, quality control, procurement, change management, procurement systems, and the integrated schedule?

- **Architecture** How should advanced software settings be set: multiple calendars, continuous vs. interruptible durations, retained-logic vs. progress-override, alternative total-float definitions, and so on?

- **Development** Who has responsibility for creation of the Execution Schedule? Who will participate in Schedule Development sessions? How will owner, architect, engineer, vendor, and subcontractors subschedules be developed and incorporated into the Project Schedule? What will the Schedule Development approach be: specific to general or general to specific? At what level-of-detail will coordination, progress monitoring, management reporting, and change management activities take place?

13

Concerning Schedule Development

Further in this chapter, under the heading "Logic Development Session," I identify a step called "Defining the Subnets." It is at that point in my description of a typical logic development session that you would expect to read about Work Breakdown Structure (WBS). Since it is noticeable by its feeble treatment there, perhaps a few words here are appropriate.

WORK BREAKDOWN STRUCTURE

In theory, the concept of a WBS makes perfect sense. WBS adopts a Newtonian view of Scheduling, proposing that one can start with one activity, "Perform Project," and repeatedly subdivide, or *decompose,* this single deliverable exponentially, one layer after another, until at some particular level-of-detail the project has been adequately subdivided.

I do not deny that this concept can, and often does, work in practice. Nonetheless, I have elected *not* to put it *matter-of-factly* into the next section in order to take an admittedly unpopular position, and that is that WBS does not work in all instances! Elsewhere in this book, I take an equally unpopular position with respect to Earned Value. Neither of these innovations of the last quarter-century is so absolute that they are *necessarily* essential for every project, no matter the type or size. Having said this, I am obligated to be thorough and to inform you that a recent attempt at a practice standard for the Scheduling Practice, developed by a leading project management association, insists that WBS is essential and that a Project Schedule produced without a WBS is simply flawed and unacceptable. It is against this absolute and sweeping insistence that I take issue; not with the general concept of the WBS. (More on this later in the chapter.)

The problems I have with WBS deal with its application, not its conceptual foundation. You may have already noticed how the human element factors into my views on virtually all aspects of Scheduling Practice. Across the project continuum, it is *people* who create Project Schedules, rely on Project Schedules, are monitored (rewarded and punished) by Project Schedules, and use Project Schedules. One of the biggest reasons Project Schedules are not embraced, I contend, is because they are thrust upon people, in one manner or another, against their wills.

For a Project Schedule to be truly *accepted* requires that the individual feels as if the Project Schedule is somehow *his*-and not something being imposed upon him. There is no better opportunity to forge a sense of ownership in the Project Schedule than during Schedule Development. But, as noted earlier, participants in logic sessions and other phases of Schedule Development are naturally skeptical, distrusting, and hesitant. This is the challenge that the Execution Scheduler must find some way to overcome, quickly and lastingly.

In two important ways, WBS *can* work at cross-purposes to that accomplishment. How so? The answer begins by recognizing that the Execution Scheduler must earn the contributor's trust. The Execution Scheduler does this by treating his contributors with respect. If he asks *them* a question, the Execution Scheduler must be prepared to work with *the contributors'* answer. The Execution Scheduler cannot try to lead the group into his way of seeing the project. Nothing offends a contractor more than to be asked a question and to give an answer, and then have the Execution Scheduler reject the answer because it doesn't fit a preconceived idea of how things ought to be. My first concern about WBS, based on years of hands-on experience as an Execution Scheduler, arises from an observation that constructors don't naturally assume a Newtonian view of the project, that they don't see the parts as comprising the whole. Instead, they adopt an even more restricted, concentric view of the project. They see *their* portion of the project with the greatest clarity, the work immediately adjacent to their own with slightly less clarity, and so on, until the work most remote to them is either unclear or unimportant, or both.

Don't get me wrong: I'm not saying that a WBS view is automatically the opposite of how the contractor looks at the job. Quite often it is very similar. But—and this is the key point—there are many times when the way contributors in the room subdivide the work is *not* compatible with the formal structure of a WBS. The problem is, if you insist on herding them back into the WBS model, you may lose their loyalty to the entire Schedule Development process!

My second concern about WBS is that, in order for it to work properly, *all* elements of the project must be subdivided consistently. In other words, once you embark on this approach, you must follow through with it, across the entire scope of the project and down to the same level-of-detail. If you do not, the fabric of WBS begins to unravel.

In the interest of fairness, let me quickly note that many of my respected colleagues will disagree with this criticism, insisting that one need not break down every higher-level activity to one contiguous lower level. In other words, there can be a jagged bottom edge to the schedule, in terms of granularity. (Note: The rolling-wave approach to scheduling readily accepts a schedule with a jagged bottom edge.)

In theory, they are correct. But again, looking at the real world, I have rarely (if ever) seen diehard WBS loyalists stop short of forcing all activities to a smooth lower level.

Early definitions of what will be considered the *functional level* become the target for all drill-down exercises.

I could stop at this point and still have a legitimate argument, but there is more. Two other complications to basic CPM methodology further compound the problem that I have described thus far, and they are Organizational Breakdown Structure (OBS) and Enterprise Project Management (EPM).

For those unfamiliar with the concept, an OBS is similar to a WBS, except that what is divided and subdivided into more and more detail is not the scope, but instead the work-performing organization. The goal is that every person on the project can be found somewhere on an extensive, often daunting, matrix.[1] More importantly, every activity in the schedule must be associated with a single individual, a specific point of accountability. This may sound innocent enough, but then an attempt is made to *merge* OBS and WBS.

Behind this attempt are two pulses. One is a belief that ultimate accountability can be achieved only if a single accountable member of the organization can be correlated for every activity in the schedule. Again, in theory, this makes a lot of sense.

The other pulse is Enterprise Project Management, which pursues an idyllic arrangement whereby all program-level resources can be allocated across multiple projects (hence, enterprise) based on where they are most beneficial. In the real world, two problems are immediately obvious. First, at the time one is creating the Execution Plan, not all players have been identified. Second, in order for there to be single-point accountability, some activities must be decomposed beyond a level of usefulness to the contractor, from a time management perspective alone. When this happens, the contractor's loyalty begins to wane. (Note: The observant reader may have noticed that I identified the Execution Plan (Strategic or Consensus) as the point when OBS is imposed into the process, even though this chapter is discussing Execution Schedule development. This is not a mistake. When an OBS is built into an Execution Plan, management will insist that it be maintained in the Execution Schedule.)

Finally, a word to my respected colleagues: please keep in mind the intended readership for this book. It is not being written for the 20-year veteran Practitioner but is instead aimed at those tasked with creating a Project Schedule who have not had years of experience or training. These individuals are most likely self-taught, and often their main sources of instruction come from software help screens or the PMBOK® Guide or some other academic writings, in which concepts such as WBS, OBS, and EPM are presented as the *best* way, and perhaps the *only way*, to do Execution Scheduling.

While you and I may intuitively understand that no one method is going to be ideal in all cases, some may not make such a distinction. In their defense, I have found a general tendency in academic writings to present these methods as being one-size-fits-all, with very few caveats that one should deliberate before choosing a method for inclusion in a project management support program.

---

[1]Often called a RAM, Responsibility Assignment Matrix.

As you read the next section, understand that use of WBS as *part* of the process of *defining the subnets* is not being discouraged; I simply don't feel that it is an *absolute*, as if to say that a Project Schedule cannot, or even should not, be created without one. I hope the foregoing explains why I am downplaying its role. It's a great concept, and it works quite well in most instances, but one time too many I have gotten bloodied up in arguments with equally passionate Practitioners who have insisted that, "without WBS, one cannot create a schedule." How do they think Project Schedules were created for the 20 years before the innovation of WBS? All I'm saying to you is to just keep an open mind. Nothing in life is that absolute. And if you do not use a WBS, then by all means, employ some other systematic method of ensuring that the project's entire scope is captured within your Project Schedule.

Equally as important, if you do use a WBS, don't lose sight of the forest. A WBS is used to subdivide and organize the Project Schedule's large number of tasks into some orderly alignment. However, it need not be a rigid standard-depth structure across the project. A WBS's bottom level should go no further than is necessary to define project scope to achieve the goals of the Schedule Performance Specifications. A WBS can also be used to get everyone onto the same page on a project.

LOGIC DEVELOPMENT SESSION

I cannot overstate the importance of Logic Development Sessions. This is when, and where, the Execution Schedule is actually developed. There is a direct correlation between the quality of the Logic Sessions and the quality of the resultant Execution Schedule. What follows are some ideas and observations, accumulated over the years, that might help you host more successful Logic Sessions. Figure 13-1 summarizes the points.

Contributors

Time and time again experience has confirmed that the best Execution Schedules are created by those who will eventually oversee the work. Recalling the well-worn adage, "*plan the work and then work the plan*," both efforts are furthered when one entity serves as the common thread. The main reason for this need for continuity is that there is often more than one "best way" to build a job.

The second observation drawn from experience is that two heads are better than one, and three are often better than two, and so on. The power of "group think" should not be understated. I continue to be amazed at the almost magical way that constructors in a group setting conceive ingenious schemes and creative notions of how to overcome the impossible, how to bring about incredible ends. Hands down, my favorite activity as a Project Scheduler is leading group-level Logic Development Sessions.

The inverse is also true and, for this reason, I cringe each time I am asked to review a Project Schedule that was created in an informational vacuum by a lone Project Scheduler hidden away in some dark closet of an office.

Figure 13-1
Schedule Logic
Session Checklist

Schedule Logic Session Checklist

Invitation List
General Orientation
Content Checklist
Define the Subnets
Construction Approach Decisions
Pound Out the Logic
Assign Activity-Durations
Add Activity Relationships
    Choose Relationship Types
    Ensure Relationship-Duration
       Realisms
    Missing Finish-to-Finish Ties
    Over-Linking/Under-Linking
    Avoid Relationship-Duration
       Extremes
    Non-Zero Finish-to-Start
       Duration
Manual Forward Pass
Subnets Development
Put It All Together
Logical Critical Path
Assorted Other Hints
    Come Prepared
    Ready the Conference Room
    Bring Food
    Establish a Timetable
    Employ Frequent Breaks

So, who should attend and participate in Logic Development Sessions? As already noted, those who will be managing the construction project should participate aggressively in the Schedule Development process. All of them! From the offices of the general contractor and construction manager, invite the project manager, general superintendent, cost engineer, estimator, and project or field engineer. Beyond them, the Logic Sessions should be attended by the highest ranking, project-specific supervisor for each of the prime subcontractors and by representatives of the critical long-lead vendors, suppliers, or manufacturers.

In an ideal world, the architect and the owner would also be present. Some of my colleagues have argued that, for contractual as well as practical reasons, session attendees may not be as forthcoming if the owner is present. I must disagree. The owner's performance on the project (directly and through his agents) historically affects every aspect of the construction process, from review and approval of construction performance plans (safety, quality, protection, and so on) and submittals to inspections and supply of owner-furnished equipment and materials.

It is essential that the owner understand his role, what is being expected of him, what he is committing to, and how his actions will impact the schedule. To make assumptions concerning the owner without the owner's input would be catastrophic to the project and diffusing to the Schedule Development effort. Just as valuable, the owner needs to hear the concerns of the constructors, so that in the event their concerns are realized later on in the project, the owner is not *surprised*.

General Orientation

Let me offer a few suggestions related to running a Logic Development Session. Start by orienting the group to what they are about to be undertaking. No one likes to be torpedoed—least of all, contractors. They're coming into the Session not just a little apprehensive. They are guarded, fearing that they'll be expected to make promises and give up their padding (float). Furthermore, keep in mind that you're working with a diverse group of experts, each with a unique and different technical orientation, yet with few having any really strong background in the Critical Path Method. You need to get everyone on the same page.

Explain what they *will* be doing and what they *won't* be doing. They *will* be sharing their expertise in their respective disciplines, and they *will* be making some commitments on behalf of their company. But those commitments will *always* be conservative, never unrealistic, adequately qualified, and rarely unchangeable.

They *won't* be asked to give away the store. They must come to understand that the purpose of the Logic Development Session is to jointly create a strategy that all participants can work to achieve, so that all are singing from the same music sheet. You will receive very little resistance from the group if you take this approach.

However, you may still experience some skepticism. Contractors who have been burned too many times before by golden-tongued Execution Schedulers aren't won over by a few opening remarks and a plastic smile. Biting the lower lip in a boyish manner may work for Bill Clinton; it won't do you any good whatsoever.

Next, quickly walk the group through the very basics of PDM scheduling. Show them how start-to-start and finish-to-finish relationships work, by demonstrating their equivalence in a standard bar chart format. Emphasize that activity-durations will be in *consecutive workdays* and not in elapsed time or calendar days.

This next point is critical. Anyone who provides you with an activity-duration estimate *must* assume the following three conditions:

1. That any preceding, constraining work has been completed and *nothing* impairs the subject activity from being completed.
2. That the work will be completed *in one continuous series of workdays*.
3. That the logic ties will create the *elapsed* duration effect they probably have in mind.

Content Checklist

Just before launching into development of logic and subnets, in some conspicuous place on the wall set forth a list of the primary parameters that should guide all Schedule Development:

- Is the contract scope fully reflected in the Project Schedule?
- Is the level-of-detail consistent with the parameters set forth in the Schedule Performance Specifications?
- Is the sequencing of the work consistent with management's execution strategy?
- Are the activity-duration estimates reasonable, achievable, defendable, and documented?
- Do activity-duration estimates derive from the same assumptions that are behind the budget's cost estimates?
- Are all contractual and negotiated milestones reflected in the Project Schedule?

Defining the Subnets

Finally, instruct the group that they will be working from general to specific, and then back again to general. Explain that the first hurdle is to agree on how the project can be logically subdivided. Often, this segmentation is done along geographic lines; less often by functional segments. Allow the group to suggest subheadings as you write them on the board.

Since this listing will also serve as the headings for the Project Schedule's subnetworks, as the Execution Scheduler, you should mentally envision how activities in different subnets can effectively and easily be linked together. If you think the proposed groupings won't work, don't hesitate to say so—just be up front as to why you need to take exception. Be persuasive. By doing so, you'll educate them a little more about the crazy world of CPM scheduling, and their respect for your technical acumen (and comfort with your operating style) will go up as well.

Once the subnets have been agreed upon, have someone write them down, erase the board (all but the first item on the list), and begin with the first of these subnets. Using the same process as before, ask the group to list the major elements of work under the first heading. If you're working on a subnet called Foundations, they might throw out such things as Spread Footings, Continuous Footings, Drilled Piers, Pile Caps, Grade Beams, Slabs-On-Grade, Underslab Utilities, and so on. At first, merely list the items in whatever order they're shouted out.

Construction Approach Decisions

With the handwritten list staring back at your group from the board, withdraw from the details and start up a discussion about the physical flow of the work. Roll out the site plans and talk about staging areas, where the tower crane will be, where trucks will offload, and where workers will park. Most importantly, decide the direction in which the structure will begin to materialize (north to south, east to west, inside to outside, and so on), and the direction in which it will finish (top down or bottom up). It is usually helpful to refer to the Consensus Plan developed earlier in the project lifecycle for insights into what was assumed going into the contract negotiations.

Pounding Out the Logic

At this point, you are now ready to start sketching logic. Return to the board and begin drawing boxes. String the activities so that they are logical (based on what makes sense from a construction perspective) and consistent with the physical direction of work just agreed upon. Don't worry about durations; that will come next.

Just diagram the logic in a flow upon which all can agree. As you draw the boxes, have someone in your group begin copying the logic onto paper or inputting it into the scheduling software. Tell them not to *get too close*, meaning not to draw the most recently created activities, since these have a nasty habit of getting changed several times before they assume their final order or sequence.

Assigning Activity-Durations

This is hardly an exact science. Let the subject matter experts at the table throw out some numbers. You'll find that on construction projects the spread between the highest and lowest durations will not be all that great. And, without your prodding, the group will pull their own extremes in toward the middle.

Justification for activity-durations ranges from scientific to educated guesses. If you are fortunate enough to be working with a group that prefers to base each activity-duration on solid backup, such as activity work scope, worker productivity rates, crew sizes, and the like, seize the moment. But, more often than not, durations are derived by "gut feel," as the superintendent for the subject work merely blurts out a number. This book assumes the latter situation.

Just be the note taker; the group will do the rest. If, by some oddity, you end up with a bunch of constructors too shy to offer an opinion, simply play devil's advocate, tossing out a number that you *know* to be too high. I guarantee that you'll get an immediate response; they'll talk you down. Now, do the same thing in reverse; they'll bring your low number up. Then restate the resultant *range* to them and ask them to accept the number in the middle. They will. (All the while, your scribe is posting the agreed-upon durations to the paper copy[2] of the subnetwork.)

Good practice encourages that a record be kept of whatever assumptions are behind the activity-durations. This includes the obvious: crew size, hours in a shift; shifts per workday, and tacit scope of work. Beyond the obvious, other assumptions might include the expected arrival of materials or equipment that some fear might arrive late. The resultant "List of Assumptions" will be invaluable to any parallel or subsequent risk management efforts.

The downside to maintaining a *Schedule Assumption Log* is that it tends to formalize the Schedule Logic Sessions, and this could be a put-off to some participants. You will notice from the previous and following paragraphs that the underlying strategy, as the Execution Scheduler, is to come across as their friend. The more you formalize the process, the less friendly you look. Try to strike the right balance.

Adding Activity Relationships

In Chapter 10, we discussed the anatomy of a relationship. I strongly encourage you to re-read that section before proceeding with overall logic development. When all is said and understood, relationship-durations are *more* ambiguous and more important than activity-durations when it comes to determining the project's critical path—and, hence, the project's end date.

I hope you found that examination of the anatomy of a relationship both interesting and insightful. As I stated before, Momentum Studies have shown that most schedule delays can be attributed to the Project Schedule's failure to allow adequate time for Administrative Actions essential to subsequent Productive Work Segment performance. Unless these Administrative Actions are started *before* the predecessor activity finishes or can be completed *during* the duration of the Productive Time Gap, the adjusted Administrative Time Gap will be overrun, and follow-on activities will be delayed.

Knowing where the problem lies is only half the battle; acting on that knowledge is the rest. I suggest that, during Schedule Development, as you discuss and determine relationship-durations and activity-durations, you diligently construct a list of *all* Administrative Actions that must necessarily precede the commencement of the Productive Work Segment. Here's a simple process:

- Use Excel or another popular spreadsheet program.
- Enter each distinct action item on a separate row.

---

[2] If your scribe is proficient in PowerPoint, he or she may choose to capture the developing logic there. This is preferable as, at the end of the Schedule Logic Session, copies of the logic can be printed and distributed to each with ease and speed. Participants will both appreciate and take pride in having a hard copy of the work they just spent hours developing.

- Alongside each Administrative Action, reference the Productive Work Segment it restrains.

- List the responsible party (usually the project manager, but not always).

- Optional: Later, back at your desk, use a database program to *link* CPM activities with the Administrative Action list. For instance, attribute to each action item the total-float value of the activity that it restrains.

- Optional: If the Administrative Actions are important enough, consider creating an activity to denote their performance, along with their associated duration and logic.

Spend adequate time with the group explaining the meaning of the three major relationship types (start-to-start, finish-to-finish, and finish-to-start), and the two possible meanings (Administrative Time Gaps and Productive Time Gaps) of relationship-durations. (For more on these terms, see the section "Anatomy of a Relationship" in Chapter 10.) Their absolute understanding of these concepts is essential to development of an Execution Schedule that is viable, realistic, understood, and supported.

Choose the Right Relationship Type

A schedule is often compared to a roadmap, but the two are very different indeed once the journey begins. While both may set forth a route *before the fact*, once the project is underway the automated schedule alone can be used to predict outcomes as well as to coordinate the work.

Ensuring Realism in Relationship-Durations

The important thing to remember about relationships and their durations is that they are simply a device for modeling the expected pace of the project. The image that comes to mind is that of the *starter* on a golf course, an individual who holds back and then releases each golf party onto the first tee. His job is to *pace* the golfers so that they don't overrun one another out on the green. A project manager employs the same technique when setting up the initial Execution Schedule. This is accomplished using the relationship types available with the Precedence Diagramming Method. Logically, it is imperative that realism be the central ingredient when determining relationship-durations.

Whenever possible, though, I encourage the use of an activity in place of a relationship-duration. In other words, try to minimize the number of nonzero relationship-durations, positive or negative. If you can define the scope that is referenced by an SS+4, then it is far better to make it visible as an activity rather than transparent and forgettable as a relationship-duration. Let a well-defined activity with correctly denoted logic be your best representation of work scope.

Missing Finish-to-Finish Ties

A common mistake among less experienced Project Schedulers is the use of start-to-start relationships without corresponding finish-to-finish relationships, or vice versa. If you stop to think about it, in the majority of cases, whatever dependent relationship exists between two activities at their starts also exists at their finishes. For instance, if it is true that Paint Wall can't *begin* until some time after Hang Drywall has been accomplished, then it follows that the completion of Paint Wall must be dependent on the prior completion of the corresponding Hang Drywall activity. If the drywall crew walks off the job (say, for a strike) midway through Hang Drywall, I'll bet you lunch that the Paint Wall activity will not continue on to completion as if nothing happened. At some point, there won't be drywall to paint!

The typical retort to this point is "scheduling overkill." The disagreeing Practitioner argues *"What's the point?"* since the follow-on activity is staggered at its start; if both proceed for the durations shown, their ends will be staggered as well. Of course, the fallacy of their argument is that it *assumes* that both will proceed uninterrupted and as planned. But if we know anything at all about projects, it is that they rarely go as planned. Projects are not predictable. Things change, often from Day One.

Over-Linked and Under-Linked Schedules

I estimate that over 90 percent of all performance patterns, as originally scheduled, are violated in one manner or another, in real life. Work starts, then work stops because design and construction issues arise or changes are effected, materials are late, work crews collide, deficient work is reworked, and the like. The primary reason for a *linked* CPM schedule—and an automated one at that—is so that, month to month, the project's current state of affairs can be recorded and analyzed. All of those open-ended activities add up to one single result: a good schedule rendered worthless when the first change from *planned* to *actual* takes place—often, as I said earlier, on Day One.

This is not to say that a schedule cannot be *over*-linked. It most surely can. Beyond a certain point, the more entwined a CPM becomes, the less valuable it is as an analytical tool. False critical-paths emerge, total-float values become obscured, and true critical-paths turn invisible. A disproportionate number of activities appear to have been started (or, less often, completed) out-of-sequence.

An example of this condition is in floor-to-floor staggering of high-rise building construction. One extreme is not to tie the floors at all. This, of course, would be a huge mistake; the resultant Execution Schedule would have similar activities occurring concurrently on more floors than the respective trades could staff, equip, or supervise.

Nearly as unrealistic as treating the floors as individual subprojects with no ties between them is where only the starting activity for each floor is tied in sequence to the one that follows. In this manner, the floors are "staggered" at their start. But again, unless the floors are similar in scope and cumulative duration, *and* unless nothing changes during construction to override the initial logic, *and* unless the work progresses uninterrupted, all kinds of unrealistic trade stacking or stand-around situations can easily result.

The other extreme is to tie floors together between every similar set of common activities. For example, all Floor Layout activities tied in series, all Erect Metal Studs activities tied in series, all Hollow Metal Frames activities tied in series, all Hang Drywall activities tied in series, and so on. This, as just mentioned, is gross scheduling overkill and results in a Project Schedule that is too convoluted to be meaningful.

What I have found works in most cases is to tie floors (or geographically distinct but contextually similar areas) at their start, in their middle, and at their end. Typically, I use Floor Layout, Hang Drywall, and Cleanup Floor to represent the start, middle, and end of each floor sequence, respectively. While this may still create trade stacking in between these hook points, the resultant total-float values will nonetheless provide the timeframe within which to "level" the resources in order to pace the work as appropriate.

Avoiding Relationship-Duration Extremes

As a final comment about relationship-durations, remember what I said at the outset of this heading: they're used to *pace* the project within the physical constraints of the project scope and design. The prudent Project Scheduler knows to temper all relationship-durations with a philosophy of moderation and reasonableness. Nothing is gained by creating an Execution Schedule that is either too fast-paced or too slow-paced. Still, within the range of what is reasonable, there is plenty of room to fail. The Execution Scheduler and project manager should listen closely to their gut feeling about the individual and collective abilities of key project players to perform in a timely, predictable, and efficient manner. All relationship-durations should be conceived accordingly.

Nonzero Finish-to-Start Durations

The default relationship between two activities in PDM is a finish-to-start with a zero relationship-duration. In other words, the successor activity can start zero days after the predecessor activity completes. It is the relationship type default because this setting represents the natural progression of logically related activities that are not overlapped.[3]

A tactic used by some Execution Schedulers is to put a positive duration on a finish-to-start tie, so that the successor activity cannot start until X days after the predecessor activity has completed (see Figure 13-2). There are many reasons why one would adopt this practice, some sinister and practically all in stark violation of the imperative Scope-Duration Correlation. Occasionally, however, a nonzero relationship-duration is innocent enough, perhaps reflecting an absolute time lag because of a physical requirement, such as not removing shoring supports until the concrete is cured.

As has been said countless times throughout this text, the duration must remain an honest reflection of the scope of work described in the activity-description. The meaning of this doctrine is not just that every activity-duration must be associated with a discrete scope of work, it also means the opposite too. Every discrete scope of work is associated with an activity-duration. I call this doctrine the Scope-Duration Correlation.

When a nonzero relationship-duration is placed on a finish-to-start relationship, such as in Figure 13-2, it suggests that there is something happening that is holding up the predecessor. In this example, Painting cannot start until 15 days after Drywall has completed. Whatever that reason is—whatever is taking place during that period of time—is work scope not captured by any activity. Granted, there may be cases where the time gap is simply that and nothing more: a gap in time. But even then, one has to wonder what is happening that makes it necessary to delay an activity's start.

---

[3]The original CPM format, ADM, had nothing but Finish-to-Start relationships!

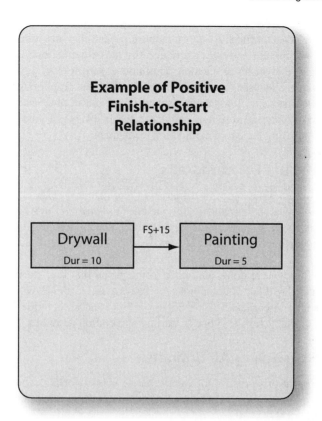

Figure 13-2
Positive Finish-to-
Start Relationship

This is another Project Scheduling tactic that, when not borne of sheer ignorance, is most often borne of questionable rather than noble motives. The reason it is so appealing to the unscrupulous is because relationship-durations aren't typically as visible as activity-durations. Most Scheduling reports don't show relationship-durations. And so, a dodgy Scheduler can elongate a schedule, or make a desired path more critical, simply by adding positive durations to finish-to-start relationships.

For equally suspicious reasons, a shady Execution Scheduler can add a negative duration to a finish-to-start relationship and cause a successor activity to start *before* its predecessor has completed. While there may be situations when such a relationship is legitimate and deserves appropriate simulation in a CPM schedule, the tenets are at once present to justify the more conventional start-to-start and finish-to-finish relationships. That is because the negative finish-to-start duration is just a convoluted way of saying that the successor activity cannot start until some time *during* the predecessor activity's life or, even less believably, *before* the predecessor activity has even started! In the case of the latter, with few exceptions, there should be no relationship at all between the successor and the predecessor.

As for the former condition, it is my opinion that one should use the far more conventional start-to-start and finish-to-finish relationships designed for this condition, if it makes sense. I have had many animated debates with much-respected colleagues, who prefer to use negative finish-to-start relationships, and they insist that negative finish-to-start relationships are perfectly legitimate. As the argument goes, their approach generates the same early dates as the more conventional start-to-start. I might concede that, in an initial (not yet statused) Execution Schedule, the dates from both approaches may be the same. But once activity status is applied to the predecessor activity, the start-float value will most likely be different (assuming the interruptible duration setting has been chosen) comparing the two diagramming techniques.

Manual Forward Pass

Now do a manual forward pass *out loud.* Do it quickly enough to get to the answer but slowly enough to allow your audience to *learn,* through observation, a little more about how earliest-dates are derived.[4] Subtly, you are teaching them CPM—in a nonintrusive, nondemanding way,—and they're soaking it up. I guarantee it!

When you're done, announce to the group that this individual subnetwork, "in a vacuum," will take *X* continuous workdays to complete. Have your scribe record the earliest-start and earliest-finish dates for a few, random activities in the subnetwork but most especially for the subnet's starting and ending activities.

Scheduling All Subnets

Repeat this process for each separate subnetwork. Do not attempt to link the subnetworks together yet. The reason for this prohibition is that if your participants can see *where this is all leading to,* it might bias their subsequent input in order to achieve the results *they* desire. The beauty of CPM scheduling, versus bar chart scheduling, is that you don't need to know how the Big Picture is going to turn out before scheduling the details. With bar charts, you have to know where to stop the pencil at the end of each bar; you can't draw a bar without knowing the duration first.

—Now forward pass each subnetwork. When this is done, you will have gotten as detailed as you will need to get during these Schedule Logic Sessions. (Note: You should be working at around Level Three.)

Putting It All Together

I find that the process of tying it all together, going from specific back to general, is the most difficult thing for novice Project Schedulers to master. At the same time, I happen to think it's the single most dramatic phase of the Schedule Development process. For here, with drums rolling and anticipation high, the answer to the one question that everyone has wondered about suddenly materializes: *Will the Project Schedule we have spent the last two days compiling get the job done by the contractual end date?*

---

[4]Though I use the term "dates" here, I refer to ordinal numbers and not actual calendar dates. It is good practice *not* to use calendar dates at this stage, because contractors tend to have preconceived ideas of when things ought to be starting or finishing. It is better to force them to think in terms of days, weeks, and months of time consumption, and then, later, ask them to "sanity check" the subnetwork lengths against this measure.

So, what is the best way to tie the subnets back together? Scheduling Practitioners tend to have their personal preferences. Mine is a two-part approach intended to get everyone involved. First, I take the photocopies of the subnetworks that my scribe has drawn and spread them out on the table. If we jointly created 11 subnetworks, then there are 11 pieces of paper on the table (or wall).

I then assign to the group the task of identifying *specific activities* that will become the *hook points* between subnetworks. Meanwhile, as they talk among themselves, I return to a clean wipe-off board and quickly sketch out a blank bar chart form: time scale along the top and subnetwork headings down the left. I'm ready for them.

As a single horizontal line, I draw to scale the first subnetwork, say Foundations, beneath the time scale. The group looks up to see that I have begun to materialize a Level Two bar chart (see Figure 13-3). I join them at the table and facilitate the discussion about how the Foundations subnetwork will "hook" into the Superstructure subnet. Based on the *hook point*, I determine how much to offset the second bar on my bar chart. And so it goes. Manually, and somewhat crudely, I compute a new forward pass through the now developing Level Two Project Schedule. On the board, the bar chart takes shape.

Figure 13-3
Building a Summary Bar Chart

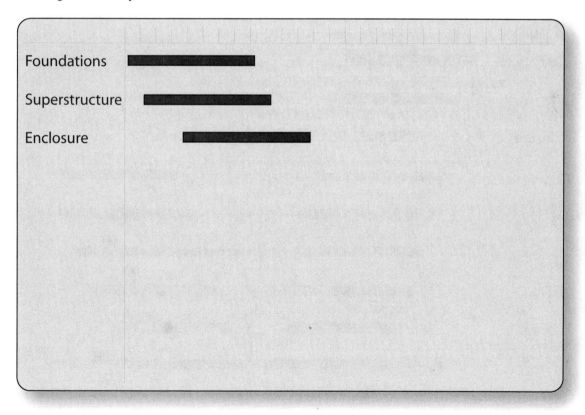

Meanwhile, the group is *learning*—they're seeing how logic can drive a bar chart. And you're learning a lot about the group. You're identifying the leaders, the followers, the confident, the arrogant, the technical, the skeptical, the dreamer, the bully, and the wimp. You and your project manager are getting a first good look at how cohesive this group is going to be over the next X months. And they're learning something about how the Execution Schedule and the Project Scheduler can factor into the way business will be done day-to-day. Imagine how beneficial these early insights can be.

Logical Critical-Path

When you're finished drawing all of the Level Two activities on the board, draw the logic ties between them. Now you have a Level Two Logic Network Diagram, or time-scaled bar chart (see Figure 13-4). Then, using a different color pen, highlight the calculated critical-path and wait for a reaction. If it agrees with the collective instincts of the group, your work is almost done, and the group is one step closer to going home.

Figure 13-4
Summary Bar Chart Takes Shape

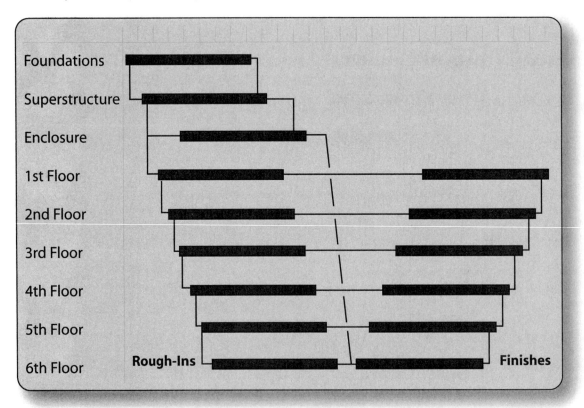

If, however, this preliminary critical-path causes group unrest and discomfort, talk through the disparities between what the logic shows and what the group *expected to see*. Revise the *hook points*, durations, and logic ties of individual activities on the Level Three subnetworks, as needed, to derive an overall Project Schedule and flow of work that all can agree to *and* feel comfortable with. Unanimous buy-in is essential!

Assorted Other Hints

Successful Schedule Logic Sessions involve far more than what these few pages convey. A good book on CPM scheduling may dedicate a few paragraphs to the Schedule Logic Session; most downplay or ignore the process altogether. But the Schedule Logic Session is, without question, the most important step in Schedule Development, and it's a big reason why your Execution Schedule will either be used or tossed in the can!

It is essential that the Schedule Logic Session is successful. You must get group buy-in, no matter what it takes. And while there is no one rule which, if followed, ensures a successful Session, the following tips will certainly increase the likelihood of a productive gathering.

Come Prepared

Nothing will enhance your credibility more than knowing as much, *or more,* about the project than anyone else in the room. Do your homework. Study the plans and specifications from cover to cover. Make a list of *all* critical submittals. Note any suspiciously long-lead items. Know the lay of the land, the layout of the structures, and their relative location to one another. Fully understand the Schedule Performance Specifications.

Ready the Conference Room

Have the room ready for the exercise. This includes having:

- A wipe-off board (not chalkboard) with pens that work
- Pads of paper and pencils for the each participant to use
- A set of plans and specs nearby
- An illustration of basic PDM concepts
- A list of frequently used CPM terms
- Plot Plans and other critical project drawings
- An equipment list with lead times
- Large butcher block paper (to draw each subnetwork)
- Copious amounts of Post-it notes (each activity gets a Post-it note)
- A laptop with scheduling software on it for the scribe
- A projector

Bring Food

People are friendlier and more cooperative when they've been fed something—anything. I often have a few liters of soda; it's inexpensive and everyone's throat gets dry eventually. Water, coffee, and tea are good choices. Donuts are nice, though messy and costly and can cause sugar-high crankiness. But always offer something for the mouth—even a pack of chewing gum, tossed matter-of-factly across the table, is a friendly gesture.

Establish a Timetable

Announce at the outset the timetable for the meeting. Don't promise a shorter meeting than is likely or worthwhile. A good Logic Session can easily span a day, sometimes two or three days. Anything less than four hours is inadequate; don't waste your time or anyone else's if you can't get the group to commit to more than four hours. If they can't—or won't—then they're not serious, and the effort won't yield anything you'll be proud of or want to hang your hat on.

Plan and Have Frequent Breaks

A trick I use is to take breaks, one half the group at a time. This may sound a bit like grade school, but hear me out. Call it the teacher's pet syndrome, but there is something kind of magical that happens when people get a chance to "talk to the prof." I see the same thing at every speaking engagement. When the speech is over, as the majority of people file out of the auditorium or banquet room, a handful make their way to the podium. There, they wait patiently to have a chance to offer their two cents: to chew the fat with the expert. I don't fully understand the underlying psychology, but it makes people feel good, maybe even special. This is particularly true if they impart a personal pearl of wisdom that draws a rise of the *expert's* eyebrows. In Schedule Logic Sessions, *you* are the *expert*.

The way I accomplish this is by announcing a short break. As the group begins to file out, if a few members of the team don't choose to stay behind on their own, I ask a few people by name if they'd hold up a minute. Then I draw them into the struggle to solve a problem or address a specific technical question concerning the Execution Schedule. By the time the others have returned, this small subgroup has succeeded in working out something that makes them feel somewhat superior to the others. They're in possession of some insider information.

They then take their break, and I repeat the process with the returned balance of the group—but on another subject, of course. Once the entire group has reconvened I ask each subgroup to explain to their colleagues what they did while the others were "in the sandbox." Believe it or not, I use this technique during every break of a two- or three-day set of Logic Sessions, and no one ever catches on that they have been subject to an intentional ploy of mine. But it works!

14

Schedule Components

The remainder of the Schedule Development process, much of which takes place inside scheduling software, is far less exciting or glamorous. Armed with the collective wisdom gleaned from the Logic Development Sessions, you return to your office psyched to put together a darned good Project Schedule—one that will actually get used! Again, a high-quality book on CPM scheduling will help you with the fundamentals if you are not already sufficiently aware of these building blocks; this book is designed merely to give you the tricks of the trade.

ELEMENTAL COMPONENTS OF THE EXECUTION SCHEDULE

There are certain elemental components of the Execution Schedule that must be fully understood by the Execution Scheduler before commencement of Schedule Development. In the following discussions, pay special attention to the human side of the business, appreciating the behavioral aspects that so often make or break our best efforts in virtually every construction or business management endeavor, Schedule Development included.

Contract Length

A project's length is directly proportional to the overall momentum to be experienced on the project. For instance, projects of short duration are almost always extremely intense. Conversely, on projects in excess of two years, it is nearly impossible to incite a fever-pitch level of urgency. Given these observations, let me offer two specific suggestions.

On projects of extremely short duration (ten months or less), give additional weight and attention to front-end activities. Their timely completion takes on added significance on shorter projects. In addition, on a longer project, a select number of deliverables are long-lead items. However, on short projects, as much as 75 percent of all deliveries can be considered long lead. Here, the word *long* is indeed relative.

Also, among early activities on short-duration projects, a greater number of submittal activities end up critical or near-critical. The timely review of drawings and submittals, an exclusive liability of the owner and its designers, becomes increasingly urgent. Finally, other front-end activities, such as the preparation of coordination drawings or exploratory demolition in renovation work, all assume greater importance on short projects.

An opposite problem occurs on extremely long projects (in excess of two years). Items easily take on the appearance of unimportance, when in fact they are indeed critical to timely completion. One must remember at all times that the critical-path concept is theoretical, never precise. No matter how exact a Project Schedule's activity-durations, and no matter how realistic its logic ties, one can never escape the ultimately "guesstimated" nature of the Project Schedule.

When all is said and done, a Project Schedule is nothing more than hundreds (or thousands) of activities, each with an *estimated* activity-duration, logically tied to show human interaction (predictions of future behavior) within the context of an overall construction approach that makes an infinite number of *assumptions* about future space, time, performance, condition, need, and surprise. The message is that we must not get too cocky in our interpretations of Execution Schedule data, especially when we find ourselves arguing over one or two days of total-float.

On extremely long projects, the "spread" between critical and near-critical total-float is proportional to the project length. Perhaps if we think in terms of percents of project length, this point might be better understood. A five-month project is roughly 150 calendar-days long. Missing the end date by two weeks represents approximately a 10 percent schedule overrun. That same two-week slippage on a four-year project equates to a 2.5 percent schedule overrun.

And so, when a selected string of activities has a total-float value only four days less than another string of activities, we must stop ourselves from asserting that one string is "critical" while the other is not. "Fair enough," you might be saying, "the lesser string is merely less critical—as opposed to not being critical at all." But let me ask you, how much is "less?" And precisely what level of attention and concern should a less critical string of activities draw?

There is a phenomenon that takes place in the minds of constructors on extremely long projects whereby they subconsciously devalue activity-durations. In other words, they become somewhat complacent with respect to schedule slippage. After all, how bad is a two-week slippage when another three years remain in the project life cycle? To be fair, if the existing three-week slippage was the project's *only* schedule slippage, then the protraction would be exceptionally small and, very possibly, recoverable. But it is highly unlikely that this will be the project's only slippage! One safeguard against such complacency comes in the form of intermediate completion milestones driven by well-placed date-constraints.

Near-Critical Activities

A few paragraphs back, I touched on the notion of *near-critical* activities—that is, activities residing on a path that is not the most critical path, but darned close to it. An often-asked question is how to determine what is near-critical. We have already noted how the dubious quality of many assumptions underlying total-float calculations makes it unwise to get too concerned about a few days difference between one path and another. That said, we shouldn't get too crazy about near-critical activities either.

For one reason, the path we are calling critical, by some other benchmark than total-float, may in fact be near-critical; and, the path we are considering near-critical may in fact be critical. For another, the concept of *near-critical* requires that we establish a total-float threshold—and that value, as well, is entirely subjective.

My rule of thumb, and it is only that, is to set the near-critical ceiling at 2.5 percent of the project length. So, for instance, on a two-year project (480 workdays), the ceiling would be 12 days. Therefore, any activities with total-float between 1 and 12, inclusive, would be considered near-critical (assuming the project has no negative total-float). On a one-year project, the cutoff would be six days. On a six-month project, near-critical would be activities with total-float between one and six, inclusive.

Activity Numbering

In the old days of Arrow Diagramming Method (ADM), there were strict rules concerning the numbering of activities, driven by ADM's mechanical limitations. Activity-numbers were generated in pairs, called I-J nodes, which had to be assigned in ascending order. Today, all such rules are gone. Except for a limitation on the number of digits in the activity-identifier—and the fact that in some software programs the first character cannot be numeric—you can do anything you want with this field.

Make Sure the Activity-Identifier Means Something

Develop a smart numbering convention, whereby each character tells something about the activity with which it is associated. One character position may tell where the item takes place (geographically), another may identify the phase of work, another may point to who is responsible, and so on.

Prominently Display the Numbering Convention Definition

Somewhere on each report that uses the activity-identifier, display the numbering convention. I usually put a legend in the footer section or under a separate heading at the back of my reports.

Don't Over-Code

Don't go crazy with trying to code the activity-identifier to death. Think about how you will eventually tailor the reports. Remember, any scheduling software worth a pound of salt will provide ample other ways besides the activity-identifier for sorting and filtering activities. All you want the activity-identifier to do is easily and succinctly inform the reader what the activity is generally about. You're simply trying to save activity-description space.

Activity-Description

No matter how powerful the scheduling software program may be, it can't change the laws of physics. There is just so much ink you can slap on a page. Before too long, any Performance Control Report will be fighting for space. Font sizes get reduced, graphics areas get shrunk, time scales get compressed, and columns get narrowed. One of the first columns to be truncated is the *activity-description*, vulnerable to downsizing simply because it's such a space hog.

Limit the Activity-Description Length

Most of today's scheduling software packages brag about activity-description fields with up to 250 characters. Don't be impressed. Anything more than roughly 35–50 characters will get truncated on reports and charts, anyway. Besides, if you need 250 characters to describe the *scope of work* of the activity, then it is probably too large of an activity and should be subdivided into several, more detailed activities. If the verbose description is intended to clarify the scope, use other fields, such as the Notes field, the Memo field, or various activity-code fields.

Use Abbreviations and Contractions Discriminately and Consistently

You will definitely need to use both in order to pack more information into a small field width. Use the most popular abbreviations for words, not just your own creations. For instance, use "bldg"for building, not "bg" or "bd" or "lg." And be consistent!

Abbreviate Common Words

Leave the less common words to be spelled out. Which of these makes more sense? "Install Variable A.D. & Grls" or "Inst Var. Air Dmprs & Grills?" Both have the same number of characters. But "Inst" is used consistently throughout the schedule. As for "Var.," once someone reads Air Dampers, they will know that the word is "variable." Again, be consistent.

The Vowel Elimination Technique

When abbreviating *less common* words, first try to get to the needed shorter length by eliminating vowels. More often than not, by removing a few vowels you can do the cutting you need to, and the description will still make sense. "You'd be srprsd hw easy it is to rd a strng of wrds wth vwls rmvd, wthout the meang being lst entrly. Of crse, you stll hve to use sme discrtn as to whch vwls to cut out & whch to lve in." For instance, say "Inst Hllw Mtl Frmes & Drs," rather than "Install H. Metal Fr/Doors." Each has the same number of characters.

Pick a Verb-Noun Order, and Stick With It

Either say "Install Millwork," "Install Glass and Glazing," "Paint Walls," "Grind Terrazzo," or reverse the order and say "Millwork Installed," "Glass & Glazing Installed," "Walls Painted," "Terrazzo Ground.' Be consistent.

Favor the Beginning of the String

On long descriptions, favor the beginning of the string, as the end may get cut off on limited-space reports. Better to say "3rd Fl Lfe Sfty Insp" than "Inspect Lfe Sfty-3rd Flr." They may never see the "3rd Flr." words.

Favor the Activity-Identifier

Never waste valuable space in a description to say something that can be conveyed in the activity-identifier. In the preceding example, the "3rd floor" notation could be handled with a single *character* in the activity-identifier. Of course, this suggestion assumes that the activity-identifier and the activity-description will *both* appear together on all reports.

Activity-Codes

Activity-codes (also called data manipulation, sort and selection, or sort and filter codes) are a powerful way to manipulate data for presentation in Schedule Extraction Reports. All popular scheduling software programs provide multiple fields for sorting and selecting.

Use them! Use them a lot! The more you tailor the massive amount of information in your Project Schedule, the more your Execution Schedule will be used. It's just that simple. I cannot emphasize this enough. If there is one *secret* more than any other, that I want to impart to you on this subject, it is to *tailor your reports.* Remember this cardinal rule for effective Performance Control Reporting: *give the people all the information they need to do their job—no more, no less, and always in a form they can readily understand and use.*

In order to accomplish this, you need to remove any information that will not benefit them or that may confuse them. You need to ensure that *all* the information that they really do need is in the Schedule Extraction in their hands. Consider including adjacent work not under their immediate responsibility yet which may affect how soon they can start, or when they must finish, their portion of the job. Consider the timing of work and how far out into the future your Extraction Report needs to go.

Manpower-Loading

I like manpower-loading, but only in certain, limited situations. This is one of those modern "bells and whistles" that sells well in a glossy advertisement in a construction trade journal but has limited application (or popularity) in the real world of construction management. Here's why I say that.

For the most part, formal, computerized CPM Scheduling is still only being performed by the larger construction management and general contracting companies but not by the little guys, the specialty trades. In either of the former instances, for construction managers (CM) and general contractors (GC), the majority of project's scope of work is brokered. That is, very little of the work is self-performed, it is subcontracted to others.

When you're not performing the work yourself, you have little need and even less interest in how many workers it will take to complete a given task. As far as the CM or GC is concerned, that's the subcontractor's problem. The CM/GC cares only that the work starts on time and finishes on time. If the subcontractor has to use twice as many laborers or a pack of mules, that's his problem! So why would a CM or GC attempt to manpower-load a CPM schedule with labor information? For the most part, he wouldn't—and typically doesn't.

When he does, it is usually for purposes of monitoring the performance of the general contractor (if he is the CM), or of the subcontractor (if he is the general contractor). By now you won't be surprised to read that I am not in favor of resource-loading, even for monitoring purposes, because it simply works at cross-purposes with the Collaborative Model. In order for project team members to respond creatively and instinctively to the daily challenges of the project, they must not be scolded for deviations from plans set on paper months or years earlier. Since schedule logic and activity-durations are all tied back to resource assumptions, you can't have flexibility in changing schedule logic or durations if you can't also change resource assumptions. How meaningful, then, is micromanagement of resources through resource-loading?

As for those who *would* gain from seeing a histogram of labor requirements *before work begins* in order to facilitate advance resource planning, they would be the smaller contractors. The vast majority of such smaller contractors do not have the skills, capital, software, or inclination to light up a CPM program and create an Execution Schedule. To them, that just seems like so much Park Avenue glitter. That's not *real* construction!

In the few instances when allocating labor quantities to Project Schedules makes sense, I caution against getting too carried away with the concept. I've seen Junior Schedulers try to allocate work down to the apprentice level. In fact, they'd go even further and assign different calendars to different trades. Before long, the resourcing effort is so elaborate that when the *resource leveling* option is executed, the results are squirrelly and the critical-path is indiscernible.

To be sure, resource-loading can be useful for area-loading concerns and craft level determination (for example, maximum number of electricians possible or available). As a general rule, I encourage you to only resource-load key or limited resources (for example, crane picks for a tower crane). See what the computer says the sequence should be and then soft-tie these crane picks to allow your Execution Schedule to depict these resource limitations. Be sure to revisit the logic frequently, however, to ensure that the Project Schedule continues to reflect reality.

Resource-Leveling

What about resource-leveling? This is where the computer uses the availability of resources, combined with each individual activity's resource requirements, to perform calculations that sequence and prioritize the Execution Schedule. Resources utilization is "optimized" by working within the available "slack" suggested by the total-float and arbitrarily assigned priorities of resource-sharing activities.

The technology is fantastic—perhaps the sharpest edge of the computerized scheduling method. I've used resource-leveling quite a bit over the years, but mostly during Strategic Planning. It allows the Commitment Planner to assess the *reasonableness* and *practicality* of a given project strategy. It demonstrates, through computer modeling, that the chosen scenario uses resources wisely.

However, I don't recommend it for the final Execution Schedule, the one that will coordinate the work in the field. In general, I discourage the use of any *button* that, once pushed, takes the decision-making out of the minds of those who are charged with managing the project and instead delegates it to a softly hissing microchip.

One additional concern with resource-leveling is that it tends to obscure the various paths (critical, near-critical, and other) of the Project Schedule. You should understand that use of resource-leveling constitutes an either-or condition with respect to who gets to exploit the Execution Schedule's total-float. If you give this power to the computer (software), no human will thereafter be able to (easily) identify or understand the total-float of activities because it obscures the various paths and, hence, one will not be able to exploit activities according to available total-float. Do you really want to surrender such power to the computer?

Cost-Loading

I'd like to bellyache about cost-loading while I'm on my soapbox. Specifically, I have heartburn over what often happens to the integrity of the Execution Schedule when it is cost-loaded. Please understand that a Project Schedule is, first and foremost, a *time management* tool as opposed to a *money management* tool. Let's be fair here. The accountants and job cost engineers have plenty of reports, tables, and tools at their disposal with which to manage the financial end of the job.

The Project Scheduler's *only* tool is the Project Schedule. More importantly, that same Execution Schedule is all that the project manager has with which to *manage* the momentum of the project. The primary tool the superintendent has with which to *run* the job is the Execution Schedule. So, please, let's not do *anything* that might erode the integrity of the Execution Schedule. Fair enough?

My experience has been that, when the financial people start messing with the schedule, quite often they end up watering it down. Here is why: A good Execution Schedule is developed with emphasis on performance of work. Activity-durations are devised based on the activity's scope. Activity-identifiers are created based on where the work is to take place and by whom. Activity-codes are oriented toward where the work will happen. Relationships deal with how the work components *relate* to one another. In short, the Execution Schedule emphasizes what needs to be done and it expresses it at a level-of-detail that supports effective communication aimed at field coordination and performance control.

The cost engineer's interest is different, however. He wants to establish consistency (a paper trail, if you will) between the contract and progress payments, between the project budget and the accounts payable ledgers. He hopes to do this by placing a dollar value on each and every activity in the CPM schedule.

For him, this makes perfect sense, since the Project Schedule is maintained monthly and is often cited as backup for the contractor's pay request. If each activity's *percent complete* amount can be multiplied times that activity's dollar value, then a combined *earned value* for all activities would essentially substantiate the progress payment request. Right? Yes, it would.

My objection is not with what cost loading accomplishes, but rather with what cost loading does to the integrity of the Execution Schedule as a Performance Control tool. In order to make the link between budget line item and payment line item, the Project Schedule is usually *modified* in order to insure that *no single Execution Schedule activity pertains to more than one line item* in the contract's Schedule of Values (budget). What this means, in practice, is that certain Execution Schedule activities must be combined, while others must be further subdivided.

The result, after the cost engineers are finished with their "modest" adjustments to the Execution Schedule, is activities that are often either too general or too minute to be useful or practical *from a time management perspective*. For instance, where, according to the original Logic Development Sessions, a single three-day activity called "Overhead Utilities-Library" makes perfect sense (and, in its own right, is about as small a duration as one would ever want), the cost engineer demands that six different one-day activities be created, corresponding to the six subcontractors doing distinctly different types of overhead utility work.

When this kind of encroachment becomes more than occasional, my recommendation is that the Execution Schedule not be used as part of cost control.[1] To be sure, the Project Scheduler has a responsibility to the project that admittedly transcends the Project Schedule, or even the time management objective. He should be performing various cost-supporting exercises as well. He must not be unresponsive to the requests or needs of the cost-oriented members of the project management team.

However, he can accommodate them and achieve the critical link between internal systems and controls by using an intervening tool of some sort. I usually employ some form of spreadsheet that provides an interface between the Project Schedule activity, the Schedule of Values line item, and the Pay Request line item. Here, roll-ups and roll-downs can be accomplished without destroying the integrity or weakening the punch of the Project Schedule.

POWERFUL SOFTWARE SETTINGS

Although, given its domination of the project scheduling market, Primavera's scheduling software programs most often come to mind in discussions of software settings that affect date, float, and criticality calculations, other programs have most of the same features that can prove equally detrimental to a good schedule, if not responsibly employed. I'd like to discuss a few of the more powerful settings that single-handedly can destroy your Execution Schedules, if not used sensibly.

---

[1]This recommendation is especially appropriate if the priority-emphasis model points to a time-sensitive, more than cost-sensitive project.

Retained-Logic vs. Progress-Override

Most popular scheduling software programs give you the choice of how the earliest-dates are to be calculated, when work has begun out-of-sequence. Figure 14-1's top panel shows a typical situation where, according to the original logic, Activity B cannot start until Activity A has finished (top panel).

Figure 14-1

Retained-Logic versus Progress-Override

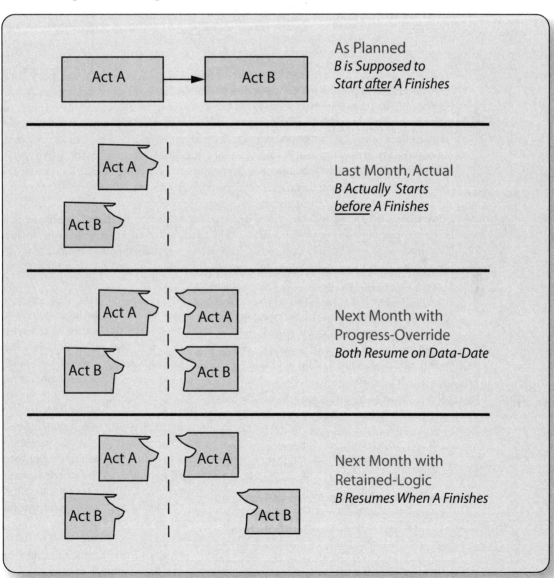

Now, suppose that, in actuality, Activity B not only starts before Activity A finishes, it starts before Activity A starts (second panel)!

How shall the program calculate the effective earliest-start for the balance of Activity B? Should the balance of Activity B be made to wait until Activity A is completed (this is called retailed-logic), or should it be shown as happening concurrent with Activity A since both are now apparently free to progress (this is called progress-override)?

Figure 14-1 shows the two options in the lower two panels. I can't give you a dyed-in-the-wool answer that works regardless of the situation. To be sure, there are occasions when progress-override makes sense. Please know that this subject is hotly debated among Scheduling Practitioners, and an equal number of them will disagree as agree with what I'm about to say.

I happen to think that retained-logic is the better way to go. I've seen too many wacky results when the progress-override option is elected. Let's face it: if the logic was faulty to begin with, then simply change the logic. You see, what often happens is that a successor activity is indeed *started* out-of-sequence but is then not continued out-of-sequence. Perhaps a portion of the activity's scope is undertaken, but the successor work quickly grinds to a halt because it really does need the predecessor activity to finish. Naturally, when we change to a progress-override setting, we abandon that relationship and the schedule calculations become faulty.

My advice is to examine each instance of out-of-sequence work and determine if the original restraint was truly valid. If, as evidenced by the fact that follow-on work did not have to wait on its predecessor's completion, it appears that the restraint was inappropriate, then modify the logic—change the logic tie.

But don't use the progress-override. Here's why I prefer the retained-logic setting. If you're going to examine all out-of-sequence activities and revisit the logic (which you should do with each Performance Control cycle), then it doesn't matter which setting you choose. But if we are concerned about the setting, it is because we envision situations where we cannot or do not perform this manual examination, and we are going to use the scheduling software's calculations of earliest and latest dates based on a setting to either retain or override earlier logic.

Think back to all that went into creating the logic in the first place, including the number of people who participated in the Logic Development Sessions, the amount of scrutiny the original logic underwent, and the extent to which logic ties and values were adjusted to achieve a reliable schedule. Are you willing to dismiss all of this thinking, especially when you consider that you don't always know why or to what extent the logic was subsequently violated in the field? No, absolutely not. It would be insulting to the people who developed the Execution Schedule in the first place.

I concede that there may be a situation where progress-override may make sense, and that is when the Execution Schedule has devolved to a state where it so radically needs an overhaul. But such overhauls, called major revisions, typically require owner approval.

If approval is not granted, or until the Execution Schedule is revised, the progress-override setting may be an appropriate stopgap measure to obtain more realistic dates. But as soon as possible, the Execution Schedule should be revised and the setting reverted to retained-logic.

Continuous vs. Elapsed Durations

The activity-duration is the most basic element of the Project Schedule. Let me repeat my four-word sermon: *keep the duration pure!* With all the professional integrity you can muster, guard the absolute integrity of the activity-duration. Improperly assigned or maintained durations will result in a worthless Project Schedule. It's that simple.

The duration is an *estimate* of *continuous-workdays* required to perform an activity. Don't miss either of the two main ingredients. Under the next heading, I will compare *workdays* to calendar days. First, let's look at the meaning of *continuous*.

One of the hardest things for old-timers trying to make the transformation from bar chart scheduling to CPM Scheduling to understand is that the activity-duration represents consecutive-workdays. You see, in bar chart scheduling the process is much simpler. You begin with a given start date and you have in mind a given end date. You pick up your pencil and you draw a horizontal line between these two points. You may cross weekends, holidays, or other nonwork days. What you're drawing is essentially an *elapsed*-duration. Consider the following example.

Let's say it takes two weeks to hang and tape a floor of drywall (see Figure 14-2), and that same amount of drywall could be painted in five days if the painting was started after all the drywall had been hung and taped (and sanded). In a bar chart depicting the two activities as overlapped, you'd see two bars, each two weeks in length, the Painting activity somewhat offset from the Drywall activity. Why is the Painting shown as a two-week bar? Not because the work requires two weeks, but because the painting can't finish any faster than the drywall that precedes it.

But in CPM scheduling we have a feature called logic ties that portrays the relationship between the two activities, and in PDM scheduling, in particular, we have unique relationship types that can depict the precise overlap between the two activities. We say, with a start-to-start of four days, the Painting activity cannot start until four days after the Drywall activity has begun. We say that, using a finish-to-finish of four days, the Painting activity will not complete until *at least* four days after the Drywall activity wraps up. Our logic reflects the relationship the old-timer understands to be true. But we keep the continuous-workday duration for Painting at five days because we want to *keep the duration pure.*

Let the logic ties do the work. Keep the durations pure. Make certain that each activity-duration represents the number of continuous-workdays required to perform that activity. This concept is so important because if the activity-duration ever stops representing the number of workdays required to perform the scope of work represented by that activity, then all of CPM's fundamental calculations are in jeopardy of becoming invalid. Plus, let's not forget that a number of other project management support methodologies depend on legitimate durations, even often requiring them to be resource- or cost-loaded.

Figure 14-2

Continuous versus Elapsed Durations

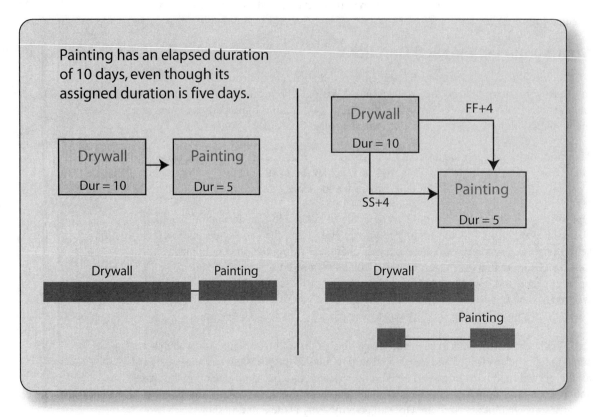

Painting has an elapsed duration of 10 days, even though its assigned duration is five days.

Continuous vs. Interruptible Durations

This feature, offered by some of the more powerful scheduling software programs, allows you to start an activity later than its earliest-start date, such that, once it starts, it can run continuously. This option was developed in response to a common condition created by the PDM method, where a successor activity has a smaller activity-duration than its predecessor activity, and the relationship between them is *both* a start-to-start and a finish-to-finish. As a result, the successor activity's *elapsed*-duration cannot be less than the predecessor's elapsed-duration. This means that the successor's elapsed-duration would be longer than its continuous-workdays duration.

Consider Figure 14-3. Activity B is shown as achievable within six continuous-workdays. Interpreting the Interruptible Condition (left panel), relying entirely on the start-to-start relationship we see that Activity B can begin as early as two days after Activity A starts. But if it does, it will come to a grinding halt at some point, because its final two days of work are restrained by the completion of Activity A.

If we set the software toggle to continuous-duration, the effect is as shown in the right panel. Even though the logic allows Activity B to start two days after Activity A commences,

Figure 14-3

Interruptible versus Continuous Duration Implications

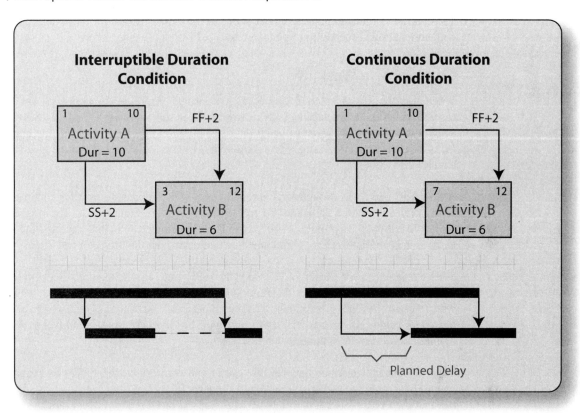

the software setting forces a planned delay, in this case equivalent to four workdays, so that the six-day activity-duration for Activity B will be continuous.

Now that you understand how it works, let me tell you why I am opposed to the continuous-duration setting. In a word, it is what I call *planned procrastination*. It is hard enough to get subcontractors to show up on site when needed. To be sure, most proactive project managers who know this will call for their subcontractors a few days *earlier* than needed. They'd rather have the subcontractor on site earlier than needed than at the last possible moment.

The continuous-duration setting essentially squanders valuable free- and total-float. I cannot understand why a project manager would want to give away float! My argument is bolstered by another realization: things rarely go as planned. That four-day period of Activity B potentially standing around waiting for Activity A to complete might not happen that way at all in real life. In the real world, Activity B might take longer than six days, maybe eight. If so, the gap between continuous- and elapsed-durations would reduce to only two days. But if the continuous-duration setting is chosen, then those extra two days (eight versus six) would result in a loss of total-float of two days. I say, why risk it?

AUTOMATED SCHEDULE CALENDARS

The concept of the automated calendar is one of the hardest things for those unfamiliar with computerized scheduling to understand.

Concept of a Workday

When an activity is assigned a duration, that duration is expressed in workdays—in all cases! Even if the contractor intends to work a seven-day workweek, and a one-week activity is expressed as seven calendar days, the duration of seven represents the number of workdays required to complete the activity. To grasp this concept, let me give you a real-world example.

A few years ago I was brought onto a federal project that appeared, by all accounts, to be significantly behind schedule. To follow this story, see Figure 14-4. The original project length was 24 months—two years. The Department of Justice retained me to analyze the contractor's Execution Schedule and determine the project's *true* status.

The two-year project began on October 1, 1995, and was scheduled to finish on September 30, 1997. The first Baseline Schedule, submitted on November 15, 1995, was rejected by the government. The contractor's next submission, which *was* approved, came out on April 1, 1996. Schedule Editions occurred monthly for nine months, from May 1996 through January 1997.

Then, in January, relations between the owner and contractor deteriorated over arguments concerning the undeniable schedule slippage. Friction was so hot among the parties that the Performance Control cycle was skipped in February. Finally, after weeks of negotiations, an agreement was reached whereby the contractor would commence working seven days a week instead of five days per week.

To reflect this decision, the contractor spent another two weeks revising the Execution Schedule. In March 1997 the first Schedule Edition using the Revised Execution Schedule was issued, and it showed the project being roughly 5.5 months behind schedule. The April Schedule Edition indicated only slightly better results, reporting the schedule overrun at 5.25 months. I arrived on the same day that the May Schedule Edition came out, at which time the project was still running five months beyond contract completion.

It didn't take me more than a few hours to figure out that the project was, in fact, only two months behind schedule. But the best news of all was that the project was most likely going to finish on schedule. Confused? Let me explain.

As I examined the originally approved Baseline Schedule and flipped through the nine subsequent Schedule Editions, I noticed that the majority of activity-durations appeared to be in increments of five, thus implying a five-day workweek. All activities used a single calendar, which employed a five-workday week, with weekends as nonworkdays.

Figure 14-4
Department of Justice Project

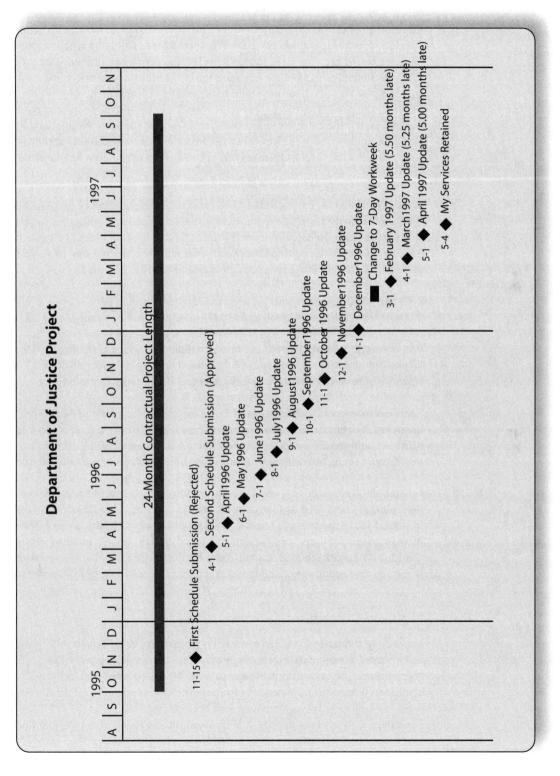

Department of Justice Project

When I looked at the Revised Execution Schedule (March 1997) and its subsequent Editions, I noticed that the activity-durations seemed to be in increments of seven, thus suggesting a seven-day workweek. Whether intentional or not, the contractor had changed the wrong value. He should have left the activity-durations as they were originally and merely changed the calendar settings to allow weekend work. Had he done so, *all* of the reported overrun would have instantly disappeared.

Instead, he left the calendar untouched, and increased the activity-durations by 40 percent (the ratio of seven to five). With the juxtaposition of seven-day activity-durations and a five-day workweek calendar, this schedule was overstating its true length almost 100 percent.

By way of example, look at Table 14-1. Imagine a single string of 28 sequential activities, each activity taking 5 days to perform. Condition A assumes that we are using a 5-day workweek. Hence, the overall Project Schedule would initially span 140 workdays, or 28 weeks. Condition D shows us that we could use a 7-day workweek and set each activity-duration to seven and get the same results, 28 weeks.

Let's see what happens when we keep the activity-duration at five, but apply all activities to a seven-day workweek calendar. According to Condition B, the 28 activities could be completed in 20 weeks. This makes sense since each five-day activity takes 0.71 weeks to perform. As for the inverse situation, look at Condition C. Here we set the activity-duration at seven and apply all activities to a five-day workweek calendar. Now, a single activity takes 1.4 weeks, and the 28 activities consume 39.2 weeks.

To reflect the owner's permission, the contractor should have left the durations at five-day increments (Condition B), *since durations are always expressed in workdays.* He should then have adjusted the *calendar* to reflect a seven-day workweek. Had the contractor done this, the remaining project length would have dropped from 28 weeks to 20 weeks.

Instead, the contractor adjusted the activity-durations to seven-day increments but left the calendar at a five-day workweek (Condition C). The effect was obvious—it increased the project length. And why shouldn't it have? Every activity's length had been increased by 40 percent—from five to seven days! The remaining project length went from 28 weeks to 39.2 weeks. When I adjusted the calendar to a seven-day workweek and the durations back to five-day increments, *the entire delay went away.*

Multiple Calendars

Scheduling software is made extremely powerful by offering this feature. But there is a catch. If you use more than one calendar in a Project Schedule, you will invariably confound critical (or any other) path delineations. This is because each activity's total-float is expressed in a unit of measure corresponding to that activity's particular calendar.

For example, two items side by side in a continuous string of activities (which, let us say, is one-week behind schedule) would show total-float values of −5 and −7 if the calendars for those activities were five-day and seven-day workweeks, respectively.

Table 14-1

Why All Durations Should Be Expressed in Continuous Workdays

	Table Contrasting Five and Seven Day Calendars							
	Condition A Activ Dur = 5 Days/Week = 5		Condition B Activ Dur = 5 Days/Week = 7		Condition C Activ Dur = 7 Days/Week = 5		Condition D Activ Dur = 7 Days/Week = 7	
Activ	Cum Dur	Wks Rqd	Cum Dur	Wks Rqd	Cum Dur	Wks Rqd	Cum Dur	Wks Rqd
1.	5	1.0	5	0.7	7	1.4	7	1.0
2.	10	2.0	10	1.4	14	2.8	14	2.0
3.	15	3.0	15	2.1	21	4.2	21	3.0
4.	20	4.0	20	2.9	28	5.6	28	4.0
5.	25	5.0	25	3.6	35	7.0	35	5.0
6.	30	6.0	30	4.3	42	8.4	42	6.0
7.	35	7.0	35	5.0	49	9.8	49	7.0
8.	40	8.0	40	5.7	56	11.2	56	8.0
9.	45	9.0	45	6.4	63	12.6	61	9.0
10.	50	10.0	50	7.1	70	14.0	70	10.0
11.	55	11.0	55	7.9	77	15.4	77	11.0
12.	60	12.0	60	8.6	84	16.8	84	12.0
13.	65	13.0	65	9.3	91	18.2	91	13.0
14.	70	14.0	70	10.0	98	19.6	98	14.0
15.	75	15.0	75	10.7	105	21.0	105	15.0
16.	80	16.0	80	11.4	112	22.4	112	16.0
17.	85	17.0	85	12.1	119	23.8	119	17.0
18.	90	18.0	90	12.9	126	25.2	126	18.0
19.	95	19.0	95	13.6	133	26.6	133	19.0
20.	100	20.0	100	14.3	140	28.0	140	20.0
21.	105	21.0	105	15.0	147	29.4	147	21.0
22.	110	22.0	110	15.7	154	30.8	154	22.0
23.	115	23.0	115	16.4	161	32.2	161	23.0
24.	120	24.0	120	17.1	168	33.6	168	24.0
25.	125	25.0	125	17.9	175	35.0	175	25.0
26.	130	26.0	130	18.6	182	36.4	182	26.0
27.	135	27.0	135	19.3	189	37.8	189	27.0
28.	140	28.0	140	20.0	196	39.2	196	28.0

Obviously, if you were to generate a report sorted by total-float, your thought being to identify the Project Schedule's critical-path, the –7 activity would be in the least-float path; the –5 activity would not.

This having been said, I am not opposed to a reasonable use of multiple calendars; being more precise with calendars makes for better schedules. Take concrete curing, for example. Concrete doesn't know the difference between weekdays, holidays, and weekends. Using a seven-day calendar for concrete curing makes perfect sense. Another great use of calendars concerns weather-sensitive items. Indoor activities are not usually subject to weather conditions the same way outside field activities are.

Workdays vs. Calendar Days

The key word of this heading is *workdays*. Even if the calendar being applied to the Execution Schedule is a seven-day calendar, and hence every calendar day is also a workday, continue to think of the activity-duration in terms of workdays, not calendar days. You may wish to refer back to the example given under Concept of a Workday earlier in this chapter to understand why an activity-duration of seven, representing a solid week of work, is not the same as an activity-duration of five, representing a solid week of work.

I have found that this concept is often hard for beginners to understand. They argue: *"If I'm going from a five-day workweek to a seven-day workweek, then I need to bump all my durations from increments of five to increments of seven."* Wrong! When I hear this I immediately question what was in the mind of the person who provided the five-day activity-duration in the first place. Did they mean that the activity would take a *week* to do? Or did they mean that it would take *five consecutive-workdays* to do? More than likely they were thinking in terms of *elapsed* versus *consecutive* workdays—which, by now, you realize is in blatant disregard to my four-word sermon: *Keep the duration pure.*

Perhaps this simple exercise will help. Instead of a single activity with a five-day duration, think of three activities, Activities A, B, and C, with durations of 2, 2, and 1, respectively. Now, let us suppose that we are told we're going to go from a five-day workweek to a seven-day workweek. Would you change the duration of Activity A, which you previously thought would take two days to perform? How about Activity C, the one-day item? Of course not!

At the time they were derived, these were reasonable estimates of workdays needed to perform the work. And those estimates are still valid. That they now might be performed on Saturday and Sunday, rather than on Tuesday and Wednesday, is no reason to change them, to bump them up. So why should a five-day activity be automatically increased to seven days? It shouldn't.

Holidays

Holidays is perhaps too specific a term. What I mean by this word is "predictable nonworkable days." In addition to holidays, other equally predictable nonworkable days are: hunting season, inaugurations, parades, Election Days, and so on. Any prescheduled nonworkable day cited on a public calendar is considered, for purposes of this discussion, a *holiday*.

So what about holidays? Do you schedule them? That all depends on the detail level at which you are performing your Execution Scheduling. It also depends on the precision of the activity-durations. For instance, if your activity-durations are rounded into increments of weeks (5, 10, 15, and so on), chances are your underlying assumption is that something scheduled to be completed in, say, two weeks will be completed in two weeks, even if overtime or weekend work is required. For this reason, in Commitment Planning, the usage of holidays is typically not necessary.

When you *do* find the need to use holidays, apply them judiciously. Not all activities are subject to these nonworkable periods. Concrete will cure on the Fourth of July just as readily as it will on the third or fifth of July. Similarly, procurement activities should not be subjected to holidays, *unless the manufacturing schedule is under the control of the contractor*, which is next to never. The reason for this is that when a supplier tells you he'll get your widgets to you in "six weeks," that's a rounded duration. In his shop (and in his head) he is committing to having those widgets delivered to your site by a *given date*, no matter what it takes, and most likely he has taken the holiday into account, when he committed to the delivery date in the first place.

Also, watch for certain "holidays" that apply to fieldwork but not to home office work. A parade at the jobsite area would be one such example; while one could expect field activities to be impacted by the parade, there is no reason why the home office, even across the street, can't still be cranking out shop drawings or why the architect in another city can't be reviewing submittals. For these reasons, I always find it odd to see an automated CPM schedule that has a five-day holiday-loaded calendar but not five-day nonholiday or seven-day nonholiday calendars.

WEATHER

What is the best way to allot for inclement weather? What? You don't allow for bad weather in your schedule? Well, you should! Whether the contract addresses the matter of weather days or not, when it comes to a claim for delay, scheduling experts on both sides of the table equally look to see whether inclement conditions *exceeded what was normal*. In other words, the general assumption is that the contractor "should have anticipated" an average, or *normal,* amount of inclement weather.

Which Activities Are Affected?

Given this, how then does the project schedule "anticipate" inclement weather? This is one of those areas where each Execution Scheduler has a preferred technique. To be sure, there are a number of equally legitimate ways to handle weather.

The science, or "art," of scheduling bad weather in advance is in knowing where to put the contingency for bad weather. But before I get into all of that, let's agree without much discussion that inclement weather only impacts certain activities. As a general statement concerning on-site activities, most outdoor activities would be subjected to, but not necessarily impacted by, foul conditions. Of course, interior activities, once the building is "dried in," would not normally be affected by bad weather. However, if the building is not sufficiently enclosed, then certain activities (perhaps those more sensitive to extreme cold or dampness) might be candidates for inclusion in the weather-sensitive group.

Offsite activities must be considered on a one-by-one basis. For instance, fabrication activities are not to be driven by a weather-coded calendar for the same reason that holidays are not applied to manufacturers. This is because when a manufacturer agrees to a completion date, he should take into account holidays and bad weather. If he experiences slowdowns in manufacturing, or even difficulties in delivering to the site on time because of them or for any other reasons, he has to make up the lost time. Plus, weather conditions at the site may be quite different from weather conditions at the fabricator's location. And it is the weather at the jobsite, not elsewhere, that the contract typically considers.

Where Do You Place the Weather Contingency?

Now comes the most difficult question: where in the calendar do you put those "11 bad weather days" that the NOAA (National Oceanic and Atmospheric Administration) tables say will likely descend upon your jobsite? Before sharing my thoughts, let's consider the options.

- **Option 1** You can leave them out of the Execution Schedule altogether.
- **Option 2** You can put the sum total of them at the end of the Execution Schedule.
- **Option 3** You can plug the sum total of them at the beginning of the Execution Schedule.
- **Option 4** You can spread them throughout the Execution Schedule.

Option 1: Leave Them Out of the Execution Schedule Altogether

Option 1 makes sense if you are putting together an Execution Schedule for a time-sensitive project and the company is committed to making the end date "no matter what it takes." In such a case, if bad weather strikes your job, the project will commit the overtime or extra forces needed to make up for the lost time. An exception to this thinking is a double-shift, seven-day workweek schedule in which you haven't allowed any "wiggle room" to make-up for weather delays. In such a schedule, you'd be wise to set a contingency for bad weather days. So, Option 1 is not such a good idea.

Option 2: Put Them at the Beginning of the Execution Schedule

Options 2 and 3 differ from Option 4 philosophically. The latter choice attempts an effort to "model" the *most likely scenario*. If it typically rains heavily during April and May, then weather days allowing for excess rain would be "allocated" during April and May. Winter weather would be "allocated" during the winter months.

So why would anyone consider *dumping* the total weather days on the end or beginning of the Execution Schedule, Options 2 and 3, respectively? The answer lies deep within management's objectives for the Execution Schedule. Most often you'll find bulk dumping of weather or other contingency days when the Execution Schedule is being used (or intended to be used) to document delays in connection with securing change orders ("extras") for time or money. To be honest, I've seen it plugged in at either end of the Execution Schedule. Either way, if the weather contingency is not allocated during the months of greatest expectation, then when the rains *do* fall, and the work is negatively impacted, the Execution Schedule will show the work falling behind.

The problem with Option 2 is that it has the effect of pushing all latest-dates to the left, and this creates an artificial squeeze on the project. As a result, during the final stages of Schedule Development, steps would have to be taken to tighten the Execution Schedule so that the earliest-dates would not exceed the more aggressive latest-dates. So, Option 2 is not a good idea.

Option 3: Put Them at the End of the Execution Schedule

Option 3 makes no sense. First, it has the effect of delaying all work from that the point of allocation forward. This creates the self-fulfilling prophecy situation we discussed earlier, concerning artificially elongated Execution Schedules. Second, once the period of allocation passes, meaning it's *turned to history,* it has no effect at all. So, Option 3 is not a good idea.

Option 4: Spread Them Throughout the Execution Schedule

That leaves Option 4, where the objective is to place the weather contingency as close as possible to the periods when the inclement weather is expected to occur. Personally, I tend to put them at the end of the month in which the bad weather is expected rather than spreading them throughout the month. This way, Performance Control Reports *during* the month will still show what *needs to be done* as if the bad weather was not expected to occur. If the bad weather does happen, then all involved will know that contingency days have been "set aside" for the disruption. In the meantime, and until the inclement weather hits, earliest-dates still stand there as goals to be met. If the team can "make up" the time without having to *tap* the weather days, then those days become available for any future disruptions, whether they be bad weather, contractor screw-ups, unreasonable inspectors, owner indecision, whatever.

Put Weather Contingency in the Calendar, Not in Durations

Finally, if it is your intent to simulate bad weather in your Execution Schedule, I should spend a moment discussing why you should put those weather days in the calendar and not in the activity-durations of likely affected activities. Believe it or not, the majority of Project Schedulers and project managers do just that: they beef up the activity-durations of the activities they consider vulnerable to the bad weather.

There are two reasons this method is completely unacceptable! For one thing, a Project Schedule is a dynamic model, and activities ebb and flow from one Performance Control cycle to the next. As they do, activities initially expected to happen in the dead of winter end up taking place in the fall or spring. When they do, the activity-durations that were inflated for the winter freeze are suddenly inappropriately "long" during the glorious days of spring. In the inverse, activities initially expected in the fall, and thus not inflated for winter, are now frozen in their tracks.

Along the same lines, there is the compounding affect. Remember that one day of bad weather may affect 50 activities. If your strategy was to artificially increase the durations on 50 activities, and then some of them actually end up impacted by the weather while others do not, you can only imagine how you have riddled your Execution Schedule with distorted durations and the effort that is now required to correct the distorted activity-durations.

The second and perhaps more important reason adjusting activity-durations for weather is an absolute no-no is that it destroys the integrity of the Execution Schedule. Remember that an Execution Schedule can never be any better than the quality of its activity-durations. Think about it: without activity-durations there would be no earliest-dates or latest-dates, and without those dates, there would be no total-float and free-float.

Total-float gives us our critical-path. Mess with the activity-durations and you've messed with the reliability of the entire Execution Schedule. When you artificially increase activity-durations for weather purposes, the duration no longer represents a purposeful balance between scope, resources, and productivity.

PRIORITY-EMPHASIS ALIGNMENT

We talked earlier about the Theory of Aligned Emphasis. Every project has an inherent urgency, a particular emphasis the owner places on one of three success criteria: cost, time, or manner. The Execution Schedule should align with this emphasis. Since I have already discussed the concept of Emphasis-Aligned Performance, here I will explore the implications of the different success criteria.

When Project Length (Time) Is Emphatic

When time is the owner's primary success criterion, activity-durations take on greater significance. To be sure, on any project and at any point along the project life cycle continuum, estimated activity-durations should fall within a range of reasonableness, as covered in our discussion of activity-durations in the previous chapter. Normally, that range can be somewhat elastic, but on time-sensitive projects reasonableness assumes a more restrictive meaning.

Start with activity-durations that are unusually small or "tight." Time-sensitive projects often bring about their own failure, by definition. Because they are understood to be "tight" right from the outset, time-critical projects tend to draw correspondingly *aggressive* activity-duration estimates. Since ambitious activity-durations stand a greater chance of being missed, they collectively raise the percentage of activities requiring make-up efforts to maintain the aggressive pace of the Project Schedule. But with time at a premium, opportunities for make-up are not as plentiful to begin with. In the end, the probability of schedule overrun is increased. It's a vicious cycle.

Now consider activity-duration estimates that are unnecessarily long. The crafty contractor may believe that he is "padding" his Execution Schedule and providing himself with a "cushion" against unknowns that will inevitably befall his project. What he fails to understand is that a padded Project Schedule is, by definition, an unrealistic Project Schedule—it does not reflect what is real.

Once we start toying with the integrity of the activity-duration, we undermine the believability and reliability of the paths defined by those activity-durations. Critical-paths become contrived, not real. Not only is the critical-path not necessarily critical, the string of activities that actually *is* critical to timely completion may be masked beyond all recognition. In the end, the project is being run without a usable Execution Schedule, and now we're back to "those who fail to plan, plan to fail."

Beyond activity-durations, the Emphasis Alignment Model should influence both the number and type of activities built into a Execution Schedule. Again, consider a time-sensitive project. The primary objective should be to finish the project on or ahead of schedule. The project manager will accomplish this by employing a well-designed, well-developed, and well-integrated Execution Schedule. He will then identify those activities that are truly most critical to timely completion and concentrate the attention of all project participants on them.

The critical-path, then, is a key to effective management on time-sensitive projects. It should be obvious that, on such projects, there can be no tolerance for mindless oversights or omissions when it comes to activity development. For example, it is the rare construction project that does not experience a few key contractor submissions going through multiple submittal-review cycles before finally being approved for fabrication or installation. Yet it is also rare to see a Project Schedule that allows for multiple iterations of the submittal process, per item. On time-sensitive projects, it is vital that at least a few submission (perhaps those with the highest probability of being rejected the first time around) be scheduled for two or even three iterations.

Another way to make a time-sensitive schedule more realistic is in the area of activity overlapping. Let me merely note that the critical-path(s) will be dramatically influenced by how aggressively activities are overlapped in a Project Schedule.

When Manner of Performance Is Emphatic

Quality-sensitive projects should employ a more relaxed activity overlap philosophy. It should assume less trade stacking (where multiple trades occupy the same area at the same time) and fewer crews per discipline. The latter point, concerning numbers of crews per discipline, has to do with learning curves. Obviously, each additional crew means an additional learning curve, and that means an additional portion of the project being subjected to "inexperienced" workers. This condition is more acute on projects with highly specialized, technical designs or components—such as special equipment, unique installations, and so on.

Quality-sensitive projects should also assume a smaller supervisor-to-worker ratio. With more supervisor attention comes slower productivity per widget. People naturally work slower when being watched, especially when they're being watched for quality mess-ups. Of course, the very fact that the worker is more attentive to details, even if supervision isn't looking over his shoulder, means that he'll be taking a little longer to "do it right the first time."

When Project Cost Is Emphatic

Cost-sensitive Project Schedules usually take longer to complete and should be depicted as such. Since labor is the largest cost ingredient, dollar savings typically come about by using less skilled, less experienced workers and subcontractors. This naturally translates into larger activity-durations (lesser efficiency during the first pass), measurable rework (additional passes), and bigger "spreads" on activity overlaps (reflecting less responsive management).

This last point, the bigger spread on activity overlaps, is the result of low-end subcontractors who are spread too thin on too many projects and who employ too few superintendents for all the work they have under contract in the area. As a result, their work force as a whole shows up on your project typically one or two days later than called for, at any given time their workforce is often 5–15 percent no-shows, and a percentage of their labor pools are therefore hiring hall substitutes.

DATE-CONSTRAINTS

Date-constraints are fixed dates arbitrarily imposed into the Project Schedule by the Project Scheduler in an attempt to alter the forward pass and backward pass calculations of dates and, thus, of total-float. A simple example would be as follows.

Based on direct logic, we cannot start the coffeemaker until we have loaded it with water and coffee grinds. But we may also set a timer on the coffeemaker, such that the machine will not turn on until a specific time, long after the water and grinds are set in place. The timer is a form of date-constraint that overrides the otherwise earlier start of the activities.

The Help Screen from Primavera's P3 5.0 provides examples of popular constraints.

Start Constraints

Primavera identifies three different Start-On Constraints.

Start On Constraint
A start on constraint is a restriction you place on an activity by imposing a start date. The start on constraint can delay an early start or accelerate a late start to satisfy the imposed date. Unlike the mandatory start constraint, which can violate the network logic, this constraint protects it.

Start On or After Constraint
A start on or after constraint is a restriction you impose on an activity that limits the earliest time it can begin. When calculating a schedule, the start on or after constraint is used in the forward pass only if the calculated early start date will be earlier than the imposed date. This constraint affects only early dates. The early start date of an activity with a start on or after constraint cannot be earlier than the imposed date, although the network logic may cause the early start to occur later.

Start On or Before Constraint
A start on or before constraint is a restriction you impose on an activity that limits the latest date it can start. When calculating a schedule, the start on or before constraint is used in the backward pass only if the calculated late start date will be later than the imposed date. This constraint may decrease total float. It only affects late dates.

Finish Constraints

Primavera identifies three different Finish Constraints.

Finish On Constraint

A finish on constraint is a restriction you place on an activity by imposing a finish date. The finish on constraint can delay an early finish or accelerate a late finish to satisfy the imposed date.

Finish On or After Constraint

A finish on or after constraint is a restriction you impose on an activity that limits the earliest time it can complete. The finish on or after constraint reduces float to coordinate parallel activities, ensuring that the finish of an activity is not scheduled before the specified date. It is usually applied to activities that have few predecessors that must finish before the next phase of a project.

Finish On or Before Constraint

A finish on or before constraint is a restriction you impose on an activity that limits the latest time it can be finished. The finish on or before constraint affects only late dates. Use this constraint to ensure that the late finish date of an activity is not later than the date you impose.

Mandatory Constraints

Primavera identifies two different Mandatory Constraints.

Mandatory Start Constraint

A mandatory start constraint is a restriction you impose on an activity that sets its early and late start dates equal to the date you specify. The mandatory early start date is used regardless of its effect on network logic. A mandatory early start date could affect the late dates for all activities that lead to the constrained activity and all early dates for the activities that lead from the constrained activity.

Mandatory Finish Constraint

A mandatory finish constraint is a restriction you impose on an activity that sets its early and late finish dates equal to the date you specify. The mandatory finish date is used regardless of its effect on network logic. This constraint affects the late dates for all activities that lead to the constrained activity and all early dates for the activities that lead from the constrained activity.

Late Constraint

Primavera identifies one popular Late Constraint.

As Late As Possible Constraint

An as late as possible constraint is a restriction you impose on an activity or work unit with positive float that allows it to start as late as possible without delaying its successors. This constraint sets the early dates as late as possible without affecting successor activities.

I am sure you intuitively appreciate that there is an inversely proportional relationship between date-constraint use and the influence of pure logic on schedule calculations. As the number of date-constraints increases, the ability of the logic to properly influence earliest and latest dates diminishes.

Avoid Excessive Date-Constraint Use

You should also be warned that some of these date-constraints conflict with one another and as a result cause unexpected and unwanted results. My advice to you is to study each date-constraint's functionality very carefully before employing them. Figure 14-5 shows a rather simple Project Schedule of only eight activities with a single date-constraint pinning the project's completion milestone. The critical path, A-C-E-G-H, bears a total-float value of zero.

Now we add two additional date-constraints, and the schedule goes crazy. Figure 14-6 shows that six of the eight activities now bear negative total-float, and another activity carries a zero-total-float. Thus, seven of the eight activities are critical, and the eighth activity is near-critical (TF = 2). There are two critical-paths (three, if you count the single zero-float activity), and both have negative total-float. There is an old expression that says, "When you have ten things to do, and all ten are Priority #1, then you have no priorities." How is this Project Schedule any different? How can the project manager concentrate on the *more* critical activities, when they are *all* critical or near-critical? Bottom line: use date-constraints with great discretion!

ALL ABOUT FLOAT

Any discussion of project float must address total-float, free-float, as well as the various software settings that affect the calculation of float.

Zero-Total-Float

Zero-total-float is a seemingly innocent-sounding option that is provided with certain scheduling software programs and has the effect of forcing an activity (or a whole string of activities) to become critical. It accomplishes this by changing the activity's latest-dates so that they are the same as the activity's earliest-dates. This, of course, reduces the activity's total-float to zero. But it also does something else. It simultaneously advances the latest-dates of all preceding activities, thereby reducing their total-float values, as well.

This feature creates an *artificial* criticality, because in reality there is still a gap between the now-earlier latest-finish of the subject activity and the latest-start of any immediately succeeding activities. So, you might be thinking, if the subject activity slips, its successors might just as possibly still be enjoying positive total-float. And you'd be correct.

That is the danger created by this option. It distorts reality, and it does so by manipulating the single most important calculation in the CPM methodology, total-float. My strong advice is not to use this feature. Moreover, if ever you are tasked with reviewing the acceptability of someone else's Project Schedule, such as would be the case if you were the owner or construction manager or a claims consultant, be on the lookout for deliberate use of this feature in order to artificially create "critical activities" where they are most advantageous for the party creating the Project Schedule.

Figure 14-5
Sample Logic; Single Date-Constraint

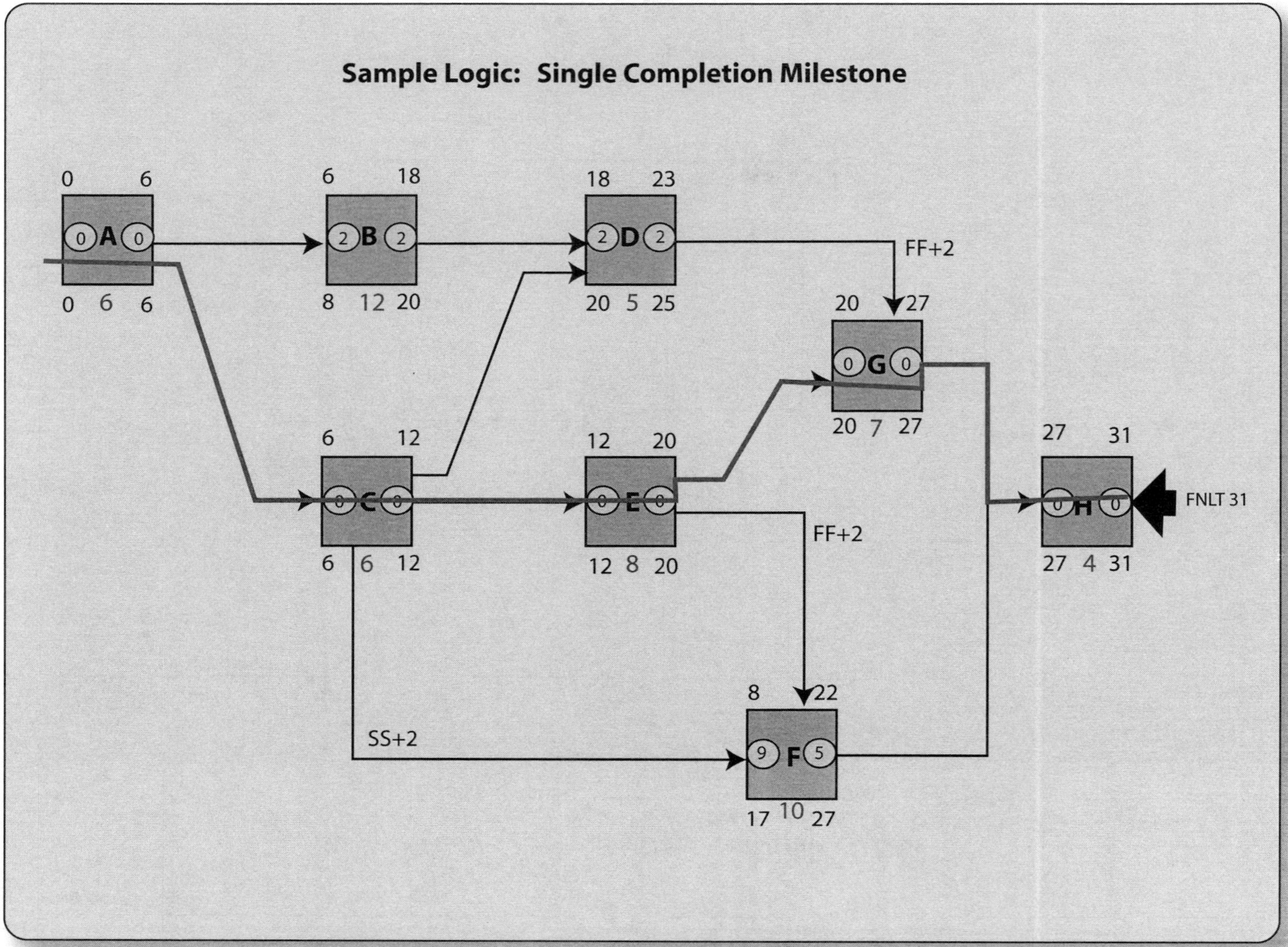

Sample Logic: Single Completion Milestone

Figure 14-6

Sample Logic; Excessive Date-Constraints

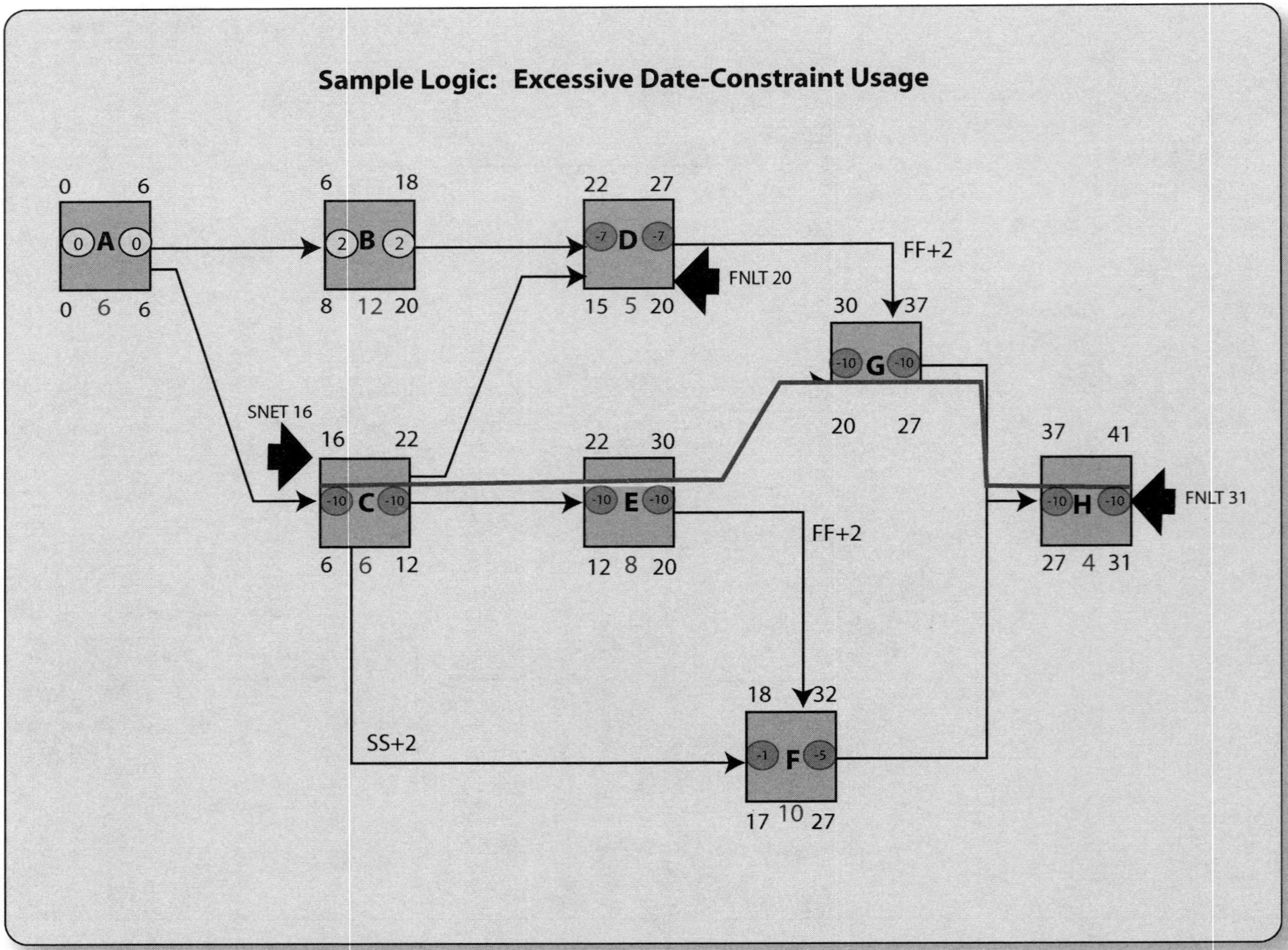

Sample Logic: Excessive Date-Constraint Usage

I can cite a real-life example of how this feature was exploited to the betterment of a contractor who had just been awarded a contract on an extremely tight project, one on which he hoped he could generate extra revenue by pursuing scope changes. In the bid documents, the owner indicated that there was a strong possibility that additional scope might be awarded at some point during the base contract work period. That extra scope was expected to involve the backstage area of a performance hall.

The contractor used zero-total-float on certain activities such that the paths leading to the backstage work had no total-float. Now, if the owner added *any* scope to these paths, the contractor would have a "justified" time extension. Of course, if this technique was later exposed, the owner might be expected to declare a false condition and deny the time extension. Therefore, the use of zero-total-float does not guarantee a time extension, but this doesn't mean the contractor wouldn't try this tactic, nonetheless.

Zero-Free-Float

Zero-free-float is an option offered by some scheduling software programs that allows you to force an activity, on a per activity basis, to start as late as possible without delaying its successors.[2] It does this by taking advantage of the free-float available to the activity.

My objection to this feature is the same as it is with the continuous-duration setting: it squanders free-float. Why would one willingly delay the start of an activity, and allow free-float to evaporate into thin air, when that free-float might be needed later? This is another case of *planned procrastination.*

Defining Total-Float in PDM

In PDM, an activity can have a different total-float value at its start than it has at its finish. This is because total-float is the difference between earliest and latest dates, both start and finish. Because of the start-to-start and finish-to-finish relationships, it is entirely possible, and quite often the case, that the number of days separating the earliest-start and latest-start dates is different than the number of days separating the earliest-finish and latest-finish dates. As a result, in PDM, each activity has *two* total float values: start-float, and finish-float. See Figure 14-7.

In most scheduling software programs, there is a choice one can make as to whether the *activity's* total-float shall be reflective of the activity's start-float, its finish-float or whichever is more critical, called least-float. If you choose either the start-float or the finish-float setting, you will have a difficult time tracing paths based on total-float. To circumvent this, choose the least- float setting, so the paths will be continuous.

---

[2]In P3 5.0, this is called the As Late As Possible constraint. We just covered this on the previous page.

Figure 14-7

Difference in Start-and Finish-Float Values

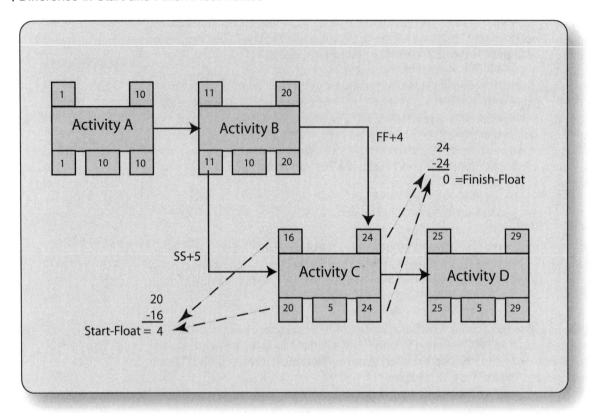

Free-Float

So that there is no confusion, let me distinguish between total-float and free-float. Both total-float and free-float apply to a *string of activities*. But whereas, in all scheduling software that I have seen, total-float is reported redundantly against *each* activity in the string, free-float is reported only against the last activity in the string.

To visualize this, Figure 14-8 represents a simple schedule containing nine activities: five on the top row (call that row String A) and four on a lower row, String B. The two strings are completely independent; both tie into a milestone called Project Complete. Each activity-duration is is five days. String A, then, would have a combined length of 25 workdays, while String B would have a length of 20 workdays. Assume that the contract length is also 25 days. Then String A would be the critical-path.

The total-float value for each activity in String A would be zero; the total-float for each activity in String B would be +5. Let me repeat the latter—each of the four String B activities would show a total-float of +5. However, these total-float values are not cumulative.

Figure 14-8
Free-Float Belongs to the Path

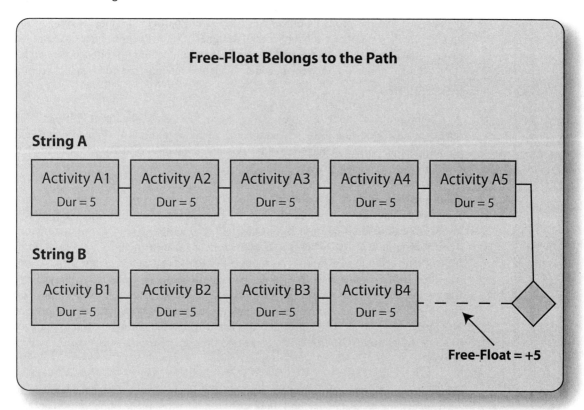

I have yet to see a definition of free-float, in any text or software help screen, which did not define it as "the amount of time any *single* activity can be delayed without affecting any subsequent activity." What I will tell you, in a minute, is that this definition is only a partial truth. But first, let us work with the popular definition. In our example, only one activity has a free-float value of +5, that being the last activity in String B. All other activities, if delayed, would impact an immediately subsequent activity. Hence, the first three activities of String B, and all the activities in String A have a free-float value of zero.

Now, back to my criticism of the popular understanding of free-float. I think a more correct definition might be this: "free-float is the amount of time that any activities of a *string* of activities can be delayed, without affecting any activities of any other string. To prove my point, consider the first activity of String B. If that activity were to delay by five days, wouldn't the "free-float" of the last activity reduce to zero? So, in other words, the free-float is being influenced by all of the activities on that string, but only reported against the last activity in the string, right? Even though String B might well have significant positive total-float, its free-float is a measure of how much unique free-float this particular string of activities enjoys.

Now, I have included a brief discussion of free-float in this text for two reasons. For one, during initial Schedule Development, free-float provides an excellent way for the astute Project Scheduler or project manager to measure or "sense" the degree of inter-dependence that the project's otherwise independent participants may have upon one another. Be they suppliers, subcontractors, designers, government agencies, or even the owner—the extent to which the project participants can potentially impact one another says volumes about the degree to which management must be focused on keeping everyone on track.

As a helpful rule of thumb, a Project Schedule with less than 30 percent of its activities having positive free-float values (versus zero), in my opinion, is a "tight" schedule and the responsible project manager must be extremely watchful of daily performance levels of all zero-free-float strings.

Additionally, free-float is a powerful tool in Performance Control Reporting. Many times, as a Scheduler, I have been asked by project managers or project directors to "mask" the total-float column from Schedule Extractions issued to subcontractors. Their reasoning was that when a subcontractor sees that his activity "has float on it" he tends to become lax. And even though the total-float refers to the excess time available to the *string* of activities and not just to any *single* activity, the subcontractor rarely elects or knows to make this distinction. Instead, he simply puts his forces elsewhere—sometimes elsewhere on your job, or, to your disappointment, elsewhere on someone else's project. And when you start beating on him to get back to work, he mutters: *"Relax, bud. I'm not holding up anybody. I've got three weeks of float."*

While I share the project manager's concern that positive total-float readings can be used against the project manager, I think that far more often those same total-float readings serve to *inspire* the subcontractor or supplier to get moving. To most subcontractors, architects, owners, and suppliers capable of reading and interpreting a CPM printout, the total-float value is a computerized "squeaky wheel." So why throw out such a powerful aid to the project manager, *just because a few crafty players use it to the project's detriment?*

That's my question. Why should we weaken the punch? I hate to see the total-float column masked, because total-float gives a sort of *perspective* to things. Remaining-durations, and even earliest-dates or latest-dates, may convey meaningful information. But total-float numbers put it all in perspective. It's CPM's best attempt to suggest priorities. Without priorities, everything is critical—and hence *nothing* is critical.

My solution to this quandary is to substitute, or supplement, the total-float column with the free-float column. Trust me on this point: *In well over 90 percent of all Project Schedules produced anywhere on the planet, greater than 90 percent of all activities have free-float values under five (5) workdays!* What this means is that, odds are, the vast majority of all activities on any given Schedule Extraction will read "critical." The squeaky wheel squeaks loud and clear, the project manager's weapon continues to fire, and the contractor's justification for being lax is removed. Try it—it works!!

Total-Float

In the following subsection, we will discuss the practical allocation of total-float, and in particular the use of time contingencies for the expectation of future delays.

Total-Float Ownership

Who owns a project's total-float? First I'll give you the official spin; then I'll give you the backroom reality. Officially, it is up to the contract. More and more, contracts are declaring up front that total-float belongs equally to the owner and the contractor. When contracts don't specifically designate the distribution, the courts have reached consensus during the final years of the 20th century that total-float belongs to the project alone. In analysis of time-related claims, though—such as for delay or acceleration—total-float is treated as having been "consumed" on a first-come-first-served basis.

If you take this arrangement to its logical extension, then if a contractor submits an *initial* schedule for review and approval, and that *initial* schedule shows one month of "float," between the projected and contractual end dates—then that *initial* float is automatically allocated between the two parties.

For this reason, no sane contractor would ever issue a schedule showing total-float in the initial submittal, unless he had already taken as much total-float as he wanted, and there was still more total-float left over. And that's the backroom reality! *In practice*, all initial total-float belongs to the contractor simply because he has the first (and, momentarily, *exclusive*) access to it—at the time the Execution Schedule is being developed.

In this sense, the contractor owns the total-float. Call it *squatter's rights*. With the Project Schedule sufficiently sprinkled with distributed total-float (in the form of padded relationship and activity durations), the project early completion might either be the same as the contractual end date, or earlier. If earlier, the contractor would be entitled to an equitable adjustment, if any owner-caused delay had prohibited him from achieving that earlier completion. There is case law on this.

Any total-float that materializes after the initial logic and durations are entered into the computer and the Calc button is pressed becomes immediately apparent to the contractor. He then has this unique, once-in-the-lifetime-of-the-project opportunity to hoard the total-float for himself. If he doesn't, it's up for the grabbing!

Owners reading this passage will no doubt take exception to my words. To them, I ask for a few more moments of tolerance; read on, please. To the drooling contractor who thinks he sees in my words a professional endorsement for "padding a schedule," wipe your mouth and read on, as well.

Within ethical limits there is a legitimate argument for burying what might *initially* be considered total-float. Beyond those limits, I believe it behooves the contractor to relinquish the surplus time as project total-float. The fundamental question, then, is what are those *ethical limits?* To answer this, I must remind the reader, at the risk of annoying repetition, that Project Scheduling is an inexact science. As I noted earlier:

No matter how exact a Project Schedule's activity-durations, and no matter how realistic its logic ties, one can never escape the ultimately "guesstimated" nature of the Project Schedule.

When all is said and done, a Project schedule is nothing more than hundreds (or thousands) of activities, each with an estimated activity-duration, logically tied to show human interaction (predictions of future behavior) within the context of an overall construction approach that makes an infinite number of assumptions about future space, time, performance, condition, need, and surprise.

It is the word *performance* in the last sentence that matters most to this discussion about total-float. Let me digress for a moment and ask you to consider what a relationship-duration is all about. In PDM, activities can be depicted as overlapping. Two activities, Activity A and Activity B, each ten days in length, can be depicted as being overlapped by five days. In PDM jargon, Activity A precedes Activity B with a start-to-start of five days.

But what do those five days represent? Two possibilities: work, or a passage of time. Both arguments have merit. In a physical sense, we are saying that 50 percent of Activity A must be completed before Activity B can be started. At least, that's how most Scheduling Practitioners would interpret the relationship. And once Activity A's remaining-duration has been reduced by five days, Activity B would be free to start.

What we need to get to, in this discussion, is what was in the heads of those creating the Project Schedule when they determined that, to some quantifiable extent, the start of Activity B should be linked to the start of Activity A. What was *their* thinking?

Again, two possibilities: either a material constraint between the elements of work represented by the activities in question, or a logistic, resource, or trade restraint between the performers of those activities. Perhaps the two activities involve the same limited physical space in which only one contractor can function effectively at a time. Or, perhaps the nature of the work is such that it doesn't make sense to "call" the second contractor until it is seen that the first contractor is "well underway" with his work.

In either of the two examples just given, the start-to-start relationship is the Project Scheduler's attempt to represent a management attitude or strategy into the computer model. If you still don't accept my argument then try defending the argument that a start-to-start of, say, four or three, or six or seven is more "right" or "wrong" than the given quantity of five (5). You can't—and that's because relationship-durations are the most subjective elements of a CPM schedule.

Subjectivity is not necessarily bad either. Opponents of PDM, diehard ADM advocates, have long argued that PDM logic fosters deception – specifically within the relationship-durations. While I am not a gun advocate, I would agree with the argument that it is not the gun, but the shooter, that kills. Similarly, it is not relationship-durations themselves, but rather their unscrupulous or irresponsible use, that distort otherwise legitimate CPM logic. And such misconduct could be perpetrated just as readily with an ADM schedule.

The prudent and responsible Project Scheduler or project manager will not create an Execution Schedule that he knows to be unrealistic. An unrealistic Project Schedule serves no useful purpose—not even if it is being created to "set up" for a downstream claim. An unrealistic schedule, rolled out in court, will be exposed for what it really is— a trumped up attempt to fake out a jury and a judge. Realism prevails in that ultimate arena—and unrealistic Project Schedules most certainly have no place or role in the hands of the project manager who sincerely wants a management tool that he can rely upon with confidence.

At the outset of this chapter I spoke of *ethical limits* to the contractor's hoarding of what might otherwise become total-float. It was in the context of the relationship-duration, and the individual justification for each relationship-duration, that I spoke of ethical limits. An initial Project Schedule can be elongated or shortened rather easily, and significantly, by merely adjusting relationship-durations ever so slightly. As long as each separate adjustment is backed by a realistic and consistently applied rationale, the resultant Execution Schedule will remain believable and entirely useful. I am not in support of arbitrary or capricious schedule manipulation for the sake of forcing a desired result.

Time Contingency

But what about the practice of *burying float* somewhere in the deep recesses of a schedule? Frankly, I'm for it! But it still comes down to why, how much, and where.

Why takes us back to the ethics question. Every construction project has a degree of unpredictability to it—if for no other reason than that the work will be performed in the future. And until humans can consistently and completely predict the future, they will have a prudent need to *plan* for the unknown. If the purpose of burying float in an Execution Schedule is to inject a time contingency factor into the Project Schedule, then I'm okay with that. It adds realism to the Project Schedule. It makes the projected end date more believable, more stable, more probable, and more likely to be achieved.

How much time should be buried? To answer this, we must separate in our minds the difference between a known-unknown and an unknown-unknown. A *known-unknown* refers to some element(s) of the project (known) about which the estimated duration is unclear (unknown). An excellent example of this is the replacement of utility lines located above a plastered ceiling. We know that *some* amount of replacement will be required, but until the ceiling is at last removed and the old utility lines exposed, it is impossible to know just how many lines will need to be replaced. We may, for purposes of the Project Schedule, estimate a two-week duration to the replacement activity, but we may be 50 percent short, or long. We may want to add some time contingency to the Execution Schedule for this known-unknown.

There is, then, the *Unknown-unknown* condition, which must always be expressed in the singular for if we can distinguish more than one then each would be a known-unknown. This unknown-unknown is another way of saying: "*I know something's gonna go wrong on this job. I don't know when. I don't know where. I don't know how big or how small. But I* know *something's gonna bite me in the behind.*" This is admittedly a very subjective position and hardly a strong rationale for burying time in a Project Schedule.

If the end date of a project is of *such* importance that many others will be relying heavily on its certainty, then it is my opinion that a small amount of time contingency is appropriate. How much is a "small amount?" My rule of thumb is somewhere between one to five percent of project length. However, I *rarely* have found justification for an unknown-unknown contingency greater than 3 percent of project length, although once in a blue moon an occasion arises which argues strongly for a hefty time contingency. On an eighteen-month project, a 5 percent contingency rate would result in a 3.9-week contingency; a 2 percent rate, 1.5 weeks.

And *where* would I recommend you bury this project-level contingency? That depends on which type it is. Unknown-unknown contingency should be buried toward the very end of the project[3]. For one thing, there can be no rationale for placing the contingency at any earlier point in the Execution Schedule, since by definition it is *unknown* when or where the calamity will hit—*if* it will hit at all.

The other reason, and the more significant one, is that you do not want the contingency to become real. If you were to locate the time contingency up front, for example, then all activities subsequent (or downstream) from the contingency would be "delayed" even before the project starts. The earliest-start dates for these follow-on activities would be later than necessary, *due to an arbitrary* and theoretical consumption of time by the contingency factor. Project participants, relying on the dates appearing in this first Schedule Edition, would plan their arrivals to site accordingly. The artificially induced delay would become a self-fulfilling prophecy.

Also, when you locate the unknown-unknown contingency at the end, it has the effect of advancing the *latest*-dates. This, in turn, would create lower total-float values and a greater sense of urgency. Project momentum would accelerate in reaction to the now-earlier latest-dates, and this would have the effect of generating the slack that the unknown-unknown will ultimately consume, if it occurs. If it doesn't occur, the project finishes a little earlier.

As for known-unknowns, the desire would be to place the contingency as near as possible to the activities to which the time contingency seems related—but always at the end of those activities, never at their start or during. The same underlying rationale applies: you don't want to artificially delay anything. Contingency is just a *bank* of time that is to be reduced *only* if an overrun occurs due to the unknown element.

As a practical suggestion concerning all buried total-float, make sure you keep a very detailed list in your Schedule Development file as to where all of the contingency amounts

---

[3]An objective and forthright way of doing this is to create an activity called "Unknown-Unknown Time Contingency," give it a duration and locate it immediately before the last activity in the schedule, called "Project Complete." Another less blatant method would be to add a nonzero duration to *all* ties linking into the Project Complete activity. This method is less preferable because it is more cumbersome to install and maintain, and because it is less visible, and hence may lead to a perception, right or wrong, of impropriety on the part of those "burying float" in the schedule. This impression would be bolstered by the absence of a descriptor, such as would have been available had a specific activity been used instead. A third option would be to block out time in the calendar.

are buried. You'll need to know this when it comes time to *draw down* on the bank, should those unknowns begin to hit your job.

To bring closure to this whole matter of total-float, clarity demands that I emphatically restate that *once time contingencies and management factors have been built into your Project Schedule, any remaining slack becomes total-float*—and, hence, is relinquished equally to the contractor and the owner, unless the contract says otherwise.

Activity Total-Float

For starters, with conventional CPM, there is no such thing! Within the science and methodology of the Critical Path Method, there is no definition of *activity total-float*. Total-float belongs to a *string of activities*, and not to any single activity.[4] Using the conventional definition that a *critical*-path is the "longest path," an activity that resides on the critical-path is deemed to be critical. But this is not to say that the activity *is* intrinsically critical, only that it resides on a critical-path. It is *critical by association*.

Consider a letter to the editor[5] that I came across recently, in which a 30-year veteran of project management contributed his "pearls of wisdom" in response to the trade journal's call for the same. One of his eight pearls read: *"There are two kinds of important matters: those intrinsically important and those in which someone important has taken a personal interest."* Here, too, importance by association is distinguished from what is "intrinsically" important.

The reason I am making a point about the nonexistence of *activity* total-float is because it is so often incorrectly cited. Please understand what I am *not* saying: I am not saying that there is no such thing as a *critical activity*. To the contrary, activities can indeed be critical. In every project, some activities are more critical than others are, and some are so critical that their performance can have profound effects on project outcomes.

The question, then, becomes: *how does one define* critical*?* In other words, what makes one activity critical and another not? And what makes one activity *more* critical than another activity? The answer to these questions is covered extensively in Chapter 16 in the section "Criticality." Here, I am concerned with the appropriateness of using an activity's mere presence on a critical-path as the sole reason for calling that activity *critical*.

Finally, you will recall that, in Chapter 7, I discussed an innovation called Discrete Activity Float. While within Momentum Science there are intricate formulas to derive this value, my point here is that the current CPM methodology doesn't define total-float for the individual activity. It merely attributes to the activity the total-float and free-float of the path on which it resides. We mustn't lose sight of this distinction.

---

[4]Except, where the activity path is comprised of only *one* activity, a fairly rare occurrence (except on over-tied schedules).
[5]Engineering News-*Record*, October 7, 1996.

Redundant Citation of Total-Float

If there is no such thing as *activity* total-float, then what about that number appearing in the "total-float" column of most Performance Control reports alongside each activity? The answer, sadly enough, is that it is blatantly misleading *in two significant ways*:

- It does not represent the *activity's* unique total-float (see previous heading).
- It redundantly cites the *path's* total-float.

A debate I had with a fellow Practitioner illustrates the second bullet. I asked him to imagine that a couple suddenly dies in a car crash and leaves behind a $1,000,000 estate. There are four offspring. What are the different possible distributions of the estate? I could think of only three:

- One child gets $1,000,000 and the other three children get zip.
- The estate is split evenly, each child getting $250,000.
- Some other, nonequal, distribution, where the total distributed amount equals $1,000,000.

"Okay," Jim said, "where's the problem?"

"Well," I responded, "an identical letter was sent by the lawyer to each of the four children, in which was a listing of the four children by name, and alongside each child's name was the sum $1,000,000. The estate *total* was never mentioned. Each child thought he/she was going to receive $1,000,000."

"So, the letter was misleading," said Jim, dismissing my example and the minor point it was making.

"But we do that with total-float, too. Ten activities comprise a single *string* of activities. The total-float value represents the maximum amount of excess time that the *string* enjoys. Yet we report the same total-float amount alongside each of the ten *activities*. At the very least, this is misleading, no?" In the faint yellow tint of a street lamp, I could see Jim starting to smile.

Conventional Employment of Total-Float is Unfair and Counterproductive

Anyone who uses the total-float value to opine on the condition of a project or the relative criticality of one activity over another is well advised to recall that *total-float belongs to the string*. When we consider how total-float is conventionally employed, two serious flaws become apparent:

- It is inherently unfair. The way we report total-float is tantamount to telling the children of the deceased couple, *"Hey, there's a million bucks here. Whoever gets here first, gets the dough. The rest of you are plumb out of luck!"*
- It encourages the squandering of total-float. That first activity on the string sees the total-float amount and thinks, *"Gee, I can relax a bit. Who can yell at me if I finish without going negative? The way I see it, it's a case of use it or lose it."*

Interpretation of Total-Float: The Weight Loss Example

Just as irrational as the idea of telling four children that each will receive $1,000,000 when the entire estate totals no more than $1,000,000 is the idea of ignoring past performance in predicting future outcomes.

Hey, I started a weight loss program four weeks ago. At the end of the first week, I had lost two pounds. In the second week, I lost an additional two pounds. In the third and fourth weeks, I lost two more pounds, each. I am now eight pounds lighter than when I began. I intend to continue with this program for another ten weeks. Assuming there is no such thing as a "plateau," what would be a reasonable expectation of the *total number of pounds I could lose by the end of 14-weeks?"*

The right answer, according to conventional interpretation of total-float numbers is (drum roll) *eight!* Yep. I have lost eight pounds to date, and even though I fully expect to adhere to the plan over the next ten weeks just as I have over the last four, I expect no further weight loss!

How is that argument, admittedly ridiculous, any different from this scenario: I update the schedule for the first four months of a project, with each update recording a separate two-day loss of total-float. The project has another ten months to go, and I project that we will finish "eight days late" because the total-float value is currently minus eight?

15 Performance Recording

Once the Execution Schedule has been developed and adopted by the project team, it goes into heavy-duty use on a daily basis—at least we hope so! Actually, a well-developed Project Schedule will almost always start out enjoying some kind of honeymoon period with the project team, for one simple reason. By definition, a "well-developed" Execution Schedule is one in which all members of the project team have had meaningful input into its creation. Like a proud parent, they each take initial delight in the product of their joint effort.

But then what? How can you ensure that the Project Schedule will be put to good use? And how can you increase the likelihood that it will remain relevant and vital for the duration of the project? Clearly, both of these questions can be answered in the context of *what comes out of the Project Schedule*—that is, the analyses, forecasts, and reports. Output will be handled in the next chapter. For right now, let's look at how to keep the schedule intact, how to preserve its integrity, and how to keep it simple. What follows is a discussion of some helpful hints, summarized in Figure 15-1, that are designed to steer you away from many common pitfalls of Performance Recording.

PERFORMANCE RECORDING ISSUES

There are a number of issues related to Performance Recording that, individually and collectively, affect the appeal and usefulness of your Execution Schedule. Here are some of the more significant ones.

Recording Frequency

As promised many chapters ago, I will now discuss the delicate balance between Performance Control frequency and the Project Schedule's level-of-detail. Of the two, the driving factor is the frequency of the Performance Control cycle.

Figure 15-1

Performance Control Helpful Hints

Establish Appropriate Update Frequency.
Sufficiently Engage Project Team.
Use Appropriate Progress Measurement Techniques.
Keep Sufficient Backups.
Predefine Conditions Warranting a Schedule Revision.
Keep All Parties, but Especially the Owner, in the Loop.
Perform Schedule Validation Checks.

There is a direct correlation between the frequency of Performance Reporting and Performance Recording. If you plan on monthly Performance Advisement, then it makes little sense to conduct Performance Recording every day, or even every week. The Performance Recording process is time consuming, expensive, and laborious. Each time you update an Execution Schedule, you run the risk of tampering with the logic, making inadvertent changes to Schedule components, and generating false or misleading information. Recording should be regarded with the same degree of respect afforded medical surgery. Don't enter into it lightly; weigh the benefits against the cost, each and every time.

The first question, then, is how often the Performance Control Reports should be issued. The answer to this one is almost always plural: different Performance Control Report types mandate different reporting frequencies. It all goes back to the *underlying* purpose for any Performance Control Advisory (whether a report, presentation, or face-to-face consulting), which is to respond to someone's need to know.

Upper management's need to know how the project is doing may arise on a monthly, quarterly, or even annual basis. By contrast, the project director's level of interest is, most often, at the monthly level as is typically the owner's upper management level of concern as well. The project manager, who receives different types of reports, might require some reports on a monthly basis, some on a weekly basis, and some as often as daily. Field superintendents of both the prime contractor and his subcontractors absolutely require information on a daily basis. Home office personnel, much like the design team, need weekly Schedule Extractions containing their commitments toward project goals and deadlines.

A general rule of thumb is to look at the shortest interval of need and move up from there, asking whether *stale* reports will do just as well. For instance, if the smallest interval is daily, then must the Project Schedule be *updated* every single day in order for the information to remain meaningful? On most projects that are scheduled in minimum activity-duration units of one-day (versus hourly scheduling, which is commonly used on maintenance, outage, or turnaround projects), the Execution Schedule need not be updated more often than once a week. The weekly Extraction Report is then *used* daily, even though Performance Recording is not conducted daily.

For most construction projects, the Execution Schedule is updated monthly with a new Performance Recording exercise, and Performance Control Reports are issued monthly, weekly, and sometimes (though not too often) daily. My advice to you is to be a bit more flexible, by considering a two-part program where the Performance Control cycle is more frequent at first and then monthly thereafter. Here's why.

Momentum Studies show that the majority of projects experiencing progress slippage during the first 10 percent of the project length complete *behind schedule*. A corollary to this is equally true. Call it the *80/20 Rule of Delay*: 80 percent of a project's delays occur during the first 20 percent of the project life cycle, as shown in Figure15-2. Together, these statistics suggest that there is great value to be gained by focusing on time-sensitive priorities during the initial period of the project. Then, once critical long leads items have been adequately expedited and once crucial submittals have been processed, the Performance Control cycle can be relaxed to a monthly rate.

Finally, in some types of work, the closeout of the project poses scheduling and timing concerns equal in importance to the issues that characterize the front end of a job. On systems-oriented projects, such as utility retrofits or projects involving major mechanical, electrical, or computer systems, the final phase of the project is performed on a system-by-system basis. Close coordination is required as the geographically aligned sequence of the earlier part of the Execution Schedule gives way to the systems-oriented closeout phase. Add to this the complex move-in requirements of an owner occupancy program, and you may need to resume a more aggressive Performance Control cycle toward the end of the project.

Who Should Participate

If Performance Recording is to be used as a part of validating progress payment requests, the broader the body of inspectors during a Performance Recording exercise, the more reliable and enduring the valuations. At a minimum, the general contractor's project manager or superintendent should accompany the subcontractor's superintendent *and* the Project Scheduler for the job progress walk-down. Ideally, both the project manager and superintendent should walk the job, and the architect and owner should join the inspection party.

The Performance Recording process is made easiest if each member of the inspection team carries his own copy of a Schedule Extraction Report especially designed for use during the job progress walk-down. This printout should be sorted first geographically,

Figure 15-2

80/20 Rule of Delay

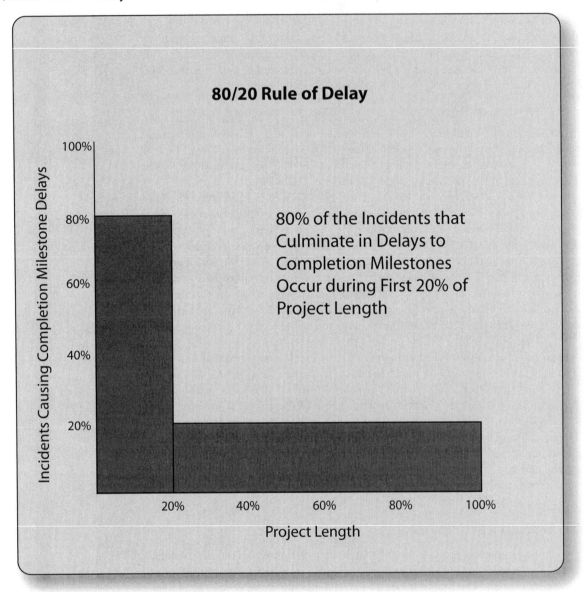

and then by earliest-start. The geographic sort allows the line items to coincide with a fixed, physical route that the inspection party takes each and every time.[1] The earliest-start subsort lists the items in their chronological order of performance. The printout should contain such information as original-duration, remaining-duration, percent-complete, and responsible party. Total-float may also appear, although this is not necessary.

---

[1]Adhering to a consistent and unwavering route facilitates meaningful comparison of visual documentation. This is especially useful when still or video pictures are taken during each update cycle.

Remaining-Duration vs. Percent-Complete

Sound Performance Recording involves establishing an appropriate progress assessment methodology, commensurate with the project's needs and the Execution Schedule's intended uses. So, which should you use: remaining-duration or percent-complete? This is another battleground among Scheduling Practitioners. Each method has a downside. Say that an activity has an original-duration of 10 days. As your inspection party stands out on the dusty floor staring upward toward some innocuous utility lines, the general consensus may emerge that the remaining work will require another two weeks. Fair enough. This is a legitimate estimate. But what percent-complete does that make the activity, assuming five days per week?

In the inverse, if you ask the other question, *"What percent complete is this work?"* the team might readily agree that the work is 60 percent complete. From this you would calculate that the remaining duration is four days. That's a long way from two weeks! So which method is correct?

I teach students in my Scheduling classes not to lose sight of the objective. We want to maintain the ability, at all times, to coordinate work and provide reliable date estimates for everything from the individual activity to the project's final completion. Of course, all estimates are based on the activity-duration—more specifically, its *remaining*-duration. Let's not forget that even on a brand new, unused Schedule, where the remaining-duration is equal to the original-duration, it is the remaining-duration (not the original-duration) that the computer uses in computing earliest-dates and latest-dates.

You'd be correct if you guessed that I favor the remaining-duration to the percent-complete method. To my thinking, the percent-complete number is a curiosity at best. True, it is utilized to calculate dollars earned (in connection with pay request reviews) in cost-loaded schedules, and it is important to Earned Value calculations. But you know how I feel about the use of the Execution Schedule to support cost-related efforts at the expense of weakening its Performance Control products and services. If these others applications can be accommodated without damaging the integrity of the Project Schedule, fine. Otherwise, find some other method; leave the Execution Schedule alone.

The percent-complete value is good to note, however. As in the preceding example where there is such a disparity between the two weeks (based on a remaining-duration approach) and the four days (based on a percent-complete approach), we need to look again at the original-duration.[2]

I encourage this kind of examination—and I'd go a step further (back at the office). If this type of disparity recurs on a number of similar activities, I'd seriously consider revisiting any other activities whose activity-durations were derived from the same source. If the source was wrong on enough activities to raise your curiosity, then what about other activities—most significantly, for future work yet to be started?

---

[2]We can bring the remaining-duration and percent-complete estimates into agreement by revising the original-duration to five weeks, or 25 days. Ten days remaining would also equal 40 percent remaining, or 60 percent complete!

"Similar" might also mean identical activities on different floors, or different activities of one contractor, or different activities in one physical area. Watch for the common denominator. It may be that the subcontractor gave you over-ambitious activity-durations during the Logic Development Sessions, or it may be that conditions in a certain geographic area of the project are such that work productivity is simply not what anyone would have expected. The problem may be more localized, meaning that maybe a certain activity is proving more difficult than initially expected. For more on this point, see Schedule Validation, later in this chapter.

Whatever the cause of the trend, investigate it. Turn it over, look at it from all angles; play with it. If you can isolate the source of the inconsistency between estimated and actual productivity, can that source be eliminated? If yes, great, because the Performance Recording process, as well as the Project Scheduler's dedication to his craft, will have benefited the project by spotting a future discrepancy before it is allowed to become a problem in reality.

If the source of the disparity cannot be discovered, then I strongly suggest that all related activity-durations in the suspect group be re-estimated in light of the trend to date. If this drives the end date out, so be it—deal with that reality! But don't sweep the information under the rug, hoping that it will miraculously cure itself. It won't. Besides, when it comes to dealing with lost time, *later is never better!!*

Performance Recording and Relationship-Durations—

Don't forget to look at these characters as well, for two reasons. First, some scheduling programs still require you to manually change relationship-durations just as you status the activity-duration. These programs tend to be less sophisticated and, by this quirk, betray their origins: they were ADM programs hastily converted to PDM programs, where nonzero relationships are nothing more than greater-than-zero dummy activities!

Second, relationship-durations require the same scrutiny given to remaining-durations. Carefully watch for disparities between the *planned* relationship-duration and the *actual* amount of time it took for a successor activity to start *after* a predecessor started. Look for patterns of inconsistency, by geographic area, by activity type, by responsibility. If you find them, re-examine all future relationship durations in light of this pattern.

Backups

Three words about back-ups: *make them—frequently!* Not only for the obvious reason that, should the computer crash, you'd lose everything, but also because of potential claims in the future. It is important to have a *separate electronic* copy of each Schedule Edition.

Be careful. Some scheduling software programs, such as P3, automatically *replace* the Project Schedule each and every time you tap the Enter button or click the mouse. It is vital that you do a *separate backup* under a different file name (perhaps one indicating the Edition number) for each Performance Control cycle. Then you'll be able to recreate the project's status at virtually any point in time. This ability will pay for itself a thousand times over should project disputes turn litigious.

SCHEDULE REVISIONS

Let's clear up some confusion in terminology: *revising* a schedule, *updating* a schedule, and *statusing* a schedule.

What Is a Revision?

Under the new Scheduling Practice Paradigm, Performance Recording includes both statusing and updating procedures. Note that Schedule Revisions are performed under Change Optimization.

They're listed here in reverse order.

- *Statusing* the schedule, something the Performance Recorder does, refers quite literally to the process of posting to the Schedule the current status of any activities that have experienced progress during the Performance Control period.

- *Updating* the Schedule, however, is broader in nature and includes walking the job to measure performance and *then* statusing the Schedule. Additionally, the scheduler will make any other *minor* adjustments to the Execution Scheduler, such as limited adjustments to activity-durations, logic ties, resource loads, calendars, and the like, to reflect reality.

- *Revisions* to a Project Schedule are, by conventional understanding, *major* changes to the *content* or *intent* of the Execution Schedule, and is also called rebaselining.

- *To Content*—in the sense of wide-scale changes in activity-durations, major adjustments to logic ties, or calendars, calculations settings, or similar.

- *To Intent*—goes to an entirely different level. Here, we're concerned with the Execution Schedule, as an overall representation of the Consensus Plan, being fundamentally *revised* to where the scope, approach, or conditions of the work is much different than previously intended.

What Precipitates a Revision?

Only one condition justifies a revision: the existing Execution Schedule is seriously out of sync with the reality of the project and/or how the balance of the project will be approached. Typically, three types of changes can precipitate a Schedule Revision: changes in scope, changes in conditions, or changes in planned, actual, or anticipated approach.

A Schedule Revision is often required when the scope of the work changes in some significant way, through one of the following:

- The addition of significant new work (not minor changes)
- A key change in requirements concerning existing work (for example, turnover sequencing)
- The removal of existing work

Similarly, if the project is so far behind or ahead of schedule that the Project Schedule's earliest-dates have no relationship to the reality beyond the jobsite trailer window, then a Schedule Revision may be in order. And, if the *actual* approach to the work (sequence, stacking, pacing, or prioritizing) differs appreciably from what the Project Schedule charted out, a revision is certainly necessary.

Keep Detailed Records

There is much one could say regarding revisions, mostly of a technical nature. In the interest of brevity, as well as to place greater emphasis on this thought, I will merely say this: keep very good records. Make sure you have a comprehensive file that details *every* change you make to the Execution Schedule—every duration change, every logic change, every description change, every coding change, and so on. Make certain that your notes are self-explanatory and will make sense to you if you don't read them again for another five years.

Keep the Owner in the Loop

As the old expression goes, *"If you're not part of the solution, you're part of the problem."* This is never truer than when it comes to keeping the owner squarely at the center of all decisions to revise the Project Schedule. The owner should be required to *authorize* and approve each Schedule Revision. Remember that revising a Project Schedule has extreme legal and contractual significance; do not enter into it lightly. Besides, many contracts require prior owner approval before making major revisions to the Baseline Schedule.

SCHEDULE PERFORMANCE ANALYSIS

A much-overlooked practice that is critical to proper Execution Schedule maintenance, as well as to ultimate Project Schedule reliability, involves constantly checking the Project Schedule for sustained dependability. The raw ingredients of all Project Schedules are estimates, assumptions, and strategies. At the outset of a project, there is often little else to go on. Durations are estimates of how long work will take to perform. Logic ties depict approaches to the work that reflect assumptions and execution strategies that are, in themselves, best guesses as to what makes the most sense in terms of project objectives.

When a given activity is one-of-a-kind, the exercise of comparing its underlying estimates, assumptions, and strategies to what, in point of fact, transpired may seem (and perhaps may actually be) more academic than beneficial. But for activities that are one of a set, the comparisons can be quite useful in sustaining or regaining the integrity of the Execution Schedule.

Imagine a 14-story building, with 14 essentially identical Floor Rough-In and Finishes subnetworks. Each subnetwork contains the same 54 activities, the only difference being the activity-durations on a few of the floors. For purposes of this example, let us consider the activity, Erect Metal Studs. Even though the activity-duration for this repeat activity is different on different floors, what if we find that on the first three floors, the contractor's *actual*-duration overran the original-duration by a consistent 15 percent? If, upon further investigation, we can find no other explanation except that the original-durations were unrealistically short, shouldn't we adjust the original-durations for the 11 identical activities that have *not yet begun*?

Similarly, what if we find that a particular relationship between two activities that exists in the original logic has not been honored in the real world? If, after ample study, we determine that the relationship tie was unnecessary, shouldn't we remove it from *yet unperformed work*?

The same question should be asked concerning relationship-durations. What if the start-to-start of five days between Erect Metal Studs and Hang Drywall has proven to be a start-to-start of seven days for three floors in a row? Shouldn't we adjust the remaining similar relationships, if further investigation suggests such an adjustment?

The idea of routinely checking the validity of initial estimates, assumptions, and strategies makes good sense. In fact, not doing so flies in the face of what Performance Control is all about. The Execution Schedule, at its core, is a project simulator. It starts out being that, and throughout the project lifecycle it is used to predict the future, based on the veracity of its depiction of future durations, assumptions, and execution strategies.

If we discover that a certain assumption was unfounded, are we not obligated by the tenets of professionalism as well as our commitment to the betterment of the project, to remove that assumption from the balance of the Execution Schedule, or replace it with a better assumption, one bolstered by real life experience?

Such modifications to future logic and activity-durations are *part* of the Schedule Performance Analysis process (or *should* be), and the changes mandated by the validation process, if major enough, might well justify a Schedule Revision, under the heading of *changed conditions*. If not so major, those changes are a part of the Performance Recording process. I treat the concept of Schedule Performance Analysis under its own heading, simply because it is so rarely done and yet is so critical to the goal of sustaining the Execution Schedule as a reliable document and dependable tool.

16 Performance Control

PERFORMANCE CONTROL, THE ULTIMATE OBJECTIVE

To this point, I have discussed the design, development, construction, and maintenance of the Project Schedule. But, unless we can derive real value from the Project Schedule, all of these earlier steps are for naught. So, in a very real sense, this entire book, dedicated to the proposition that Project Schedules actually will be *used*, boils down to *how* they will be used.

Performance Control involves three separate sets of procedures, each labeled as a different subspecialty. Performance Analysis encompasses a set of diagnostic exercises performed on information obtained during Performance Recording. Change Optimization uses the assessments reached during Performance Analysis to identify and select appropriate responses to changes in scope, conditions, or execution approach. Whether the full impact of such changes is blatant or transparent at the site level, Performance Analysis will reveal their presence. The decisions reached during Change Optimization determine how the project will proceed in light of these changes. Performance Advisement entails the communication of those decisions, in the form of Performance Control Reports and Consulting.

Examples of meaningful Performance Control Reports include:

- **Resource Performance Reports** A set of reports designed to critique and coordinate resource performance on the project. Resources include contractors, suppliers, design professionals, equipment, manpower, materials, and so on.
- **Management Performance Reports** A set of reports designed to critique and coordinate project management performance. Project management includes all nonproduction, project management personnel on the project who give direction and provide coordination or support those functions.
- **Schedule Performance Reports** A set of reports designed to critique the performance of the Project Schedule as a reliable and effective management tool.

- **Critical Issues Rack-Up** A report or report segment that summarizes the project's most critical issues in terms of time-sensitive goals achievement.
- **Hot Spot Highlights** A report or report segment that highlights the project's most significant problem areas, uncovered through Performance Analysis.

At their most succinct, Project Schedules are used for two primary reasons: to *understand* and to *communicate*. The combined efforts of Performance Recording, Performance Analysis, and Change Optimization help foster understanding of the project dynamics by way of measuring progress, analyzing reality, and optimizing future actions. Meanwhile, Performance Advisement communicates vital information, so that the project manager can effectively inform, coordinate, direct, and control actual performance.

USING THE PROJECT SCHEDULE TO UNDERSTAND

I happen to think that Performance Analysis is at the very epicenter of the Scheduling Practice. Here's why I say this: every project is dynamic, and it is riddled with surprises. The project manager's number one challenge is anticipating and coping with such surprises. He looks to the Project Schedule to give him as much advance warning as possible about upcoming surprises. And when he struggles to find a clever response to a surprise, he turns to the Execution Schedule again.

If the Project Schedule is not going to be useful *during* the project, then why bother having one at all? There is a wealth of invaluable information in the Execution Schedule, the majority of which is not apparent at the start. Only after the Execution Schedule is statused are certain important indicators detectable. A rigorous and consistent set of analytic processes is required to mine the critical information inherent within the Project Schedule. If pains are taken to extract this information, the project will surely benefit.

If you want to talk about what it takes to create Project Schedules that *"they'll actually want to use,"* then try telling the project management team something they didn't already know! The way that most of today's Scheduling Practitioners operate, Project Schedules are statused and printouts are issued—and little more. Whether they are Earned Value metrics or total-float reports, the traditional Scheduling reports rarely do more than report yesterday's sports scores; that is, what went up and what went down, who gained and who lost. But if the project manager is worth his salt, *he already knew* that his project had problems, and he already knew who the culprits were.

Solid analytic methods, like the ones covered in the next few pages, are guaranteed to yield information your project manager did *not* know. Innovative techniques like Dilemma Forecasting and Soft Ground Advisories can tell the project manager where the smoke is *going to* appear.[1]

---

[1] Let alone not waiting for signs of flames, these methods will detect conditions conducive to fire, even before the smoke appears.

This book is about creating Execution Schedules that will actually be used. It is not meant to provide an in-depth treatment of analytic methods.[2] What follows is merely meant to wet your whistle, to enhance your awareness of other techniques and methods that are available to you. I encourage you to investigate these powerful approaches and not to settle for the same old set of tired standards, ones that only yield sports scores!

Using the Schedule to Measure Progress

Perhaps the most frequently asked question on a project is, *"How's the job doing?"* Pushed to be more specific, the inquiring executive, probing for assurance that the project is performing pretty much as expected, rewords his question: *"How far along are we?"*

Types of Percent Complete

If we encourage our curious customer to be more specific still, he might say: *"What percent complete are we?"* But even if he isn't this specific, we can assume that that's what he is asking about, and so we couch our answer in terms of percent-complete estimates. But does a single value really exist that can accurately and fairly represent a project's true status? I say, *no.*

Consider each of these different ways of describing a project's status, all expressed as percent-complete estimates.

Project Length   This percent-complete calculation identifies where we are along the project timeline. Using the project start date as 0 percent complete, and the project (contractual) end date as 100 percent complete, if we are at the end of the sixth month of a 12-month project, in terms of project length, the project is at the 50 percent point.[3] Much like, *"Oh my gosh! The day's half over!"*

Labor Consumption   This percent-complete calculation compares *earned* labor hours to total estimated labor hours. Alternatively, it compares spent labor dollars to total estimated labor dollars. Either approach speculates on project percent-complete, assuming that there is reliability in both the estimate of total labor hours or labor dollars required to perform the complete scope of the project, and the estimate of percent-complete for each progressed activity to date, as determined through Performance Recording.

Capital Consumption   Similar to labor consumption, this percent-complete calculation compares actual costs to planned costs.[4]

---

[2]The third book in the Momentum Management set, *How to Get the Most Out of Project Schedules,* will provide an in-depth treatment of Performance Control.

[3]This is not to imply that 50 percent of the work has been put in place.

[4]Both this and the previous method are often by-products of the Earned Value Management System.

Earned Duration-Days This percent-complete calculation compares duration-days completed (earned) to the aggregate of all activity-durations in the schedule. It reflects project status in terms of work performed, as opposed to labor or capital expended.[5]

Weighted Quantities This percent-complete calculation attempts to measure project status in terms of work in place. Every activity is associated with a quantity of work. Then, using some technique for weighting the relative value of such work, a percent-complete estimate is derived by comparing the aggregate of all work to be installed with the value of work thus far completed.

Activity Count Admittedly unsophisticated, some organizations simply divide the number of activities completed by the total number of activities in the Project Schedule to derive a crude percent-complete estimate.

Observation-Based Status This percent-complete method only works on certain kinds of projects, those where the scope of the project is predominantly one type of work. Examples include tunneling, roadwork, software development (not design), report writing, high-rise structural work, and the like. The idea is that one can make a percent-complete determination based on what is observed. If tunneling has reached the halfway point, it is 50 percent complete. If a report-writing project has completed rough text for half of the proposed outline, it is 50 percent complete.

It should be obvious that each percent-complete method comes with its own limitations, just as it has its own significance and usefulness. But what should we make of contradictions between the findings of different methods? Obviously, such disparities can be insightful. If we are only 25 percent complete according to weighted quantities, activity count, and earned duration-days, but we're 50 percent complete according to labor and capital consumption, we know where at least a part of the problem lies.

The main point I'm trying to make under this heading is to use only those methods that are appropriate for the type of work involved and for the project's success criteria. For example, if the owner is more concerned about time than money or quality, then percent-complete estimates should be formulated *in terms of time*. Using duration-days to measure percent complete would be far more pertinent than using consumed labor hours. This, of course, argues against relying too heavily on Earned Value's Schedule Performance Index as opposed to statistics derived directly from the Execution Schedule itself, when the Emphasis Alignment Model puts the red dot nearest the time vertex.

Performance Measurement

The primary goal of any performance measurement system is to provide useful information supportive of the project management effort. Management's key functions involve decision-making, problem solving, troubleshooting, and general program facilitation. Performance measurement and reporting should contribute to management's ability to perform these critical activities.

---

[5]Earned Duration-Days are a measure of *Performance Intensity* and are derived using Momentum formulas.

What Performance Is It That We Are Measuring and Reporting?   In a gross over-simplification, it is *project* performance that should be the target of our measurement and reporting. Yet no single unit of measure has been found that sufficiently measures the entire project. Rather, individual project components have been proven to be measurable and reportable.

Causes and Effects   I think it is important to distinguish between causative variables that *create* Project Momentum and resultant variables that reflect the *effects* of such causes. Since causative variables call upon us to speculate on the effects that might emanate from a cause, whenever possible, it is most desirable for performance analyses to measure and report on resultant variables, not causative variables.

Examples of *resultant variables* are Milestone Date (slippage or gain), Budget Goals (overruns or underruns), activities completed, milestones achieved, work completed, and so on. Examples of *causative* variables include man-hours consumed, dollars expended, days elapsed, and so on.

Earned Value as a Performance Indicator   Traditional Earned Value computations measure and report on causative variables, from which conclusions are *inferred* concerning probable outcomes. So conducted, Earned Value is an indirect method that interpolates project performance from specific resource consumption rates.

Furthermore, Earned Value can be rendered less reliable under circumstances where the underlying baseline values fail to inspire sufficient confidence. Typically, R&D programs make poor candidates for Earned Value computations, where historical data from other programs prove inadequate to bolster the baseline assumptions of the subject program.

Not all of its proponents realize that Earned Value implicitly relies on a concept known as the "measured mile." A clearly definable portion of the project is declared the *standard*, or "measured mile" and, against this segment, all other similar work is compared. This apples-to-apples comparison is a fundamental aspect of Earned Value. However, on projects where there is little repetitive work, the applicability of Earned Value is dramatically reduced. This point was amply discussed in Chapter 14.

Other Performance Indicators   For management to acquire the broadest understanding of project performance, a *number* of performance gauges are required, each with unique measurement and reporting features. Some gauges monitor *causative* variables; others monitor *resultant* variables. Only through multiple perspectives can project management "vector in" on the project's most critical performance achievements, anomalies, and obstacles.

It would be difficult to overstate the significance of this point. Achieving successful projects requires project management to be responsive to such anomalies and obstacles. Needed then are sensors and tell-tales that provide the earliest reliable notice of impending danger. To this end, I encourage you to employ an intelligently cross-referenced *set* of performance monitoring methods and tools, rather than putting all your eggs in one basket (such as we do with unidimensional Total-Float Reports).

To give you some food for thought, I recommend you study the value of multiple, well-established performance measurement methods/tools, such as the following:

- Program Health Number
- Percent Complete Comparisons (seven different percent completes, discussed earlier)
- Quantity-based Measurement
- Momentum Analytics
- Manpower Profiles
- Labor Statistics
- Schedule Credibility
- Schedule Vulnerability
- Schedule Resiliency
- Schedule Relevancy
- Cash Flow Profiles
- Performance Intensity

In terms of information reporting, emphasis *must* be *pro*active, rather than *re*active. The ultimate objective should not be forgotten: to help Management effectively perform its decision-making, problem solving, troubleshooting, and project facilitating duties. Sports casting, reporting yesterday's wins and losses, does little to help the project manager deal with tomorrow's issues. For this, I suggest management-targeted reports, such as the following:

- Dilemma Forecasting
- Soft Ground Advisories
- Momentum Tracking
- Critical Issues Rack-up
- Management Performance Report
- Contractor Performance Report
- Delay Mitigation/Avoidance Report

Using the Project Schedule to Analyze Reality

The new Scheduling Practice Paradigm introduced by this book expands our understanding of *realty* beyond mere field performance. We are equally concerned with the performance of management, as well as with the Execution Schedule as a reliable management tool. In the following subsection, we will consider different ways to measure and analyze Schedule Compliance.

Schedule Compliance

This is an area of Performance Control that is rarely discussed in texts on project management or project scheduling. Yet, there is a rather ordinary, almost instinctual interest in how closely the Execution Schedule is being *followed*. This interest is greatest during post-project analyses for or against allegations of delay, acceleration, or loss of productivity. But even *during* the project life, there is a natural reaction, positive and negative, to how well project participants align their actions with the sequencing and pacing required by the Execution Schedule.

We should also keep in mind the distinction between causative variables and resultant variables when measuring and reporting progress. Whenever possible, it is most desirable for Performance Analyses to measure and report on resultant variables, not causative variables. Consider the ways in which the contractor's performance is monitored in terms of the Project Schedule:

- Will the activity start on time?
- Will the activity finish on time?
- Will the activity complete within the number of days allowed by the activity-duration?
- Are activities being performed in the same sequence as depicted in the Execution Schedule?
- Are the contractor's human and other resource commitments commensurate with what was originally estimated and promised?
- Are the contractor's declarations of activity completeness consistent with the understood activity scope at the time the Project Schedule was created?

The questions asked during claims analysis are not much different, long after all project dust has settled. In order to prove (or defend against) allegations of delay, acceleration, or loss of productivity, the claims consultant will consider the following:

- Did the activity start on time?
- Did the activity finish on time?
- Did the activity complete within the number of days allowed by the activity-duration?
- Were activities performed in the same sequence as depicted in the Execution Schedule? Were any activities performed out-of-sequence?
- Did the contractor provide human and other resources in amounts greater than or equal to what was estimated and promised?
- Was the contractor's declaration(s) of activity completeness consistent with the understood activity scope at the time the Project Schedule was created?

Okay, so compliance with schedule assumptions is of great interest both during and after the project. But is such compliance inherently important? What should we make of evidence that the Execution Schedule was *not* followed or, worse, abandoned altogether? The reason I am wasting ink on this entire heading is because I have seen too many instances where wrong or unbalanced assumptions were made. Now, given that this is a book about *using* the schedule, I will drop all concern with this issue's influence on claims work and instead limit my comments to the interests of project management. Accordingly, then, how would misinterpretation of schedule noncompliance affect the utility of the Project Schedule?

Flexibility   One answer has to do with the concept of flexibility and lies in an often-understated need for the Project Schedule (and those who use it) to remain flexible. When I was a boy, my father (a Golden Gloves boxer) explained the meaning of the expression *roll with the punch*. In the ring, fighters bounce on their toes and slowly rotate in a counter-clockwise direction. From one side to the other, the boxers shift their balance from one leg to the other. But it is the *left* leg that is always ready to spring the body to the right and backward, so that when the opponent throws his right punch, he can *roll with the punch* and lessen the impact to his body.

The wise constructor will watch for opportunities to exploit the project. But unless his workforce is flexible, ready to *roll with the punch,* what good is such alertness? Ask 100 Scheduling Practitioners or claims consultants whether they consider work performed out-of-sequence as either good or bad, and 90 percent will say, *"Bad."* But doesn't the answer depend on *why* the work was performed out-of-sequence?

I can think of countless reasons why it would be more responsible, prudent, and beneficial to perform work differently than scheduled, whether that means out-of-sequence, slower than scheduled, faster than scheduled, or with different resources than scheduled. And every one of those reasons would appeal to the common sense of a concerned owner or a fair-minded jury.

Most contracts impose a requirement on the contractor to *mitigate* delay. *"Time is of the essence"* is a phrase commonly inserted into most construction contracts. The contractor that does not think on his feet and compensate for sudden surprises on the project is to be criticized, not praised.

In my opinion, the number one reason for ignoring an Execution Schedule element (interdependency, activity-duration, activity start date, and so on) is because the assumptions behind that Execution Schedule element were flawed in the first place or didn't anticipate a change (in scope, approach, or conditions) now facing the project. Of the two primary categories of Execution Schedule elements, durations and logic, the latter is more often flawed from the get-go. This should make sense since activity-durations are mostly based on known, measurable quantities, while most interdependencies are far more subjectively assigned.

In Chapter 10, I discussed the important difference between Administrative Time Gaps and Productive Time Gaps. From that section you should now appreciate why relationships and their durations are so often wrong to start with. So, when a contractor violates a logic tie, does this necessarily evidence incompetence or insubordination?

Finally, the reader is encouraged to be forever mindful of the different conditions that logic ties are called upon to simulate. I can think of four:

- Material Constraints
- Logistic Constraints
- Resource Constraints
- Administrative Constraints

A *material constraint* is one in which Activity B is restrained by Activity A in some material way (some call this a "mechanical lock"). I don't mean "material" in the sense of physical materials that the two activities share. Rather, I mean that there is something inherently dependent between the two activities in terms of the work itself. Perhaps Activity B involves painting a wall, and Activity A entails the erection of that wall. Or, Activity B is the laying of pipe, and Activity A is the excavation of the trench.

Another popular constraint is the *logistic constraint*, where Activity A and Activity B cannot be in the same room at the same time. So, the Execution Scheduler links the two activities sequentially. In reality, it doesn't matter (materially) which one goes first. It should follow, then, that if a subsequent out-of-sequence condition evolves, where Activity B happens before Activity A, there is nothing particularly wrong with this reversed order of attack.

A third use of interdependencies is to depict a *resource constraint*. Here, we refer to two activities that require the same resources. Obviously, if you are using the mobile crane at one end of the site, I cannot be using it at the other end of the site. Like the logistic constraint, the particular order chosen during Schedule Development may not be the same as what evolves in the field. But this out-of-sequence condition is not necessarily indicative of incompetence or blatant disregard for the Project Schedule.

Finally, there are *administrative constraints*. These are interdependencies introduced into the Execution Schedule to reflect the will of the project management team, including the owner. Perhaps it has been decided that the work will flow west to east. Perhaps floor finishes are to be completed from the top floor, downward.

Realism   There is another reason for Performance measurement, however, which *only* applies during the life of the project, not afterward. The Project Schedule is, above all else, a computer model. To be a reliable one, as realistically as possible it must represent the execution strategy for the remaining work of the project. As the project progresses and as departures from planned durations and logic naturally occur, the portion of the Execution Schedule covering the project's yet-unfinished scope of work should be re-examined in light of these departures. This point was discussed at length in Chapter 15, "Performance Recording." Here, let me just say that if a particular subcontractor's activity-durations are consistently overrunning by 20 percent for the first third of the project, they'll probably be overrunning by 20 percent for the other two-thirds of the project.

Trending   I tip my hat to EVMS because it at least tries to look at project performance as an evolving trend and not as a series of independent snapshots. Sadly, CPM does the latter. You will recall my earlier comments about the silliness of ignoring trends. A project loses one week per month for the first three months of a two-year project. At the end of the third month it has a project total-float of –15 days. The conventional interpretation of this value is that, 21 months later, the project will finish 3 weeks late. This blatantly ignores the project trend. At a loss rate of one week per month, shouldn't we expect the project to finish 24 weeks late?

There are many other trends one can watch, as well. Per contractor, or per geographic area, watch for changes in the percent of activities starting on time, of work completing within their original-durations, of subcontractors using planned resources (minimally), or relationship-durations proving adequate, and so on.

Criticality

It seems to me that this is the most-used expression in construction. Given the phenomenal influence of the *Critical* Path Method, I guess this is not surprising. The problem is that Criticality is *only* defined in terms of the critical-path, and that to me is unfortunate. Let me give you a few reasons why I say this:

1. Just because an activity resides on a critical-path doesn't make the activity critical. Just because I attend a Senate hearing doesn't make me a Senator.

2. Even if every activity on a path is automatically critical just because the path is critical, I'm not convinced that the path itself is necessarily critical just because it has the lowest total-float value. This book is overflowing with reasons why total-float values are among the least reliable indicators in the entire CPM methodology. With accuracy swings as great as 30 percent[6] across the span of a project, it becomes laughable to split hairs over one or two days here or there. And yet, so terribly often only a few days distinguish "critical" from "noncritical" paths.

3. Total-float values are unstable; they change with every update, and paths (as defined or ranked by total-float) flip around like a snapped power line thrashing randomly in the night. One minute an activity is *critical,* and the next minute it is not. Is this any way to manage a project?

4. Criticality ought to be defined in terms of the Emphasis Alignment Model, and that doesn't *always* translate into a timely project completion date *only*. What if the owner is more concerned about saving money than finishing sooner? In that case, performing as many labor-intensive activities as possible before labor rates go up, even if those activities are *not* on the project's critical-path, may make a lot of sense.

5. One man's *critical* is another man's *optional*. We have discussed elsewhere in this book that each participant to the project arrives at the jobsite with his own agenda, his own priorities, and his own fears. Take, for example, the project manager who is called back to the home office for three days to help put together a bid on another job. For three days, his responsibilities at the jobsite will slip. But what is more critical to the project manager, protecting the ephemeral critical-path, or keeping the president of the construction company on his good side, and perhaps lining up his next job assignment in the process?

Another example can be found with the subcontractor who needs a concrete mixer on another project, where the financial stakes are higher if he finishes late. So, on your job, he accelerates his work on all activities that require the concrete mixer, even if these activities have significant positive total-float.

---

[6]From Momentum Studies.

I have spent over 20 years studying the concept of Criticality and have developed a number of different standards by which an activity can be classified as *critical,* all beyond total-float. Here are just a few.

Activity Placement   Compare two activities on the same path, each with the same total-float value; let's say, +2. Assume that one activity occurs within the first week of the project, while the other one occurs within the last week of the project, and that the job is two years long. Which activity is more critical? I hope you agree that the one toward the end of the project is because, if it slips by even a day, there is essentially no time left to make up for any slippage that might occur so late in the project lifecycle.

You may be thinking that the timing of an activity within the network is of only theoretical importance since the typical use of float is to ignore *distant* activities and compare contemporaneous *present* activities. But my illustration may have clouded the point. Consider a Project Schedule that contains five contractual milestones, the first of which is approaching within two weeks. The short path, spanning from project start to this first milestone has a total float of +5. Another path, completely unrelated and also bearing a total-float of +5, spans from project start to project completion, two years away. Two activities, one on each path, are both to be completed this week. Which is more critical? Now do you see my point?

Relationships Aggregation   Two activities have the same total-float. But one activity is followed by 9 downstream activities, while the other has 27 activities following it. This is not the same as the *Activity Placement* condition. There, we were concerned with the cumulative duration-days between the activity in question and the deadline it leads to (and against which total-float is measured). Here, we are concerned with the number of activities that depend on its timely performance. The reason activity count is significant is fascinating (at least it is to me).

Which of the following has a greater chance of schedule slippage, one 10-day activity, or 10 one-day activities? The latter, because the presence of 10 activities implies 10 different players, or at least more than one player, right? And even if one player performed all 10 activities, the nature of the activities would be different, right? Otherwise, why would we divide a single activity performed by a single player into 10 activities?

So, whether what is changing per activity is scope or performer, the more activities per path length, the greater the likelihood of *hand-offs.* And each hand-off also kicks off a learning curve. Each learning curve represents an unmeasured amount of inefficiency, different types of equipment and material, and increased probability of surprises, the key cause of delay.

And there is yet another reason why multiple activities create more risk to deadline achievement than a single activity of equal length: Administrative Time Gaps. We will establish later in this text that *every* activity is prevented from starting until one or more Administrative Actions take place. We have already noted elsewhere in this book that the majority of project slippage occurs *between* activities, mostly due to belated or incomplete performance of Administrative Actions.

So, measured against the standard of *Relationships Aggregation*, it may be more *critical* to the overall health of the project to complete an activity with a total-float value of +26 than one with a total-float value of +2. Surely you recognize that this measure of Criticality supports proactive management of the project. In firefighting, it is sometimes more prudent and *critical* to fall back from the fire line and perform a controlled burn a half-mile away, in order to create a fire break, than it is to continue pouring water on the raging fire.

Confluence Aggregation   Picture an activity standing at the start of a path that is 31 activities long. Now picture another activity that precedes three 10-activity paths. In either case, the activity affects the start of 30 subsequent activities. But is one configuration more conducive to slippage than the other? I think the latter condition is more challenging to the Project Schedule, because it introduces the concept of concurrence. With three paths running concurrently, supervision requirements increase, and turf battles for limited real estate increase as well.

If the three paths are all being performed by the same organization under the auspices of the same supervisor, then his oversight is being spread three times thinner than if the work were drawn out in one long path. If each of the three paths is being performed by three different organizations, then competition for space, access, traffic, staging, common utilities, and management support (for example, design conflict resolution) may all pose threats to the smooth and timely performance of the work. Measuring against the standard of *Confluence Aggregation*, it may be more critical to complete an activity with 19 downstream splits than one with only 3 splits downstream, even if the latter has a lower total-float value.

Schedule Resiliency   Every Execution Schedule has a limited ability to recover from incurred delay. I call this ability *resiliency*. Just how resilient a Project Schedule is can be measured. A resiliency value can be ascertained for the entire Execution Schedule or for any given path in the Project Schedule. A path resiliency value can be assigned to each activity on that path, much the same way we currently assign a path's total-float to all activities on a path.

An activity with a very low *Activity Resiliency* value means that if an activity is delayed, the ability of the activity to recover from the delay is remote. So, is it more urgent that a project manager focus attention on an activity with total-float of +35 but potential resiliency of 4 percent, or should he focus on an activity with total-float of +6 but with potential resiliency of 95 percent? Your answer will depend on how much importance you place on acting preemptively. The former is more proactive, the later more reactive.

Discrete Activity Float (DAF)   I am perhaps quite proud of this improvement to the Scheduling Practice, one that took me years to develop. To describe the concept in a nutshell, each activity is given a proportional *share* of the path's combined total-float and free-float amounts. I call this value Discrete Activity Float, or DAF. Don't kid yourself; the mathematical algorithms to achieve this seemingly simple exercise are immensely complicated. It took me nearly five years to develop the correct arithmetic rules to achieve a model of predictive merit and quantitative integrity.

Without exposing the gory insides of this beast, simply consider Table 16-1, which is an example of a noncritical path having five activities and a total-float of +30.

Activity	Duration	Path Percent	Discrete Activity Float	Total Float
Activity A	5	10%	3.0	30
Activity B	12	24%	7.2	30
Activity C	10	20%	6.0	30
Activity D	15	30%	9.0	30
Activity E	8	16%	4.8	30

Table 16-1

Discrete Activity Float; Non-Critical Path

Under the conventional CPM methodology, all five activities would be reported as having total-float of +30. Yet, based on the DAF value, Activity A is three times more critical than Activity D.

Now, let's introduce the Project Schedule's least-float path (bearing a positive total-float of +9), therefore constituting our Schedule's critical-path. It is comprised of the two activities, as shown in Table 16-2. Next we want to combine the two paths, critical (X, Y) and noncritical (A, B, C, D, E). If we combine all seven activities, we can see how DAF helps us prioritize activities that, according to total-float alone would lead us to an entirely different understanding of Criticality.

In Table 16-3's right panel, we see that using the measure of *total-float,* we can only separate the seven activities into two groupings. We are also under the impression that Activity X and Activity Y are more critical than Activities A through E, since the former two activities have the lesser total-float. By comparison, using DAF, the seven activities are individually ranked by Criticality.

There are several observations we can make as we compare the results of the two ranking methods:

- The total-float method yields higher numbers in general, which can lead to a false sense of confidence. Let's face it, is there really any reason to panic when an activity has 30 days of total-float?
- The DAF method takes into account the number of activities that share the path's total-float values. This creates lower DAF values, in turn creating a naturally higher sense of urgency among the activities' performers.
- The DAF ranking factors the relative size of activities, in terms of activity-duration. Smaller activities tend to have lower DAF values. This is preferable, because there

Activity	Duration	Path Percent	Discrete Activity Float
Activity X	10	33%	3.0
Activity Y	20	67%	6.0

Table 16-2

Discrete Activity Float; Critical Path

Table 16-3

Discrete Activity
Float and Total
Float Contrasted

Activity	Discrete Activity Float	Activity	Total Float
Activity X	3.0	Activity X	9.0
Activity A	3.0	Activity Y	9.0
Activity E	4.8	Activity A	30.0
Activity Y	6.0	Activity B	30.0
Activity C	6.0	Activity C	30.0
Activity B	7.2	Activity D	30.0
Activity D	9.0	Activity E	30.0

is strong evidence to support the need for management to keep a closer eye on smaller activities than larger ones, for two reasons:

- Every activity has a learning curve. Learning curves are *not* a function of the percent of an activity's duration, but rather a function of time itself. Hence, on a 10-day activity, the learning curve may be one day, or 10 percent. On a two-day activity, the learning curve may be a half day, or 25 percent. Typically, however, as the activity-duration shortens, the learning curve becomes a larger percent of the overall activity-duration.

- A delay that is incurred on a short activity has less remaining-duration available to it for delay recovery. If you are only 50 percent productive on the third day of a four-day activity, you have one day to make up the deficiency. If you are only 50 percent productive on the third day of a 20-day activity, you have 17 days to make up the difference.

- The DAF method promotes fairness among activity performers. By allocating to each activity only that portion of the path's free-float and total-float to which it has exclusive claim, contractors are less inclined to use "someone else's float." By contrast, with the conventional measurement of total-float, the first activity feels it has the "right" to take the *entire* path float for itself. One is hard-pressed to tell a contractor he cannot use the total-float that appears in a report that you gave him, one that showed him having nine days of total-float alongside his activities.

The point of this heading, "Criticality," is that there are many ways to determine what is critical. We must be careful not to assume that total-float is the *only*, or even the *best*, way to define Criticality. When we stop to consider the importance to the overall project management effort of knowing what is critical or not, the significance of this single subject cannot be overstated.

Using the Schedule to Optimize the Future

Change Optimization is a major subspecialty of the Scheduling Practice and is conducted as part of Performance Control. A skilled Change Optimizer will use information uncovered during Performance Recording and Performance Analysis to determine the optimum response to changes in scope, approach, or conditions. The work products of Change Optimization are various optimization scenarios, including those discussed in the next subsections.

Workarounds

Schedule workarounds are group-developed execution strategies designed to offset the effects of changes in scope, approach, or conditions. I encourage you to not codify theoretical modifications as a Schedule Revision unless such is truly needed. For instance, if you are merely trying to bring the project back on schedule and have developed an interim piece of logic that, if followed in the field, will do just that, it doesn't necessarily constitute a Schedule Revision. A helpful rule of thumb for knowing when a deviation from plan constitutes a Schedule Revision is whether it crosses two update periods.

Short-term workaround and catch-up strategies, even if they take the form of a handy little logic diagram, can be used outside the Execution Schedule in an effort to support its compliance and sovereignty. But don't be greedy—don't push the envelope too far. A few weeks of sidebar work plans is probably okay. But a month? That's pushing it. More than a month? You're looking at a Schedule Revision.

What-If Studies

One of the most overlooked uses of an automated CPM schedule is as a feasibility tool, useful in reasonably and easily projecting likely outcomes of different optimization scenarios. If the Execution Schedule has been properly maintained through Performance Recording, and if its representation of remaining work is as real as can be simulated, then the Execution Schedule stands ready to extend the power of computer modeling to problem-solving on the jobsite.

Performing what-if studies is no more difficult than making a backup copy of the Execution Schedule under a different file name and then *playing with it*. Don't be afraid to mess with the logic. Consider tightening up interdependencies. Look at doubling up crews or double shifting. Try changing to a six-day workweek. The possibilities are all in your head; use the computer to evaluate the merits of each of them.

Don't get too literal on the critical-path. Remember the margin of error inherent in all CPM schedules. But for a little duration adjustment here and a little logic snipping there, the critical-path could vary widely. Play with the Project Schedule and become a far more powerful Project Scheduler as you do. Just remember to keep detailed notes of all changes, so if you decide to go forward with all or some of them, you know what changes you made.

USING THE SCHEDULE TO COMMUNICATE

The other main use of the Project Schedule is to communicate vital information to the project team.

Using the Project Schedule to Inform

There are different communication uses of the Project Schedule, one being to inform.

What Constitutes Good Information?

It follows that the project manager's performance—as problem-solver, decision-maker, facilitator, or trouble-shooter—can be no better than the information he depends upon to perform those functions. Clearly, then, nothing should be more important to the project manager than the preservation of the informational integrity of the Project Schedule. In a nutshell, for information to be good it must be reliable. The criteria for reliable information are as follows in the next subsections.

Accuracy   Any information that is purported to be factual must be accurate. All else should be clearly identified as speculative—for example, conjecture, opinion, or theory. Good information will not contain data that is redundant, missing, conflicting, or technically flawed.

Timeliness   Because the project is a living, breathing, and constantly changing organism, what is true today may not be true tomorrow—or even this afternoon. Information must be timely.

Level-of-Detail   Information must match its intended use in terms of content and specificity. When information is too detailed, end-users are forced to generalize. When information is too general, they are forced to interpolate. Either way, inappropriate levels-of-detail can lead to misinterpretation, misunderstanding, distortion, subjectivity, or false impressions.

Dependability   Information useful during the execution stage of a project should be issued cyclically. The frequency of such communication cycles should be commensurate with the shelf life of the information, as well as the recipients' need to know. This requirement implies a reliability of the *process*—that it will consistently and fully maintain the communication regimen.

Integration   Information derived separately but amalgamated into a more encompassing data set must be validated after the transition. All too often, information that may be correct at the point of origin no longer makes sense within a different, or modifying, context.

Management Reports

As stated previously, the Performance Recording cycle should correspond to the Performance Reporting cycle in some supportive and collaborative way. But beyond this, I feel it important to point out that, based on the number of times I've seen abuses along these lines, *any and all management reports and communication documents that speak about scheduling issues should derive their facts from the Project Schedule.* To do otherwise not only makes a mockery of the Execution Scheduling and Performance Control processes, it invalidates the Execution Schedule by inference. By this, I mean that people have a logical right to assume that when a project manager states a scheduling *fact* in a letter or report, he derives his information from the Project Schedule. Later on, when reality looks nothing like the prediction, the critic wrongly assumes the faulty information came from the Execution Schedule and the Project Schedule may then receive ridicule for being flawed and unreliable.

Let me digress for a moment to give this point some life. A few years back, my company was retained to provide aggressive Scheduling support services on a high-rise project that was nearing completion. The project was both grossly over-budget and extremely behind schedule. I spent just under three weeks pulling together a fairly detailed Recovery Schedule and, based upon it, determined that the project was far less than 90 percent complete, as was the current belief of the Vice President of Operations, the fellow who had retained my services. Once I had aligned all of my Scheduling ducks in a row, I wrote a report which concluded that the project was only 68 percent complete and would likely finish no earlier than the following August. On November 15, I issued this report by mail to a number of people throughout the organization, most notably the VP who retained me.

Imagine my surprise when I came in the next morning and found in my In basket a copy of the VP's report to *his* bosses. Apparently our reports had crossed in the mail. In his report, however, also dated November 15, he announced to God and the world that the project was "nearly done and we'll be off the job in three weeks." You may be wondering how we could be so far apart in our views. The answer is simple.This company had never built a high-rise building before; they were power plant builders. I, on the other hand, had extensive experience in building construction, with a special emphasis on high-rise construction. When did the project finish? August 8.

The point is that by not waiting or even asking for the Project Scheduler's input, the Vice President not only made himself look stupid, he invalidated the Scheduling effort as well. As you may have guessed, the VP took one step after another to point the finger my way. At first, he claimed that I didn't know what I was talking about when I projected an August completion. Then, as the weeks and months dragged on, he changed his story. He next insisted that his report was based on information I had sent him in a memo (which—surprise, surprise—he was unable to produce). In the end, though, he dismantled the entire Scheduling Department. I was released from service. (Not to worry, I had plenty of other clients, and a very strong reputation.) Bottom line: make sure all schedule-related pronouncements are founded on proper Performance Control procedures.

Narratives

Narratives are an often overlooked yet extremely powerful form of reporting. What they offer that no other reporting format offers is context. Extraction (tabular) Reports are great for sorting, grouping, and presenting large listings of information. Metrics, fancy graphs, and charts, are great for depicting trends and comparative performance. Logic diagrams are great at mapping the interdependency and complexity of the project elements. But none of these formats explains *why* things are the way they are.

A well-written narrative will answer questions that the other formats simply cannot. In fact, many of the questions a good narrative can answer are those that the other formats have raised! Narratives provide context, and context provides fairness and perspective. Let me give you an excellent example of this.

About 25 years ago, I was promoted from *senior scheduler* to *scheduling manager* for a national construction management company. Over a period of three months, I offloaded my direct Execution Scheduling responsibilities to subordinates, thus freeing me up to handle the new managerial role. One project, a government office building, was assigned to Sharon, a Junior Scheduler with about two years of Scheduling experience under her belt.

At the time of the handoff, the project was running about five weeks behind schedule. As part of the Performance Reporting process, I required all Project Schedulers to write a narrative report that would accompany any other scheduling work products, as well as to present their findings orally at the monthly project meeting with the owner (and other key project players). Of course, I insisted on reviewing the rough drafts of these reports before they were finalized and published.

Late into the night, I sat at my desk reading the two dozen narratives stacked before me. Most were acceptable but not great, but it was Sharon's that got my blood boiling. In her narrative, she gave a scathing critique of the project manager's performance. She cited the Project Schedule reporting a total-float of –24! To bolster her position, she found ample evidence of activities performed out-of-sequence, overrun original-durations, and excessive rework.

The next morning I called her into my office. I asked her if she had spoken with the project manager. "Why should I?" she responded. "The facts speak for themselves." As I dropped her narrative in a basket on my credenza, I asked her not only to speak with the project manager, but to make a special trip to the jobsite, 140 miles away. I requested a briefing from her immediately on her return.

Two days later, the woman sitting before me was not the same person who was so indignant only a few days earlier. "So," I began, "how did it go?" Her response, which took a good 15 minutes and was peppered with apologies and embarrassment, convinced me that she had learned a valuable lesson about the importance of context.

What she reported, which of course I had known all along, was that this was a Murphy project, having been hit by one calamity after another. The original general contractor defaulted three months into the job, and the replacement contractor had a string of incompetent project managers passing through the jobsite as if it were a revolving door.

Things only began turning around when the current project manager arrived on-site four months ago. At that time, the project was more than three months behind schedule. In a remarkable display of ingenuity and charisma, he was able to motivate the nine prime subcontractors to turn around the job. In a matter of 16 weeks, he had reduced the negative total-float from –65 to –19.

"Then, last week," she wrapped up her review, "the project got hit by a 50-year rainstorm, and the basement was flooded out. The project lost another week, and the total-float went to negative 24." It was clear that Sharon had learned the importance of context. But she learned something else, too.

"So," I inquired, "tell me what you think the narrative's job is."

"That's easy," she quickly replied. "If I can be distracted and misled by *the facts* in the other reports, so can others. The narrative is needed to provide context to the readers of those other reports." Bingo! She got it—and, now, you do, too.

Figure 16-1

Seven M's of Momentum Management

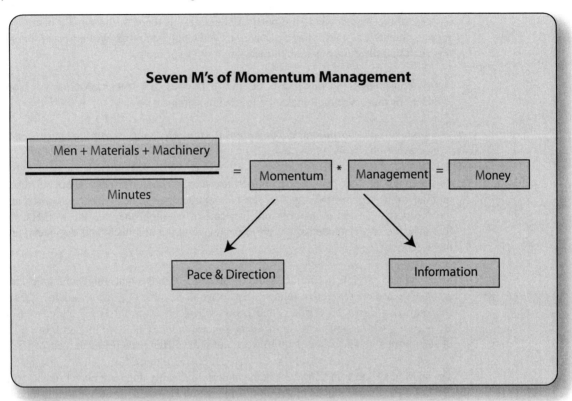

Using the Project Schedule to Coordinate

The coordination of project activities is *one* of the most, if not *the* most, important functions of the project manager, and to accomplish this the Execution Schedule is an essential tool. Effective coordination is also why I invented Momentum Management, which can also be thought of purposeful coordination. Allow me to explain.

Typically, when I speak on the subject of Momentology, I have a small segment entitled *"The Seven M's of Momentum Management."* (Please indulge me as I substitute a few common terms for less used ones, in order to derive the seven "M's.") See Figure 16-1 for the following discussion.

You and I agree that all construction projects involve "labor, materials, and equipment[7]," right? Okay, so with a minor change in wording, we have:

---

[7]By "equipment," I am referring not to the installed equipment that is part of the project design and scope, but rather to the construction equipment used to place the work of the project in its final location. This includes everything from bulldozers and dump trucks to man hoists, compressors, and hand tools.

Men, Materials, and Machinery

Every project is the amalgamation of labor, materials, and equipment—in motion! That is, these three key elements are not just standing out there in the middle of a field. Rather, humans are assembling the materials and using equipment in a purposeful manner, such that the design is transformed into a physical product.

Action consumes time; this is a basic law of physics. So, if we substitute the word Minutes for time, we could make the following statement.

> *A project is the purposeful combination of Men, Materials, and Machinery, acting over a period of time (Minutes).*

The humans that we have just identified are those who perform the work. In terms familiar to us, organizationally they are the contractors, the designers, the owner, and their respective levels of supervision. In terms of position, they are the workers, the foremen, the superintendents, the project managers, the architects and engineers, and the executives.

So let me ask a simple question. Assuming all of these individuals (and companies) are competent at their respective trades, why do we need others to oversee them? If each subcontractor *knows his business* and knows where he fits in the Big Picture, why do we need a *general contractor* or *construction manager*? Can't we just let loose a set of subcontractors and allow them to work out their differences between them?

The answer, as you well know, lies in the underlying reality that each player on the project has at least two agendas: the project's agenda and his own agenda. And it is the latter agenda that motivates individuals and organizations to act in ways that are not always in the best interest of the project.

The role of Management is to keep the parties primarily focused on the project's agenda and on its objectives. The common thread that weaves its way through all of the project manager's responsibilities and that also (not coincidentally) characterizes the single greatest source of conflict on the project is Momentum. This is because Momentum is the result of action. And when all parties are acting in a mutually compatible manner, Project Momentum is enhanced, but when their respective actions are in conflict, Project Momentum suffers. So, to further our formula for effective Momentum Management, let's now say:

> *A project is the purposeful combination of Men, Materials, and Machinery, acting over a period of time (Minutes). That action creates a project Momentum, and Management's goal is to influence that Momentum.*

Finally, while there may be many other reasons companies and individuals participate in projects, the vast majority of times it is for financial gain. I use the word *money* to provide the seventh "M," but the word is a metaphor for whatever are the priorities of the owner, as depicted in the Emphasis-Alignment Model. To complete our formula for Momentum Management, consider this:

A project is the purposeful combination of Men, Materials, and Machinery, acting over a period of time (Minutes). That action creates a project Momentum, and Management's goal is to influence that Momentum so that project objectives (Money) are realized.

The key point of this section is that the project manager's job is to influence Project Momentum by simultaneously influencing the individual and interrelated actions of its many conflicting parties. There is a word for this attempt to influence actions: *coordination.*

The Project Schedule, if it is to be of help to the project manager in this regard, must reflect an execution strategy that strikes a workable balance between project objectives and competing player objectives.

Using the Project Schedule to Direct

Here, the Project Schedule is used to communicate executable details of the overall strategy. The coordination function discussed under the previous heading manifests itself in the communication of to-do lists, specific directions as to what needs to be done, in what order, at what time, by whom, for how long, and in what manner.

Using the Project Schedule to Control

Finally, the Execution Schedule sticks around to see that the *directions* discussed under the previous heading are achieved. One of the first things you learn in public speaking classes is that the speaker is responsible for all three parts of the communication process: what is said, what is heard, and what is understood. It is not enough to simply pronounce words through a microphone. You must also study your listeners' faces and test their comprehension of what you are saying.

Likewise, it is not enough to merely generate a Schedule Extraction Report, distribute it, and have it referenced in the weekly progress meeting. It is necessary to monitor the work, compare actual performance to what was planned and expected, and pursue explanations and responses for disparities between the two. That is the essence of *control.* As has been said elsewhere, when we use the word *control,* we really mean *influence.* All actions on a project come down to the actions of individuals, and the individual alone controls his own actions. The rest of us can only hope to influence his decision to act one way or another.

The project manager can use the Execution Schedule to gain insights into where such influence will be most beneficial. Performance Control, however, provides systematic and reliable analyses of project performance designed to ensure that the benefits of effective performance are being realized.

Project Schedule Support of Pay Requests

The only thing I want to say here is that by not incorporating the Performance Control functions into the approval process for contractor pay requests, project management misses a golden opportunity to bring closure to the entire scheduling effort. The incorporation I refer to works like this:

- The Performance Control is administered on a regular basis, with Performance Recording being performed by a committee of involved participants, including the general contractor and/or construction manager, the design professional(s), the owner, and the key subcontractors.

- The Execution Schedule's activities will have been cost-loaded, such that the aggregate value of all such activity costs equals the approved contract value, including approved change orders.

- With each Performance Control cycle, an *earned* dollar value can be computed and used to validate and authorize the contractor's monthly request for payment.

When a contractor realizes that he will be compensated only for what work the Execution Schedule confirms he has completed, he will pay far more attention to the Execution Schedule—during its development, during its usage, and from its reports. Money has a way of getting people's attention, especially contractors, for whom the bottom line is not only their lifeblood but also the only barometer of success that really means anything to them. Don't miss the antithesis to this: if the contractor can get paid independent of Performance Control, then why does he need to worry about the Project Schedule at all?

THE ELEMENT OF SURPRISE

Of all of the ways to describe or confirm a Project Schedule's failure to perform adequately, the most frequently mentioned is *project or schedule delay.* When a project overruns its allotted time, we naturally look to the Execution Schedule for answers to the underlying question: *why?* Claims consultants make a living answering that one-word question. Of course, their answers are specific to the given project.

I pose the same question on an across-the-board level. What is it about projects that they seem so impossible to adequately plan for and predict that there always seem to be "surprises," these things that no one could anticipate? Is that necessarily true, that they *couldn't* anticipate the surprise? Perhaps they just *didn't* anticipate the eventuality that, with sufficient experience and focus on detail, they most certainly *could have!*

Momentum Studies conducted on the Project Schedules of hundreds of failed projects have led me to a few conclusions on this all-important subject. Under this heading, I hope you will find the following short discussion instructional as to how to create better schedules in the future, schedules that do a far better job of eliminating "surprises." In Chapter 6, where we explored the world of Dilemma Control, we learned that it is the mass of small surprises, and not the few whopping risks, that kill most Project Schedules. Here we will examine some of the causes of dilemmas.

Delay is a Delta

When I speak of a delay, I am really talking about something taking longer than expected. In this sense, the word *delay* refers to the difference, or *delta*, between two points in time: when something was *expected* to occur and when it actually *did* occur. These points in time are often expressed in terms of calendar dates, but durations also define a culminating moment in time. For instance, an activity bearing a five-day activity-duration is expected to complete at a moment-in-time five days later than when the activity began. If it takes seven days to complete, then the moment-in-time when the activity completed was delayed by two days. So, delay is a word or concept that represents the delta between what was expected and what occurred.

Identifying the Sources of Divergence

When there is a difference between two durations (whether activity-durations or relationship-durations), such that the actual-duration is greater than the original-duration, there are three possible explanations:

- The original-duration was reasonable, but the actual-duration was greater than what was reasonable.

- The actual-duration was reasonable (meaning, that it truly couldn't have occurred sooner), but the original-duration was unrealistically short to begin with.

- The original-duration was unreasonable *and* the actual-duration was greater than what was reasonable.

In claims work, all three possibilities are considered, but during the life of the project, it is most often assumed that the original-durations are correct, and it is assumed that any divergence is due to inadequate performance (the first bullet in the preceding list).

Momentum Studies have shown that the third bullet best reflects what happens on projects with slipped Execution Schedules. This should be good news to us because it means that we have a legitimate basis for optimism. If all delay causes were outside our control, then we would have no choice but to simply accept them and struggle to deal with them. Instead, we learn that there is indeed much we can do to reduce delays on our projects. In particular, we can do a better job of *anticipating surprises*. In Momentology jargon, this is called Dilemma Forecasting.

Where Improvement Opportunities Reside

Of course, improvement opportunities reside where the durations reside; this is obvious. But we have already learned that there are two primary categories of durations: activity-durations and relationship-durations, and each has a unique set of conceptual and functional criteria. Let's examine each group separately, with an eye toward better understanding how dilemmas can be (and *should* be) anticipated.

Anticipating Activity-Tenure Surprises

We need to get a bit esoteric in our discussion, so please bear with me as we drift into a highly theoretical examination of how activity-durations and relationship-durations are derived *in the real world.* Let's start with activity-durations.

Imagine an activity called Set Brick-North Wall. About this wall we have precise dimensions, including all openings for doors and windows. We can estimate the number of bricks down to the gnat's behind. We also have very good historical performance data on the very same individuals who will comprise the bricklaying crew—masons and laborers. The wall is not very high, so there is no need to factor in height as a productivity variable.

If I've left out any other key pieces of information, forgive me. The condition I'm trying to depict is one where, at the time we derive the activity-duration, we have *all* the information that we need to develop a *very* accurate, yet theoretical, estimate of the amount of time to perform the scope of work expressed by the activity-description. Let's call this a scope-limited duration.

Based on all of this wonderful and highly reliable information, we estimate a scope-limited duration of four workdays. If I were to ask you, the reader, how confident (expressed as a percent) we should be that the work *will* complete within four days, how would you answer? Would you answer 100 percent? Why not? We know precisely what is involved, and we know just how quickly our crew works. Why shouldn't we have 100 percent confidence that the activity will complete within four days?

Your answer, if it is like the overwhelming majority of people to whom I have posed this same scenario and question, is that there are unknowns lurking out there that might affect the crew's ability to perform the work by the *theoretical,* scope-limited duration we have estimated. And *theoretical* is the operative word.

"Fair enough," I respond. Then, let me ask a different question: *What level of confidence would you put on the scope-limited duration of four days?*

This book is not interactive, so I can't wait for your response, but if I had to guess, you are thinking something along the lines of 90–95 percent.[8] Your answer is based on years of experience, and your "gut feel" is that the odds of *some* surprise are great, but the odds of a *major* surprise are slim.

"Now," you add, "if the activity had had a longer duration, say two weeks, I might drop that confidence to 80 percent." You might be interested to know that there is a technical foundation for your last comment. The larger a duration is, the further it extends into the future. Empirical data from the Momentum Studies show that the future component of an activity-duration is inversely proportional to the activity-duration's confidence level. This also makes good common sense, doesn't it? If 90 percent of an activity's

---

[8] Of course you would never be foolish enough to go to 100 percent, no matter how confident you are.

duration is in the future, and only 10 percent is in the present (very near future), aren't we less confident about that activity-duration than with one in which 90 percent of the duration is in the present and only 10 percent is in the future?[9]

So, let's put all this theoretical chatter to work in the real world. As the project team sits around the Logic Development table, we jointly agree that the Set Brick-North Wall activity should have an activity-duration of five days. Here's how we derived that value: we strongly (90 percent) believe that the work can and will complete in four days, but we want to add a 10 percent contingency to derive a duration worthy of near 100 percent confidence. Ten percent of four is 0.4, and so we round up to one-day and end up with a duration of five, with a nearly 100 percent confidence factor.

As for another masonry activity, Set Brick-South Wall, which has an 80 percent confidence level on a 10-day (two week) scope-limited duration, we might add 2 extra days to represent the 20 percent lack of confidence, in order to derive an activity-duration with a near-100 percent confidence. I call this additional duration boost a Duration Confidence Factor (DCF). Further, I use the term Composite Duration to mean the activity-duration that is derived from the aggregate of the scope-limited duration *plus* the DCF. That is:

Composite Duration (CD) = Scope-Limited Duration + Duration Confidence Factor

Let's return to our discussion about surprises. Assuming we were to create Composite Durations for all activities in the Project Schedule using the preceding process, I have two questions:

- Does the preceding process threaten the inherent integrity of the Project Schedule, specifically the principle of keeping the activity-duration as pure as possible?
- Would this yield a Project Schedule with a near-100 percent confidence level on the project's predicted completion date?

Maintaining Duration Purity

A Scheduling purist would argue that the inclusion of contingency in an activity-duration to represent the likelihood of minor activity-tenure surprises violates the sacred principle of restricting the activity-duration to the time actually needed to perform the work. I disagree because any activity-duration is an estimate of how long something will take. Arms need not be swinging a hammer every minute of an activity's duration for it to be legitimate. Included in every commercial productivity rates table I have ever seen is allowance for toilet breaks, foot travel time to secure materials and bring them to the area of operation, and so on.

The kinds of activity-tenure surprises that the DCF seeks to anticipate are of the same nature. Maybe the lumber pile has fallen over and the 2×6's can't be found. Maybe the laborer cut his finger and has gone to the trailer for a bandage. Maybe there is a dimensional conflict and the masonry activity has come to a halt, awaiting the arrival of the architect.

---

[9]For purposes of this premise, I define the present (near future) anything within the current week (five workdays).

I think inclusion of a DCF that allows for the likelihood of minor surprises—as long as it is limited, justified, and fully documented—makes for a more realistic duration. Conversely, I think that not including a DCF leads to an unrealistic activity-duration and hence to an unreliable Execution Schedule.

Project Completion Date Confidence Factor

The other question is this: is the cumulative reasonableness of all activity-durations the only driving factor in the reasonableness of the Project Schedule itself as a project end date predictor? I think not. I think that other factors beyond what the Composite Durations can simulate also influence the end date's achievement. I have practical reasons for saying this, but your reasons for feeling the same way may well be rooted in experience and that so-often-right *gut feeling.*

Since we are speaking in arcane terms, here is a good place to challenge the conventional definition of the critical-path as being the *longest* path. Technically speaking, for this rule to be true, all paths would have to start at the beginning of the schedule and terminate at the Project Schedule's end. It has been my experience, after reviewing hundreds of Project Schedules that conditions quite often exist where elements of the project scope are *not* included in the Execution Schedule, except as single-activity deliverables.

For instance, projects often have owner-furnished equipment and materials. Perhaps to save on sales taxes or to spare a contractor mark-up or (more often the case) to preorder long lead equipment even before the general contract is awarded, the owner purchases such equipment and materials. In the Project Schedule, the equipment delivery is shown as a single activity with no predecessor, but instead with only a date-constraint, signaling that the delivery will occur "no-earlier-than" a given date.

There can be any number of other reasons why a string of activities might start "in the middle" of the Execution Schedule and not at its start. It is entirely likely, and quite often the case, that one of these activities heads a path that is last to complete, thus driving the project end date. Other paths might very well be longer, in terms of consecutive durations (relationship-durations and activity-durations), and those paths commence earlier than the date-constrained path discussed previously.

The undeniable fact is that a project's end date is dictated by completion of one or more paths (strings of activities) yielding the latest completion date. And, to answer the second question—about whether the cumulative reasonableness of all activity-durations is the only driving factor in the reasonableness of the schedule itself as a project end date predictor—since every path of two or more activities contains one or more relationships, and since both relationships and activities have durations, schedule-tenure surprises can strike activities, relationships, or both.

Moreover, similar to activity-durations, relationship-durations are subject to both relationship-tenure surprises and schedule-tenure surprises. So, the answer to the second question is that, even if both relationship-tenure surprises and activity-tenure surprises are contemplated and offset by respective DCFs, the relationships and activities are still vulnerable to project-tenure surprises. This means that even if all Composite Durations, whether relationship or activity, carried a 99 percent confidence factor, the project end date may still not enjoy an equally high rating. What to do to increase project-tenure confidence in the Project Schedule is treated next.

Anticipating Relationship-Tenure Surprises

Elsewhere in this book we held a comprehensive discussion of the proper way to derive relationship-durations. We agreed that a relationship-duration is a *Time Gap,* and that there are two types of Time Gaps, administrative and productive. Let's refresh our memory of those terms.

A Productive Time Gap (PTG) represents a period of time by which a Productive Work Segment is restrained from starting until one or more predecessor Productive Work Segments complete. We also noted that this coincides with the generally understood interpretation of start-to-start and finish-to-finish logic ties, that Activity Y cannot start until so many days after Activity X has started; or, Activity Y cannot complete until so many days after Activity X has completed.

Administrative Time Gaps (ATG) are numeric values representing the amount of time a Productive Work Segment is restrained from starting because prerequisite Administrative Actions must be performed. For the following discussion, refer to Table 16-4. As with Composite Activity Durations, it is critical that relationship-durations be derived as scientifically as possible and that we apply a DCF to offset relationship-tenure surprises.

We accomplish this by first itemizing the Administrative Actions that restrain the commencement of an activity (lines 8–10) and then make our best guess as to how long these typically concurrent actions will take to complete. We derive a scope-limited

Line	Relationship	Activity	Rel Type	Rel Dur
0	**PTG Calculation**			
1	Predecessor	Activity B	SS	3
2	Predeccesor	Activity C	SS	4
3	Predeccesor	Activity D	FS	0
4	Predeccesor	Activity E	SS	2
5		Maximum PTG		4
6				
7	**ATG Calculation**			
8	Admin Action	Call for Sub		4
9	Admin Action	Clear Area		1
10	Admin Action	Get Inspector		5
11		Maximum ATG		5
12		Rel Dur DCF	20%	1.0
13		Adjusted ATG		6
14	**Composite Relationship Duration**			6

Table 16-4

Example of ATG and PTG Calculations

duration that carries an 80 percent confidence factor among the participants at the Logic Development Session (line 11). To this value we add a 20 percent DCF (line 12) and call the result an *adjusted ATG* (line 13).

Next, we consider the Productive Time Gap requirements for the subject activity (lines 1–4) and determine the largest PTG (Line 5). Finally, of these two, line 5 and line 12, we take whichever is greater, the largest PTG or the adjusted ATG, and use this as our Composite Relationship Duration (Line 15). The Composite Relationship Duration is then substituted for the largest PTG. In this example, Activity C's SS4 would now become an SS6.

This process generates a value that is definable, measurable, and fully documented. A Composite Relationship Duration so derived contains a time safeguard to offset predictable (yet not measurable) relationship-tenure surprises.

Bolstering Project-Level Confidence in the Schedule

With DCFs built into both activity-durations and Administrative Time Gaps, the only remaining surprises for which no offsetting protection has been created are at the project level. By that I mean that such surprises are expected to affect more than one activity and more than one relationship. Even project-level surprises can be further subdivided, based on how we might anticipate and allow for them. Risk analysts have names for these two categories: known-unknowns, and unknown-unknowns.

It is chiefly because of the unknown-unknown, which can affect both relationship and activity durations, that most seasoned construction professionals are unwilling to grant more than a 95 percent confidence factor to any projected end date, *even if every relationship-duration and activity-duration in the schedule carries a 99 percent confidence factor (with DCFs increasing such durations from 90 percent confidence to 99 percent confidence).*

Ideally, and only if the Project Schedule can tolerate the addition, it would be nice to place a single activity at the end of the Execution Schedule called Project-Level Unknown-Unknown Contingency. A carefully conceived and rigidly enforced policy would control who could authorize reductions in this contingency, under what circumstances, and what to do subsequently to recover the contingency drain. Unfortunately, most construction projects are simply too tight at the outset to have "room" for a 5–10 percent contingency for the unknown-unknown. And so, notwithstanding everything else we may do to ensure reasonableness, even including slightly padded relationship-durations and activity-durations, the Project Schedule simply cannot guarantee a project end date with 100 percent confidence.

That's just the cold, hard truth!

Part 5 Epilogue

Well, we made it. Congratulations!

It has been quite a journey that we have traveled together; to be sure, we covered a lot of ground. We started out by looking at the environment in which we struggle as Scheduling Practitioners to make a difference on the projects we serve. We acknowledged the many distinct and contrasting customers we have and the many disparate requirements imposed on our Execution Schedules, as well as on the various Commitment Plans and even on ourselves as Scheduling Practitioners.

We took an introspective look at our Practice and concluded that it *isn't* a profession. Our field suffers from a lack of consistent terminology or of a professional nucleus. The state of the Scheduling Practice calls out for stewardship, and toward that end I proposed a new Scheduling Practice Paradigm, a new project management system (Dilemma Control), and a new project management methodology (Momentology).

At last, we turned our attention to the murky details of Project Schedule design, development, maintenance, and usage. Along the way we studied the anatomy of a relationship and learned about the potent and corrosive effect of Administrative Actions performed belatedly or not at all. We discussed Time Gaps, both Administrative and Productive, Duration Confidence Factors, and Composite Durations.

We learned about Discrete Activity Float and the significance of Performance Analysis, including Schedule Performance measures such as Density, Buoyancy, Potency, and Schedule Resiliency, Vulnerability, and Credibility. We acknowledged that no review of project performance, as a general category of study, would be comprehensive (or therefore reliable) unless it equally examined Management Performance, Schedule Performance, and Execution Performance.

To a fair extent, this text is really two books in one. It is a *how-to-better-our-Scheduling-effort* book that addresses the mechanics of Execution Schedule Design, development, maintenance, and usage. But it is also a *how-to-better-our-Practice* book that addresses numerous ailments, deficiencies, and impediments that block our collective path and prevent us from working cohesively or presenting a consistent face to our customers and stakeholders, or from ever becoming a true profession.

As I think about it, it seems to me that there is a common thread weaving through both subbooks: the *human* element. Certainly, the overall message in the Scheduling how-to book is to never forget that project management is really *people* management, and that as we do what we do as Scheduling Practitioners, we must also do whatever it takes to gain the support and involvement of the people we work with.

But as a member of the Scheduling Practice, each of us is being called upon to join hands with fellow Practitioners in an effort to give our discipline a comprehensive makeover, to re-engineer it so that it will be capable of supporting the new Project Management Paradigm, which also puts the greater emphasis on *people*, rather than on processes or statistics.

As you know, I have been involved in the College of Scheduling's efforts to write "best practices" for the Scheduling world. The word "best" is surely a subjective one, and that begs the question: *what is to be used as the sliding scale that spans from bad to good to best?* "Good" is both a subjective and, I will add, contextual concept. Is the crescent wrench a *good* tool? It was a *great* invention to be sure, a vast improvement over the centuries-old pliers. But the crescent wrench makes for a lousy hammer; it is designed for twisting bolts, not pounding spikes or nails.

The gradual disintegration of our craft, at its most general or most specific, centers on us getting clear about the limitations inherent in our tools and methods, and rethinking the connection between our products and services and our customers whose informational needs and wants we seek to supply. When you step back and look at what has happened to the Scheduling Practice over the decades, it is easy to see that we have blurred, or allowed to blur, the distinction between *time*-oriented Project Scheduling practices and other practices that serve often-competing interests.

Can we reverse the tide of encroachment or is it too late? Some leading experts are of the mind that things have gone too far astray; that those other interests who have commandeered Project Scheduling for their purposes will never agree to release the grip they have on what are now perceived as "traditional" methods and practices. I am too much of a pragmatist (and cynic) to venture a guess.

One thing is for sure: the Scheduling Practice, as we currently know it, *is* going away. Either we, as a collective whole, will do nothing to reverse the current, devastating trends and thus the Practice will implode (from the tension of too many competing forces pulling on us from different directions), or we will change ourselves sufficiently to become and remain responsive to the new Project Management Paradigm. Either way, in another few years, we won't look very much like we look today.

What troubles me is that, as I pan the landscape, I cannot seem to spot the nexus from which such radical changes will emerge. To be sure, some organizations offer cause to be optimistic, but each of them still has a long way to go. I know of no current Scheduling organization with the necessary passion and strength of character to fight the political battles that are inevitably required to force a cultural revolution. For an assortment of unrelated reasons, those who would be adversely affected if "business as usual" were to be significantly altered, dominate today's Scheduling and project management associations.

A new generation of leaders is needed—*now*. The Old Guard has had its time on the bridge, at the helm. Because it is more than apparent that what we *are* doing isn't working, it is time for a new generation of leaders to guide us to our destiny, to question the motives behind established practices, to follow the money, to challenge the status quo, and to think outside the box.

And the next generation of leaders must come from the ranks, from the trenches. We have had our fill of claims consultants, lawyers, cost engineers, and project managers who have appointed themselves as custodians of our Practice. With our collective vote, it is time for us to wrestle control from these surrogate protectors (no matter how sincere their motives) and restore control in the hands of fellow Schedulers. This rescue is desperately needed, and long overdue.

Early on in the development of this book I made a bold decision: to use this book as the platform for a verbal campaign intended to stimulate debate, provoke thought, and encourage action, to be a catalyst for the types of radical changes that our Practice urgently demands, if we are to survive at all. At first, it might seem that my philosophical musings have little to do with a solitary Project Scheduler's struggle to produce a great Execution Schedule for his project manager. But, if you stop and think about it, the two subjects of this book are intimately and integrally tied. That individual Project Scheduler depends on the backing of a Scheduling Practice to validate his recommendations on the project. And the Practice in turn depends on the collective stewardship of Scheduling Practitioners to advance the trade.

And so that brings us to the end. On the last few pages I will summarize what you need to know about creating Project Schedules they'll actually want to use. I hope this book has proved helpful. Most of all, though, I hope it has tantalized you enough to want to read upcoming books on Momentum Theory and Application. Whether or not you adopt Momentum, I encourage you, in your ongoing quest for personal improvement, to investigate all the different ways we can practice time-centered Project Scheduling. We are indeed so fortunate to be in this field; it is so rich with challenge and opportunity. And on a more cosmic level, each of you reading this book finds yourself at the right time and place to make a lasting difference. Let us not blow the chance!

Best of luck to you,
Murray

17

Creating Schedules They'll Actually Want to Use!

We have covered a lot of material in this book, and as we bring it to a close, I would like to summarize the main points we have covered. The main objective of this text was to provide you with meaningful advice on how to more effectively design, develop, maintain, and use your Execution Schedules so that the project manager will be the most avaricious consumer of your handiwork. To boil down the hundreds of key points covered in this book, I thought it might be interesting to borrow from David Letterman and present a Top Ten list of what *not* to do. In other words, if you want to create a Project Schedule that *no one* will want to use, then just follow this recipe for disaster.[1]

But this book also covers many other topics not directly related to schedule design, development, maintenance, and usage, so I thought it might be helpful to provide a per-chapter summary of the book's messages, which I present just after the Top Ten List.

TOP TEN TECHNIQUES FOR SABOTAGING YOUR SCHEDULING EFFORTS

See Figure 17-1 for a helpful tear-out page to tape to the side of your computer monitor or the inside lid of your traveling briefcase.

Technique #10: Disconnect the Project Schedule from All Other Project Management Support Functions

Operate the Execution Schedule in a vacuum. Allow other project management support systems to opine on time-management issues without regard for what the Project Schedule says. Generate conflicting information from these independent systems and confuse the project stakeholders. For its part, deprive the Project Schedule of critical information it requires that can only be derived from these other project management support systems (such as cost data).

---

[1]These techniques are listed in reverse order of impact on schedule effectiveness.

Figure 17-1

Top Ten Techniques for Sabotaging Your Scheduling Efforts

#10.	Disconnect the Execution Schedule from all other project controls functions.
#9.	Don't safeguard duration purity.
#8.	Employ poor reporting techniques.
#7.	Fail to adhere to sound updating practices.
#6.	Mismanage activity relationships.
#5.	Choose improper scheduling software settings.
#4.	Ignore the Theory of Aligned Emphasis.
#3.	Ignore project momentum.
#2.	Force the Project Schedule to satisfy too many different uses/objectives.
#1.	Entirely omit, or inadequately perform, Schedule Design.

Technique #9: Don't Safeguard Duration Purity

Allow the activity-duration to represent different things to different people. Let it represent *elapsed* time on some activities and continuous-workdays on others. Base some activity-durations on the scope of work entailed in the activity, yet establish other activity-durations with little or no regard for crew configurations, productivity rates, scope quantities, or working conditions. Arbitrarily reduce or increase activity-durations to achieve desired milestone dates or to manipulate total-float values. Assign relationship-durations that fail to take into account prerequisite Administrative Actions. Don't use Duration Confidence Factors (DCFs) in establishing relationship-durations and activity-durations.

Technique #8: Employ Poor Reporting Techniques

Don't worry about who will be reading the reports, what information they need, how often they need it, how much detail they require, or the form in which they would like to see that information. Generate canned reports and force readers to *make do*. Restrict your reports to one or two basic formats and force everyone to get the information from these limited outputs. Produce volumes of printouts and graphs that depict *what* is happening on the project, but don't produce narratives that explain *why*. And most certainly don't waste time analyzing project data before issuing reports.

Technique #7: Fail to Adhere to Sound Performance Recording Practices

Don't strive to be as accurate as possible when assessing activity progress in the field. Don't be concerned about whether percent-complete and remaining-duration estimates yield different results. When statusing the Execution Schedule, don't bother with investigating the reasons why activities started out-of-sequence; simply let the software override or retain the logic. Allow the Execution Schedule to gradually depart from reality by not performing routine, minor schedule adjustments of logic and durations. Don't validate actual dates, but instead rely on guesstimates of when activity start and finish dates were achieved.

Technique #6: Mismanage Relationships

Pepper the Project Schedule with dangling activities; omit critical logic ties. Link activities with a start-to-start tie, but forget to include the corresponding finish-to-finish tie. Constrict the Execution Schedule with excessive logic ties or, alternatively, fail to adequately depict important relationships. Use date-constraints in lieu of sound logic as a fast way to throw a Project Schedule together.

Technique #5: Choose Inappropriate Scheduling Software Settings

Don't bother to understand how the scheduling software computes critical data or how the various settings affect those calculations. Use advanced settings to manipulate the Project Schedule, to distort or obscure the critical-path, to arbitrarily alter total-float or free-float values, or to force unnecessary loss of total-float. Use too many calendars. Fail to allow for weather and other predictable threats to timely performance.

Technique #4: Ignore the Theory of Aligned Emphasis

Disregard the owner's wishes and build the project in accordance with your own objectives and priorities. Fail to take into account that the owner is focused on certain project success criteria and that prudent project management involves making them your highest priorities. Employ standard forms, reports, and procedures mandated by your Home Office; the owner will eventually come to realize the wisdom of your ways, and the folly of his own!

Technique #3: Ignore Project Momentum

Completely disregard the ever-present influence of project dynamics, in particular Project Momentum. Manage the project as a series of only marginally related activities without understanding how overall Project Momentum is affected by individual decisions. Believe that project dynamics can be *controlled*, even though they can never be more than *influenced*.

Technique #2: Force the Schedule to Satisfy Too Many Different Uses/Objectives

Insist that the Project Schedule function as a jack-of-all-trades. Expect it to meet everyone's informational needs. Allow everyone to influence the content, structure, and use of the Execution Schedule. Make it into a one-size-fits-all tool. Ignore the uniqueness of projects and create all Project Schedules according to a general set of standards that applies to most projects most of the time.

Technique #1: Entirely Omit, or Inadequately Perform, Schedule Design

Launch into Schedule Development without ever performing Schedule Design. Create the Project Schedule before first understanding who will use the Project Schedule, how they wish to use it, and how other project management support systems will interface with it. Hold no discussions with end users to reach agreement on expectations, but then blame their subsequent disappointment in the Project Schedule on their failure to make their wishes known.

CHAPTER-BY-CHAPTER SUMMARY OF THE BOOK'S ESSENTIAL COMMENTS

What follows is a convenient per-chapter summary of the book's main messages. I hope that, by consolidating the most important points discussed in this book, you will more easily be able to incorporate into your Project Schedule the many hundreds of ideas and tricks of the trade contained on these pages.

Part 1: Keeping Your Eye on the Donut

Only by understanding the challenges facing the project manager as he struggles to maneuver his project through tumultuous political, social, economic, technical, and functional waters can the Project Schedule, created to serve him, be of any real value. Part 1 explores the many diverse and often conflicting elements that either influence or are influenced by the Project Schedule's design, development, maintenance, use, and quality.

Chapter 1: The Allure of the Project Schedule

Can the Project Schedule really make a difference? In other words, will a project really be better off when a good Project Schedule is in play? The answer is an emphatic "yes," but the secret lies in what makes for a good Project Schedule.

A Project Schedule's ultimate quality, utility, and value is affected by many variables, including its timing and content, the format of its work products, user resistance, upper management support, the expertise of those developing the Project Schedule, the relationship between the Project Schedule and other project control systems, and the understanding of those using the Project Schedule.

To its credit, the automated Project Schedule offers a number of impressive strengths. It is a picture capable of conveying complex concepts in an intuitive style. This picture format fosters lucid perceptions and facilitates group consensus. It not only transitions seamlessly from a Strategic Plan to an Execution Schedule, it also gives direction, supports resource optimization, provides irrefutable historical documentation, and represents a dynamic model of reality.

Chapter 2: Understanding the Scheduling Theater

Creating good Project Schedules requires a full appreciation for the settings in which the Project Schedule must operate. Specifically, one should understand the operating environment of the project (the stage), those who will interact with the Project Schedule (the actors and audience), and how the Project Schedule itself will be used (the script).

The Stage   In construction, each project is unique in design, size, purpose, location, surrounding community, management control requirements, and financing strategy. As a result, the project control systems appropriate for each project are unique. A project is also a dynamic organism, where a multitude of competing interests struggle to work toward common goals. As they do, they create a Project Momentum; but they also create friction.

As an environmental variable, project management exists to positively influence that Momentum and temper that friction. This challenge is made more difficult because the project manager wears two competing hats. On the one hand, he is the facilitator of the work (hoping to inspire), while on the other hand he is a contracts administrator (needing to control).

He overcomes this obstacle by adopting dynamic project management techniques. Dynamic project management boils down to four key concepts: Planned Resources, Objective Judgments, Effective Communication, and Troubleshooting. Together, these key functions spell PROJECT.

Finally, scheduling software constitutes a very real and influential "environment" in which the Execution Schedule must operate. For this reason, it is essential that the software's computational and operational functionality be understandable and actually understood by those who use it, that unnecessary bells and whistles are avoided, and that the scheduling process be constantly monitored for evidence of unscrupulous schedule manipulation.

The Actors   Many people interact with the Project Schedule, including those who do the physical work, those who supervise the physical work, the project manager, those who support the project manager, those who oversee the project manager, and other project stakeholders, such as those who supply the project or monitor the work.

The Script   Finally, there is the Project Schedule itself. Getting the most out of the Project Schedule requires putting the right things into the Project Schedule. We begin by understanding what the Project Schedule is capable of doing. To be sure, the Project Schedule is quite versatile, able to serve in many different capacities and being the tool of choice for planning; coordination; communication; work organization; resource management; performance measurement, forecasting, and reporting; contracts administration; cost control; marketing; financial planning; record keeping; and dispute resolution.

Chapter 3: Why Our Schedules Disappoint Our Customers

That our Project Scheduling efforts often disappoint our customers is sadly all too well known. As to why this is so, three major reasons are identified: we use confusing terminology, we have lost sight of our customer's informational needs and wants, and the design and quality of our work products have gradually become obsolete through years of custodial neglect.

Concerning terminology, the Scheduling Practice employs a handful of overworked terms to describe the many diverse work products and technical processes described in Chapter 2. In so doing, we create confusion among our stakeholders, thereby cultivating unreasonable expectations in their minds, which eventually lead to disappointment.

Given the complex environment in which the Project Schedule is called upon to function, and given the many diverse and contrasting ways the Project Schedule can be utilized, we have to ask whether one Project Schedule can really do it all? The answer is that it can't, if left as just one huge Project Schedule. However, it can satisfy its many users and serve in multiple capacities if it is intelligently designed, thoughtfully developed, attentively maintained, and skillfully used (including the use of Schedule Extractions).

To these ends, we must perceive our various products and services as dividing into three distinct specialties, each requiring a different set of unique skills: Commitment Planning, Execution Scheduling, and Performance Control.

Chapter 4: The Changing Style of Project Management

Meanwhile, the field of project management is presently undergoing a major paradigm shift. Since its inception, project management has been held in the unyielding grip of the Newtonian Model. But now, for the first time, it is beginning to adopt different strategies for managing projects, influenced by lessons learned from the New Sciences.

The relevance of the New Sciences (which include physics, biology, chemistry, psychology, and mathematics) to project management is that they each provide a unique view into the composition and functionality of "complex adaptive systems," which characteristically match the typical construction project.

The New Sciences suggest an entirely different, refreshing, and vital approach to project management in the form of different understandings about the nature of projects. They tell us that there is no such thing as objective reality; that projects operate chaordically (according to the Chaos Theory of bounded disorder); that projects are naturally self-renewing (if we step out of the way and allow them to do so); that our pursuit of the "bottom line" is futile because "there is no such thing as ever *fully* knowing;" that humans have a limited capacity for change and respond by practicing Complexity Reduction; that such Complexity Reduction hides from us 90 percent of the project's essential information; and that every project is subtly sparked and influenced by hidden fields of energy and influence.

As of this writing, the transition from the Newtonian-influenced Management style of Command-and-Control to the New Sciences-influenced Collaborative Management style is well on its way. It is easy to spot which management style is employed on a given project by observing characteristic behaviors, which in turn are inspired by underlying beliefs. For instance, Command-and-Control managers believe that controlling a project requires controlling all parts of the project, that the worker is not to be fully trusted or respected, that you must plan your work and work your plan, and that order and structure are essential to successful management. By contrast, the Collaborative Model manager believes in a balance between accountability and authority, that the worker on the front line possesses the best answers, that there is power in synergy, and that preparedness trumps prediction every time.

All around the world, the new Project Management Paradigm is causing seismic attitudinal changes: in purpose, from control to facilitation; in emphasis, from activities to relationships; in authority, from top-centered to bottom-shared; in perspective, from deterministic and linear to chaordic and complex; in forecasting, from prediction to early warnings; in reaction, from planned responses to spontaneous skilled responses; and, in focus, from compliance to creativity.

Part 2: Creating a Penchant for Change

Admittedly, Part 2 takes a detour from the main purpose of this book, that being to explore ways of creating better Project Schedules that in turn will lead to faster flowing projects. Here, I propose sweeping changes in how the Scheduling Practice is organized, presented and perceived; what we offer as our work products; and, what words we use to describe ourselves, our processes, and our products and services.

Chapter 5: The New Scheduling Practice Paradigm

One of the reasons that Project Schedules fail is that they are being pulled in too many different directions in order to satisfy too many different users. In some ways, the Scheduling Practice is like a country without a government. In this chapter I propose a crystal clear definition of the Scheduling Practice so that we know what *is* contained within it and what is not. I call this crystal clear definition the *Scheduling Practice Paradigm*.

To be sure, the Scheduling Practice is suffering from decades of custodial neglect, but we cannot fix what we cannot or will not acknowledge as broken. Viewed honestly, we will see that our terminology, areas of specialty, position titles, deliverables, and primary roles all call for serious academic and intellectual treatment. Professionally, we lack cohesion, are not a profession per se, and lack standardized processes or best practices; in addition, our educational wells of new talent are characterized by disconnected and conflicting emphasis and content.

The Scheduling Practice Paradigm, as a remedy for these ailments, provides a discipline with defined specialties, procedures, deliverables, roles, and so forth. Specifically, I propose the acknowledgement of three specialties: Commitment Planning, Execution Scheduling, and Performance Control.

This Scheduling Practice Paradigm makes good sense for several reasons. It clears up our terminology quagmire; it structures and organizes Scheduling products and services; it clarifies what Scheduling Practitioners do; it provides a framework for future academic development and collegial unification; it is compatible with the new Project Management Paradigm; and it supports the creation of a true profession, one that bridges industry differences.

Chapter 6: Introduction to Dilemma Control

Dilemma Control deals with planning for and responding to project dilemmas. Risk Management differs from Dilemma Control in these important ways: Risk Management focuses on major issues (risks), whereas Dilemma Control focuses on minor issues (dilemmas); Risk Management is primarily a pre-project planning methodology, whereas Dilemma Control is primarily a real-time methodology during the project; Risk Management is concerned with project objectives, whereas Dilemma Control is concerned with Project Momentum; Risk Management is oriented around events, whereas Dilemma Control is oriented around people; Risk Management is based on speculation and subjectivity, whereas Dilemma Control is triggered by empirical data and formulas; Risk Management's scope is finite, whereas Dilemma Control's scope is infinite; Risk Management monitors the project against a pre-project Watch List, whereas Dilemma Control monitors Performance Analytics for signs of impending dilemmas; Risk Management's responses are pre-planned (and thus outdated), whereas Dilemma Control's response are skilled and spontaneous; and Risk Management is a complex, cumbersome set of processes, whereas Dilemma Control's processes are lean, simple, and responsive.

Dilemma Control entails Extemporaneous Response Training, Dilemma Forecasting, Dilemma Response Options, Dilemma Mitigation, and Dilemma Repair and Recovery programs. The obvious benefit of Dilemma Control is that it fills a current void in the project manager's informational quiver. Sophisticated Performance Diagnostics can provide management with early warnings about impending dilemma likelihood.

Chapter 7: Introduction to Momentology

Every project dances to an invisible Momentum. Momentology is based on the notion that if its Momentum is managed, a project's *time* objectives can more effectively be influenced and reasonably ensured. The major components of Momentology, or Management by Momentum, are Momentum Theory, Momentum Science, and Applied Momentum.

Momentum Management's main features include a measurable rate of project Performance Intensity; proportional (free and total) float allocation per activity (Discrete Activity Float); the ability to determine a project's Schedule Achievement Potential; several innovative and powerful definitions of Criticality; a structured process for defining relationship-durations; a methodology for control of field administrative responsibilities; an ability to predict schedule slippage before it happens; the ability to influence outcomes in a way never before possible; and the generation of project outcome projections, sooner and more accurately.

Momentum Theory begins with the Theory of Workload Backlog, which states that, in order to meet time objectives, work must progress steadily on all activities in a Project Schedule, not just critical ones. If not, then, with the passage of time, the ratio of remaining work volume to remaining available time to perform that work dramatically climbs. At some point, the volume of work simply cannot be completed in the allotted time, and schedule slippage will result.

To measure and depict this concept, a unit of measure called Performance Intensity (PI) compares planned and actual Momentum and yields the required (catch-up) Momentum needed to sustain a project's time goals.

Momentology also contains other innovations, such as a new graphical look to the Project Schedule (including Waterways, Momentum Control Points, and Topographical Maps), a developed understanding of the nature of activity relationships (including Administrative and Productive Time Gaps and relationship-durations), and distributed total-float and free-float, called Discrete Activity Float.

Momentum Science refers to the technical application of Momentum Theory in ways that yield meaningful products and services of value to project management. Performance Diagnostics, performed in conjunction with the routine Performance Control cycle, take today's simplistic schedule updating procedures (which monitor execution efforts alone) and extend them to the monitoring of management and Project Schedule performance, as well.

Momentum Science recognizes that this three-front approach to Performance Control is only as good as the Project Schedule upon which it is based. Thus, Momentum Science uses complex formulas to ensure the schedule's ongoing viability by monitoring indicators of Schedule Credibility and Schedule Achievability. In turn, Schedule Credibility derives from separate assessments of Schedule Relevance and Schedule Volatility, whereas Schedule Achievement Potential is based on measures of Schedule Vulnerability and Schedule Resiliency.

Momentum Management, or Applied Momentum, converts Momentum Science into practical project management programs. Specifically, Momentum Controls involves Momentum Planning, and Momentum Controls Design and Development. Momentum Analytics entails Momentum Diagnostics, Dilemma Forecasting, Flow Rate Metrics, and Momentum Reporting. Momentum Management, at the project manager level, involves Preventive Administrative Actions, Priority-based Decision-making, Momentum-focused Coordination, Criticality-oriented Problem solving, and Proactive Project Management.

Chapter 8: Recap of New Concepts and Terminology
For easy reference, this short chapter provides a concise recap of the new concepts and terminology introduced in the previous three chapters.

Chapter 9: The Scheduling Practice and Faster Projects
Applying the Scheduling Practice Paradigm to the goal of better Project Schedules and faster projects, Commitment Planning produces deliverables that are of value to downstream Execution Scheduling and Performance Control. For its part, Performance

Control is extremely important to the ultimate goal of this book, because thoroughly administered Performance Reporting, Performance Analysis, Change Optimization, and Performance Advisement are central to how Project Schedules are ultimately used.

The Scheduling Practice Paradigm also includes an interesting characterization of the Scheduling Practitioner as playing nine different roles in the course of performing his duties, these being educator, strategist, interpreter, scribe, investigator, analyst, adviser, diplomat, and communicator.

Part 3: Preserving Project Schedule Integrity

Before immersing ourselves in the details of Commitment Planning, Execution Scheduling, and Performance Control, we need to get two important topics out on the table. First, we need to adopt a fresh perspective on the makeup of the CPM schedule, with particular emphasis on its two most basic building blocks: activities and relationships. Second, we need to be alerted to potential threats to Project Schedule integrity.

Chapter 10: Anatomy of a Schedule

A CPM network is a simulation model of a project that employs a sophisticated symbolic language. In terms of the anatomy of an activity, whether in ADM or PDM format, the Project Schedule's activity graphically depicts scope, duration, starting moment-in-time, and ending moment-in-time. As for the anatomy of the relationship, a relationship is not just an interdependency statement between two activities, it is also a forced gap of time, imposed by the Project Schedule's developers.

Activities are comprised of one or more Productive Work Segments. When a Time Gap is inserted to represent the restraint of an activity start by the prior completion of productive work, it is called a Productive Time Gap. When the gap is intended to allow time for the performance of prerequisite Administrative Actions, it is called an Administrative Time Gap.

To be sure, the battle between ADM and PDM advocates rages on. PDM supporters contend that PDM is easier to interpret, handles corrections more easily, reduces activity count, and achieves contractor buy-in more readily. By contrast, the ADM proponents complain about PDM's nonspecific start-to-start, negative lags, and overlapping activities.

When we think of a Project Schedule that has failed us, we most often think of a project that ran longer than desired. We call this schedule slippage. If we are precise in fixing blame, we will agree that there is a difference between the estimated length of a project and the actual length of a project. Since it is just as likely that the estimate is unrealistic as it is that the performance is inadequate, one must be careful before pointing fingers when the two don't coincide.

Momentum Studies show that, of the two, more often the culprit is initial duration estimates that are too small. Surprisingly, though, it is not the activity-duration but rather the relationship-duration that is the real source of the problem. For the most part, relationship-duration estimates fail to consider the time requirements of Administrative

Time Gaps. If Administrative Actions are performed but time is not allocated in the Project Schedule, the Execution Schedule elongates. Worse, though, is when Administrative Actions are not performed and the activities that legitimately required their completion suffer inefficiencies that translate into schedule slippage.

Chapter 11: Working at Cross-Purposes

There are unforeseen forces that threaten the integrity of the overall Project Scheduling effort. In this chapter, we look at harmful Project Scheduling practices, competing project controls, and the presence of flawed definitions.

Concerning harmful Project Scheduling practices, we are advised not to use total-float as the only statement of activity criticality, overlook the equal importance of the relationship-duration relative to the activity-duration, or rely exclusively on reports sorted by total-float. Especially on time-sensitive projects, we are warned not to let the needs and interests of other project control systems weaken the power of the Project Schedule as a time management tool.

Two popular methodologies that can cause this type of erosion are Earned Value and Critical Chain Project Management. Though an excellent cost management methodology, the Earned Value Management System is weak in its time management features. Furthermore, even with respect to its ability to evaluate the performance of resources, it is weakest on projects that are not extensively familiar and highly repetitive in nature.

Critical Chain Project Management is innovative in its focus on cumulative project float and how that float is derived and used. However, the underlying rationale for the methodology makes several false assumptions, such as: every project's primary objective is to finish as soon as possible; all parties to the project share the project's goal of finishing as soon as possible; left unmanaged, workers will drag out the project as much as they can get away with; activity durations, as typically developed, are twice the size justified by the work scope; start and finish dates constitute "distractions" to timely completion of work; and unexpected schedule gains are rarely exploited by management.

Aside from building on unfounded assumptions, other concerns about CCPM include that it demeans the importance of duration purity, ignores the project's operating context and environment, creates project delay, is only applicable to time-sensitive projects, and fails to deal with the true causes of project delay.

As for flawed definitions, we note two important changes in the Scheduling Practice over the decades that many scholars overlook: that PDM has replaced ADM (and, thus, there are four relationship types to contend with, not just finish-to-start) and that the use of date-constraints has increased dramatically over the years.

These two changes in CPM usage lead to new truisms that did not exist 30 or more years ago, such as: start-float and finish-float are not always the same; float paths need not pass entirely through an activity; and the critical-path can have positive total-float, may not terminate at the project's end, and need not be the path with the least total-float or the longest path in the Project Schedule.

Part 4: Execution Scheduling and Performance Control

In the following five chapters, we carefully examine the many processes and techniques involved in Execution Scheduling and Performance Control.

Chapter 12: Schedule Design

Competent Schedule Development is *always* preceded by competent Schedule Design because a full appreciation of what the owner wants is critical to successful Execution Scheduling and Performance Control.

The Theory of Aligned Emphasis helps us to understand what the owner wants and insists that there must be complete alignment between the owner's project success criteria and the contractor's performance emphasis. On every project, the owner favors one project outcome over the other two: cost, time, or manner of performance. Whichever value is most important to the owner should also be most important to those performing the work.

The purpose of Schedule Design is to establish the performance requirements for the ensuing Project Schedule. The steps involved include Intelligence Gathering, a focal Schedule Design Summit, and creation of Schedule Performance Specifications.

The Schedule Design Summit should be attended by all project stakeholders and should consider all factors potentially affecting the Project Schedule's use. Included in these factors are: understanding the project's nuances, acknowledging the need for emphasis-aligned management, and settling on plans for organizational structure and resources utilization. In addition, decisions should be made as to how other project control functions will be implemented and how those functions will interface with the scheduling program. Specifically, attention should be given to cost management, risk management, procurement management, and communications.

Special thought should be given to the question of the Project Schedule's level-of-detail, which will differ in design based on the prevailing management style, Command-and-Control or Collaborative. Schedule Design should reflect the relative importance that management places on different core functions, including: planning, coordination, direction, work organization, resource management, compliance measurement, contract management, cost control, record keeping, and dispute resolution. As a helpful guide, this chapter contains the SmartStart program, complete with SmartMaps, SmartGrids, and SmartSpecs.

The key deliverable of Schedule Design is the Schedule Performance Specification, which established the criteria with which the quality of a schedule's performance ultimately will be measured, including end use objectives, maintenance requirements, project controls features, physical architecture, development process, and level-of-detail for both content and reporting. Finally, the Schedule Performance Specifications should take into account the anticipated project management style to insure compatibility.

Chapter 13: Schedule Development

The Schedule Development effort results in a logic diagram, complete with activities, activity-durations, relationships, relationship-durations, subnetworks, date-constraints, and software settings. The final work product is a computer-resident Project Schedule with an end date that satisfies contract requirements. Typically, the first step in Schedule Development is creation of a Work Breakdown Structure, followed by Logic Development Sessions, in which those who will ultimately build the project collaborate on the Project Schedule's content.

A Logic Development Session involves these steps: general orientation of the group to the process, defining subnets, deciding on construction approach, crafting the precise logic, assigning activity-durations, adding relationships and their durations, performing a manual forward pass, scheduling all subnetworks, and identifying the critical-path. In cases where the computed project end date is beyond the contractual project end date, steps should be taken to optimize the Execution Schedule.

Chapter 14: Schedule Construction

Schedule Construction takes the work products of the Logic Development Session, adds important architectural features, and creates the final CPM schedule. Specifically, the Execution Scheduler addresses activity-numbering, activity-descriptions, activity data manipulation codes, manpower-loading, resource-leveling, cost-loading, and various software settings.

The more critical software options to be set are retained-logic versus progress-override, continuous-durations versus elapsed-durations, continuous-durations versus interruptible-durations, zero-free-float, zero-total-float, nonzero finish-to-start relationship-durations, and how total-float is defined by the software. Other considerations crucial to the integrity of the Project Schedule are the use of automated calendars, the treatment of weather and holidays, workdays versus calendar days, and the inclusion of excessive date-constraints.

During Schedule Development, free-float provides an excellent way for the astute Execution Scheduler or project manager to measure or "sense" the degree of interdependence of the project's otherwise independent participants upon one another. Free-float is also a powerful tool in Performance Control reporting.

As for total-float, one of the first questions is "who owns it?" There is the formal answer, and there is the real world answer. Since the contractor creates the initial schedule and has a preemptive opportunity to bury float, in a very real sense he owns the project total-float. I encourage the responsible use of time contingencies in Schedule Development.

Chapter 15: Performance Reporting

Performance Reporting is concerned with preserving the integrity of the Project Schedule. It does this in two important ways. First, it continually updates the contents of the Project Schedule so that it accurately reflects both the facts of the past and the intentions of the future. Second, it ensures that the content of the Project Schedule is at all times reliable.

Performance Reporting is the process of determining the current status of activities and posting the same to the Project Schedule. Updating, which includes statusing, encompasses making minor adjustments to logic, durations, calendars, and software settings. A Schedule Revision is in a dimension all its own and entails major changes to Execution Schedule content or intent.

Chapter 16: Performance Control

We create Project Schedules for the information they can give us, information that is derived through in-depth analysis and then communicated through reports. Performance Recording measures progress, Performance Analysis closely examines the current reality, and Change Optimization determines the optimum use of future expenditures of critical resources. Performance Advisement provides reports and presentations designed to support management efforts to coordinate, direct, and control work activities. This chapter provides useful advice on how to accomplish Performance Control, as described in the next subsections.

Performance Reporting   Be aware of seven methods for determining percent-complete: project length, labor consumption, capital consumption, earned duration-days, weighted quantities, activity count, and, observation-based status.

Performance Analysis   Watch for performance trends and maintain a balanced sense of what is truly critical. Much like percent-complete, there are several ways to determine what is or is not critical. In addition to an activity's place on the critical-path, other methods of defining Criticality exist, including location of activity, magnitude of dependents, magnitude of path splits, potential resilience, and Discrete Activity Float.

Change Optimization   An Execution Schedule that accurately reflects reality, including past performance, provides an excellent tool for strategizing and planning responses to the kind of surprises that infect every project. Specifically, short-term work-around schedules and what-if studies are frequent uses of the Schedule as situations warrant.

In terms of communication, the Project Schedule must contain good information, which implies accuracy, timeliness, appropriate level-of-detail, dependability, and full integration with the information derived from other project control systems. An often under-utilized, but highly effective report format is the narrative. It allows the reader to understand why things are the way they are. All other report formats merely describe the current status.

Glossary

This Glossary contains Meaning Clarifications, which have, as their underlying rationale, the collective reasoning discussed in Chapter 11. If you find yourself not understanding a Clarification, please re-read Chapter 11's section "Arcane Term Meaning Clarifications." In the following table, I will concisely state the Clarifications that I propose for adoption by the Scheduling Practice.

Please note that Meaning Clarifications are not the same as *definitions*, per se, as I have not taken the time to wordsmith each Clarification with focused attention on the many possible nuances of meaning in each combination or choice of words. That is why I call these Meaning Clarifications—simply because I wish to convey the *spirit* of the meaning, rather than the linguistic construction of a carefully worded definition.

In particular, any terms falling within the context of the Scheduling Practice Paradigm are offered as fodder for subsequent academic efforts to develop a coordinated set of definitions that will eventually earn universal recognition and respect. As previously noted, the leading initiatives along these lines, including those most recent, still fall short of providing a comprehensive set of definitions (for example, they don't even define the two most fundamental terms to the Practice: planning and scheduling.).

80/20 Rule of Delay	**Clarification** A rule of thumb that states that 80 percent of a project's delays occur during the first 20 percent of the project life cycle.
activity	**Clarification** This is the basic project work element. The *activity-description* should define the portion of project work scope represented by the activity. **Cross-Reference** See Chapter 11.
activity-description	**Clarification** A short description of the general scope of work to be accomplished by the *activity*. **Cross-Reference** See Chapter 11.
activity-duration	**Clarification** A more complete name for what is commonly known as the duration. Because *Momentology* uses the term *relationship-duration* in lieu of the more confusing leads, lags, and lag values, it's necessary to put a modifier in front

of the activity-duration, so as to distinguish it from the *relationship-duration*.

Each *activity* is assigned a numeric value that estimates the amount of time required to perform the activity work scope, assuming a particular workforce configuration, worker and team productivity, resource availability, and so on.

Cross-Reference See Chapters 10 and 11.

activity-duration variances

Clarification *Momentology* processes that monitor, measure, and report variances between planned and actual *activity-durations*. Contributes to formula for *Schedule Relevancy*.

Cross-Reference See Chapter 7.

activity placement

Clarification During *Resiliency Diagnostics*, *Momentology* calculations that evaluate an activity's ability to recover from a time impact by considering its location along the project timeline continuum. During *Vulnerability Diagnostics*, *Momentology* calculations that evaluate an activity's likelihood of being time-impacted by considering its location along the project timeline continuum.

Cross-Reference See Chapter 7.

Activity Profiles

Clarification *Momentology* calculations that categorize and characterize an activity according to performance timing and uniqueness attributes. Contributes to formula for *Vulnerability*.

Cross-Reference See Chapter 7.

Activity Resiliency

Clarification *Momentology* calculations that compute an activity's ability to "bounce back" from a time impact, based on various statistical factors, including *Criticality*, *Relationships Aggregation*, *Confluence Aggregation*, and *activity placement*. Contributes to formula for *Waterway Resiliency*.

Cross-Reference See Chapter 7.

activity-tenure

Clarification The period of time spanning between the start of an *activity* and the completion of an *activity*, inclusive.

Cross-Reference For a full discussion, see Chapter 16.

Activity Vulnerability

Clarification *Momentology* calculations that compute an activity's likelihood of incurring a time impact, based on various statistical factors, including *Criticality*, *Relationships Aggregation*, *Confluence Aggregation*, *Activity Placement*, and *Activity Profiles*. Contributes to formula for *Waterway Vulnerability*.

Cross-Reference See Chapter 7.

ADM

Clarification Stands for *Arrow Diagramming Method*, an earlier graphical method of depicting Critical Path Method logic.

Cross-Reference See Chapter 10.

administrative constraint	**Clarification** One of four reasons for tying two activities together; the others are *material constraint*, *logistic constraint*, and *resource constraint*. Two activities are linked to simulate an administrative constraint, when the intent is to reflect an execution strategy of the project management team. Perhaps it is decided that the work will flow west to east. Perhaps floor finishes are desired from the top floor, downward. **Cross-Reference** See Chapter 16.
Administrative Time Gap	**Clarification** A gap in time required for the completion of Administrative Actions that are prerequisites to a *Productive Work Segment*. **Cross-Reference** See Chapter 10.
Applied Momentum	**Clarification** The practical application of *Momentum Theory* and *Momentum Science*. Its systems include *Momentum Controls*, *Momentum Analytics*, and *Momentum Management* (also called *Management by Momentum*). **Cross-Reference** See Chapter 7.
Approach Optimization	**Clarification** As part of the new *Scheduling Practice Paradigm*, procedures that evaluate the acceptability of actual performance variances from plan, as well as the merits of future variances from plan. **Cross-Reference** See Chapter 5.
Arrow Diagramming Method	**Clarification** An earlier graphical method of depicting Critical Path Method (CPM) logic. This book considers ADM obsolete and has retired arcane terms exclusive to ADM (for example, dummy, node, and so forth). **Cross-Reference** See Chapter 10.
ATG	**Clarification** Stands for *Administrative Time Gap,* which is the gap in time required for the completion of Administrative Actions that are prerequisites to a *Productive Work Segment*. **Cross-Reference** See Chapter 10.
Atmospheric Maps	**Clarification** One innovation of *Momentology* is a new graphical presentation of schedule logic in the form of *Topographical Maps* and Atmospheric Maps. The inherent logic in the Project Schedule defines the outer profile of the "land mass," while high and low points correspond to *Momentum Control Points*, *Capitals*, and *Regions*. **Cross-Reference** See Chapter 7.
Authorization Planner	**Clarification** As part of the new *Scheduling Practice Paradigm*, a functional position within the *Authorization Planning* subspecialty responsible for *Feasibility Planning* and *Master Planning*. **Cross-Reference** See Chapter 5.

Authorization Planning	**Clarification** As part of the new *Scheduling Practice Paradigm*, one of two subspecialties of the *Commitment Planning* specialty, the other being *Execution Planning*. Authorization Planning involves two procedures: *Feasibility Planning* and *Master Planning*. The ultimate goal of Authorization Planning is a decision whether or not to proceed with the project. The primary deliverables of Authorization Planning are the *Feasibility Plan* and the *Master Plan*. **Cross-Reference** See Chapter 5.
Authorization Plans	**Clarification** As part of the new *Scheduling Practice Paradigm*, the primary deliverables of *Authorization Planning*, which includes the *Feasibility Plan* and *Master Plan*. **Cross-Reference** See Chapter 5.
bounded disorder	**Clarification** From the *New Sciences*, Chaos Theory teaches that *Complex Adaptive Systems* are bound at one level to rules of conduct and, at a more detailed level, they are disorderly. This behavior is also called *chaordic*. Supports the *no objective reality* postulate. **Cross-Reference** See Chapter 4.
Brooks	**Clarification** Any string of logic-tied activities. *Waterways* are ranked by their significance to schedule deadlines. In declining order of significance, they are *Rivers*, *Streams*, *Creeks*, and *Brooks*. *Inlets* are small activity sets that spring from and return to a single *Waterway*. **Cross-Reference** See Chapter 7.
buoyancy	**Clarification** For *Resiliency Determination*, *Momentology* calculations that express *Discrete Activity Float* as a percent of a *Composite Duration* and determine the probability of recovery from a time impact accordingly. For *Vulnerability Determination*, *Momentology* calculations that express *Discrete Activity Float* as a percent of *Composite Duration* and determine the probability of time impact accordingly. Contributes to formula for *Criticality*. **Cross-Reference** See Chapter 7.
Capitals	**Clarification** An innovation of *Momentology* is a new graphical presentation of schedule logic in the form of *Topographical* and *Atmospheric Maps*. The inherent logic in the schedule defines the outer profile of the "land mass," and high and low points correspond to *Momentum Control Points*, *Capitals*, and *Regions*. Capitals are *MCPs* that have been identified as being more significant to schedule stakeholders.
Change Optimization	**Clarification** As part of the new *Scheduling Practice Paradigm*, one of four subspecialties of the *Performance Control* specialty, the others being *Performance Recording*,

Performance Analysis, and *Performance Advisement*. Change Optimization is a set of strategic processes that uses raw and developed data ascertained during *Performance Recording* and *Performance Analysis*, respectively, in an effort to develop optimum responses to changes in project scope, approach, or conditions. Change Optimization involves four procedures: *Scope Optimization*, *Approach Optimization*, *Conditions Optimization*, and *Execution Schedule Amendment*.
Cross-Reference See Chapter 5.

Change Optimizer   **Clarification** As part of the new *Scheduling Practice Paradigm*, a functional position within the *Performance Control* specialty responsible for *Change Optimization*.
Cross-Reference See Chapter 5.

Change Science   **Clarification** From the *New Sciences*, a new field that studies how humans handle the phenomenon of change, the rate of which is exponentially increasing over time. Change Science evolved the concept of *Complexity Reduction*.
Cross-Reference See Chapter 4.

Changes to Calendars   **Clarification** *Momentology* processes that monitor, measure, and report the extent to which changes have been made to calendar settings originally incorporated into the logic. Contributes to formula for *Schedule Volatility*.
Cross-Reference See Chapter 7.

Changes to Constraints   **Clarification** *Momentology* processes that monitor, measure, and report the extent to which changes have been made to arbitrary *Date Constraints* originally incorporated into the logic. Contributes to formula for *Schedule Volatility*.
Cross-Reference See Chapter 7.

Changes to Durations   **Clarification** *Momentology* processes that monitor, measure, and report the extent to which changes have been made in the number, type, and level of detail of both *relationship-durations* and *activity-durations*. Contributes to formula for *Schedule Volatility*.
Cross-Reference See Chapter 7.

Changes to Logic   **Clarification** *Momentology* processes that monitor, measure, and report the extent to which original schedule logic has been modified. Contributes to formula for *Schedule Volatility*.
Cross-Reference See Chapter 7.

Changes to Settings   **Clarification** *Momentology* processes that monitor, measure, and report the extent to which changes have been made to schedule *software settings* originally incorporated into the logic. Contributes to formula for *Schedule Volatility*.
Cross-Reference See Chapter 7.

chaordic   **Clarification** From the *New Sciences*, describes the natural behavior of *Complex Adaptive Systems* as simultaneously

chaotic and orderly; hence, chaordic. See also *bounded disorder*.
Cross-Reference See Chapter 4.

Collaborative Management (or Model)

Clarification A new project management style that is currently displacing the prevalent *Command-and-Control Model* (which has been in place for centuries). Collaborative Management fosters team ownership and administration of the project. Part of the *Project Management Paradigm Shift*.
Cross-Reference See Chapter 4.

Command-and-Control Management (or Model)

Clarification A label to describe a management style prevalent for many centuries, influenced by the *Newtonian Model*, and only now being replaced by the *Collaborative Model* (influenced by the *New Sciences*). Supports the belief that one can collectively control the project itself by dictating and controlling the behavior of each and every activity on the project. Conventional CPM scheduling supports the Command-and-Control Model. Part of the *Project Management Paradigm Shift*.
Cross-Reference See Chapter 4.

Commitment Planner

Clarification As part of the new *Scheduling Practice Paradigm*, a functional position within the Commitment Planning specialty responsible for *Authorization Planning* and *Execution Planning*.
Cross-Reference See Chapter 5.

Commitment Planning

Clarification As part of the new *Scheduling Practice Paradigm*, one of three specialties of the Scheduling Practice, the other two being *Execution Scheduling* and *Performance Control*. Commitment Planning involves two subspecialties (*Authorization Planning* and *Execution Planning*) that share the overall goal of forging commitment among project participants, either in the form of demonstrating why the project is worth performing or outlining how the project will unfold.
Cross-Reference See Chapter 5.

completion milestone

Clarification Any activity whose timely completion is defined by an imposed *date-constraint* is a completion milestone, regardless of the value of the *activity-duration*.
Cross-Reference See Chapter 11.

complex adaptive systems

Clarification Derived from the *New Sciences*, a project is a complex adaptive system because it possesses these attributes: it is an open system, it is comprised of a large number of interdependent parts, it is characteristically dynamic, and it cannot be understood simply by understanding the parts.
Cross-Reference See Chapter 4.

Complexity Reduction

Clarification From the *New Sciences* field of *Change Science*, this theory argues that humans have a maximum

capacity for change, and when change volume exceeds this capacity, humans invoke techniques of complexity reduction. Supports the *no objective reality* postulate.
Cross-Reference See Chapter 4.

Composite Duration

Clarification An *activity-duration* value that is comprised of a *Scope-Limited Duration* plus the *DCF*.
Cross-Reference See Chapter 16.

Conditions Optimization

Clarification As part of the new *Scheduling Practice Paradigm*, adjustments to future plans necessitated by changes in conditions. In this context, *conditions* include site conditions, weather conditions, availability of labor, materials or other resources, and so forth.
Cross-Reference See Chapter 5.

Confluence Aggregation

Clarification For *Resiliency Determination*, *Momentology* calculations that evaluate an *activity* in terms of the number of paths emanating from the *activity*. For *Vulnerability Determination*, *Momentology* calculations that evaluate an *activity* in terms of the number of paths upon which it is influenced.
Cross-Reference See Chapter 7.

Consensus Plan

Clarification As part of the new *Scheduling Practice Paradigm*, the primary deliverable of *Consensus Planning* based upon the foundational work contained in the *Strategic Plan*.
Cross-Reference See Chapter 5.

Consensus Planning

Clarification As part of the new *Scheduling Practice Paradigm*, one of two procedures performed during *Execution Planning*, the other being *Strategic Planning*. The purpose of Consensus Planning is to formalize the assumptions, primary strategies, and other strategic considerations identified during *Strategic Planning*. The primary deliverable of Consensus Planning is the *Consensus Plan*. The Consensus Plan is used as the springboard for a subsequent *Execution Scheduling*.
Cross-Reference See Chapter 5.

Contractor Performance Reports

Clarification A set of reports designed to coordinate and critique contractor performance on the project, and as part of *Execution Performance*, a component of *Performance Diagnostics*.
Cross-Reference See Chapter 7.

Creeks

Clarification Any string of logic-tied activities. *Waterways* are ranked by their significance to schedule *completion milestones*. In declining order of significance, they are *Rivers*, *Streams*, *Creeks*, and *Brooks*. *Inlets* are small activity sets that spring from and return to a single *Waterway*.
Cross-Reference For further details, see Chapter 7.

critical	**Clarification** With *Criticality* based on one or more criteria (not just *total-float*), the word *critical* should not be used in isolation but only as a modifier, such as *critical-activity* or *critical-path*. **Cross-Reference** See Chapter 11.
critical-activity	**Clarification** An *activity* that is deemed *critical*, according to one or more measures of *Criticality*, one of which might be total-float. **Cross-Reference** See Chapter 11.
Critical Issues Rack-Up	**Clarification** A Performance Advisement report, or report segment, that summarizes the project's most critical issues. **Cross-Reference** See Chapter 7.
critical-path	**Clarification** The combination of *activities*, *relationships*, *durations*, *date-constraints*, *calendars*, and *software settings* that establishes a *completion milestone's* earliest possible completion date. Note: The term *critical-path* should always be associated with a specific *completion milestone* and, therefore, accompanied by a modifier in all cases. For example, Project Critical-Path or Dry-In Critical-Path. **Cross-Reference** For further details, see Chapter 11.
Criticality	**Clarification:** Refers to a measure of activity of path importance, based on various Criticality Factors, that reflect a weighted average across density, buoyancy, and potency and that determine an accordant probability of time impact. **Cross-Reference** See Chapter 7.
Criticality Factors	**Clarification** A set of standards against which the *Criticality* of the project is measured and reported. The term *Criticality* loosely represents a half-dozen different ways to define criticality. For *Resiliency Determination*, *Momentology* calculations that compute a *Momentum Control Point's* likelihood of recovering from a time impact, based on the cumulative probabilities of its tributary *Waterways*. For *Vulnerability Determination*, *Momentology* calculations that compute a weighted average across *Density*, *Buoyancy*, and *Potency* and determine the probability of time impact accordingly. **Cross-Reference** See Chapter 7.
date-constraint	**Clarification** Any arbitrarily imposed date on, before, or after which an *activity* may or may not start or finish. Common date-constraints include Start On, Start On or After, Start On or Before, Finish On, Finish On or After, Finish On or Before, Mandatory Start, Mandatory Finish, and As Late As Possible. Date-constraints have the power to override logic in forward and backward pass calculations. **Cross-Reference** See Chapter 14.

DCF   **Clarification** See Duration Confidence Factor.

Density   **Clarification** For *Resiliency Determination*, *Momentology* calculations that express the *activity-duration* as a percent of the *Composite Duration* plus *Discrete Activity Float* and determine the probability of recovery from a time impact accordingly. For *Vulnerability Determination*, Momentology calculations that express the *activity-duration* as a percent of the *Composite Duration* plus *Discrete Activity Float* and determine the probability of time impact accordingly. Contributes for formula for *Criticality*.
Cross-Reference See Chapter 7.

dependency   **Clarification** Rejected term; do not use. Use *interdependency* instead.
Cross-Reference See Chapter 11.

Dilemma   **Clarification** Unexpected minor developments that can affect the success of the project if not anticipated and adequately managed.
Cross-Reference See Chapter 6.

Dilemma Control   **Clarification** From *Momentology*, a set of concepts and procedures that will better prepare the project manager to anticipate, mitigate, respond to, and recover from *Dilemmas* that strike the project.
Cross-Reference See Chapter 6.

Dilemma Forecasting   **Clarification** From *Momentology*, a programmatic way of reasonably predicting where schedule slippage will occur in the future. Assessments are given along a severity continuum ranging from watches to warnings to advisories. Assessments based on *Performance Diagnostics*, *Schedule Achievement Potential*, and *Schedule Credibility*.
Cross-Reference See Chapter 7.

Discrete Activity Float   **Clarification** A numeric value assigned to an *activity* that represents a proportional allocation of some combination of *total-float* and *free-float*.
Cross-Reference See Chapter 16.

Duration Confidence Factor   **Clarification** An amount of time added to an *activity-duration* in order to derive an *activity-duration* with a near-100 percent achievement confidence rating. Abbreviation is *DCF*.
Cross-Reference See Chapter 16.

Duration-Day   **Clarification** The amount of work performance required to reduce a remaining-duration by one workday. Can be thought of as a crew day.
Cross-Reference See Chapter 7.

Dynamic Nature of Projects   **Clarification** A revelation by the *New Sciences* that projects are *Complex Adaptive Systems* and thus entirely and extremely dynamic and interactive.
Cross-Reference See Chapter 4.

Dynamic Project Management

Clarification The project manager's primary functions can be distinguished in the context of an ever-changing environment, that is, in the context of a dynamic project. The acronym PROJECT can help us to remember the four main elements of Dynamic Project Management: *Planned Resources, Objective Judgments, Effective Communication,* and *Troubleshooting.*
Cross-Reference See Chapter 2.

Earned Value Management System

Clarification Popular project management system for evaluating resource performance and efficiency. Abbreviated as *EVMS.*
Cross-Reference See Chapter 11.

effective communications

Clarification The project manager's primary functions can be distinguished in the context of an ever-changing environment, that is, in the context of a dynamic project. The acronym PROJECT can help us to remember the four main elements of *Dynamic Project Management: Planned Resources, Objective Judgments, Effective Communication,* and *Troubleshooting.*
Cross-Reference See Chapter 2.

EPC

Clarification Engineering/Procurement/Construction; a type of project delivery method where one party is responsible for all three components of the project.
Cross-Reference See Chapter 2.

EVMS

Clarification See *Earned Value Management System.*
Cross-Reference See Chapter 2.

Execution Performance

Clarification *Momentology* calculations that compute a project's overall *Execution Performance* in terms of *Performance Intensity* and *Performance Coordination.* Contributes to formula for *Performance Diagnostics.*
Cross-Reference See Chapter 7.

Execution Performance Analysis

Clarification As part of the new *Scheduling Practice Paradigm,* one of three procedures performed during *Performance Analysis,* the others being *Schedule Performance Analysis* and *Management Performance Analysis.* The purpose of Execution Performance Analysis is to ensure that the work is being performed efficiently and confidently and is consistent with the *Execution Schedule.*
Cross-Reference See Chapter 5.

Execution Planner

Clarification As part of the new *Scheduling Practice Paradigm,* a functional position within the *Execution Planning* subspecialty responsible for *Strategic Planning* and *Consensus Planning.*
Cross-Reference See Chapter 5.

Execution Planning

Clarification As part of the new *Scheduling Practice Paradigm,* one of two subspecialties of the *Commitment*

Planning specialty, the other being *Authorization Planning*. Execution Planning involves two subspecialties (*Strategic Planning* and *Consensus Planning*) that share the overall goal of forging commitment among project participants as to how best to execute the project for the maximum mutual benefit of all parties.
Cross-Reference See Chapter 5.

Execution Schedule **Clarification** As part of the new *Scheduling Practice Paradigm*, the primary deliverable of *Execution Scheduling*. The Execution Schedule is used for coordinating, directing, monitoring, and troubleshooting project execution and is the foundational basis for subsequent *Performance Control*. Also called the *Project Schedule*.
Cross-Reference See Chapter 5.

Execution Schedule Amendment **Clarification** As part of the new *Scheduling Practice Paradigm*, the processes needed to develop *Execution Schedule Revisions*. Examples of *Execution Schedule Revisions* include recovery, acceleration, or workaround schedule releases.
Cross-Reference See Chapter 5.

Execution Schedule Editions **Clarification** As part of the new *Scheduling Practice Paradigm*, replaces the conventional term *update*, represents each unique cyclical issuance of the Execution Schedule, and contains the latest Performance Recording entries.
Cross-Reference See Chapter 5.

Execution Schedule Extractions **Clarification** As part of the new *Scheduling Practice Paradigm*, refers to printed reports that contain subsets of the entire Execution Schedule database. Examples include Submittal Reports, Key Deliveries Reports, Total-Float Reports, Earliest-Start Reports, and so on.
Cross-Reference See Chapter 5.

Execution Schedule Revisions **Clarification** As part of the new *Scheduling Practice Paradigm*, a major modification of the *Execution Schedule* performed during the *Execution Schedule Amendment* proce- dure, such that it replaces the Baseline Schedule (or latest Execution Schedule Revision) as the primary basis for comparison during *Performance Control*.
Cross-Reference See Chapter 5.

Execution Scheduler **Clarification** As part of the new *Scheduling Practice Paradigm*, a functional position within the Execution Scheduling specialty responsible for *Schedule Design* and *Schedule Development*.
Cross-Reference See Chapter 5.

Execution Scheduling **Clarification** As part of the new *Scheduling Practice Paradigm*, one of three specialties of the Scheduling Practice, the other two being *Commitment Planning* and

Performance Control. Execution Scheduling is designed to deliberate upon, develop, and reach consensus about the details of project execution. The resultant work product is the *Execution Schedule*, also called the *Project Schedule*. It is developed at a greater level-of-detail than its predecessor the *Execution Plan*. While both may contain dates, it is the *Execution Schedule's* dates that constitute performance goals binding upon all project participants. It is the *Execution Schedule* against which another *Scheduling Practice* specialty, *Performance Control*, evaluates performance.

Cross-Reference See Chapter 5.

Extreme Data

Clarification An element of the *NERD Threshold*, which is a theoretical level-of-detail beyond which the benefits to the project are more than offset by loss or distortion of critical information. Stands for *Nutshell Data*, *Extreme Data*, and *Remote Data*.

Cross-Reference See Chapter 4.

Feasibility Plan

Clarification As part of the new *Scheduling Practice Paradigm*, the primary deliverable of *Feasibility Planning* and the foundation for the subsequent Master Plan.

Cross-Reference See Chapter 5.

Feasibility Planning

Clarification As part of the new *Scheduling Practice Paradigm*, one of two procedures performed during *Authorization Planning*, the other being *Master Planning*. The purpose of Feasibility Planning is to eliminate any projects whose stated objectives are determined to be impossible or impractical to achieve. It serves the project management goal of eliminating unviable projects by providing management with the ability to make informed decisions with respect to authorizing the project, or not (often called the Go/No Go decision). The primary deliverable of Feasibility Planning is the *Feasibility Plan*.

Cross-Reference See Chapter 5.

Fields Theory

Clarification From the *New Sciences*, this theory states that all around us are invisible fields of energy that cause living organisms to behave in ways that have nothing to do their own mental thoughts. Supports the *no objective reality* postulate.

Cross-Reference See Chapter 4.

finish-float

Clarification The numeric difference between an activity's earliest-finish and latest-finish values, according to the formula:

finish-float = latest-finish minus earliest-finish

Cross-Reference For a full discussion, see Chapter 11.

Flow Rate Metrics

Clarification From *Momentology*, a unique set of graphic

formats that visually convey the ebbs and flows of activity *paths*, pressures against *Momentum Control Points*, and so on.
Cross-Reference See Chapter 7.

fractals | **Clarification** From the *New Sciences*, fractals contain a large degree of self-similarity as if they are comprised of little copies of themselves, and this teaches us not to become too obsessed with our quest for greater precision, because there really is no precise answer. Supports the *no objective reality* postulate.
Cross-Reference See Chapter 4.

Hot Spot Highlights | **Clarification** From *Momentology*, a report or report segment that highlights the project's most significant problem areas, per schedule analysis.
Cross-Reference See Chapter 7.

Inlets | **Definition** From *Momentology*, any string of logic-tied activities. *Waterways* are ranked by their significance to schedule *completion milestones*. In declining order of significance, they are *Rivers*, *Streams*, *Creeks*, and *Brooks*. *Inlets* are small activity sets that spring from and return to a single *Waterway*.
Cross-Reference See Chapter 7.

interdependency | **Clarification** A term that reflects the nature of the *relationship* between activities and implies that no one *activity* is superior or subordinate to another. This term replaces *dependency*, *lead*, and *lag*, all of which are considered obsolete by this book.
Cross-Reference See Chapter 11.

known-unknowns | **Clarification** Some element of the project (known) about which the estimated duration is unclear (unknown).
Cross-Reference See Chapter 9.

lag | **Clarification** Term rejected; do not use. Use *interdependency* instead.
Cross-Reference See Chapter 11.

Lag Value | **Clarification** Term rejected; do not use. Use *relationship-duration* instead.
Cross-Reference See Chapter 11.

Lead | **Clarification** Term rejected; do not use. Use *interdependency* instead.
Cross-Reference See Chapter 11.

Lead Value | **Clarification** Term rejected; do not use. Use *relationship-duration* instead.
Cross-Reference See Chapter 11.

logistic constraint | **Clarification** One of four reasons for tying two activities together; the others are *administrative constraint*, *material constraint*, and *resource constraint*. Two activities are linked

to simulate a logistic constraint when they cannot share the same physical space. With logistic constraints, it doesn't matter which one goes first.
Cross-Reference See Chapter 10.

Management by Momentum	**Clarification** Another name for *Momentum Management*. **Cross-Reference** See Chapter 7.
Management Performance	**Clarification** *Momentology* calculations that compute project management's overall performance in terms of PROJECT performance criteria: *Planned Resources*, *Objective Judgments*, *Effective Communications*, and *Troubleshooting*. Contributes to formula for *Performance Diagnostics*. **Cross-Reference** See Chapter 7.
Management Performance Analysis	**Clarification** As part of the new *Scheduling Practice Paradigm*, one of three procedures performed during *Performance Analysis*, the others being *Schedule Performance Analysis* and *Execution Performance Analysis*. The purpose of Schedule Performance Analysis is to ensure that project management is performing its duties efficiently, competently, and completely. **Cross-Reference** See Chapter 5.
Management Performance Reports	**Clarification** From *Momentology*, a set of reports designed to coordinate and critique project *Management Performance*.
Master Plan	**Clarification** As part of the new *Scheduling Practice Paradigm*, the primary deliverable of *Master Planning*, based upon the foundational work contained in the *Feasibility Plan*. **Cross-Reference** See Chapter 5.
Master Planning	**Clarification** As part of the new *Scheduling Practice Paradigm*, one of two procedures performed during *Authorization Planning*, the other being *Feasibility Planning*. The purpose of Master Planning is to formalize the assumptions, primary strategies, and other strategic considerations identified during *Feasibility Planning*. The primary deliverable of Master Planning is the *Master Plan*. **Cross-Reference** See Chapter 5.
material constraint	**Clarification** One of four strategies for tying two activities together; the others are *administrative constraint*, *logistic constraint*, and *resource constraint*. Two activities are linked to simulate a material constraint when there is something inherently dependent between the two activities in terms of the work itself. You cannot paint a wall until it has been erected. **Cross-Reference** See Chapter 10.
MCP	**Clarification** See *Momentum Control Point*.

MCP Resiliency	**Clarification** *Momentology* calculations that compute a *Momentum Control Point's* likelihood of recovering from a time impact, based on the cumulative probabilities of its tributary *Waterways*. Contributes to formula for *Schedule Resiliency*. **Cross-Reference** See Chapter 7.
MCP Vulnerability	**Clarification** *Momentology* calculations that compute a *Momentum Control Point's* likelihood of incurring a time impact, based on the cumulative probabilities of its tributary *Waterways*. Contributes to formula for *Schedule Vulnerability*. **Cross-Reference** See Chapter 7.
Momentology	**Clarification** Represents the entire combination of *Momentum Theory*, *Momentum Science*, and *Applied Momentum*. **Cross-Reference** See Chapter 7.
Momentum	**Clarification** An informal expression reflecting the idea that the rate of performance of disparate project activities, in a synergistic way, creates an intangible, yet very real "current" among all involved activities. See also *Performance Intensity*, the formulaic expression of *Momentum*. **Cross-Reference** See Chapter 7.
Momentum Analytics	**Definition** A set of analytic methods that measure and evaluate various aspects of *Project Momentum*. Contributes to *Performance Analytics*. Coincides with traditional *Performance Control* and entails *Momentum Diagnostics*, *Dilemma Forecasting*, *Flow Rate Metrics*, and *Momentum Reporting*. **Cross-Reference** See Chapter 7.
Momentum Control Point	**Clarification** A point of confluence where multiple *Waterways* come together in a schedule. Various *Momentum* readings are taken at each defined *Momentum Control Point* and, much like meteorologists who gather wind and precipitation readings from all around town, an overall sense of schedule-level conditions can be gleaned from the readings at key *Momentum Control Points*. **Cross-Reference** See Chapter 7.
Momentum Controls	**Clarification** Coincides with traditional project controls development and involves *Momentum Planning*, *Momentum Controls Design*, and *Momentum Controls Development*. **Cross-Reference** See Chapter 7.
Momentum Controls Design	**Clarification** The processes involved in designing the precise configuration of *Momentum* processes and technologies consistent with the directives of *Momentum Planning*. Part of *Momentum Controls*; other parts being *Momentum Planning* and *Momentum Controls Development*. **Cross-Reference** See Chapter 7.

Momentum Controls Development	**Clarification** The processes involved in constructing the precise configuration of *Momentum* processes and technologies consistent with the performance parameters of *Momentum Planning* and the structures of *Momentum Design*. Part of *Momentum Controls*; other parts being *Momentum Planning* and *Momentum Controls Design*. **Cross-Reference** See Chapter 7.
Momentum Diagnostics	**Clarification** A set of measurement and reporting processes and variables specifically focused on *Momentum* flow implications. **Cross-Reference** See Chapter 7.
Momentum-Focused Coordination	**Clarification** Perhaps the single most important role a project manager plays is to coordinate the disparate activities of all project participants. Momentum-Focused Coordination is directed at influencing the pace of each participant's performance, so that the current of the *Waterways* upon which the participants flows arrives at *Momentum Control Points* as required. **Cross-Reference** See Chapter 7.
Momentum Management	**Clarification** A set of principles, theories, concepts, processes, procedures, technologies, and management practices, appropriately applicable on projects that are time-sensitive. Momentum Management operates under the premise that a project's time objectives can be best ensured by constantly monitoring and influencing the *Momentum* of its various participants and performers. **Definition** The practical synthesis of *Momentum Science* and *Applied Momentum*. Subsets of *Momentum Management* are *Preventive Administrative Actions*, *Priority-Based Decision Making*, *Momentum-Focused Coordination*, *Criticality-Oriented Problem Solving*, and *Proactive Project Management*. **Cross-Reference** See Chapter 7.
Momentum Planning	**Clarification** The processes and decisions involved in determining the level of *Momentology* application appropriate and desired for the project. Part of *Momentum Controls*; other parts being *Momentum Controls Design* and *Momentum Controls Development*. **Cross-Reference** See Chapter 7.
Momentum Reporting	**Clarification** Communication options employed to convey to schedule stakeholders the true state of the project from a *Momentum* perspective. Incorporates *Momentum Diagnostics*, *Dilemma Forecasting*, and *Flow Rate Metrics*. **Cross-Reference** See Chapter 7.
Momentum Studies	**Clarification** My work in the area of *Momentology*, which began in the spring of 1983, has followed a genuine fascination

with the invisible dynamics alive on every project that force project *Momentum* to ebb and flow. As part of my research, I studied the as-built schedules of over 200 projects that failed to meet their contractual *completion-milestones*. Numerous important and invaluable statistics were gleaned from these studies.

Sadly, the many boxes of printouts, schedules, and detailed work products were lost in a cross-country move. As a result, I do not have the tangible evidence to support many of the facts and figures attributed to Momentum Studies throughout this book.

For this reason, I actively encourage professional scheduling societies to sponsor studies of their own, which I am confident will reaffirm what I have already determined to be true. Even without the scientific backup, however, this book still enjoys a solid foundation of common sense backed by universally shared experiences. The feedback I have consistently received following speaking engagements on *Momentology* is that the principles described in this book ring true in the ears of those with dirty boots and callused hands.

Momentum Theory	**Clarification** A set of axioms, algorithms, principles, and formulas that are concentric to the notion that a state of performance completeness travels down each *Waterway* (string of connected *Activities*) in a schedule much like a boat drifting down a river. The drift rate reflects the current of the *Waterway*. The current of the *Waterway*, *Momentum*, is regulated by the collective achievement of the *Waterway's Activities*. **Cross-Reference** See Chapter 7.
Momentum Tracking	**Clarification** A set of procedures designed to monitor and measure project *Momentum*. Coincides with traditional *Performance Recording*. **Cross-Reference** See Chapter 7.
Monte Carlo Simulation	**Clarification** A statistical modeling technology that generates values randomly for certain variables (such as *activity-durations*)—over and over—in order to calculate the probability of different outcomes.
NERD Threshold	**Clarification** A theoretical detail threshold of a schedule below which the benefits to the project are more than offset by lose or distortion of critical information. Stands for *Nutshell Data*, *Extreme Data*, and *Remote Data*. **Cross-Reference** See Chapter 4.
New Sciences	**Clarification** Refers to major discoveries that have emerged virtually simultaneously in five separate traditional sciences: physics, chemistry, biology, psychology, and mathematics. **Cross-Reference** See Chapter 4.

New Sciences Model	**Clarification** Counters the *Newtonian Model*, as an influence on project management philosophy, approach, and style, and includes revelations such as: *No Objective Reality*; *Bounded Disorder, Fractals, Change Science,* and *Complexity Reduction.* **Cross-Reference** See Chapter 4.
Newtonian Model	**Clarification** In the seventeenth century, Sir Isaac Newton gave the world a systematic way to understand complex systems or entities by breaking them down into smaller and smaller subelements. The whole can be understood (or controlled) by understanding (or controlling) the parts. The *Project Management Paradigm Shift* is moving project management from the Newtonian Model to the *New Sciences Model.* **Cross-Reference** See Chapter 4.
no objective reality	**Clarification** A discovery from the *New Sciences* which states that, quite possibly, what we have always believed to be reality is not, and what we thought was unreal, is. This conclusion is supported by *Observation Theory, Water Molecules Studies, Pygmalion in the Classroom,* and *Time Irreversibility Rule.* **Cross-Reference** See Chapter 4.
Nutshell Data	**Clarification** An element of the *NERD Threshold*, which is a theoretical level of detail beyond which the benefits to the project are more than offset by lose or distortion of critical information. Stands for *Nutshell Data, Extreme Data,* and *Remote Data.* **Cross-Reference** See Chapter 4.
Objective Judgments	**Clarification** The project manager's primary functions can be distinguished in the context of an ever-changing environment in the context of *Dynamic Project Management*. The acronym PROJECT can help us to remember the four main elements of dynamic project management: *Planned Resources, Objective Judgments, Effective Communication,* and *Troubleshooting.* **Cross-Reference** See Chapter 2.
Observation Theory	**Clarification** From the New Sciences, Observation Theory says that the very act of observing something causes that something to alter its own behavior. This theory supports the *no objective reality* postulate. **Cross-Reference** See Chapter 4.
Optimized Approach Scenarios	**Clarification** As part of the new *Scheduling Practice Paradigm*, the key deliverable of *Approach Optimization*. **Cross-Reference** See Chapter 5.
Optimized Conditions Scenarios	**Clarification** As part of the new *Scheduling Practice Paradigm*, the key deliverable of *Conditions Optimization*. **Cross-Reference** See Chapter 5.

Optimized Scope Scenarios	**Clarification** As part of the new *Scheduling Practice Paradigm*, the key deliverable of *Scope Optimization*. **Cross-Reference** See Chapter 5.
Out-of-Sequence Work	**Clarification** *Momentology* processes that monitor, measure, and report incidences of work being performed out-of-sequence. Contributes to formula for *Schedule Relevancy*. **Cross-Reference** See Chapter 7.
P3	**Clarification** *Primavera Project Planner*; scheduling software, produced by Primavera Systems, Inc..
path	**Clarification** Any combination of associated, sequential, and proximate *activities*, *relationships*, *date-constraints*, and *software settings* that form a cohesive work execution stratagem. In order to form a "cohesive stratagem," these components must be associated, sequential, and proximate—the latter term meaning, "very near or next, as in space, time, or order." **Cross-Reference** See Chapter 11.
PDM	**Clarification** See *Precedence Diagramming Method*. **Cross-Reference** For a full discussion, see Chapter 10.
Performance Advisement	**Clarification** As part of the new *Scheduling Practice Paradigm*, one of four subspecialties of the *Performance Control* specialty, the others being *Performance Recording, Performance Analysis*, and *Change Optimization*. Performance Advisement is a set of processes that accomplishes a thorough exchange of information between the Scheduling Practice and project management with respect to project performance goals, achievement, and optimization opportunities. Performance Advisement involves two subspecialties (*Performance Reporting* and *Performance Consulting*) that share the overall goal of communicating performance-related information from the Scheduling Practice to project management. **Cross-Reference** See Chapter 5.
Performance Advisor	**Clarification** As part of the new *Scheduling Practice Paradigm*, a functional position within the *Performance Control* specialty responsible for *Performance Advisement*. **Cross-Reference** See Chapter 5.
Performance Analysis	**Clarification** As part of the new *Scheduling Practice Paradigm*, one of four subspecialties of the *Performance Control* specialty, the others being *Performance Recording, Change Optimization*, and *Performance Advisement*. Performance Analysis is a set of analytic processes that uses raw data ascertained during *Performance Recording* to fully understand the realities of the project. Performance Analysis involves the three procedures: *Schedule Performance Analysis, Management Performance Analysis*, and *Execution Performance Analysis*. **Cross-Reference** See Chapter 5.

Performance Consultant	**Clarification** As part of the new *Scheduling Practice Paradigm*, a functional position within the *Performance Advisement* subspecialty responsible for *Performance Consulting*. **Cross-Reference** See Chapter 5.
Performance Consulting	**Clarification** As part of the new *Scheduling Practice Paradigm*, one of two procedures performed during Performance Advisement, the other being *Performance Reporting*. Performance Consulting provides for a collaborative exchange of ideas enduring project troubleshooting and decision-making. **Cross-Reference** See Chapter 5.
Performance Control	**Clarification** As part of the new *Scheduling Practice Paradigm*, one of three specialties of the Scheduling Practice, the other two being *Commitment Planning* and *Execution Scheduling*. **Cross-Reference** See Chapter 5.
Performance Controller	**Clarification** As part of the new *Scheduling Practice Paradigm*, a functional position within the Performance Control specialty responsible for *Performance Recording*, *Performance Analysis*, *Change Optimization*, and *Performance Advisement*. **Cross-Reference** See Chapter 5.
Performance Recorder	**Clarification** As part of the new *Scheduling Practice Paradigm*, a functional position within the *Performance Control* specialty responsible for *Performance Recording*. **Cross-Reference** See Chapter 5.
Performance Recording	**Clarification** As part of the new *Scheduling Practice Paradigm*, one of four subspecialties of the *Performance Control* specialty, the others being *Performance Analysis*, *Change Optimization*, and *Performance Advisement*. Performance Recording refers to the maintenance activities performed by the during the cyclical *Performance Control* cycle. **Cross-Reference** See Chapter 5.
Performance Reporter	**Clarification** As part of the new *Scheduling Practice Paradigm*, a functional position within the *Performance Advisement* subspecialty responsible for *Performance Reporting*. **Cross-Reference** See Chapter 5.
Performance Reporting	**Clarification** As part of the new *Scheduling Practice Paradigm*, one of two procedures performed during Performance Advisement, the other being *Performance Consulting*. The responsibility of Performance Reporting includes production of various *Performance Reports* and *Presentations*, in addition to production of cyclical *Execution Schedule Editions* and *Execution Schedule Extractions*. **Cross-Reference** See Chapter 5.

Planned Resources	**Clarification** The project manager's primary functions can be distinguished in the context of an ever-changing environment, in the context of a dynamic project. The acronym PROJECT can help us remember the four main elements of *Dynamic Project Management*: *Planned Resources*, *Objective Judgments*, *Effective Communication*, and *Troubleshooting*. **Cross-Reference** See Chapter 2.
PMBOK® Guide	**Clarification** The *Project Management Body of Knowledge Guide*, a flagship work product of the Project Management Institute.
Potency	**Clarification** For *Resiliency Determination*, *Momentology* calculations that express *Discrete Activity Float* as a percent of worst *Discrete Activity Float* and determine the probability of recovery from a time impact accordingly. For *Vulnerability Determination*, *Momentology* calculations that express *Discrete Activity Float* as a percent of worst *Discrete Activity Float* and determine the probability of time impact accordingly. Contributes to formula for *Criticality*. **Cross-Reference** See Chapter 7.
Precedence Diagramming Method	**Clarification** The current, most popular graphical method of depicting Critical Path Method logic. For a full discussion, see Chapter 10.
Preventive Administrative Actions	**Clarification** A structured process whereby *Administrative Activities* (that are necessarily precedents to *Productive Work Segments*) are accounted for and incorporated into the project schedule and project management reporting and administration. **Cross-Reference** See Chapter 7.
Primavera	**Clarification** Primavera Systems, Inc, is producer of the leading scheduling software, Primavera Project Planner (P3).
Priority-Based Decision-Making	**Clarification** A technique whereby decision-making on the part of the project manager is based on the measured priorities of *activities*, according to an established priority ranking system. **Cross-Reference** See Chapter 7.
Proactive Project Management	**Clarification** The cumulative effect of applying *Momentum Theory* and underlying *Momentum Science* in such a way that the project manager confronts problems before they manifest into crises. **Cross-Reference** See Chapter 7.
Productive Time Gap	**Clarification** A *Time Gap* required by the completion of a prior *Productive Work Segment*. **Cross-Reference** For a full discussion, see Chapter 10.

Productive Work Segment

Clarification An *activity* portion having a distinct restraint at its start. Such restraints are typically tied to other, preceding *Productive Work Segments*.
Cross-Reference For a full discussion, see Chapter 10.

Program Health Number

Clarification From *Momentology*, a convenient single number that amalgamates the values of various supporting statistics and presents an encapsulated measure of overall project condition from a time perspective.

Project Controls

Clarification A popular label for a group of project management support systems, typically including cost and schedule and occasionally including other support systems such as estimating, quality control, contracts, and procurement. Since I do not believe there is such a thing as project control, per se, throughout this book I have substituted the label *Project Management Support Systems*.

Project Facilitation

Clarification A possibly better (future) name for the *Scheduling Practice Paradigm*, this still embodies *Commitment Planning*, *Execution Scheduling*, and *Performance Control* as its three specialties.
Cross-Reference See Chapter 5.

Project Management Paradigm Shift

Clarification A current trend in project management away from *Command-and-Control* style of management to *Collaborative Management*. Entails sweeping changes in attitude with respect to purpose, emphasis, authority, perspective, future views, reaction, and focus.
Cross-Reference See Chapter 4.

Project Management Support Systems

Clarification See *Project Controls*.

Project Momentum

Clarification See *Momentum*.

Project Momentum Management

Clarification See *Momentum Management*.

Cross-Reference For a full discussion, see Chapter 7.

Project Schedule

Clarification See *Execution Schedule*.

PTG

Clarification See *Productive Time Gap*.

PWS

Clarification See *Productive Work Segment*.

Pygmalion in the Classroom

Clarification Psychologist Robert Rosenthal, a researcher from Harvard University, published this controversial study in which he argued, "When teachers expect students to do well and show intellectual growth, they do; when teachers do not have such expectations, performance and growth are not so encouraged and may in fact be discouraged in a variety of ways." Supports the *no objective reality* postulate.
Cross-Reference See Chapter 4.

Regions	**Clarification** An innovation of *Momentology* is a new graphical presentation of schedule logic in the form of *Topographical Maps* and *Atmospheric Maps*. The inherent logic in the schedule defines the outer profile of the "land mass," and high and low points correspond to *Momentum Control Points*, *Capitals*, and *Regions*. *Regions* are defined as those *Activities* and *Waterways* that feed a *Capital MCP*. **Cross-Reference** See Chapter 7.
relationship	**Clarification** The graphical and agreed upon basis of an *interdependency* between two *activities*. The term *relationship* should replace confusing terms like *leads*, *lags*, and *dependencies*. **Cross-Reference** See Chapter 11.
relationship-duration	**Clarification** A numerical value assigned to a relationship that approximates a *Time Gap* between the start or finish of one *activity* and the start or finish of another *activity*. **Cross-Reference** See Chapters 7 and 11.
Relationship-Duration Variances	**Clarification** *Momentology* processes that monitor, measure, and report variances between planned and actual *relationship-durations*. Contributes to formula for *Schedule Relevancy*. **Cross-Reference** See Chapter 7.
Relationship-Tenure	**Clarification** The period of time spanning between the start of a *relationship* and the end of a *relationship*, inclusive.
Relationship Type	**Clarification** CPM uses four different relationship types: finish-to-start, start-to-start, start-to-finish, and finish-to-finish. **Cross-Reference** See Chapter 11.
Relationships Aggregation	**Clarification** For *Resiliency Determination*, *Momentology* calculations that evaluate and describe an *Activity* in terms of the number of activities dependent upon its performance. For *Vulnerability Determination*, *Momentology* calculations that evaluate and describe an *Activity* in terms of the number of activities upon whose performance it depends. **Cross-Reference** See Chapter 7.
Remote Data	**Clarification** An element of the *NERD Threshold*, which is a theoretical level-of-detail beyond which the benefits to the project are more than offset by loss or distortion of critical information. Stands for *Nutshell Data*, *Extreme Data*, and *Remote Data*. **Cross-Reference** See Chapter 4.
Resiliency Diagnostics	**Clarification:** Resiliency Diagnostics refer to *Momentology* calculations that compute a Schedule's likelihood of recovering from a time impact, based on the cumulative probabilities of its subordinate *MCPs*. **Cross-Reference** See Chapter 7.

resource constraint	**Clarification** One of four strategies for tying two activities together; the others are *administrative constraint*, *material constraint*, and *logistic constraint*. Two activities are linked to simulate a resource constraint when they require the same resources. Obviously, if you are using the crane, I cannot be. With resource constraints, it doesn't matter which one goes first.
Resource Performance	**Clarification** *Momentology* calculations that incorporate and summarize various *Resource Performance* indices, including *EVMS* statistics. Contributes to *Performance Diagnostics*. **Cross-Reference** See Chapter 7.
revising	**Clarification** Revisions to an Execution Schedule are, by conventional understanding, major changes to the content or intent of the schedule and are often called rebaselining. Revisions to content incorporate wide-scale changes in *activity-durations* or *relationship-durations*, major adjustments to logic ties or *calendars*, *software settings*, and so forth. Revisions to intent go to an entirely different level. Here, we're concerned with the Execution Schedule as a Change Optimization work product, reflecting major changes to project scope, approach, or conditions. **Cross-Reference** See Chapter 15.
Rivers	**Clarification** Any string of logic-tied activities. *Waterways* are ranked by their significance to schedule *completion milestones*. In declining order of significance, they are *Rivers*, *Streams*, *Creeks*, and *Brooks*. *Inlets* are small *Activity* sets that spring from and return to a single *Waterway*. **Cross-Reference** See Chapter 7.
Schedule	**Clarification** The short name (nickname) for the *Execution Schedule*, which is the key deliverable of the *Execution Scheduling* specialty within the *Scheduling Practice*. **Cross-Reference** See Chapter 5.
Schedule Achievement Potential	**Clarification** *Momentology* calculations that compute a schedule's probability of achieving its time-based objectives based on the cumulative determinations of *Schedule Vulnerability* and *Schedule Resiliency*. Contributes to *Dilemma Forecasting*. **Cross-Reference** See Chapter 7.
Schedule Credibility	**Clarification** *Momentology* calculations that compute a schedule's overall believability by considering *Schedule Relevancy* and *Schedule Volatility*. Contributes to *Dilemma Forecasting*. **Cross-Reference** See Chapter 7.
Schedule Design	**Clarification** As part of the new *Scheduling Practice Paradigm*, one of two subspecialties of the *Execution*

Scheduling specialty, the other being *Schedule Development*. Schedule Design is an essential precursor to *Schedule Development* and establishes the context and objectives of subsequent *Performance Control*. The primary deliverable of Schedule Design is the *Schedule Performance Specifications*.
Cross-Reference See Chapter 5.

Schedule Development

Clarification As part of the new *Scheduling Practice Paradigm*, one of two subspecialties of the *Execution Scheduling* specialty, the other being *Schedule Design*. Schedule Development entails the various processes involved in project schedule production. The primary deliverable of Schedule Development is the *Execution Schedule*.
Cross-Reference See Chapter 5.

Schedule Effectiveness Paradox

Clarification An apparent contradiction of observable "facts," which show that projects which use *CPM* scheduling tend to overrun their deadlines more often than projects that don't use network-based scheduling as a project management approach.
Cross-Reference See Preface.

Schedule Performance Analysis

Clarification As part of the new *Scheduling Practice Paradigm*, one of three procedures performed during Performance Analysis, the others being *Management Performance Analysis* and *Execution Performance Analysis*. The purpose of Schedule Performance Analysis is to ensure the *Execution Schedule's* ongoing functionality, viability, and integrity.
Cross-Reference See Chapter 5.

Schedule Performance Specifications

Clarification As part of the new *Scheduling Practice Paradigm*, the primary deliverable of Schedule Design which sets the functional parameters for the *Execution Schedule*.
Cross-Reference See Chapter 5.

Schedule Relevancy

Clarification *Momentology* calculations that evaluate the ongoing relevancy of the schedule by considering the frequency and magnitude of out-of-sequence work, and/or significant variances between planned actual *relationship-durations* and *activity-durations*. Contributes to formula for *Schedule Credibility*.
Cross-Reference See Chapter 7.

Schedule Resiliency

Clarification *Momentology* calculations that compute a schedule's likelihood of recovering from a time impact, based on the cumulative probabilities of its subordinate *MCPs*. Contributes to formula for *Schedule Achievement Potential*.
Cross-Reference See Chapter 7.

Schedule Volatility

Clarification *Momentology* calculations that evaluate the ongoing stability of the schedule by considering changes to

logic, changes to durations, changes to settings, changes to *date-constraints*, and changes to calendars. Contributes to formula for *Schedule Credibility*.
Cross-Reference See Chapter 7.

Schedule Vulnerability

Clarification *Momentology* calculations that compute a schedule's likelihood of incurring a time impact, based on the cumulative probabilities of its subordinate *MCPs*. Contributes to formula for *Schedule Achievement Potential*.
Cross-Reference See Chapter 7.

Scheduling Practice

Clarification As part of the new *Scheduling Practice Paradigm*, a combination of specialties, roles, skills, processes and procedures, concepts, terminology, and deliverables that jointly produces vital Project Scheduling products and services for the construction industry. The Scheduling Practice is comprised of three specialties: *Commitment Planning*, *Execution Scheduling*, and *Performance Control*.
Cross-Reference See Chapter 5.

Scheduling Practice Paradigm

Clarification A new way to view the entire scope, context, and composition of the *Scheduling Prac*tice. This book introduces the new Scheduling Practice Paradigm.
Cross-Reference See Chapter 5.

Scope-Duration Correlation

Clarification A doctrine stating that each *activity-duration* must be associated with a discrete scope of work, as described by the *activity-description*.
Cross-Reference See Chapter 13.

Scope-Limited Duration

Clarification The unadjusted *activity-dur*ation based solely on pure scope. A *Duration Confidence Factor* is added to the scope-limited duration to yield the *Composite Duration*.
Cross-Reference See Chapter 16.

Scope Optimization

Clarification As part of the new *Scheduling Practice Paradigm*, procedures performed to determine the best way to respond to changes in scope. Contemporaneous Time Impact Analyses (TIAs) are performed during Scope Optimization.
Cross-Reference See Chapter 5.

self-reference and self-renewal

Clarification From the *New Sciences*, a discovery that *Complex Adaptive Systems* seem to "know" when they are out of sync (with the outer boundaries of *Bounded Disorder*) and correct themselves.
Cross-Reference See Chapter 4.

Seven Ms of Momentology

Clarification A project is the purposeful combination of Men, Materials, and Machinery, acting over a period of time (Minutes). Such action creates a project *Momentum*, and Management's goal is to influence *Momentum* so that project objectives (Money) are realized.
Cross-Reference See Chapter 7.

Soft Ground Advisories	**Clarification** *Momentology* reports, or report segments, that highlight areas in the schedule which are most prone to slippage.
software settings	**Clarification** All scheduling software programs provide a host of optional settings, applicable globally or per activity, which can affect the results of basic CPM calculations of *earliest-dates* and *latest-dates*, as well as *total-float* and *free-float*. Examples of such settings include *zero-free-float, zero-total-float, retained-logic, progress-override, contiguous-durations, interruptible-durations, start-float, finish-float, least-float, calendars*, and so on. **Cross-Reference** See Chapter 11.
start-float	**Clarification** The numeric difference between an *activity's* earliest-start and latest-start values, according to the formula: *start-float = latest-start minus earliest-start* **Cross-Reference** For a full discussion, see Chapter 11.
statusing	**Clarification** Something the *Performance Recorder* does, statusing refers quite literally to the process of posting to the *Execution Schedule* the current status of any activities that have experienced progress during the reporting period. One of four major steps in *Performance Control*. **Cross-Reference** See Chapter 15.
Strategic Plan	**Clarification** As part of the new *Scheduling Practice Paradigm*, the primary deliverable of Strategic Planning and the foundation for the subsequent Consensus Plan. **Cross-Reference** See Chapter 5.
Strategic Planning	**Clarification** As part of the new *Scheduling Practice Paradigm*, one of two procedures performed during *Execution Planning*, the other being *Consensus Planning*. The purpose of Strategic Planning is to provide an opportunity for those you will perform the work of the project to identify the ideal strategic plan, one that yields the maximum mutual benefit for all parties. The primary deliverable of Strategic Planning is the *Strategic Plan*. **Cross-Reference** See Chapter 5.
Streams	**Clarification** Any string of logic-tied activities. *Waterways* are ranked by their significance to schedule deadlines. In declining order of significance, they are *Rivers, Streams, Creeks*, and *Brooks. Inlets* are small activity sets that spring from and return to a single *Waterway*. **Cross-Reference** See Chapter 7.
task	**Clarification** Obsolete term that referred to a project work element that comprises a portion of an *activity*. Typically, tasks are useful in breaking down the work for *Execution*

Planning and *Performance Recording* but are not necessary for coordination or reporting level efforts. Considered obsolete in this book.
Cross-Reference See Chapter 11.

Theory of Aligned Emphasis

Clarification A *Momentum Theory* that states, "No matter what the project type, location, size, design, function, or purpose, on every project, one of three qualifiers (cost, schedule, or manner) is of a greater priority to the owner than the other two."
Cross-Reference See Chapter 12.

Theory of Workload Backlog

Clarification *Momentum Theory* is based on the notion that unperformed but scheduled work results in an increasing ratio between Required Performance and Time Available to perform the required work.
Cross-Reference See Chapter 7.

Time Gap

Clarification An imposed delay to the commencement of a *Productive Work Segment*.
Cross-Reference See Chapter 10.

Time Irreversibility Rule

Clarification From the New Sciences and often explained as "you never step into the same river twice," this rule asserts that both you and the river are always changing. Supports the *no objective reality* postulate.
Cross-Reference See Chapter 4.

To-Go Basis

Clarification A project analytic and reporting focus where the perspective and emphasis is on the work yet to be performed, as opposed to the work already completed.

Topographical Maps

Clarification An innovation of *Momentology* is a new graphical presentation of schedule logic in the form of Topographical Maps and *Atmospheric Maps*. The inherent logic in the schedule defines the outer profile of the "land mass," and high and low points correspond to *Momentum Control Points*, *Capitals*, and *Regions*.
Cross-Reference See Chapter 7.

total-float

Clarification The lesser (lowest total-float value) as between an *activity's start-float* or its *finish-float*.
Formula The difference between early and late dates.
Cross-Reference See Chapter 11.

troubleshooting

Clarification The project manager's primary functions can be distinguished in the context of an ever-changing environment in the context of a dynamic project. The acronym PROJECT can help us to remember the four main elements of *Dynamic Project Management*: *Planned Resources*, *Objective Judgments*, *Effective Communication*, and *Troubleshooting*.
Cross-Reference See Chapter 2.

unknown-unknown	**Clarification** Always expressed in the singular, it is a label representing the probability that something will befall the project that cannot be anticipated or quantified.
updating	**Clarification** Broader in nature than mere *Performance Recording (statusing)*, updating includes walking the job to measure *Execution Performance* and then *statusing* the schedule. Additionally, the *Performance Analyst* will make any other minor adjustments to the schedule, such as limited adjustments to *activities, activity-durations, relationships, relationship-durations*, resource loads, *date-constraints, calendars, software settings*, and the like, in order to better reflect reality. A set of processes that spans *Performance Recording* and *Change Optimization*. **Cross-Reference** See Chapter 15.
Vulnerability Diagnostics	**Clarfication:** Refers to *Momentology* calculations that compute a Schedule's likelihood of incurring a time impact, based on the cumulative probabilities of its subordinate *MCPs*. **Cross-Reference** See Chapter 7.
Water Molecules Studies	**Clarification** From the *New Sciences*, Dr. Masaru Emoto made great strides in understanding the behavior of water molecules when being observed and discovered that water molecules "react" to the vibrations emanating from humans, the wave patterns of which change with different emotions within the human. His work supports the *no objective reality* postulate. **Cross-Reference** See Chapter 4.
Waterway	**Clarification** Any string of logic-tied *activities*. *Waterways* are ranked by their significance to schedule *Completion Deadlines*. In declining order of significance, they are *Rivers, Streams, Creeks*, and *Brooks*. *Inlets* are small activity sets that spring from and return to a single *Waterway*. **Cross-Reference** See Chapter 7.
Waterway Resiliency	**Clarification** *Momentology* calculations that compute a *Waterway's* likelihood of recovering from a time impact based on the cumulative probabilities of its resident activities. Contributes to formula for *MCP Resiliency*. **Cross-Reference** See Chapter 7.
Waterway Vulnerability	**Clarification** Momentology calculations that compute a *Waterway's* likelihood of incurring a time impact, based on the cumulative probabilities of its resident activities. Contributes to formula for *MCP Vulnerability*. **Cross-Reference** See Chapter 7.
WBS	**Clarification** Work Breakdown Structure.
Work Breakdown Structure	**Clarification** A systematic way to decompose the scope of a project into increasingly more finite elements.

Index